THE HUMAN DIMENSIONS
OF NATION MAKING

THE HUMAN DIMENSIONS
OF NATION MAKING

Merrill Jensen: A Personal Comment

E. James Ferguson

MERRILL JENSEN grew up on a small farm in South Dakota. After graduating from the local high school, he taught for a couple of years in a one-room grade school. Then he took the train for Seattle, Washington, the farthest point away his money would carry him, and enrolled at the University of Washington. To support himself he worked at odd jobs like painting and refurbishing houses. He caught the attention of Professor Edward McMahon, chairman of the history department, a roughhewn but deeply idealistic man who had worked his way up from the lumber camps. Recognizing Jensen's potential as a historian, McMahon became his friend and benefactor. Encouraged by his prospects at the university, Jensen returned to South Dakota to rescue his fiancée from life on the prairie. He had gone to school with Genevieve, the charming daughter of a neighboring farmer. They were married, and they both attended the University of Washington.

Jensen received his master's degree in 1931, whereupon McMahon directed his prize pupil to his own alma mater, the University of Wisconsin, to study for the doctorate. Finances, however, remained a problem. The country was sinking into economic depression, and jobs of any kind were scarce. Jensen found employment at the State Historical Society of Wisconsin calendaring portions of the famed Draper Manuscripts, and was subsequently appointed to a teaching assistantship at the university.

3

Until the birth of their daughter, Genevieve worked part-time to help out, but the young family was financially hard pressed. Within three years Jensen completed the requirements for the Ph.D. and wrote his thesis. He had finished, however, at a most unfortunate time. The depression had deepened; there were few academic openings; and some Ph.D.'s were turning to the Works Progress Administration for work. Finally, after months of harrowing uncertainty, Jensen received the offer of an instructorship at the University of Washington.

Course loads at the university were heavy, involving a five-day teaching schedule. Besides teaching, Jensen took over the managing editorship of the *Pacific Northwest Quarterly*, changing the format and former title of the journal, and with Genevieve's assistance assuming virtually sole responsibility for its publication. Personal illness sharpened the unavoidable stress of these early years. Genevieve on one occasion spent nearly a year confined to bed, and Jensen himself suffered from a heart condition. He eventually recovered from it, but in those days just climbing stairs wore him out, and he kept a cot in his office to lie down on when attacks occurred. Nevertheless, he persevered in scholarly work, writing several important articles, two of which appeared in the *Mississippi Valley Historical Review*, and in 1940 published *The Articles of Confederation*, which won national recognition among scholars. He also brought a high level of professionalism to his teaching, particularly in graduate instruction. The graduate school at the University of Washington was small and the students heterogeneous, but a number of them from this period moved on to successful academic careers, and a few eventually became scholars of reputation.

Although Jensen registered for the draft in 1940, his heart trouble ruled out any possibility of military service when the United States entered World War II. During the war years universities tended to become backwaters with so many of the intellectually motivated students gone and the classes converted into auxiliaries of officers' training programs. Jensen finally gained leave from the university in 1944 to go to Washington, D.C., where he worked as a historian for the Air Force. The same year, however, a decisive turn came in his career with an appointment at the University of Wisconsin.

The postwar years were a high point in the development of the

University of Wisconsin. The history faculty was among the best in the nation, and the institution attracted its full share of that exceptional college generation of returning GI's, young men raised during the economic depression for whom service benefits suddenly opened higher prospects. The university administration and, behind it, the state legislature were committed to the idea that research was a primary function of universities. Time for personal study and frequent research leaves were granted to the faculty. In this hospitable environment Jensen devoted himself to works that steadily enhanced his reputation. Signal marks of recognition soon followed. In 1949 Oxford University appointed him Harmsworth Professor, and in the next few years he was invited to teach at the State University of Ghent and the University of Tokyo. Since 1955 he has been a regular consultant of federal government agencies and the Japanese government on educational exchanges between the two countries and has frequently taught in Japan. The University of Wisconsin conferred its highest honor in history on him in 1964 by naming him Vilas Professor, and in 1969 his fellow historians elected him President of the Organization of American Historians. Disinclined to rest on his laurels, Jensen continued research on the second volume of a large-scale history of the American Revolution, and in 1971 took over the editorship of two important historical editing projects: the Documentary History of the Ratification of the Constitution and the Documentary History of the First Federal Elections. In 1974 he was summoned before the House of Representatives in Washington, D.C., to address that body on the observance of the bicentennial of the American Revolution.

In the course of a life of scholarly accomplishment and ramifying worldly experience, Jensen, as could be expected, has moved a long way from his youthful background. Although he is essentially pragmatic, disdainful of ideology, and would reject any classification of himself, his intellectual antecedents can probably best be described as vaguely Populist, combining a sympathy for the common man with a realistic sense of human motives and a hardheaded recognition of how the loaves and fishes are divided. Imposed on this structure of attitudes, however, and most instrumental to his scholarship is a steadfast commitment to "scientific history," which was dominant during the years of his professional training. In Jensen's thinking about the past, the fact, not the

word, is paramount. His criterion of historical writing is verisimili-
tude: did what historians say really exist? Or is it the corollary
of some abstract proposition or generated by the implication of
words? Although duly aware of the subjective element in the writing of history, Jensen as a matter of principle and so far as possible
tries to keep interpretation out of research, to employ strictly
inductive methods, and to let interpretation flow out of source
materials.

His teaching follows the same pattern. In class lectures he
ordinarily presents a body of data, often an unelaborated narrative. Although aware of the implications which the students
may reasonably draw from the material, he nevertheless hands out
no generalization and, in fact, leaves plenty of room for variant
formulations of the evidence. Similarly, in graduate instruction
Jensen has been known to set students at just reading primary
sources on the supposition that without prior hypotheses they
would be free to pick up fresh insights from exposure to the past.
The inductive method, it must be said, is not the quickest or most
efficient way to produce doctoral dissertations and get books published, but the contribution Jensen's students have made to historical scholarship suggests that his techniques are highly effective.

Jensen's own scholarship bears the same marks. He is usually
classified as the leading, currently active, spokesman of the Becker-
Beard school of historical interpretation. Jensen does not repudi-
ate this categorization, but he is rather amused by it; he does not
regard himself as a member of any school. Abiding by his precepts
and despite swirls of revisionism rising about him, Jensen over a
long period has merely stuck, as he would say, to recording the
facts, aware of, but undistracted by, shifting fashions of interpretation. To critics his only rejoinder is to keep reciting unem-
broidered facts about the past and their common-sense implications. It has no doubt been personally gratifying to him that
recent interpretation has swung back toward his own, rendered
more fully dimensional by its excursions perhaps, but nonetheless
broadly consonant with his own emphases.

Jensen also tries to apply the ideal of objectivity to his dealings
with students. Their political ideologies, for example, have never
interested him, except as pardonable aberrations of youthful
minds of which the investigation of historical fact is the surest cor-

rective. During the era of Joseph McCarthy and the Un-American Activities Committee investigations, Jensen was loftily disdainful of meddlers into academic freedom and did not care whose list his students were on. By the same token, he has always distinguished carefully between his personal likes and dislikes and his professional evaluation of students. His only standard is their scholarship, a fact of which they are never left in doubt.

Such detachment was hard to sustain at the University of Wisconsin because the graduate school was and, in spite of its enormous growth during the 1960's, still is a master-disciple system characterized by close social relations between faculty and graduate students. Jensen pursued this tradition in his early years of teaching at the University of Washington, where he often held seminars in his home. At Wisconsin the Jensens entertained frequently, usually holding dinner parties for a mixed crowd of professors and students. The mistress of this company was Genevieve, an excellent cook and gracious hostess, who imparted a warm and civilizing element to the academic scene. In recent years the Jensens have continued to entertain much as before, but they now harbor visiting Japanese with their families who have to be met at the airport and who stay for a week at a time while they look for quarters.

Although Merrill Jensen likes company and has many old friends, he evidently feels a periodic need for solitude. At home he spends many evenings listening, without conversation, to classical music. Nearly every summer he and Genevieve drive halfway across the continent to the Pacific Northwest. In his early years at the University of Washington Jensen bought a piece of land on Whidbey Island, which lies in Puget Sound and was then sparsely settled and remote. Jensen has considerable craft skills and a highly developed artistic sense; with the fine lumber providentially afforded by two enormous abandoned chicken coops that came with the property he built an elegantly simple cottage on the edge of a cliff overlooking a broad salt-water channel and forested hills beyond. Moved by an abiding attachment to the house and to the Pacific Northwest, Jensen went back year after year to enjoy the solitude and the opportunity for uninterrupted writing. Recently, as the suburban sprawl from Seattle crept out to Whidbey Island and weekend residents overran nearby property, Jensen, feeling crowded, sold the house and built another and larger one on distant, rocky Orcas Island far out in Puget Sound, where he is said to reside each summer in baronial splendor.

Although Merrill Jensen has reached the age of retirement at the University of Wisconsin, his scholarly activities show no signs of abating. He is fully engaged in ongoing research and historical editing. The sum of his achievements is already monumental. Throughout his long career he has taught and practiced a straightforward technique founded upon tireless research and careful interpretation. In some areas of history his books stand alone, but it is finally indicative of the man that everything he has written is substantial, authoritative in the field, and of enduring importance.

The Human Dimensions of Nation Making:
Merrill Jensen's Scholarship and
the American Revolution

James Kirby Martin

IN 1962 historian Jack P. Greene thought he heard the death knell sounding for the scholarship of individuals conveniently called "progressive" historians. Greene claimed that this group, "represented by Carl Becker, Arthur Schlesinger, Sr., John F. Jameson, and Merrill Jensen," had been interested mainly in the "social and economic divisions within the colonies in an effort to discover what was revolutionary about the Revolution," and had been undermined by post-World War II thrusts in scholarship. The current interpretive mood, labeled "neo-whig," was offering abundant new evidence which made "progressive" writings seem dated, narrow, perhaps even ahistorical. Greene was optimistic that "neo-whig" interpretations would "produce a greater awareness of complexities, a more precise formulation of issues, and a deeper understanding of the pattern, process, and causes of the American Revolution."[1]

But scholarly excavations since the early 1960's have effectively buried Greene's prophecy. Critical methodological breakthroughs were not foreseen then, but they have had significant historiographical impact as yet another and sometimes younger group of his-

---

[1] "The Flight From Determinism: A Review of Recent Literature on the Coming of the American Revolution," in the *South Atlantic Quarterly*, 61 (1962), 235–259. See also Jack P. Greene, ed., *The Reinterpretation of the American Revolution, 1763–1789* (New York, 1968), 2–74.

torians began drawing upon knowledge from other academic disciplines, especially the social sciences. The application of theoretical systems about human behavior, multidimensional comparative models, statistical techniques, and quantifiable measures to historical problems has resulted in "newer" findings which more often support "older" conceptualizations about eighteenth-century provincial society and the American Revolution.[2] The ongoing scholarly dialectic now is corroborating less of the post-World War II premises of consensus and more of the interpretive insight of such notable and pioneering historians as Merrill Jensen.[3]

*   *   *   *

Through several scholarly books and articles of far-reaching implication, Merrill Jensen has unfolded the drama and tension that was the American Revolution.[4] It has been the exciting story of human beings interacting with other human beings, of individuals quarreling over and trying to resolve basic issues of government and society, of a diversity of peoples seeking to articulate the goals and ideals of a new nation struggling over its initial identity. It has been the story of conflict, bitterness, and internal divisiveness at a time when so many citizens felt the agonizing travail of national birth. It has been the story of a successful, though hardly orderly realization of certain forms and practices in the configuration of American institutions. It has not been the story of a united people marching forward together into a harmonious future; rather it has been the story of citizens and leaders contending with each other while seeking solutions to problems which seemed almost insurmountable during their time.

[2] For summaries of recent "new" scholarship conclusions see George A. Billias, "The Revolutionary Era: Reinterpretations and Revisions," in George A. Billias and Gerald N. Grob, eds., *American History: Retrospect and Prospect* (New York, 1971), 34–84; Jack P. Greene, "The Social Origins of the American Revolution: An Evaluation and an Interpretation," in the *Political Science Quarterly*, 88 (1973), 1–22; Kenneth A. Lockridge, "Social Change and the Meaning of the American Revolution," in the *Journal of Social History*, 6 (1973), 403–439.

[3] Merrill Jensen constantly reminded his students that convenient historiographical labels tend to mute the real nuances of historical interpretations. In that context I am only borrowing from others who have used such terms as "neo-whig," "consensus," and "new conservative." My intention is to define a group of scholars who agree on basic assumptions, even though their work admittedly displays a rich multiplicity of interpretive and thematic variations.

[4] A full bibliography of Merrill Jensen's publications appears at the end of this volume.

The human dimensions of nation making described by Professor Jensen during his early professional career in *The Articles of Confederation: An Interpretation of the Social-Constitutional History of the American Revolution, 1774–1781* (1940), and *The New Nation: A History of the United States During the Confederation, 1781–1789* (1950) filled a gaping chasm in knowledge about what had transacted among American citizens between the signing of the Declaration of Independence and the writing of the Constitution of 1787. Merrill Jensen's research revealed that Revolutionary leaders were more concerned with opportunities for profits from land speculation, to take one example, than with ratifying the Articles of Confederation. The Founding Fathers turned out to be men with specific and mundane programs and goals which would benefit themselves as much as the yearling nation. More layers of mythology had been swept away.

Such conclusions disturbed historians of the immediate post-World War II years. These scholars disdained the research conclusion that Americans had been contentious and divisive in their revolution; moreover, they did not believe that the struggle among socioeconomic groups which Jensen dubbed "the internal revolution" was a vital, formative agent in giving impetus to the independence movement before 1776. According to John Higham, these scholars in their writings began to homogenize the American past; they performed "a massive grading operation that smoothed and flattened the convulsive dialectic of progressive history." They found "an unsuspected degree of uniformity and agreement . . . in the welter of America's historical experience. Instead of a polarized culture—a culture eternally divided between over- and underprivileged groups, between a party of the past and a party of the future, between noble ideals and ignoble interests—young scholars glimpsed an essentially homogeneous culture full of small, impermanent variations."[5] Insignificant divisiveness versus formative internal social upheaval became the issue.[6]

[5] With Leonard Krieger and Felix Gilbert, *History: The Development of Historical Studies in the United States* (Englewood Cliffs, 1965), 214. It is not my purpose to discuss the contemporary circumstances leading to this shift in historiographical emphasis, but the issue of being influenced by the times is there and has been commented upon by others. John Higham, for instance, offered the following as a partial explanation for the shift: "Historians in an age of unceasing international peril, when national security and the capacity for survival are fundamental concerns, can hardly avoid a somewhat conservative view of their country's history. They can hardly avoid

The post-World War II group seemed to coalesce around three premises. First (and a necessary precondition for the others), there was the widely-accepted conclusion that prerevolutionary America was fundamentally a middle-class society. Ownership of property was widespread; most adult white males could vote. Fulfilling "stake in society" requirements and being able to act through franchise rights in the political arena, middle-class provincials lacked reasons to struggle among themselves. Having property and the franchise (apparently the *summum bonum*), there appeared to be no basis for internal revolution with lower-class have-nots struggling against better-placed haves and demanding broader sociopolitical rights as part of the Revolution.[7]

Second, since the socioeconomic basis for internal conflict was absent, the insurgency movement seemed to have resulted from the introduction of stricter imperial regulations after 1763, when the Paris peace settlement ended the Seven Years' War and signaled a new departure from the general policy of "salutary neglect." Anglo-Americans rallied together against more stringent

---

an appreciation of its more cohesive and deeply rooted qualities. Nevertheless, they may trace those qualities to quite diverse sources, and they may disagree widely on the worth and durability of such homogeneity as they perceive. In rejecting a simple cleavage between the two Americas, some historians may be most impressed by the wholeness of the national fabric, others by the looseness and multitude of its many strands. Their common concern is with the nature and degree of stability in American experience." See *History*, 221. Staughton Lynd, representing another point of view, wrote the following: "These overtones are the more apparent when it is recalled that sustained criticism of [Charles A.] Beard's work is largely a product of the Cold War years. At a time when the politics of dead center and an end to ideology prevailed in American society at large, historians rather suddenly discovered that Americans had always shared a consensus about fundamentals that enabled them pragmatically to muddle through." See *Class Conflict, Slavery, and the United States Constitution* (Indianapolis, 1967), 5.

[6] "Neo-whig" historians often have accused "progressive" historians of writing in a quasi-Marxist sense when discussing tensions among social groups. For a summary see Richard B. Morris, "Class Struggle and the American Revolution," in the *William and Mary Quarterly*, 3rd Ser., 19 (1962), 3–29.

[7] The work of Robert E. and B. Katherine Brown became the scriptural source of middle classness. See in particular *Middle-Class Democracy and the Revolution in Massachusetts, 1691–1780* (Ithaca, 1955), and *Virginia, 1705–1786: Democracy or Aristocracy?* (East Lansing, 1964). In 1962 Bernard Bailyn discussed the influence as follows: "All arguments concerning politics during the prerevolutionary years have been affected by an exhaustive demonstration for one colony [Massachusetts], which might well be duplicated for others, that the franchise, far from being restricted in behalf of a borough-mongering aristocracy, was widely available for popular use." See "Political Experience and Enlightenment Ideas in Eighteenth-Century America," in the *American Historical Review*, 67 (1962), 339–351.

controls. Focusing exclusively on Great Britain and Parliamentary legislation, provincial Americans went to war to defend the openness of their society, which seemed, in their perceptions, to be under attack by corrupted home ministers. The issue was home rule and defense of liberties; other matters dwindled to meaninglessness, except for the launching of republicanism.[8]

Internal social and political upheaval directed against the American governing group—the question of who should rule at home—lost out to images of rebellious Americans defending an internal order of openness. Thus, third, Americans were united by the Revolution and began to institutionalize the unique reality of their society. For some historians in the post-World War II group the Revolutionary generation had been engaged in a search for principles; to others they had been ratifying previously inchoate but unique patterns of existence. By the end of the Revolutionary years and through the writing of the Constitution of 1787, the colonial American War for Independence had culminated in the legitimation of a truly different society among the nations of the world. Institutions, ideals, and cultural norms now were codifying the partially defined reality of eighteenth-century America.[9]

[8] There is a decided split among the post-World War II group as to why Americans went to war. According to Robert E. Brown, Americans fought "to *preserve* a social order rather than to change it." See *Middle-Class Democracy*, 405. But to Bernard Bailyn, the American independence quest grew out of the late colonial mind and a commonly held world view, more so than out of institutional relationships. In *The Ideological Origins of the American Revolution* (Cambridge, 1967), 95, Bailyn explained as follows: "It was this—the overwhelming evidence, as they [the colonists] saw it, that they were faced with conspirators against liberty determined at all costs to gain ends which their words dissembled—that was signaled to the colonists after 1763, and it was this above all else that in the end propelled them into Revolution." For some, then, *unity* came from the necessity to maintain the uniqueness of the socioeconomic order; for others that unity took form from ideas, ideology, and belief systems. Whatever the source, there was little room for internal divisiveness or internal revolution in these causal explanations.

[9] Some "neo-whigs" have argued that the Revolution was conserving in the use of its energy. See comments by Robert E. Brown in footnote 8. By comparison, Edmund S. Morgan summarized the results of the Revolution as follows: "It is worth pointing out, however, that if the Revolution was a struggle to make property secure, the Constitution was the final fulfilment of that struggle. If the Revolution called for the coupling of taxation with representation, the Constitution made the central government representative before giving it powers to tax. If the Revolution was built upon the principle that all men are created equal, the Constitution gave men a more equal share in the national government than the Confederation did. If the Revolution opened for Americans the discovery of their own nationality, the Constitution gave them the instrument for expressing it. If the Revolution taught them the danger of

The critical starting point in this interpretive revisionism was the presumption of widespread and fairly even property distribution (the image of middle classness in provincial America as compared to the highly stratified, feudal world of early modern Europe). Middle classness became the new article of commitment, the tacit assumption which various "neo-whig" historians accepted with interpretive caveats.[10] The grievances of such well-known groups as the marching Paxton Boys, the rioting tenant farmers associated with William Prendergast of New York, and the disrupting North Carolina and South Carolina Regulators, to name but a few sources of internal disagreement, became minor perturbations, hardly significant enough examples of sociopolitical tension to imply some form of impending internal revolution or to reflect, among other conditions, widespread unevenness in the over-all distribution of wealth, property, and political rights.[11] For those bent on homogenizing the past that was discredited thinking.

Confidence in the structural soundness of the "neo-whig" edifice reached its zenith at the very time that new methodological approaches were beginning to influence still another group of historians. Interested in varieties of structures and their nature

tyranny, the aim of the Constitution was to prevent tyranny." See *The Birth of the Republic, 1763–1789 (The Chicago History of American Civilization*, Chicago, 1956), 156–157. Morgan saw the results of the Revolution as both conserving and liberating, establishing old as well as new principles. Bernard Bailyn pictured the Revolution more as "radicalizing" in "that intellectual developments in the decade before Independence led to a radical idealization and conceptualization of the previous century and a half of American Experience, and that it was this intimate relationship between Revolutionary thought and the circumstances of life in eighteenth-century America that endowed the Revolution with its peculiar force and made it so profoundly a transforming event." See *Ideological Origins*, vi–vii.

[10] Many examples of middle classness acting as a tacit assumption in research design may be found. The late Richard Hofstadter stated in his last volume, *America at 1750: A Social Portrait* (New York, 1971), 131, that "what we must envisage in order to comprehend eighteenth-century America is a middle-class world." Apparently this assumption would have affected the multivolume history of the United States that Hofstadter intended to write. To take another example, Bernard Bailyn wrote in *Ideological Origins*, vi, that his study of pamphlets "confirmed my rather old-fashioned view that the American Revolution was above all else an ideological, constitutional, political struggle and not primarily a controversy between social groups undertaken to force changes in the organization of the society or the economy."

[11] Middle classness even became a characteristic of prerevolutionary crowd action, though systematic research into the social origins of mob leaders and participants still is sparse. For assumptions affecting conclusions though, see Pauline Maier, *From Resistance to Revolution: Colonial Radicals and the Development of American Opposition to Britain, 1765–1776* (New York, 1972), 12–13.

and significance in the human experience, some in this group devoted long research hours to the question of opportunity in early America. Working on discrete communities and sorting through local records that could be quantified, these historians did not support images of middle classness in their published writings.

Recently one scholar summarized their basic findings and postulated that Anglo-American society after 1720 could be characterized by the following:[12] rapid population growth (population doubling every twenty to thirty years); growing population density, including attendant problems of "overcrowding" in older seaboard settlements; greater horizontal mobility, reflecting population density pressures in older settlements; increasing concentration of wealth, especially in older settlements where many younger inhabitants were being forced out because they could not sustain themselves at even subsistence levels on overly subdivided family plots; greater social polarization and social differentiation, reflecting the ability of some individuals to gather in overly subdivided land, thereby increasing personal wealth vis-à-vis others in such communities; and growing commercialization as a reflection of greater dependency on a market economy, yielding geographic concentrations of wealth and other forms of dependency, such as more precise elaborations of stratifying economic roles and functions.[13] Dynamic flux in all regions and increasing interdependence and socioeconomic stratification, especially in terms of levels of wealth and economic roles, cast serious doubts on the value of static images of middle classness.

With such "unprecedentedly acute interpersonal and interregional differences in wealth, in social status, in political power, in economic interest and in material prospects" which became more pervasive after 1720,[14] historians once again have to deal with several phases of Revolutionary activity within the structural context of differently placed sociopolitical groups vying among themselves on the American landscape. Real as well as perceived differences among inhabitants of regions at different stages of development need further scrutiny if historians are to understand more fully the varieties of reactions by citizens and governing groups to

---

[12] Lockridge, "Social Change and the Meaning of the American Revolution," 403–439.

[13] *Ibid.*, 405–409.

[14] *Ibid.*, 423.

new assertions of imperial authority. Scholars must still grapple with patterns of consensus and disagreement between leadership cadres and the increasingly undeferential generality of citizens in an increasingly stratified society. These suggestions at their base represent a recognition that concepts about formative social stress and internal revolution, so skillfully explored by Merrill Jensen, deserve further elaboration, not abandonment.

Jensen uncovered sociopolitical tensions as he investigated the sources and broadened rather than summarily rejected the insights of scholars writing prior to him. Today the latest research efforts verify the essential premise that "social change was in several ways a major energizer of intricate exchanges which ultimately and half-inadvertently gave us the Constitution [of 1787]."[15]

*   *   *   *

If the *sine qua non* of the "neo-whig" position provides a misleading perception of socioeconomic development in prerevolutionary America, then the remaining two premises may also be overstatements. The second premise is that a united Anglo-American citizenry went to war to protect the openness of their society and with fears that a corrupted ministry would bury Americans in political tyranny. The primary characteristic is that of a citizenry which acted in concert out of a commonly held world view of liberty being threatened by sycophantic, power-hungry, tyrannical ministers and their political hirelings in the provinces.

By juxtaposition, one hallmark of Merrill Jensen's research has been its appreciation of the importance of petty party factionalism in building images of tyranny and generating revolution. Sometimes the factionalism reflected deep socioeconomic fissures in the provincial population; at other times it was a product of groups which took opposing positions on aspects of imperial policy, depending on local circumstances in each colony. Jensen, in *The Founding of a Nation: A History of the American Revolution, 1763–1776* (1968), takes an exacting look at political factionalism in the provinces. He captures in bold relief the types of petty vituperativeness which men such as the legendary Samuel

---

[15] *Ibid.*, 405. Jack P. Greene, "The Social Origins of the American Revolution," 1–22, also samples the new literature but concludes that research results are too inconsistent in terms of themes to prove a relationship between social tension and the American Revolution.

Adams used in battling against imperial programs not only to resist perceptions of tyranny but also to smash down longtime political opponents like Thomas Hutchinson. He demonstrates, as no other has, how the various Parliamentary programs after 1763 impacted and intensified the increasingly bitter recriminations of Anglo-American political factionalism. For "popular leaders" home government mandates served the purpose of uniting popular feeling in isolated areas and among specific groups, making it possible to undercut "enemies of America" who found themselves in the untenable position of defending imperial programs. Popular leaders did not react to the unified calls of universally well-informed constituents; they organized opinion.

Even though everyone today agrees that voting rights were more widespread among colonial white adult males than once assumed, Professor Jensen was among the first to appreciate the limitations of this finding as it affected actions in the pre-1776 political arena. It certainly did not mean that voting constituents controlled the function of decision-making or that leaders acted when well-informed constituents spoke out. As Merrill Jensen pointed out, researchers into eighteenth-century American franchise levels forgot that few offices were elective, or presumed that the ones that were elective were the most influential and important. They seemingly forgot that inhabitants had little if any role in the nomination process for elective offices, that voting was by viva voce, and that everyday citizens with modest holdings tended, though decreasingly, to assume that it was the function of the "better sort" to provide the broad parameters of leadership and act in the most enlightened fashion, regardless of public opinion. The infrastructure of the modern democratic paradigm was lacking; procedures militated against direct popular decision-making through the hierarchical channels of governments.[16]

Thus it remained the push of popular leaders shoving against their enemies or the "out-of-doors" activities of such dissident groups as the Paxton Boys that resulted by sheer inadvertence and by volition in an expansion of ways and means for meaningful popular participation in political decision-making after 1776. However unintended, popular sovereignty and greater democracy

[16] See in particular "Preface to the Third Printing," appended in 1959 to *The Articles of Confederation*, xv–xxiii.

was the legacy of the turmoil. Above all, Merrill Jensen found that the American Revolution was revolutionary.[17]

From still another angle Merrill Jensen was instrumental in developing scholarly appreciation for the importance of the anxiety among some upper-class provincial leaders that the generality would get out of control through revolution, seize too much authority, and convulse a society in chaos. Nearly paranoic fears of popular licentiousness caused many elite leaders, many of whom became reluctant revolutionaries and later fathers of the Constitution of 1787, to resist the undercurrent that became part of the Revolutionary tide. John Dickinson exemplified those men caught in the middle. As one who was most anxious about the disruptive potential of the generality, Dickinson and others fought against the independence question. Such men did not see how internal political chaos could be avoided without the stabilizing influence of central imperial authority, represented by the discredited King and Parliament.[18]

Dickinson and others of his persuasion were certainly not of an American intelligentsia which was willing to respond uncritically to constituency demands. Merrill Jensen showed how such men sought to stem popular feeling. It was Dickinson who played a large role in the first drafting of the Articles of Confederation. It was Dickinson and others of his cautiously conservative persuasion who were losing out in 1776 to popular leaders assembled in the Continental Congress. The popular leaders did not deal with the generality out of fear; rather they devoted themselves to drafting the final version of the Articles and establishing a relatively powerless central government. Merrill Jensen called that final draft "a constitutional expression of the philosophy of the Declaration of Independence," a document which institutionalized "the idea of the supremacy of the local legislatures," meaning that "'state sovereignty'," as an expression of the ideal of popular sovereignty had been triumphant in the first phase of the Revolution.[19] It was the clash of nearly irreconcilable political interests that resulted in this first, liberating constitutional settlement.

---

[17] Merrill Jensen, "Democracy and the American Revolution," in the *Huntington Library Quarterly*, 20 (1957), 321–341, and "The American People and the American Revolution," in the *Journal of American History*, 57 (1970), 5–35.

[18] Jensen, *Articles of Confederation*, 88–139.

[19] *Ibid.*, 239.

Conflicting internal interests, epitomized for convenience here in men like Samuel Adams and John Dickinson, cannot be graded away by assurances that "the most radical change produced in Americans by the Revolution was in fact not a division at all but the union of three million cantankerous colonists into a new nation."[20] That union, and its haphazard development, cannot be understood without investigating the areas of disagreement. It was the thrashing out of differences which Merrill Jensen discovered in the sources, and which he argued gave true form and character to the Revolution both before and after 1776.

Through his acceptance of the basic complexities that pervade human relationships, Merrill Jensen has offered other historians a rich explication of the subtleties of those social, societal, and political tensions that formed such a large part of the relentless dynamism of a resistance movement that somehow spilled over into revolution. No doubt many British ministers, even King George III himself, evidenced a narrowness of vision about America's potential in supporting more demanding imperial legislation. That program, though, did not unite all Americans in opposition. As Professor Jensen has written, imperial legislation was only one basis for instigating and intensifying internal cleavage over future possibilities for the Anglo-American polity. At first the imperial program heated up petty party factionalism; ultimately it made it possible to dispose of those who would defend King and Parliament against provincial interests. After 1774 the clash moved beyond momentary concerns and resulted in a full-scale internal power struggle between those who could envision the people as the basis of government and those who could not. The debate was by no means over with the completion of the Articles of Confederation. Americans would have to fight a war in the midst of a rancorous dispute over how open their society should be.[21]

*   *   *   *

Differing viewpoints over the role the generality should have in government and society was the critical problem facing men in

---

[20] Morgan, *Birth of the Republic*, 100.

[21] Whereas *The Founding of a Nation* stresses party factionalism in the context of imperial legislation after 1763, Professor Jensen's *Articles of Confederation*, 16–53, looks at the internal socioeconomic basis of that factional conflict.

the Continental Congress who were trying to thrash out a national constitution. Some of these gentlemen, most notably former "popular leaders" according to Professor Jensen, feared with good reason a distant central government; that would be substituting one form of tyranny for another. Swept up in colony-centered parochialism and believing that power somehow had to be kept closer to themselves and to the people who supported them, they formed the driving wedge that stripped the Continental Congress under the Articles of real vestiges of authority. Merrill Jensen named Samuel Adams, Patrick Henry, Richard Henry Lee, George Clinton, James Warren, Samuel Bryan, George Bryan, Elbridge Gerry, and George Mason as *representative* of "true federalists [who] believed that the greatest gain of the Revolution was the independence of the several states and the creation of a central government subservient to them."[22]

On the other side of the ledger were the real *nationalists,* though they performed political artistry during the later Confederation years by calling themselves "federalists." Frustrated by the first constitutional settlement and desiring a strong central government to foster orderly and stable national development, they had few doubts that the nation-making experiment could survive very long with "no check upon the actions of majorities in state legislatures" and without a "central government to which minorities could appeal from the decisions of such majorities, as they had done before the Revolution." Robert Morris, John Jay, Gouverneur Morris, James Wilson, Alexander Hamilton, Henry Knox, James Duane, George Washington, and James Madison *represented* many others who would devote themselves in various ways after 1776 to bringing constitutional order out of their perceived fears of chaos and doom, given the sharp shift toward greater authority in the hands of the people through the first state constitutions.[23]

Indeed, it was this nationalist perception, based on desires for orderly economic development (and personal profit), on concerns about convulsive state actions, and on fears of a tyrannical majority, that led John Fiske in *The Critical Period of American History, 1783–1789* (1888) and so many other commentators to conclude that the Confederation years were "critical" and to envision

---

[22] Jensen, *The New Nation*, 424.
[23] *Ibid.*, 425.

"unselfish patriots [who] rescued the new nation from impending anarchy, if not from chaos itself."[24] Professor Jensen in distilling the sources concluded that explanations of the Confederation years reflected nationalist musings and writings. Quasi-historians like Fiske had underrated the accomplishments of those years which were made despite the enormous obstacles which confronted citizens who tried to make the Confederation work. What emerges from Jensen's writing is the vigor and determination with which the nationalists pursued their desires for a powerful central government. Merrill Jensen virtually brought to light divisions over the Articles of Confederation, virtually discovered the "nationalists," and made the 1770's and 1780's into a recognizable period of history. Moreover, Professor Jensen demonstrated that the Constitution of 1787 was a political document, a product of its time, as its framers always knew it to be.

But the nationalist victory in 1787 was more than a counter-revolution, or a backward-looking *coup d'état*. In his most recent volume Professor Jensen describes the nationalists' work as "The Revolution of 1787." These constitution makers "adopted the theory of the Continental Congress in 1776: the sovereignty of the people." They had learned through their struggles that there was no retreating from that principle. Merrill Jensen explains further: "The people were sovereign, they [the nationalists] argued, and could delegate their sovereign power in any way they chose: to the state governments, to Congress under the Confederation, or to the government provided for by the Constitution. The adoption of the basic theory of the Revolution of 1776 to justify the Revolution of 1787, one designed in part at least to thwart the sovereignty of the people in practice, . . . placed the opponents of the Constitution in the impossible position of having to deny the very sovereignty of the people they declared they were defending."[25]

The Revolution in its last stages, then, did much more during the Confederation years than confirm previously ill-defined and unrealized patterns of openness, the third "neo-whig" premise. It forced some men, despite their standing, to adopt ideas that were anathema to them; in the process prominent nationalists found

---

[24] *Ibid.*, xii–xiii.
[25] *The American Revolution Within America* (New York, 1974), 214–215. See also Merrill Jensen, *The Making of the American Constitution* (Princeton, 1964).

themselves trapped into working with the very generality they mistrusted and disdained. The ground rules were marked out through the revolutionary process; in time the commitment in writing would become the governing reality.

Merrill Jensen's writings reveal that the Revolution in America framed a totally new set of possibilities, defying the stratified nature of prerevolutionary government and society. The Revolution created possibilities that would be more fully actualized as the new nation aged.

*   *   *   *

In his *The American Revolution Within America,* an outgrowth of Professor Jensen's Anson G. Phelps Lectures at New York University in 1973, the following 1786 quotation from a letter from John Adams to David Ramsay appears:

> There have been in fact 13 Revolutions, for that number of established governments were overthrown and as many new ones erected. For this reason I think that a complete history of the American Revolution can never be written until the history of the change in each state is known, nor can any man be competent to the general undertaking who is not master of the particulars.[26]

Through a lifetime of demanding scholarly inquiry, research, and writing, Merrill Jensen perhaps more than any other person has come to know those particulars that were the American Revolution. New thrusts in scholarship are sustaining his appreciation of the subtleties and complexities of the Revolutionary process as it developed into a movement of grand proportions, despite the willfulness of many of its participants.

It is unlikely, as John Adams suggested, that anyone will ever know the full story. Professor Jensen would be the first to admit that. But in the continuing quest historians will find Professor Jensen's published works of enormous value. Those books and scholarly articles deal with the stuff of history—people as people, not people as we idealize them to be. In the years ahead all we can ask is that Merrill Jensen keep presenting us with the results of his research, as we know he will in the finest tradition of scholarship.

---

[26] Quoted in *American Revolution Within America*, 1.

The Trials of Sir Edmund Andros

Stephen Saunders Webb

In reviewing the long public career of Sir Edmund Andros, we are struck not less by the amount of work which he performed than by the censures which his services entailed. He was the Governor at times of every Royal Province on the main-land, and exercised a larger influence than any of the other of the rulers sent thither by Great Britain. He was repeatedly accused of dishonesty and oppression, yet he passed harmless through repeated examinations only to receive fresh promotion . . . thus holding office under four successive monarchs. Surely there must have been some noble traits of character in a man thus perpetually involved in contests and thus invariably successful.

W. H. WHITMORE[1]

ON October 27, 1663, Ensign Edmund Andros of the Guards and six musketeers of his company took a political prisoner from the Tower to be questioned at Whitehall. Andros's prisoner was Colonel Thomas Hutchinson, renowned as the parliament's governor of Nottingham during the civil wars. He had been seized at

---

[1] Whitmore's concern to rescue Andros from the unthinking calumnies of Boston did not lead him to discuss Sir Edmund's "repeated examinations." Most of them lay beyond the bounds of *The Andros Tracts Being A Collection of Pamphlets And Official Papers Issued During The Period Between The Overthrow Of The Andros Government And The Establishment Of The Second Charter Of Massachusetts* (Boston, 1868–1874), I, xxxvi.

his home by royal troops on the night of October 11, suspected of complicity in a republican rising. Captured without a warrant, transported to London without arraignment, held in the Tower without any charge being made against him, Hutchinson died in captivity eleven months after this interrogation by Ensign Andros. Yet the colonel admiringly recorded Ensign Andros's military caution and legally skillful interview.[2]

The dexterity of the twenty-five-year-old ensign in balancing the demands of the royal prerogative and the forms of law was again displayed when next this army officer appeared as an officer of royal justice. To swear in Major Edmund Andros as their "baliff," or president, the "jurats," or judges, of the Royal Court of Guernsey met in a special session on Monday, June 29, 1674. The constitutional and circumstantial conditions which the new baliff found in Guernsey were very similar to those which later evolved in other overseas outposts of England's empire. The island was subject to parliamentary statute only when specifically named. Like the American colonies, Guernsey was named in the acts of trade and navigation so hated by the Guernseymen, whose trade was largely with French neighbors and American associates. Guernseymen were further governed by a local law code, in part customary, Norman, and Calvinist, and in part legislated. They were also commanded by a royal military executive who administered the various types of law, but who was especially concerned to enforce the commercial monopoly claimed by England, to collect the resulting royal customs which paid his salary, and to insist upon the spiritual rights of the Church of England despite the islanders'

---

[2] Henry Gee, "The Derwentdale Plot, 1663," in Royal Historical Society *Transactions*, 3rd Ser., 2 (1917), 137n; Lucy Hutchinson, *Memoirs of the Life of Colonel Hutchinson, Governor of Nottingham*, Rev. Julius Hutchinson, ed., revised by C. H. Firth (London, 1806, 1906), 322, 326, 327–330, 331–336, and esp. 351–354. The King issued an order (not a warrant), dated October 25, 1663, to the lieutenant of the Tower, to closely imprison Hutchinson for treasonable practices. Historical Manuscripts Commission [HMC], *Manuscripts of the Duke of Leeds* (London, 1888), 6; *Calendar of State Papers, Domestic Series* [*Cal. S.P. Dom.*], *1661–1662*, F. H. Blackburne Daniell et al., eds. (London, 1888), 327, 329. Andros is the "Andrews" of Hutchinson's narrative, having been commissioned an ensign in the Guards, June 4, 1662. As late as November, 1663, he was the only "Andros" or "Andrews" in the commission registers. Charles Dalton, ed., *English Army Lists and Commission Registers, 1661–1714* (London, 1891–1904), I, 28, 37, *passim*; Sir F. W. Hamilton, *The Origin and History of the First or Grenadier Guards* (London, 1874–1877), I, 4. Andros served in the Guards until he was commissioned major of the Barbados Regiment, September, 1667.

traditional Calvinism. Proud of their autonomy, yet dependent upon England for military and naval security against their French neighbors and Dutch rivals, the people of Guernsey were in a situation very similar to that of England's American dependencies. As one of the fifth generation of his family on the island, successor to his father as seigneur of Sausmarez, and baliff of the royal court (which he headed for forty years), Edmund Andros must be cleared of the accusations of American historians that he "lacked understanding of business affairs and Puritan psychology," or that his "aristocratic background allowed him little faith in democratic institutions." Andros's Guernsey inheritance and experience thoroughly equipped him to understand the colonial constitution, economy, dissenting religion, and—not "democratic institutions," for the seventeenth century admitted none—representative government.[3]

In the case of courts and law, however, it was true, as his Presbyterian opponents on the bench of the royal court of Guernsey said in 1674, that Major Andros had "noe experience at all in Judicial proceedings or laws or customs, though he might in other things," such as arrests and interrogations, London riot control, martial law in the West Indies, the law of marine salvage in the Netherlands, diplomacy for James Stuart, and garrison government of English towns, of Barbados, and of the Leeward Islands. On the civil bench, Major and Baliff Andros did not always respect the distinction between his own arbitrary judgments and those based on Guernsey's local laws or customs. But it was not at all clear which were arbitrary rulings and which were based on local laws and customs. These constitutional foundations had been reshaped and reinterpreted on a case-by-case basis for centuries by shifting

---

[3] See Jonathan Duncan, *The History of Guernsey* . . . (London, 1841), 443–462; John Uttley, *A Short History of the Channel Islands* (New York, 1966), esp. 41–66, 77, 79–82, 85–94, 97. See also William Berry, *The History of the Island of Guernsey* . . . *to the year 1814* (London, 1815); A. J. Eagleston, *The Channel Islands under Tudor Government: A Study in Administrative History, 1485–1642* (Cambridge, 1949). On the Andros family in the islands, the best study, and one which relies on documents now destroyed, is Edith F. Carey, "Amias Andros and Sir Edmund His Son," in Guernsey Society of Natural Science and Local Research *Transactions*, 7 (1913–1916), 38–68. A notably fair-minded estimate of Andros is given by Viola Florence Barnes in Allen Johnson and Dumas Malone, eds., *The Dictionary of American Biography* (New York, 1928–1936), II, 300–301. On Andros's swearing-in, see W. Beauvoir to Viscount Hatton of Kirby, July 7, 1674, in Additional Manuscripts [Add. MS] 29554, 364–364b, British Museum.

majorities of Guernsey jurats. Where some "customary" invention or recollection would not serve to preserve the hegemony of the local elite against the commands of the English king or against lower-class levelling, simple falsehood served Guernsey's need: "the people are made of fraud." In the relationships of royal prerogative and local self-government, or of law and lying, Andros's royalist background, unique in Guernsey, anticipated his American experience. Then too, his court appearances on both sides of the Atlantic were deeply dyed with religious hatred.[4]

The supreme head of the Church of England, King Charles II, asserted that the islanders' "dissenting in manner of worship and church government . . . was the chief if not the only cause of the late disorders," that is, of Guernsey's "having submitted to the usurping powers . . . and quitted their duties to their native sovereign." It was the King's dean of the church in Guernsey who reminded royal officers "that the way to establish yourself is by taking care of God's worship"; who called on Edmund's father, Baliff Amias Andros, to help discipline "those that oppose conformity," whether religious or political; who insisted that no minister of God should be "a trumpet of sedition" against the King's officers; and who rejoiced that "the honorable defunct [the late Amias Andros], hath left worthy offsprings of his most Noble and Illustrious family" to continue the imposition of religious and political obedience on the dissident islanders.[5]

In order to succeed his father, Major Andros presented the assembled jurats of the royal court the dean's fulsome testimony to his religious conformity, along with the king's warrant appointing him baliff of Guernsey. The new baliff of the royal court began his first session by naming as lieutenant baliff his uncle, that veteran royalist soldier Charles Andros. Then Major Andros read an order of the privy council "much to the disadvantage of our Court," as the leader of the Presbyterian "faction" put it, "& to the Baliff power and exaltation." The judges of the court

---

[4] Beauvoir to Hatton, July 27, 1674, *ibid.*, 376–378; Adrian de Saravia, quoted by A. J. Eagleston, "Guernsey under Sir Thomas Leighton (1570–1610)," in Guernsey Society *Trans.*

[5] The King to Hatton, July 15, 1663, quoted in Duncan, *Guernsey*, 342; Order of the King in Council, August 18, 1660, quoted *ibid.*, 107; *ibid.*, 342–350; 8 Proverbs 15; A. E. de Sausmarez to Hatton, August 18, 1671, July 18, 1672, in Add. MS 29553, 229; Add. MS 29554, 7–7b; Havilland to same, March 2, [1673/1674], in Add. MS 29553, 391.

were told that they must support the dignity of the baliff, or his lieutenant, "as representing his majesty's person, and being his chief minister of justice" by their personal attendance. As one jurat complained, "if he goes out to make water, we must attend him" or be imprisoned at the baliff's pleasure. Institutionally, the locally selected jurats lost to the royally appointed baliff "the power to fine, suspend, depose, and punish" not only the members of the royal court, but also "the King's Subjects here, who ought by all our Laws, Liberties, Charters, Privileges, to be judged and punished by the King's Royal Court alone, [but] are left to the arbitrary judgment of a single man alone . . . divesting the King's Court here of Lawfull authority to place it on himself for his mere ambition & covetousnesse."[6]

The reaction of Edmund Andros's Guernsey opponents in the royal court anticipated in detail that of his American enemies. The "anti-Androsites" argued that, unless the King were misinformed, he would not have violated their chartered liberties by appointing Andros baliff or enlarging his powers. They sought to deny registration and refuse obedience to Andros's commission until the King could be correctly informed. Andros's reaction to dissidence and debate was characteristic. "The Bailly often interrupted me," complained the leader of the opposition, "telling me I was not there to make harrangues [*sic*], but to say in a few words whether [the order] should be registered or not." "As judge," Andros's opponent claimed "that I was to have my freedom of expression." But opinion did not prevail against numbers. Two brothers, a cousin, and a nephew, to count only the closest Andros kin on the court, helped carry the vote which registered the privy council order. It made their seigneur the most powerful official in the province and it made them Guernsey's oligarchs.[7]

Andros and his deputies did not neglect the material advantages of judicial position any more than they neglected to enforce the royal prerogatives which were the basis of their profit and power. The baliff was registrar of all sales of property, which some Guern-

[6] The Order of the King in Council, July 4, 1674, is reproduced in Duncan, *Guernsey*, 114. The French military career of Charles Andros is noted by Carey, "Andros," 40. Andros's warrant as bailiff is in *Cal. S.P. Dom., 1673–1675*, 95. W. Beauvoir complained to Lord Hatton, July 7, 1674, in Add. MS 29554, 364. See also *ibid.*, 261, 363.

[7] W. Beauvoir to Lord Hatton, July 7, 27, August 14, 1674, *ibid.*, 29554, 364–364b, 376–378, 388.

seymen found as onerous as New Englanders would. He recorded all commercial contracts, received the royal customs duties and quit rents, and was licensed to import English wool for the island knitters. The baliff won from the English government permission for the free import of salt for the island fisheries, as he was to do for the fishermen of New York and Maine. He sought wheat to feed both handicrafters and fishermen. Likewise, it would be the need of maritime Massachusetts for Connecticut bread that encouraged Andros to seek the union of their economies. The baliff of Guernsey also supervised trade with Newfoundland, New England, and Virginia in servants, fish, tobacco, and (illegally) in European manufactured goods. In all these transactions—as well as in acting as the champion at court of a local currency, inflated in relation to sterling, the model for his later fiscal requests for New York and New England—Edmund Andros served the needs of Guernsey's colonial economy, enriched his family, friends, and political supporters by special privilege, and illustrated the identity of imperial issues throughout England's Atlantic empire. Baliff Andros's comprehensive understanding and relatively successful management of American colonial economies was the result of that island experience, and of military missions that involved him in the supervision of commercial exchanges in both commodities and merchandise, which rebuts historical allegations of Major Andros's supposed soldierly limitations. His background was far broader than his detractors have recognized.[8]

In the same summer of 1674 when he capped his long association with Guernsey by becoming its civil head, Major Edmund Andros was commissioned by the Duke of York to govern his province of New York. Andros's ties to the duke dated back fifteen years. Linked with the youthful duke's first government, Jersey, in 1649, Andros followed the Stuarts into exile, where he became

---

[8] Andros's support of the wool trade appears in Add. MS 29558, 38, 51, 66; Add. MS 29559, 413. On the relation of wheat, meat, fisheries, and the potential of the Dominion of New England as a large free trade area, see Andros to Blathwayt, March 30, August 17, 1687, in the Blathwayt Papers III, 3, Colonial Williamsburg, Inc. See also same, October 4, 1688, *ibid.*, 5. New York's fur trade, fisheries, customs-free salt, colonial currency inflation, and direct trade with the Dutch were discussed by Andros with the Duke and his household commissioners; E. B. O'Callaghan, ed., *Documents Relative to the Colonial History of the State of New York* [*NYCD*] (15 vols., Albany, 1853–1887), III, 230–231, 233–234; W. Noel Sainsbury, ed., *Calendar of State Papers, Colonial Series (America and West Indies)* [*Cal. S. P. Col.*] (London, 1860–1939), *1669–1674*, no. 1313; *ibid.*, *1675–1676*, no. 796.

cupbearer to the duke's aunt, "the winter queen," Elizabeth of Bohemia. After the restoration of the Stuarts, Andros had left Elizabeth's household to become ensign to another retainer of the Stuarts, Sir John Talbot of the Grenadier Guards. Following extensive service in English garrisons and in the West Indies, Major Andros married into the family of the Duke of York's most faithful military servant, the Earl of Craven, formerly the financier, master of the ceremonies, and perhaps second husband of Elizabeth of Bohemia, and afterwards colonel of James II's Grenadier Guards. In Major Andros, then, James Stuart found a tried royalist and a veteran soldier, with English and American experience in garrison government, and an administrator familiar with the constitutional peculiarities of the overseas dominions, as manifested in Guernsey.

In New York as the duke's governor, as in Guernsey as baliff, Edmund Andros presided over governing bodies of local magnates. In form as well as in function, the New York council resembled the royal court of Guernsey. The New York court of assizes carried out similar quasi-legislative functions to those undertaken by the States of Guernsey. In both cases, the standing court or council was annually augmented by representatives of the several parishes or townships. Andros proposed that the duke make these two sets of provincial institutions nearly identical by conferring the political functions of the assizes on an assembly whose township members would, as in Guernsey's parishes, be elected by major property holders. As in Guernsey, or in England, this New York "court of parliament" would be composed of the head of government, his councilors, and elected representatives of those districts which now sent their justices of the peace as judges of assize. These representatives would, as the duke remarked, "in all likelihood be the same men" who now sat in the assizes. As Andros knew from his Guernsey experience, however, elected delegates would constitute "an afforcement of the court," able to give "the consent of the community" to the court-legislature's taxes and laws.[9]

Andros's proposed expansion of political participation seemed

[9] Andros's commission for the government passed July 1, when he was in Guernsey; C.O. 5/1311; *NYCD*, III, 215. See also, *ibid.*, 261; *Cal. S. P. Col. 1669–1674*, nos. 1313–1318. On the augmentation of the court, see J. H. LePatourel, *The Medieval Administration of the Channel Islands, 1199–1399* (Oxford, 1937), 117–118, and the Duke of York to Andros, April 6, 1675, January 28, 1675/1676, in *NYCD*, III, 230, 235.

to the Duke of York only nominal in form but really dangerous in effect, "nothing being more knowne than the aptness of such bodys to assume to themselves many priviledges which prove destructive to, or very oft disturbe the peace of the governmt wherein they are allowed." Andros was left to control New York's court and council as he had Guernsey's, using authority derived from the crown to confer economic privilege and social status on politically loyal and obedient members of the local elite. Those who resisted the taxes, laws, and decrees of the assize court and the council were beaten down by the governor's garrison of English regulars. It was Major Andros's redcoated regulars who captured the defendant and enforced the decisions of the court of assizes in the most dramatic of the New York trials by which the major asserted his master's prerogative and his own power.[10]

Sir Edmund Andros returned from furlough in England to New York in August, 1678. Newly knighted by the King, the governor was full of the prerogative prescriptions associated with the Earl of Danby's ministry and was emboldened by the magnified political influence of the Duke of York. Andros's letters home were suddenly full of criticisms of "petty independent governments," of their military imbecility, destructive economic rivalries, and independence from royal authority. An example was near at hand. The duke had lopped lands from New York to reward the loyalty of his favorite courtiers, Sir Edward Carteret and Lord John Berkeley. But Carteret had presumed to govern as well as to own the lands granted him, and Berkeley had sold out his acres to Quakers. The Duke of York's secretary had warned his governor of New York that these dangerous divisions of his command were only temporary. Should Sir George Carteret's "foote chance to slip, those who succeed him must be content with less civility yn we show him . . . since yn we should exercise yt just authority his Rll Highness hath without such reserves, as though intended but favours now, may, if confirmed, redound too much to ye prejudice of yor colony."[11]

[10] York to Andros, *idem.* For the exemptions, see Werden to Andros, September 15, 1675, in *NYCD*, III, 233, and for the fishery company see *ibid.*, 234. For repression of the English towns of Long Island and the New York City Dutch see *ibid.*, 230, 233, 254.

[11] Andros left New York on November 16, 1677 (*ibid.*, 257) and returned on August 7, 1678 (*ibid.*, 271). See his letters to Blathwayt, September 16, October 12, 1678, March 25, 1679, in *NYCD*, III, 271–273, 277-278; C. O. 5/1111, 40–42, 43–44, and to the lords

As soon as the news of Sir George's death reached Andros in March, 1680, he wrote to Philip Carteret "to forbear and not to presume further to assume or exercise distinct or any jurisdiction over his Majesty's subjects, or any person." Carteret and his councilors feared that Andros was poised to invade New Jersey "with your sloops and a considerable number of soldiers," but they clung to political authority in New Jersey. Andros's agents then lobbied the prospective members of the New Jersey assembly. Carteret canceled their meeting. Suddenly, Governor Andros himself appeared at Elizabeth Town. He was surrounded by his military officers, councilors, and merchants, but had none of the "offensive forces" against whom Carteret had assembled "150 men in arms." Andros proclaimed his authority by publicly reading his commissions. Carteret still refused to retire from the government. Sir Edmund quietly returned to New York. At midnight, April 30/31, 1680, soldiers from Andros's garrison broke into Philip Carteret's home. They "seized him naked, dragged him through the window, struck and kicked him terribly, and even injured him internally. They threw him, all naked as he was, into a canoe . . . and carried him in that condition to New York, where they furnished him clothes and shoes and stockings, and then conducted him to the fort and put him immediately in prison."[12]

Five weeks later, Sir Edmund Andros summoned the court of assize to give a legal gloss to his seizure of Captain Carteret and to the authority Andros had forcibly assumed over New Jersey. Heralded by three trumpeters, Sir Edmund took the president's seat, "high up above all the others." He charged that the prisoner, Captain Philip Carteret, had exercised royal authority although he was simply the de facto leader of a private settlement. In reply,

---

of trade and plantations, April 9, 1678, esp. clauses 8–9, 12, in *NYCD*, III, 262–264, C. O. 5/1111, 31. On the Duke's grant of lands to Carteret, just as Andros was to sail for New York, see *Cal S. P. Col., 1669–1674*, no. 1331. Werden's warnings to Andros, February 13, 1674/1675, August 31, 1676, are in *NYCD*, III, 229, 240.

[12] E. Andros, "To Governor Philip Carteret," March 8, 1679/1680, and proclamation, March 13, 1679/1680, are in Aaron Leaming and Jacob Spicer, eds., *The Grants, Concessions, And Original Constitutions of The Province Of New Jersey . . .* (Philadelphia, 1752; Somerville, N.J., 1881), 673, 675–676. The correspondence of these principals is contained *ibid.*, 674–678, as are the orders by "Sir Edmund Andross, Knight, Seigneur of Sausmarez, Lieutenant and Governor General and Vice Admiral under his Royal Highness JAMES Duke of York and Albany, &c." to Capt. James Collyer to seize Carteret, *ibid.*, 679–680. Carteret (*ibid.*, 678) confirms Bartlett Burliegh James and J. Franklin Jameson, eds., *Journal of Jasper Danckaerts, 1679–1680* (New York, 1913), 241.

Carteret protested "against the jurisdiction of this court, where his imprisoner and accuser is to be the judge." The defendant insisted that the King "is the only proper decider of this matter." But Andros forced Carteret to plead, and he did: "not guilty." Andros himself, Carteret then pointed out, had recognized his right to rule New Jersey. He pulled from his pocket Andros's letters addressed to himself as "Governor of New Jersey." Sir Edmund replied that his calling Carteret "governor" did not make him so, an observation true but not forcible, and one which only reinforced Carteret's contention that the King alone could decide the dispute. The jury declared *"the prisoner at the bar not guilty."* Repeatedly, Andros sent the jury back to reconsider their verdict, the third time with "threats that they should look to what they did, as there was too much depended upon it, for themselves their entire condition and welfare." The utmost Sir Edmund could bring the jury to do was to advise Carteret to return to private life, giving bond "not to assume any authority or jurisdiction . . . civil or military, in New Jersey," until the crown declared who should govern its people.[13]

Captain Carteret obeyed the court order and abandoned his government for the time being. He "was compelled to do so" by Andros's armed forces. But Carteret hoped to join others aggrieved by Andros in capitalizing on changed political conditions in England, and on influential personal connections there, to make the duke reverse the verdict of Sir Edmund's court.[14]

Carteret's shotgun appeal—to kinsfolk, to customs commissioners, to friends at court, and through them all to the Duke of York and his household officers—coincided with other complaints against Andros. West New Jersey Quakers, whose local leader Andros had imprisoned for more than two years for claiming political and fiscal authority on the Delaware, had acquired powerful access to the Duke of York through William Penn. The influential father of an officer of Andros's garrison, whom the governor had cashiered for connivance with the Quaker settlers, demanded that

---

[13] Danckaerts' trial description is augmented by the official record, dated May 28, 1680, in Leaming and Spicer, eds., *Grants*, 678–680, and Carteret's own report, July 9, 1680, *ibid.*, 683–685.

[14] James and Jameson, eds., *Danckaerts*, 253; Andros to New Jersey Assembly, June 2, 1680, in Leaming and Spicer, eds., *Grants*, 680–681.

Andros himself be called to account. Andros's opponents in New York persuaded their business partners in London to approach the Duke of York with reports that his governor's favors to certain merchants, his trading on his own account, and his permitting direct trade with the Dutch had ruined the duke's revenue while enriching Governor Andros. James was too weak politically to defend Andros against all these attacks. The Duke of York, caught in the Exclusion Crisis, which was designed to prevent his succession to the throne, and repeatedly exiled by the King, needed both the support of Andros's enemies and the revenue they promised him when Andros was out of the way. In May, 1680, the duke recalled Sir Edmund to answer the accumulated charges against him.[15]

The duke himself was faced with such strident accusations in Parliament that the King did not allow him to come home from exile until February, 1680. Then Charles warned his brother that he would have to leave England again before the legislature reconvened in October, months before Andros returned. Little time remained for James to rally his political resources to resist exclusion and to recruit the physical means to fight the civil war which would follow his degradation. Hastily, before James left for exile in Scotland and months before Sir Edmund arrived to defend himself, the duke disavowed Andros's action in New Jersey, passed political authority to the Quakers, and sent out an accountant, John Lewin, who was badly biased against Andros and in favor of Lewin's own secret commercial partners, the anti-Androsite merchants. In January, 1681, as soon as Lewin's investigation of the New York government was finished, Andros sailed for Eng-

---

[15] Carteret's appeals are in Leaming and Spicer, eds., *Grants*, 684–685. On the Fenwick case, and William Penn's warning to James that England's religious dissenters would measure their likely fate, should he come to the throne, by his treatment of the Quakers in the Jerseys, see Charles M. Andrews, *The Colonial Period of American History* (New Haven, 1937), III, esp. 164; Vincent Buranelli, *The King and the Quaker* (Philadelphia, 1962), 64–65; and Werden's letters to Andros, August 31, 1676, May 7, 1677, August 12, 1678, in *Cal. S. P. Col.*, no. 1024; *ibid., 1677–1680*, nos. 222, 778. James's recall of Sir Edmund, May 24, 1680, and Werden's explanation, with its veiled warning of Lewin's bias, are in *NYCD*, III, 283–284. See also Werden to Andros, January 31, 1676, in *Cal. S. P. Col., 1675–1676*, no. 803. On the Christopher Billop case and the military politics of the garrison, see York to Andros, January 28, 1675/1676; Werden to same, August 31, 1676, March 10, 1678/1679, in *NYCD*, III, 235, 239, 276–277; same to Billop, August 31, 1676, in *Cal. S. P. Col., 1675–1676*, no. 1025.

land. No sooner did he reach London than he re-embarked, going to Scotland early in March to pay his respects to the Duke of York at Edinburgh. On April 4, the duke ordered the commissioners of his household to countenance no charges against Andros unless both the plaintiffs and plain proofs appeared before the commissioners.

The charges against him were, as Sir Edmund said to the duke's commissioners, broad and vague, but from them emerged two clear facts. First, news of the Duke of York's political weakness in England had unleashed in New York the social and political dissidence endemic to Anglo-American society in this period. This turbulence was especially stimulated in New York's recently arrived English merchant community by Sir Edmund's cultivation of the older Dutch provincial establishment. Second, the enemies of authority had seized on the weakness of the heir apparent to the throne not just to attack his governor but also to reject the attributes and functions of monarchical government itself.[16]

Republican politics and racial hatred alike emerged from the case of *Milbourne v. Andros* when it was heard in London in 1681. Jacob Milbourne, the plaintiff, alleged that in December, 1678, the governor of New York, Sir Edmund Andros, twice "with force and armes &c did make an Assault upon the plt & him then and there did beat, wound, evilly intreat & imprison & him in prison agt the law of England did detain." Milbourne said that Andros jailed him for twenty-four hours on the first occasion and for six days on the second, at a cost to Milbourne of 1000 pounds in lost business.[17]

Andros's defense was narrowly legal in its premises but broadly political in its conclusions. Sir Edmund presented the court his commission from the duke to govern New York and the duke's grant of authority from the King. Under these general commissions to preserve the king's peace, Andros, like every English governor, asserted his legal right, political responsibility, and military duty to examine all travelers passing through the headquarters of

---

[16] F. C. Turner, *James II* (London, 1948), 175, 180; James to Andros, May 24, 1680, in *NYCD*, III, 283; Andrews, *Colonial Period*, III, 153; Leaming and Spicer eds., *Grants*, 685–687; Sir Charles Littleton, former deputy governor of Jamaica, to Hatton, March 11, 1681, in Add. MS 29577, 3, 21; The Answer of Sir Edmund Andros, in *NYCD*, III, 312.

[17] Jacob Milbourne plt Sr. Edmond Andross Deft., London SS, in *NYCD*, III, 301.

his command. Milbourne had been told by the customs officials to report to the governor. He had refused, according to Andros, saying the governor had no power over him, "thereby encouraging others to be mutinous." An officer of the garrison marched Milbourne to the governor and his council, "who by the laws of the country are justices of the peace & chief magistrates there." By their order, Milbourne was jailed overnight, it being ten in the evening at the time of the commitment.[18]

Having explained his authority and described the incident, Sir Edmund then expanded on his reasons for thinking Milbourne a threat to the peace of New York, who deserved public humiliation and disgrace. These reasons said something about the social divisions and discontents which heated Anglo-American politics. Jacob Milbourne, Sir Edmund told the court, was a "person of noe credit, but one that hath been bought as a servant in Barbadoes & New England and by reason of his stubbornesse & disobedience to his Masters hath severall times been transferred from one Master to another." That a rebellious servant should sass the seigneur of Sausmarez (whose overpopulated Guernsey estates provided scores of servants such as Milbourne to labor in the colonies) was shocking in itself. Still worse, Sir Edmund said, was the threat that such impudent men represented to the king's peace. Milbourne was making trouble, the governor pointed out, in a colony still agitated by insurrections in Virginia and Maryland. From the events of 1689, Milbourne emerged to lead the New York phase of the revolution against Andros's Dominion of New England. Milbourne's platform—anti-Catholic and antimonarchical, proprovincial autonomy and proassembly—was taken directly from the Exclusion Crisis and the anti-Androsite campaign. The republicanism of Jacob Milbourne, ideologue and secretary of

[18] *Ibid.* The Guernsey parallel appears in Add. MS 29577, 261, 304, 485; Add. MS 29559, 298, 429; and in State Papers Group 44, Piece 68, 161, Public Records Office [PRO]. A classic example at York is discussed in James J. Cartwright, ed., *The Memoirs of Sir John Reresby . . . , 1634–1689* (London, 1875), and ed. by Andrew Browning (Glasgow, 1936); Cartwright, 256–257, 258; Browning, 226, 227, 271–272, 273. Authority "to keep the keys" was the essence of gubernatorial power. Major Richard Elton, *The Compleat Body of the Art Military Compiled for the Foot* (London, 1649, 1659), 189, 190. The Duke specifically authorized Andros to use garrison troops to police the port (Werden to Andros, August 31, 1676, in *NYCD*, III, 239) and made Andros his vice admiral for New York and its dependencies in May, 1678 (*Cal. S. P. Col., 1677–1680*, no. 708).

Leisler's Rebellion, would authenticate Sir Edmund's apprehension.[19]

But Andros could not tell the court of Milbourne's most immediate menace. No sooner had this republican arrived in New York than there spread the news of the Popish Plot, an engine of anti-Catholic hysteria which was designed to fell first James Stuart and then the English monarchy. Jailing Jacob Milbourne in James's own province had not sufficed to squelch rumors so satisfying to the enemies of the duke's government and Andros's authority. These were the aspirant, middling merchants and craftsmen. Their hopes for enhanced social status and economic opportunity lay in legitimizing their own wider participation in politics. To rise, the "middling sort" had to reduce the royal prerogative which kept them down and which elevated Dutchmen and courtiers to be their social superiors and economic masters.[20]

These ambitious men emerged from obscurity to testify against Governor Andros and his New York establishment. The Duke of York had had no such intention in ordering the inquiry. He merely wanted to assess the plausibility of the out-merchants' proposal to purchase the farm of his New York revenue. They offered to pay him more from the profits of New York than his governor admitted collecting altogether. The fiscal impossibility of so doing did not deter the merchant faction, for their true motives were rooted in English politics. The result was a political inquisition in New York. John Lewin, the auditor appointed to investigate the New York accounts, admitted as much when he reached New York. He declared that Andros was recalled and that Sir Edmund would never return if only the antiprerogative party turned out in force to testify against the governor. The English-born merchants who accepted this invitation shared commercial partnerships with Lewin himself and with the would-be revenue farmers in London. They were associates of the Quakers, of Fenwick in particular, who had invested in New Jersey. They were to be the lifelong rivals

---

[19] *Milbourne v. Andros*, in *NYCD*, III, 301. Werden warned Andros of the Baconian danger, November 30, 1676, "as they may have scattered about to debauch the fidelity or attract the pitty of the neighbor colonies"; *ibid.*, 245. As Andros's secretary, Edward Randolph, wrote to a New York correspondent after the revolution in 1689, "Your rebels are no changelings"; *Cal. S. P. Col., 1689–1692*, no. 664.

[20] The testimony of the grand jury and the court of assizes as to merchant political participation is in New-York Historical Society *Collections*, 45 (1913), 14–18. On the origins of the Lewin inquiry, see Sir John Churchill's remarks in *NYCD*, III, 315.

of the wealthiest merchants of New York, the Dutch-born magnates whom Andros had appointed to his council, named as judges, and, in all likelihood, joined in trading ventures. The victim of political hatred directed against his master, the duke, and of social competition which existed regardless of his actions, in December, 1681, Sir Edmund Andros at last exposed his opponents' motives. The movement to exclude the Duke of York from the succession had failed. Now it was personally and politically safe for Andros to say, publicly, what had been the subterranean truth of the New York inquest from its inception. It was, Sir Edmund testified, "a consequence of former practices under pretence of his Royal Highness's service against the Authority there [in New York] to overthrow his Royal Highnesses Revenue and Authority in the said parts, which was effected during Mr. Lewin's being upon the place and after my being commanded thence & returne home, as may appear upon due examination."[21]

Due examination before the duke's commissioners proved Andros's arguments accurate. The charges against him were the usual colonial combination of economics and politics.[22]

It was alleged that Andros had taxed the colonists without their consent to build and fortify the new breakwater and dock. In reply, he asked who objected to a levy of labor and materials which had produced an immediate profit to the community. No objectors could be found.[23]

It was also charged that the governor had misspent the duke's revenue to strengthen the citadel of New York, Fort James. Andros offered the usual governor general's reply, one which sounded self-evident to a board of commissioners, all of whom were royalist veterans of the civil wars and several of whom, as garrison governors, had themselves held down hostile townspeople on behalf of royal authority. The new armory in the fort, Sir Edmund said, secured the store of weapons which had to be available to arm the militia against foreign invasion or Indian upris-

---

[21] See the limitations in the Duke's instructions to Lewin, May 24, 1680, *ibid.*, 279–282. Andros's report of Lewin's remarks, *ibid.*, III, 309, is supported by the assize court's testimony, N.Y. Hist. Soc. *Colls.* (1913), 16.

[22] John Lewin's Report, in *NYCD*, III, 306–308.

[23] Andros also noted that his warehouse construction was part of this public works program which, he claimed, had multiplied both the trade and revenue of New York tenfold; *ibid.*, 312–313.

ing, but had to be protected from domestic dissidents. The new kitchen in Fort James, Andros alleged, fed more effectively the garrison of his government, the troops who preserved the peace in the duke's colonial capital and who were the first defense against French aggression or Indian treachery as well.[24]

The governor's accusers then insisted that the revenue was less than it should have been, whether because of his favor to his Dutch councilors or because he discouraged commerce by his severity in collecting customs from English-born opponents. It was logically and legally hard to have it both ways, although it may well have been true both that customs enforcement did discourage trade and that Andros did not collect as rigorously as he might have from those whom he did not want to discourage.

"5thly," Governor Andros's accusers alleged "That ye governor obstructed ye trade, encouraged the Dutch & connived at bringing in contraband goods; and told the inhabitants that if they knew wt lres he recd from the Duke they would find their privileges hung on but a slender thread." Only the lesser merchants' combined hatreds—of regulation, of the Dutch, of the duke, and so of his governor who disciplined them, distinguished the Dutch, and defended the duke's authority—explain the juxtapositions of items in this article. The provable substance of the charge was: (1) lest the commercial reputation of New York's staple trade suffer, the governor had forced a baker to take back a shipment of bad bread intended for the West Indies; (2) Andros had limited fur trading to merchants resident at Albany and permitted only residents of New York City to mill wheat. The governor replied that the fur monopoly was his way of obeying the duke's instructions to favor Albany, the entrepot of the Iroquois trade, trade which secured the loyalty of the most militant people in North America. Likewise, milling regulations were Andros's response to the duke's orders to enrich the urban center of the colony, in accordance with the metropolitan preoccupations of Yorkists and of garrison government.

Most serious, because it was purely political and implicated the duke directly in Andros's authoritarian behavior, was the penultimate charge. It was alleged that during the trial of Philip Carte-

---

[24] [Sir] J[ohn] Churchill to the . . . Commissioners of his Royal Highness Revenue, *ibid.*, 314–316; The Answer of Sir Edmund Andros, *ibid.*, 311.

ret, one of the jury "speaking to the governor said that he hoped they had the same privileges as the other plantations. The Governor answered that their Privileges hung on a slender thread, & that he was chidden for giving them such liberties." No witness could be found to support this charge before the Duke of York's commissioners. Several officers of Andros's government swore that they were present at the trial but had heard him say nothing to this effect. Neither Lewin nor any other of the composers of the accusations against Andros would make the charge his own and so risk Andros's libel suit. Therefore, the article was dismissed by the hearing board, together with a final, frivolous allegation that the governor had committed lese majesty by demanding a jury trial of all the charges against him. No one in authority imagined that Sir Edmund Andros would prefer a jury (no matter how pleasantly packed by the new Tory sheriffs of London) rather than the understanding assessment of his fellow servants to his royal highness. These commissioners formally concluded that the case against the governor of New York, whether for fraud in the duke's revenue or for mismanagement of his political authority, had failed for lack of evidence. Not content with this negative judgment, the duke's commissioners reported to their master that Sir Edmund and his subordinates "have behaved themselves very well in their severall stations."[25]

Yet while Sir Edmund Andros and his associates were being exonerated and commended in England, the mass of their opponents were busy dismantling the structure of ducal authority in New York and the Jerseys. Deprived of Andros's unflinching support for the prerogative, Sir Edmund's deputy, Captain Anthony Brockholes, had simply ceased to do anything to which the antiprerogative party objected. He did not collect customs or taxes. He neglected the fort and fortifications. He ended regulation of the economy. Brockholes stopped governing.[26] And he permitted his subordinates to be indicted for treason by New York juries for presuming to act without an authority approved by the antiexecutive factions, that is, without laws newly passed by an assembly elected by all men of property. An assembly, the disgruntled New

---

[25] See notes 22 and 24 above.

[26] See note 16, above, and the Proceedings of the Governor & Council & Assembly of New Jersey, October 19–December 2, 1681, in *NYCD*, III, 293. York's yelp to Brockholes, August 8, [1681], is *ibid.*, 291–292.

Yorkers made plain, had been promised them by Lewin as their reward for allegations against Andros. The court of assizes now told the Duke of York that, for want of an assembly, the colonists "have Grond Under Unexpressible Burdens by having an Arbitrary and Absolute power Used and exercised over us by which a Yearly Revenue is Exacted from us against o[r] Wills o[r] trade Grievously Burdened with undue and Unusuall Customs imposed on o[r] merchandize without o[r] consents o[r] Libertyes and freedomes Intharled and the Inhabitants wholly shut out and deprived of any share Vote or Interest in the Government to thier [*sic*] Great Discouragement and contrary to the Laws, Rights, Liberties and Privilege of the Subject. . . ."[27]

No more exact picture than this has ever been drawn of the aspirations of middling men for status and self-determination, the root of American rebellions for a century, 1676–1776. No prince has ever been more determined than James Stuart to deny such aspirations as anarchical, even impious. As Sir Edmund Andros's trial and its aftermath showed, the strong hand was both resented and required in New York, as it was in those other colonies which had tried to replicate the English constitution. Yet in New York's government—as in that of every royal colony during the Exclusion Crisis—a political impasse had overtaken both ambition and authority. The ambitious colonists still depended on England and found political support at the center of English politics. Their authoritarian English rulers lacked the physical power and the consent of the political nation which were prerequisites for coercion of the colonists. The Duke of York could not govern despotically for many reasons: he felt real responsibilities toward his overseas dominion; he hoped for tangible rewards from it; he was constrained in imperial authority by domestic politics; and he was confronted by colonial stubbornness. Therefore he was forced to grant some "share Vote or Interest in the Government" of his colony to more of his subjects. This was the advice of the Earl of Halifax, who had spoken powerfully in the House of Lords to save James from exclusion and the country from a crisis of authority.

[27] Court of assizes to the secretary of state, enclosing the grand jury bill against Capt. William Dyre; Brockholes to Andros, September 17, 1681, in *NYCD*, III, 287–289; petition of Dyre to the privy council, August 3, 1682, *ibid.*, 319–321; C. O. 5/1111, 54–56; Proceedings of the General Court of Assizes, October 5–6, 1681, in N.Y. Hist. Soc. *Colls.* (1913), 16.

Now he insisted that the constitutional balance must be struck in the empire as well by weighting the representative side of the political scale. As soon as the trial of Sir Edmund Andros was over, and the ducal prerogative thereby confirmed, James ordered the same imperial constitutional compromise to be applied to New York that his brother the King had allowed for Jamaica and Virginia. The military executive of the colony was to be restored in all its authority. Every one of the policies by which Andros had applied the duke's instructions within the colony was reconfirmed. By the same instructions, however, the freeholders of the colony were permitted to elect an assembly, if that assembly in turn voted taxes sufficient to pay the costs of the duke's governor and garrison. The assembly might legislate on any matter of local concern, but it was summoned, prorogued, or dissolved by the governor, and its bills could be amended or rejected by the governor's council, vetoed by the governor, and disallowed by the duke. Thus from the trials of Sir Edmund Andros emerged the assembly of New York. Trials and assembly were parts of the imperial constitutional settlement of 1681, a settlement which would prevail for almost a century.[28]

It may have been November, 1683, before Andros was formally exonerated, but six months previously King Charles had appointed Sir Edmund a gentleman of his household, perhaps of his bedchamber. This was a sensitive post at the side of the dying King for a servant of the heir to the throne. Sir Edmund was in attendance when Charles II died and the Duke of York succeeded to the throne as James II. Andros was one of the household servants whom James dispatched to defend him against Monmouth's

---

[28] On Halifax's position, see J. P. Kenyon, *Robert Spencer, Earl of Sunderland* (London, 1958), 48, 55–60; Gilbert Burnet, *History of My Own Time . . .* , Osmond Airy, ed. (Oxford, 1897), 339–340; H. C. Foxcroft, *The Life and Letters of . . . First Marquis of Halifax* (Oxford, 1897, 1898), I, 225–228. Notice to Andros of the Duke's release of both Jerseys and the Delaware, with full political rights to Penn, followed within three days the King's concessions regarding Jamaica; *Cal. S. P. Col., 1677–1680*, nos. 1570–1571, 1579–1580. Only Andros's councillors and partners were named as members of the council of Sir Edmund's successor; *NYCD*, III, 333–334. In fortification, urban monopolies, and land regulation, the new governor was "particularly to observe how it was in Sr Edmd Andros his time." The pretentions of Pennsylvania and New Jersey were resisted, and a mint for New York considered, again on Andros's recommendation; *ibid.*, 350–351; Add. MS 24927, 49, 52; *Cal. S. P. Col. 1681–1685*, no. 1563. On the revenue-representation tradeoff, see the letters from [Werden] and York. February 11, March 28, 1682, in *NYCD*, III, 317–318.

invasion and the rising of the West Country. The King gave
Andros a bodyguard of cavalry and sent him riding west to advise
a local militia lieutenant in the work of suppression. Three weeks
after the rebellion was crushed at Sedgemoor, King James II commissioned Sir Edmund Andros as lieutenant colonel of a regiment
of dragoons, a military unit designed for political police work.[29]

During the suppression of Monmouth's rebellion, the governor
or general designate of New England, Colonel Piercy Kirke, had
shown himself to be a bit independent of royal commands. As
soon as the rebellion was defeated, King James nominated Sir
Edmund to succeed Colonel Kirke in command of New England.
Since 1635, and with increasing frequency after 1664, English imperialists had tried to eliminate the autonomy of Puritan Massachusetts. When James Stuart came to power in 1682, almost three
years before he formally succeeded to the throne, the destruction
of the Massachusetts charter government was again put in train.
In 1684 it was legally concluded. A provisional regime was hastily
organized to set the stage for the imposition of garrison government on Massachusetts and, subsequently, its extension south to
the Delaware under Sir Edmund Andros. But the crises of secession, rebellion, and repression produced a year-long neglect of
American affairs. Sir Edmund's commission and instructions were
not completed until the spring of 1686. It was December before
he and his garrison—the characteristic instrument of an Andros
administration—landed in "this distant, & generally plenty, but
otherways poor place much obliged to fishermen."[30]

Andros did not long enjoy his new command. The military

[29] *Cal. S. P. Col., 1681–1685,* no. 1415, assigns this date to the report printed in
NYCD, III, 314–316. Whitmore, ed., *Andros Tracts,* I, xlvii–xlix; Dalton, ed., *Army
Lists,* II, 9, 14. My discussion of the general relation of this repression to imperial
government is given in " 'Brave Men and Servants to His Royal Highness': The
Household of James Stuart in the Evolution of English Imperialism," in *Perspectives
in American History,* 8 (1974), 47–89.

[30] On Kirke, see Lt. Col. John Davis, *The History of the Second Queen's Royal
Regiment* (London, 1881), esp. II, 38–39; State Papers, Group 44, Piece 56, 260, 266,
268; War Office, Group 4, Piece 1, 12–13, PRO. Andros's commissions are listed in
Jeanne Gould Bloom, "Sir Edmund Andros: A Study in Seventeenth Century Colonial
Administration" (doctoral dissertation, Yale University, 1962), 89–90. The fourth
clause of the declaration of the Massachusetts revolutionaries, April 18, 1689, notes
that the garrison of redcoats was designed to impose Andros's commission on New
England, "not without repeated Menaces that some hundreds more were intended for
us"; Whitmore, ed., *Andros Tracts,* I, 13; *Cal. S. P. Col., 1689–1692,* no. 261.

coup which overthrew King James in the winter of 1688 had its counterpart in Massachusetts in the following spring. In the overseas dominion, as in the realm of England, members of the traditional, locally-rooted ruling elites had either been dispossessed or were fearful of being ousted from authority by the obedient, statist, bureaucratic or militaristic servants of Stuart sovereignty. These local elites allied themselves with the established, politicized, Protestant clergy whose religious hegemony was threatened by the Trojan horse of Catholic James's tolerance. Magnates and ministers played upon the Protestantism (and Francophobia) of the armed forces, already restive under the imposition of modern military discipline by a soldier-sovereign's professional officers. Military discipline endangered both popular liberty and aristocratic social dominance. That the standing forces of royal authority were also increasingly representative of the British Isles' racial and religious minorities added the bite of racism and bigotry to the fears of militarism's potential for social leveling and political absolutism.[31]

The resulting revolt of the Massachusetts militia found the governor general of New England militarily helpless. Most of his officers and all but a corporal's guard of his garrison were dispersed on the northern frontiers of New England to provide the military leadership New Englanders lacked and the core of the garrisons for the outposts they would not willingly defend. On the rumor of the English upheaval, Sir Edmund Andros returned to Boston from his winter campaign against the natives. But, in a decision as politically disastrous as it was militarily correct, he left his redcoats behind to protect his subjects. To command Boston on the morning of April 18, 1689, he had but a dozen soldiers in Fort Mary. Another dozen regulars isolated on Castle Island, three miles across the harbor. Sir Edmund's soldiers were too few to guard the walls of his newly built citadel, much less quell the carefully organized militia rising which overwhelmed his capital. Taken prisoner, Andros was locked up for nine months,

---

[31] The Declaration of April 18, 1689, *Andros Tracts*, I, 11–19. On the destruction of clerical monopoly, see also Toppan and Goodrich, eds., *Randolph*, IV, 163; Michael Garibaldi Hall, *Edward Randolph and the American Colonies, 1676–1703* (Chapel Hill, 1960), 114–117. On the composition and use of the Declaration, see especially Viola Florence Barnes, *The Dominion of New England: A Study in British Colonial Policy* (New Haven, 1923), 241–242.

several of them in winter and in a wet dungeon on Castle Island. Finally, in February, 1690, the self-restored charter government of Massachusetts dispatched evidence, prosecutors, and prisoners on long winter voyages to royal judgment.[32]

Sir Edmund Andros landed in Bristol at the end of March, 1690. Reaching London on April 6, he found that the coup of 1688 had not displaced many of his patrons or any of his policies. His regiment had been one of the first to go over to William of Orange. The new King's privy council, before whom Andros's case would be heard, was presided over by Thomas Osborne (the former Earl of Danby, now Marquess of Carmarthen), whose politics were Sir Edmund's own. Sir Edmund's long-time ally and patron, Daniel Finch, now Earl of Nottingham, was the secretary of state who assumed control of colonial affairs just as Andros arrived. As lord keeper, Finch had supported Andros's Guernsey pretensions. Together, they had been listed among Danby's courtiers. Both had served in agencies associated with the Duke of York. Deeply identified with the Church of England, Nottingham, like Andros, had nonetheless remained to the end loyal to James. When Sir Edmund came home, the secretary, a member of the privy council, was "caballing" with the council's president to pro-

---

[32] The fatal indiscipline of the militia and the essential services of the regular soldiers and their brutal officers, can be observed in *Cal. S. P. Col., 1689–1692,* nos. 152, 286 I, 310, 311, 316, 319, 407, 482, 509, 513, 740, 742, 763, 773, 783, 788, 802, 884–885, 899, and especially in Andros's own summary, *ibid.,* 901–902. See also *ibid.,* 904–906, 912–913, in particular, 939, 1000; "A Particular Account," in Charles M. Andrews, ed., *Narratives of the Insurrections, 1675–1690* (New York, 1915), 198, 204–205, 209; Andros's report, *ibid.,* 234; "New England's Faction Discovered," *ibid.,* 260–261, 263, 265–267; "Reflections upon the Affairs of New England," in Connecticut Historical Society *Collections,* 21 (1924), 328. As always, the militia was more powerful politically than militarily. See *Cal. S. P. Col., 1689–1692,* nos. 306, 885. For the number of Andros's guards see *ibid.,* no. 261. The revolutionary leadership spoke of the rising as one the "prior motion of which we were wholly ignorant" (*ibid.,* 261 II; *Andros Tracts,* I, 20), but see not only the authoritarians (Andrews, ed., *Narratives,* 196, 232, 257, 259) but, conclusively, the balanced account of Samuel Mather, whose name proclaims his allegiance and descent (*Andros Tracts,* III, 145). Mather records the prior preparation of the Declaration to cover a rising seen by some colonial leaders as precipitate but unavoidable. See also Barnes, *Dominion,* 237–238. Not until June 28, 1689, did the committee of safety allege that Andros's acceptance and execution of supposedly illegal commissions to govern them was the reason for his continued imprisonment; *Cal. S. P. Col., 1689–1692,* no. 286 II. On October 10, 1689, the general court (*i.e.,* assembly) finally authorized the continued detention of the prisoners seized the previous April 19; *ibid.,* 512, 512 II, 522. See also Andrews, ed., *Narratives,* 260; Bloom, "Andros," 137–139; Barnes, *Dominion,* 253–255; Whitmore, ed., *Andros Tracts,* I, 26, 174–175; III, 111–113, 151.

tect Charles II's and James II's old servants from whig attacks. Nottingham's chief subordinate, the clerk of the privy council—and thus the arranger of Andros's forthcoming trial—was Andros's old associate in imperialism, the secretary for war and plantations, William Blathwayt. Only two months before Andros returned to London, the King himself had turned to a political coalition dominated by Sir Edmund's tory patrons, Carmarthen and Nottingham. When Sir Edmund reached London in April, 1690, the new parliament, "which are most Church men where nothing amongst them has been moved Concerning New England" and the restoration of its charter, had been in session a month. Its conservatism was already apparent. Its business was the King's proposals that parliament pass an indemnity for all past political offenses, minimize the acts of revolutionary conventions, and force no officer to abjure the former King. "The Agents of New England," as the spokesmen for the current government of Massachusetts styled themselves, discovered that, to put it mildly, "greater malefactors yn Sr Edmond could be represented to be in the utmost imagination were not hastily proceeded against."[33]

The trial of Sir Edmund Andros took place on Thursday, April 17, 1690. The privy council chamber was divided by a long table, "the council board." At its head sat the lord president; at the foot was the clerk of the council. Around the table were ranged chairs for the committee of the council for trade and plantations, and for such other privy councilors as chose to attend. On one side of the council chamber stood the four agents of the acting government of Massachusetts Bay: the influential Presbyterian Sir Henry

---

[33] Elisha Cooke to Simon Bradstreet, London, October 16, 1690, Massachusetts Historical Society *Proceedings*, 45 (1911–1912), 644–645; Dalton, ed., *Army Lists*, II, 9. Shrewsbury was ill during the spring and resigned in June; William A. Aiken, comp., *The Conduct of the Earl of Nottingham . . .* (New Haven, 1941), 45–47, 54–55, 63–64, n. 61, n. 65; Henry Horwitz, *Revolution Politicks: The Career of Daniel Finch, Second Earl of Nottingham, 1647–1730* (Cambridge, 1968), 57, 83, 102, 104, 106, 107, 111, 115; Stephen Saunders Webb, "William Blathwayt . . . ," in the *William and Mary Quarterly*, 3rd Ser., 26 (1969), 373–374, 377–378; and the extraordinarily valuable account of Thomas Brinley to Francis Brinley, May 28, 1690, printed with Increase Mather's notes (from the back of the charges against Andros) as "Sir Edmund Andros's Hearing before the Lords of Trade and Plantations, April 17, 1690," in ed. and intro. by Theodore B. Lewis, American Antiquarian Society *Proceedings* (1973), 241–250. Dr. Lewis very kindly permitted me to read a larger version of his introduction to these documents. I am also in his debt for a personal communication on the subject of the charges against Sir Edmund.

Ashurst; the Reverend Increase Mather, who had spent the past year at court lobbying against the government of Sir Edmund Andros; and the newly arrived champions of the old charter and the puritan society it symbolized, "the two doctors," Elisha Cooke and Thomas Oakes. With them stood distinguished counsel, the leading whig partisans, Sir John Somers and Edward Ward. Against these prosecutors stood "Sir Edmund, and the [seven or more] Gentlemen Concerned with him on the other side of the Board and about twenty Gentlemen and merchants accompanying him." Sir Edmund's supporters included a number of New England's wealthiest traders as well as leading Guernseymen. Sir Edmund was flanked by his defense counsel, the present and former attorneys general, Sir George Treby and Sir Robert Sawyer.[34]

Despite all this evidence of Sir Edmund's forethought and self-assurance, Dr. Cooke was astonished that Sir Edmund "came prepared with a charge against the colony for rebellion against lawful authority, for imprisoning the King's governor &c." Suddenly, the defendant had become the prosecutor. Before the colonial agents could charge Sir Edmund with anything, the lord president of the privy council permitted Sir Robert Sawyer to read Andros's accusation. Then he allowed Sawyer to support Sir Edmund Andros's counterattack with a legally irrelevant but politically effective summary of Massachusetts' sins against English authority: defiance of the crown's commands; disobedience of the parliament's acts of trade; disrespect toward the Church of England. Sawyer was well-qualified to denounce the Massachusetts dissidents. He had prosecuted the original writ against the Massachusetts charter in 1683. Only two months prior to the present hearing, Sawyer had convinced this very committee of the privy council that the revocation of the Massachusetts grant was legal, and that Sir Edmund's commission to govern the colony was likewise legitimate. In December, Sir Edmund Andros's other counsel, the current attorney general, had reported to this council committee that the collection of taxes in Massachusetts by authority of Andros's commission and at his orders was altogether legal and unactionable. Recent precedents, plus quick action by Andros, his attor-

---

[34] In addition to Brinley's, Mather's, and Cooke's accounts, another, seemingly eye-witness account is reprinted in Carey, "Andros," 59–60. Here see *ibid.*, 59; Cooke, *Mass. Hist. Soc. Proc.*, (1911–1912), 645–646; *Cal. S. P. Col., 1689–1692*, no. 817; Hall, *Randolph*, 131.

neys, and the lord president of the council, had turned the tables on the colonial agents.[35]

The "Matters objected against Sir Edmond Andros" now had to be presented not as accusations but rather as justifications for rebellion against the Dominion of New England and the imprisonment of its governor general. Read without sympathy by the clerk of the council, William Blathwayt, the first of these charges was that the governor general had ordered New Englanders to resist "his present Maties" invasion and had stifled news of its success by imprisoning the bearer of William's declaration. Secondly, the agents asserted that Andros governed "without forme or colour of legal authority," and in particular that he illegally taxed the colonists and usurped the right to patent lands. This set of accusations concluded with the infamous charge that the governor general, "during the time of actuall war with the Indians . . . did supply them with ammunition, and severall Indians declared that they were encouraged by him to make war upon the English, and he discountenanced making defence against the Indians." Finally, a third paragraph implicated all the other dominion officials imprisoned by the revolutionaries as "Accomplices and confederates with Sr Edmund Andros." Some were councillors who "joined with him in his Arbitrary Lawes and Impositions, & in threatening and imprisoning them who would not comply" with Andros's taxes. Others were executives under Andros, such as Deputy Secretary West, whose words "shewed himself no friend to the English." Government attorneys were "concerned in illegal proceedings destructive of the Propertie of the subject." Sir Edmund's sheriff "impaneled Juries of strangers who had no freehold in that Country, and extorted unreasonable fees."[36]

The first article against Andros was the only one of substance. Replying to it, Sir Robert Sawyer observed that "his present Majesty" was not yet King when Sir Edmund issued "King James Proclamation against a foreign Invasion which was Proclaimed all over England at that time and in London." Proclaimed, although Sawyer did not say so, by some of the lords now sitting in judgment. In thus warning his people against a possible invasion, Sir

---

[35] Cooke to Bradstreet, 646–647; Carey, "Andros," 59–60; "Reflections," Conn. Hist. Soc. *Colls.* (1924), 327; Whitmore, ed., *Andros Tracts*, II, 174; *Cal. S. P. Col., 1689–1692*, nos. 25, 28, 152, 676; Colonial Office, Group 5, Piece 905, 253–254, cited by Bloom, "Andros," 301n, 304n.

Edmund "did butt his duty as being Governour their [*sic*] and Commander in chiefe." To this self-evident statement there could be no reply. But Sir Robert moved onto stickier soil when he defended the governor general against an accurate charge. The first man to bring to Boston William of Orange's declaration *had* been promptly jailed for spreading a "treasonable libel," and he was refused bail. Sawyer said that this charge "was false and [he] would Prove it so," but, for the moment, begged leave to dispose of the remaining charges.[37]

Sir Edmund's attorney was not going to have any difficulty in doing that. The bulk of articles two and three really were either erroneous or false. They had been previously so judged by lords of the present committee. The lords had already decided that Andros's taxation, land regulation, and his officers' enforcement of them by arrest, fine, and imprisonment were legal. Several of the lords had been members of the committee when it rejected Massachusetts' previous presentation of the profoundly hypocritical, false, and ungrateful libel that Sir Edmund Andros, the most successful Indian figher in the history of New England, had betrayed them to the natives. The remainder of the indictment concerned excessive fees extorted by Sir Edmund's executives and juries packed by his sheriff. These allegations were literally true, but legally unprovable.[38] The head of the restored charter govern-

[36] The proceedings are reconstructed from the two conflicting accounts by Brinley (Lewis, ed., Am. Antiquarian Soc. *Proc.* [1973], 241–250), and Bradstreet to Cooke (Mass. Hist. Soc. *Proc.* [1911–1912], 644–645). See West's reply on the peculiar Massachusetts mentality which assumed that they were the only Englishmen, natives of England being regarded as "strangers" or foreigners; Whitmore, ed., *Andros Tracts*, II, 185–186. The charges against Andros are printed *ibid.*, 176–177. The disposal of them is recorded *ibid.*, 173–174, 177. In general, the defendants made the obvious point that *their* English liberties had been violated by the colonists, not the reverse.

[37] Besides Bradstreet and Brinley, see Barnes, *Dominion*, 239–240, on the arrest of John Winslow (but the Declaration he carried came from Virginia, not from Nevis).

[38] See the privy council's hearing, in response to Andros's petition, of the Massachusetts charge that he connived in the supply of munitions to King Philip, and note the humiliating rebuff to the colonial agents on that occasion; *Cal. S. P. Col., 1677–1680*, nos. 654, 655, 669, 677–678. Since 1676, Andros's French and Indian diplomacy had been misinterpreted and his military skill maligned by those merchants of Massachusetts (led in 1689 by Thomas Hutchinson's grandfather, John Foster, who built the Foster-Hutchinson mansion out of the profits of supplying the eastern Indians against New England's frontier) who were themselves shamefully compromised in arms sales to hostile natives; Andrews, ed., *Narratives*, 198, 198n; Whitmore, ed., *Andros Tracts*, II, 88–89, 216–217; *NYCD*, III, 581, 724; Bloom, "Andros," 135–136; Barnes, *Dominion*, 227–230, 239–240, n. 22, n. 24. For views of the house, and for its destruction, see Bernard Bailyn, *The Ordeal of Thomas Hutchinson* (Cambridge, 1974), 10–11, 35–37.

ment, Simon Bradstreet, had admitted as much when he wrote Increase Mather to apologize that "the informations and evidences we have gathered up against Sir Ed. Andros [and sent over with Drs. Cooke and Oakes] fall greatly short of what might have been procured" had the revolutionaries only been able to find some incriminating papers. But the Massachusetts regime could find nothing. They assumed that the Dominion officials had burned the evidence, or hidden it, or that "many of their actings in things that would make them most obnoxious were . . . not committed to writing that might otherwise rise up against them." Their assumptions, however, were not admissible evidence.[39]

Now the embarrassed agents of the revolution in Massachusetts realized before the privy council the "great difference between clamour and legal evidences." What they had scraped up "might have served a turn before a propitious judicatory, especially if saying without proving might have gone for ay," but the lords of the privy council, dominated by noblemen sympathetic to Andros, expected proof. The colonial agents found to their sorrow the "difference between talking high at home and doing business at White[h]all."[40]

Leaping on the apparent weakness of the agents' political position and legal case, Joseph Dudley, the president of Sir Edmund's council for New England, interrupted the proceedings to ask that the lord president of the privy council demand the agents' credentials, that is, to find out for what legal government they made these charges. If the agents' authority to make any accusations was established, Dudley asked Carmarthen to insist that the agents sign the charges and so assume legal liability for them. Agreeing to President Dudley's request, "My Lord President asked them [the agents] if they came from any Governor and Counsell or any General Assembly. They answered from the People. From what People Said my Lord. From the whole body of the People. . . . Then said Sir Robert Sawyer they come from the Rabble my Lord." The agents' attorney, Sir John Somers, solicitor general and the brains of the whig party, tried to rescue the situation. He

---

[39] Simon Bradstreet to the Rev. Mr. Increase Mather, January 29, 1689 [1690], in [Thomas Hutchinson, ed.], *A Collection of Original Papers Relative to the History of the Colony of Massachusetts Bay* (Boston, 1769), 575; "Reflections," Conn. Hist. Soc. *Colls.* (1924), 327.

[40] "Reflections," *ibid.*

explained to the lord president that "the country, my lord, oppressed by an arbitrary government did as we did here . . . rose as one man. . . ." The lords of the council laughed aloud. They knew about the conspiratorial origins of revolution from their own experience, and they saw in themselves and in the groups on either side of the board the partisanships masked by Somers's homogenization. When order was restored, the lord president demonstrated a degree of legalistic impatience with Somers's ingenuous explanation of the revolutions of 1688–1689. "You say it was the country and the people," said his lordship, "that is nobody; let us see A, B, and C, the persons that will make it their case. Here is a charge against the King's governor, but nobody has signed the paper." And nobody did.[41]

One agent, either Cooke or Oakes, whispered to Sir John Somers that the agents would sign if they must; but Sir John knew that Mather and Ashurst had refused to sign the charges, refused because they did not believe Cooke and Oakes when they said the charges could be proved before the privy council in England, whatever Massachusetts opinion might be. So Somers simply said, "If they wish to bring us off thus they may." That is, if the privy councilors wished to avoid reopening their own political wounds by avoiding a vote, it was easiest to do so by declaring that the plaintiffs had no standing to sue. Such a solution both evaded the necessity of declaring the colonial version of the English revolution illegal and avoided the admission that colonists had risen with impunity against an honest and capable English governor.[42]

The governor general could not be criticized for carrying out the crown's legal orders, but neither could the revolution be undone. It already had had important results in securing for

---

[41] Cooke to Bradstreet, Mass. Hist. Soc. *Colls.* (1911–1912), 648; Brinley in Lewis, ed., Am. Antiquarian Soc. *Proc.* (1973), 248–250; *Cal. S. P. Col., 1689–1692*, nos. 267, 884. Sawyer had been a follower of Danby at least from 1677, and Nottingham's association was as ancient; Andrew Browning, ed., *English Historical Documents, 1660–1714* (New York, 1953), 237, 247. On the other side, Somers would lead the whig attack on Andros as a way of reaching Blathwayt in 1696–1698; Webb, "Blathwayt," 399–401.

[42] Cooke to Bradstreet, in Mass. Hist. Soc. *Proc.* (1912), 649. Randolph had predicted this result to the Governor General of Barbados as early as May 16, 1689; Hutchinson, ed., *Original Papers,* 572. Whitmore concludes that "Andros had committed no crime for which he could be punished and that he had in no way exceeded or abused the powers conferred upon him"; *Andros Tracts,* I, xxxiii.

Massachusetts royal promises of inclusion with Jamaica, Virginia, and New York in the restored 1681 constitutional settlement. It would never be acknowledged as legitimate, however, nor would the governor general be condemned by a privy council committee dominated by royalists and imperialists. Belatedly realizing this, the agents cut their political losses and avoided personal liability for the charges by denying that "they were any wayes concerned for New England, and that if Sir Edmund &c. had nothing to say against them, they had nothing against him, and as for the said objections, they would not owne them." Thereupon, the lord president said, "wee must take a Minute that there is an Accusation or objection brought against Sir Edmund Andros &c. by nobody, and so commanded the Chamber to be cleared." Three days later the committee recommended to the King in council "that the said Sr Edmond Andros and other persons lately imprisoned in New England and now attending upon your Matie, be forthwith discharged and set at liberties, and the said Paper or Charge which has not been signed or owned, may be dismissed, inasmuch as nothing has been objected against the said Sr. Edmond Andros and others, by the present Government of the Massachusetts Bay or their Agents. . . ."[43]

As one whig lord told the agents, politically "they had cut the throat of their country" by refusing to sign the articles against Andros. Mather himself admitted that "the Toreys insult [us] saying the N[ew]-E[ngland] Agents put in a Libell which they darst not signe and that the things were false that Sr. E[dmund] was charged with." King William appeared to agree with the tories. He accepted the recommendation to dismiss the charges. Then, at the instance of "many great Lords and Noblemen," the Earl of Nottingham chief among them, the King received Sir Edmund and seventeen of his Dominion officials with extraordinary marks of favor: "the King, hearing they were come, immediately left all the Court and came out to them, and they all kissed his hand." King William was as impressed as the agents had been dismayed by the number and quality of Andros's party. "His Majesty

---

[43] Carey, "Andros," 59–60; Whitmore, ed., *Andros Tracts*, II, 173–176; *Cal. S. P. Col., 1689–1692*, nos. 830, 846; Brinley in Lewis, ed., Am. Antiquarian Soc. *Proc.* (1973), 249, 250.

asked Sir Edmond if all these Gentlemen came from New England with him. He told him they did and had served his Majesty their [*sic*] in severall Imployments. Coll. Dudley Prayed his Majesty would thinke of New England to settle them again, which he most Graciously said he would take care of them."[44]

The settlement of New England and its imperial officials meant consultations in which "Sir Edmund is almost every day with the King and is sent for [by] him often," while "the agents are never since seen about the Court and no news of the Charter." Instead, King William accepted Sir Edmund's argument that the current Massachusetts leadership, having by "insurection" managed the "subversion of the Government," could not surmount its leaders' suicidally selfish desires to sell to the Indians the food and firearms which fueled the natives' devastation of the New England frontiers. Elevated by a militia mutiny against frontier service, the would-be leaders of Massachusetts could not make the militia defend the people and so could not claim the people's obedience. After the trial of Sir Edmund Andros, the King came to believe that if he agreed to the political proposals of the Massachusetts agents, "the Kings Governour would be made a Governour of Clouts." Therefore William gave Massachusetts very little more in the way of self-government than the assembly which he permitted to every colony.[45]

As for the colony's alleged oppressor, not only did acquittal lead once again to Sir Edmund Andros's personal vindication and to the reiteration of the imperial policies whose enforcement was his lifework, but it led to professional advancement. King William commissioned Andros captain general and governor-in-chief of

---

[44] The number, quality, and wealth of Andros's court party—a surprising number of whom accompanied him to England, to his trial, and to his vindication by King William—were as much an embarrassment to the revolutionary regime and to their agents (Bradstreet to Mather, in Hutchinson, ed., *Original Papers*, 576) as they were a support to Andros at his trial (Brinley in Lewis, ed., Am. Antiquarian Soc. *Proc.* [1973], 249), impressive to the King (Carey, "Andros," 59–60), and a powerful argument in favor of Andros's prescriptions for colonial government (*Cal. S. P. Col., 1689–1692*, no. 1439). See also *ibid.*, 740–743, 1390–1393, 1404, 1418–1420, 1431–1432, 1440; Bloom, "Andros," 303–304n; Hall, *Randolph*, 125–126.

[45] On the charter negotiations, besides note 44, see Cooke to Bradstreet, in Mass. Hist. Soc. *Colls.* (1912), 650, 651; Webb, "Blathwayt," 378; Whitmore, ed., *Andros Tracts*, III, 19, 165. On the force and acceptance of Andros's view, see *Cal. S. P. Col., 1689–1692*, nos. 901–902, 912, 913, 939; "Reflections," in Conn. Hist. Soc. *Colls.* (1924), 328; *NYCD*, III, 722.

Virginia, one of the most lucrative and least onerous imperial commands.[46]

Sir Edmund's appointment testified to the peoples of England's empire that changed rulers did not mean changed imperial policies; that King William was a Protestant King James; that, as Lord Halifax observed, "when the people contend for their liberty, they seldom get anything by their victory but new masters." Or, after the trials of Sir Edmund Andros, they got the old one back again, and again.

In Andros's person there appeared in provincial America a new class of royal executive: the militarily and administratively experienced, socially well-connected, garrison governor. Each of the governor general's characteristics warred with the civilian, middle-class, anti-institutional aspirations of colonists unqualified to rule by any criteria but their own ambition and the widening social and emotional distance between England and her diverse colonies. Governors general like Sir Edmund Andros created the "old Empire." Their successors alienated the leaders of the American Revolution. Both creative imperial coercion and rebellious colonial reaction found prophetic voice in the trials of Sir Edmund Andros.

---

[46] It was widely rumored that the King would return Andros to New England; Brinley in Lewis, ed., Am. Antiquarian Soc. *Proc.* (1973), 250; Bloom, "Andros," 301–302n. Sir Edmund's appointment to Virginia, February 4, 1692, is noted in *Cal. S. P. Col., 1689–1692,* nos. 2045, 2050, 2097–2101. Note that the commission as captain general and governor in chief, given by William III to Andros, was identical to that issued by James II to Lord Howard of Effingham. Compare the latter (August 3, 1685, in Colonial Office, Group 5, Piece 1357, 1–39), to the former (March 1, 1691/1692, *ibid.,* Piece 1359, 15–18), as evidence of the continuity of imperial policy through the revolution of 1688–1689.

The Distribution of Property
in Colonial Connecticut

Jackson Turner Main

Purposes and Sources

SYSTEMATIC ANALYSIS of the distribution of property during colonial times is in its infancy. We confront several theories, each resting upon inadequate evidence and in part contradictory. One holds that a truncated version of the European class structure was transplanted to America, characterized by inequality and rigidity. The democratizing influence of the frontier environment gradually created an equalitarian social order with high mobility, and the Revolution (according to one subspecies) preserved social democracy. A counter-hypothesis postulates a fairly equal distribution of property at first, under frontier influences, and subsequently a trend back toward European conditions of economic inequality and decreasing mobility, with the Revolution (again per a subspecies) designed to halt this retrogression. A third suggestion, as yet incompletely formulated, works backward in time from a quite stable and high concentration of wealth during the nineteenth century and predicts the same situation earlier. We therefore ask whether in Connecticut we can discern any consistent change in the level and distribution of property. In addition, we will examine some of the reasons for the patterns of wealthholding, especially the correlation of wealth with age, marital status, residence, and occupation. For lack of space we will omit a description of the relationship between property and social class or prestige, and between property and political power. We will

AUTHOR'S NOTE: I particularly wish to thank James Henretta, James Kirby Martin, and Gary Nash for their meticulous criticism of this essay.

also forego any discussion of social mobility (important though that is) and of the effect of heredity upon wealth.

This analysis will depend upon two major sources: tax lists and inventories of estates. Both have virtues and drawbacks. Tax lists, as compiled in colonial Connecticut, included almost every man in the community, even if he owned no property.[1] If the surviving form enumerates the taxpayers' names and indicates the number of polls—men sixteen and up—for whom they paid a tax, we can obtain a close estimate of the population at that time. Assessed property included oxen, certain other farm animals, improved land, and the profits of nonagricultural enterprises, such as innkeeping or shoemaking (a tax on "faculties"). We therefore can derive some notion of the distribution of property and, if a series of lists survive, of changes over time.

Unfortunately we cannot rely upon these lists for an analysis of property holding. First, only a scattered few exist—far too few to answer our questions satisfactorily. Second, many important forms of property escaped taxation, such as household goods which made up over one-third of the people's personal estates, debts receivable, and buildings. Third, laws assigned set values to property which really varied greatly in quality. The trend was toward a uniformity which disguised the very real differences in wealth. Fourth, people sometimes concealed property and assessors may have abetted the practice. Fifth, unless we possess the full assessment list (which is rarely), naming each taxpayer and specifying the number of polls for which he or she was responsible, we cannot distinguish the tax on polls from the rest of the tax. This hinders us from obtaining a correct count of the adult men and from accurately studying the distribution of property.[2] Finally, the tax system was regressive in that the property which escaped taxation belonged mostly to the rich. Therefore the lists understate the property held by the wealthiest citizens, making the distribution appear more equal than was really the case. All in all,

---

[1] The important exceptions were ministers and men in military service, who were regularly excluded; sometimes transients; and occasionally a poor family or one stricken by some disaster. Men over sixty paid no poll tax. Dependent polls, whose tax a father or master paid for them, included servants and slaves as well as sons or other relatives.

[2] Thus a man with two sons who was assessed for £30 in property would pay a tax on £84 (at £18 per poll), placing him among the top 20 percent of wealth holders, whereas he really stood near the median.

tax lists are more useful in affording us occasional counts of the male population, of the proportion of landless, and of men's occupations than in studying the distribution of wealth. For that we turn to estate inventories.

Inventories in Connecticut included all property, real and personal, usually priced item by item.[3] Taken in conjunction with wills and accounts of administration, they furnish an extraordinary picture of the people's lives and possessions. Unfortunately inventories, like tax lists, have certain defects.

First, not every estate entered probate, but only 40 to 90 percent of them, varying with time and place. Until 1700 or even later the proportion for Connecticut as a whole approached nine out of ten, but then declined to less than two-thirds by midcentury. Luckily this deficiency does not create a serious bias in the records other than the flaws presently described.

Second, since prices changed considerably over time after about 1710, we cannot compare inventory values without drawing up a price index. Even then our figures will remain approximate rather than exact, adding to the imprecision caused by the appraisers' carelessness. We must also adjust for the different kinds of money: the "country pay" which was standard until after 1700, the "cash," "lawful," or "proclamation" money worth one-third more, the English sterling, and the inflated "old tenor" of the first half of the eighteenth century. We will translate everything into country pay as of about 1700 (see methodological note at the conclusion of this essay).

Third, the inventories obviously recorded the property of men at the moment of their death. Since the average age at death exceeded by twenty-five years the average age of the adult males then living, we are studying the wealth of older men who usually had acquired more property than the younger. Therefore we must adjust for age bias and translate from the distribution of wealth among the probate population to that of the living population, by which we mean adult men (see methodological note).

Finally, probate records usually involve a wealth bias in which the more property a person left, the more likelihood that the

---

[3] That often means every cow, each pair of sheets, every kitchen utensil, each article of clothing, and every book, but the degree of detail differed with the appraisers, the copyist, and local custom.

estate would enter probate. Recourse to tax lists permits us to estimate the degree of error because we can determine what estates escaped being inventoried and estimate also what proportion of the living population had little or no personal property or lacked land.

Since tax lists supply the accurate count of men which we need to correct the biases in probate inventories, and since the latter furnish the full and reliable description of property lacking in the former, a combination of the two permits the description which follows. Our account will open with some general observations about Connecticut's society and wealth and continue with a more detailed analysis of the property, examining some of the major variables affecting the distribution of wealth.

General Distribution of Wealth

The colony-wide assessment lists reveal that at first the richer towns lay in Hartford County, which received an early influx of well-to-do immigrants. Those of New London district ranked close behind. Fairfield came next and New Haven County last. Trading centers such as Hartford, New London, and New Haven contained only average amounts of taxable property, probably because despite the presence of rich men, the poor were also more numerous than in most communities. In 1676, just before King Philip's War, the mean assessment was £65 (country pay) or, subtracting polls, £50 per taxable inhabitant. By 1700 the tax base declined to a mean of £55 or only £37 without the polls, and in 1756 dropped still further to about £43.

Probate records show a mean level of total wealth for the adult men in Hartford County of about £280, including £120 in personal property and £160 in real estate (ignoring changes over time). Is this high or low? We might judge by some comparisons with other colonies, using for this purpose the mean value of the decedent's personal estates (not the property of the average living man), which in the Hartford area was £150 in 1700. This exceeds, by a small margin, the means for Hampshire and Suffolk counties, Massachusetts (exclusive of Boston) and for Gloucester County, New Jersey, but falls below those for the relatively rich farming areas of Burlington and Salem counties, New Jersey (£275 and

£200). In Maryland it was about £150 sterling, or £267 Connecticut money, and in the rich Virginia county of Westmoreland roughly £300, while Boston's mean was even higher.

What do these figures mean for people's standard of living? A farmer of 1700 would require a farm of at least fifty acres (the median was ninety) worth, with house and barn, between £100 and £150. He would need, in livestock, a yoke of oxen (£10) and a few other animals such as a milk cow, a heifer, a calf, and a horse, totaling another £10. Farming implements such as a plow, kitchen utensils, household furniture, and the man's clothing together with his other personal possessions should equal £20— his wife's apparel, children's clothes, and quite often other articles belonging to them or needed for subsistence did not appear in the inventories. Thus the minimum for survival would come to £40 in personal estate, which was, incidentally, a frequent requirement for voting rights. Comfort probably demanded at least the famous eighty acres, including some land of better quality, with superior buildings, worth in all £250 or more, and a personal estate of at least £100.

How many of Connecticut's men attained these levels? According to the inventories, about one-third fell short of the £40, but most of these were young and single. The general median personal wealth for men in their forties and fifties (1650–1750) was about £120, which suggests that a majority provided well for their families. But these single figures reveal little about the distribution of wealth.

Tax lists suggest that during most of the colonial period, about one-third of the adult men owned very little property. Of these, half paid no tax at all, their poll tax being assessed against someone else, usually a father. These men held no land and formed a class of dependent laborers. In addition one-eighth were taxed for under £20 (not counting their poll tax) and must have lived near the margin. Practically all such men were in their twenties or thirties and had not yet married. At the other end of the spectrum 4 or 5 percent owned estates valued at over £100.

Probate records reveal the same distribution. Table I, which includes 360 inventories, exaggerates the people's wealth, because it is based on the holdings mostly of older men. It must be adjusted to show the distribution of property among the living members of society (see methodological note) so we can answer the major question: did a few men own most of the wealth or did everyone have a proportionate share, as such things go? Table II reveals the general distribution among all living adult men, ignoring place and other variables, in percentages, pounds in country pay as of 1700.

TABLE I

DISTRIBUTION OF PROBATE WEALTH, HARTFORD COUNTY, 1690–1709

	Personal (%)	Real (%)	Total (%)
£ 1–49	31.4	22.0	10.3
50–99	26.1	16.3	14.2
100–199	28.9	24.2	19.2
200–299	6.6	16.6	17.3
300–399	2.8	8.2	11.4
400–499	1.7	4.8	8.9
500–999	0.8	6.5	12.5
1,000 +	1.7	1.4	6.4
Total	100.0	100.0	100.2
Mean £	143	213	356
Median £	90	140	230

TABLE II

GENERAL DISTRIBUTION OF WEALTH (PERCENTAGES)

	Personal			Real			Total		
	Hartford	All Conn.		Hartford	All Conn.		Hartford	All Conn.	
	1650–1753	1700	1750	1650–1753	1700	1750	1650–1753	1700	1750
£ 1–49	41	34	39	40	40	36	22	19	22
50–99	27	27	26	16	16	13	15	15	13
100–199	21	21	21	20	20	15	22	22	19
200–299	6	9	7	10	10	11	15	16	13
300–499	3	5	5	7	7	11	14	15	16
500–999	1	2	2	5	6	11	8	9	13
1000 +	1	2	0	2	1	3	4	4	4
Total	100	100	100	100	100	100	100	100	100

Obviously few residents owned estates which would classify them

as well-to-do, even if we lower the requirement of £2,000, stated
in an informed survey, to £1,000. Also, the number of the really
poor was quite limited.[4]

The same conclusion follows from studying the concentration
or dispersion of wealth. There exist several methods of evaluating
relative degrees of concentration, but the simplest both to understand and to execute is to determine the share of total wealth
held by some significant segment of the population. We will use
a decile system, and determine the share held by the richest 10
percent, and so on down to the poorest. In an absolutely equal
distribution, each decile would own 10 percent of the wealth.
Probably the figure almost never falls below 30 percent simply
because men acquire more property as they grow older, and
because inheritances and native abilities differ. Generalizing without fear, anything under 40 percent may be considered equal,
anything over 50 percent, unequal and over 60 percent—which
became usual during the nineteenth century—highly concentrated.

The following estimates serve as a rough guide:[5]

Place	Time	Type of Estate	Top 10% Own
Rural Suffolk County, Mass.	1650–1719	personal inventory	40%
Burlington County, N.J.	1710–1775	”	45%
Maryland, tobacco area	1660–1720	”	55%
Virginia	1763–1789	”	55%
Boston	1763–1789	”	60%
United States	1850–1960	general	56 to 70%

In Connecticut, the concentration in Hartford County exceeded
that of the rest of the colony. During the period taken as a whole,
one out of ten adult men owned 45 percent of the total wealth.
Another 10 percent also held substantially more than their
share—about one-sixth. Then followed half of the men possessing
around one-third of the property, and three out of ten with only

---

[4] Figures for Hartford County omit inventories 1720–1749 because currency fluctuations hinder precision. Using the entire set of inventories, instead of those from a
particular decade, minimizes the effect of exceptional estates or abnormal time
periods. The adjustment for age bias in records other than Hartford County rests not
upon precise information concerning the ages of decedents but assumes a situation
similar to that of Hartford.

[5] Material for the period before 1800 comes from extensive analysis of probate
records by Gloria L. Main and myself. Sources for the more recent period differ in
particulars but agree in a figure of about 70 percent for the nineteenth century, and
a decline in the middle decades of the twentieth.

5 percent. That top group would own over £1,300 apiece, the second around £500 each, the central half £220, and the poorest class well under £50. Our understanding of these crude figures and our interpretation of whether this distribution was equal or unequal depends upon further analysis, particularly with regard to the relationship between property and age or marital status.

Variables 1 and 2: Age and Marital Status

One reason for the concentration of wealth and for what seems at first glance a large number of poor men lies in the correlation between age and wealth. Historians seem to have neglected this life-cycle. They have lamented a high proportion of nearly propertyless polls appearing on tax lists, which reached over 40 percent in some rural communities and even more in the larger towns, without perceiving that most of these were just entering manhood and that many were being supported by parents. Yet upon consideration the sequence becomes obvious. Most of Connecticut's adult males were poor when young and single, increasingly prosperous as they married and grew older and had children, and finally, in some cases, poor again as the boys married and left home with their shares of the family inheritance.

Connecticut's tax lists indicate that about 36 percent of the adult men were between the ages of twenty and thirty, over half of them single. At least half of these young single men lived with their parents. The colony contained relatively few orphans, for fathers usually lived to see their children grown: once a man survived childhood diseases and the ravages of war while retaining the vigor necessary for a parent and breadwinner, he ordinarily lasted until he was over fifty. Besides, widows commonly remarried. According to the tax lists, about one-tenth of Connecticut's adult males lived with their parents or (rarely) with a master. These owned almost no personal property and rarely any real estate. Their deaths might escape the notice of the probate courts, especially during the late colonial period, appearing sometimes when they had inherited land, or died as soldiers or sailors leaving behind their wages due, prize money, and perhaps some clothes together with a few articles given them by their fathers. They paid no tax, but instead their parent or master was assessed for £18,

which represented the estimated return from their labor.[6] Slaves
and indentured servants belong to this same category. Slaves
formed only a small part of Connecticut's population, rising from
1 percent in the seventeenth century to 3 percent by 1770, and
indentured servants also were rare.

The rest of the colony's young single men paid their own tax,
thus establishing themselves as independent. Generally that
involved the acquisition of a house of sorts and a little land, for
the towns periodically distributed ungranted land to all of its taxpaying residents, no matter how poor. Such men would also own
some personal estate consisting primarily of consumption goods—
clothing and household furnishings. Those who planned to
become farmers would be buying some livestock, raising their first
crops, and obtaining farm implements. The others would invest
in the tools of a trade and the appropriate supplies—a loom and
yarn for the weaver, lasts and leather for the shoemaker. Only a
few men remained poor and single all their lives; before 1700 it
was almost unheard of, after that date still unusual. Among all
of the men in their twenties, the mean personal inventory wealth
was £40, compared with a general (Hartford) average of £140;
they owned £60 in real estate as against the usual £200; and they
left at death less than 4 percent of the total property.[7]

Marriage involved not only a social but a major economic
change. The responsibility required income and property beyond
that of mere subsistence. The farmer must own sixty to eighty
acres of land, livestock, and agricultural implements; the artisan
needed tools and a shop; the trader required capital or credit and
a supply of goods; all relied upon considerable skills and maturity.
Always the married man added the articles necessary for a "householder," like kitchen utensils, tableware, and furniture, together
with certain amenities such as pewter instead of wood for dishes:
indeed the inventory clearly distinguishes the husband from the
bachelor. The acquisition of land especially identifies the family
man, for the average young married couple owned from the start
£75 worth, which meant a house, barn, home lot, and some additional acres for livestock. The change of condition from single

---

[6] The basic minimum wage was two shillings per day, or about £30 per year, from
which must be subtracted living costs, evidently judged at £12.

[7] Because of the wealth bias inherent in the probate data, the means of the living
population would be even lower among these young men.

to married therefore involved an economic and social metamorphosis from an almost propertyless dependent, whose status and sustenance derived solely from his parent, to the propertied independent householder with his own individual possessions and reputation.

For some years thereafter the new husband advanced very slowly, because the economic liability of small children nearly counterbalanced any increase in his income. But when the children—especially the boys—reached about the age of sixteen, the value of their labor exceeded their cost. At that point the father began to pay the poll tax, acknowledging the added wealth now contributed by the son's labor. Usually by that time the father had reached the mid-forties and he doubled, tripled, or quadrupled his own still vigorous labor as his sons reached maturity. Men with economically useful children made up about two-fifths of the probate population and held three-fifths of the property.

The final stage in this economic life-cycle began as the grown sons left home. This involved not only a loss of labor for the parent but a transfer of property. The increase of wealth ended, and in extreme cases a man of seventy or more might return to his old starting point—without land and owning but little personal property, sometimes being relieved of all taxes because of his poverty or dependent condition. Not everyone completed this last stage, of course, for some fathers held on grimly to their land until they died, others survived their children, some never produced any sons, and a few acquired enough wealth to withstand such divisions.

Poverty in colonial Connecticut, then, was less associated with class bias than with age. Characteristically around one-fourth of the men owned under £50, nearly forty percent under £100. But of the first group three-fifths were in their twenties and of the second, well over half. That poorest class, which contemporaries often disenfranchised as lacking the desirable stake in society, thus included only 13 percent of the men over thirty. Just 28 percent of the married men held under £100, and among these a few had formerly possessed large estates and had given them away. Tax lists confirm the evidence of inventories. For example, the farming town of Windsor, with about 300 adult men in 1702, contained over 100 assessed for under £10, of whom probably two-thirds were young, single men, so that the genuine class of poor—those who were old enough to have acquired property but had failed—did not exceed 12 percent or, if one establishes the dividing line at £20 worth of taxable property, 23 percent, and two or three points less if one excludes the aged. If one also excludes those men in their early thirties who had not yet become established but might yet succeed, the town's economic failures included only one-tenth at the lower definition, under one-fifth at the higher.[8] This age difference certainly does not explain the distribution of property in Connecticut. Within each age and marital group, great differences in wealth occurred. It does however account for most of the smallest properties and helps us to understand both the nature of poverty and the life-history of the colonial.

Variable 3: Occupation

Just as age and marital status divided the colonists into an economic hierarchy, so also occupation separated them into distinctive groups. Among the people comprising Connecticut's society, perhaps half of the men derived their principal income through their possession of a farm, and 30 percent worked as farm laborers. Most of the last were farmers' sons, hired help being uncommon. Of the remaining 20 percent, half belonged to that broad category called "artisans and mechanics" or "craftsmen," skilled workers who generally owned a little shop and had their own tools, the most common being smiths, coopers, carpenters of various types, shoemakers, tailors, and weavers. Some of the smiths belonged to a separate group who ran larger business enterprises requiring capital and often hired laborers. Let us call them manufacturers. The remaining 10 percent engaged in trade, practiced a profession, or belonged to a miscellaneous category including retired men and soldiers.

At the top, at least from an economic point of view, stood men engaged in commerce, including the "merchants" who exported or imported, "traders" who limited their activities as a rule to the local area, and retail "shopkeepers." Judging from probate records, the first-named owned three times as much real and six or

[8] By the end of the colonial period the proportion had risen by 50 percent in the old town of Wethersfield, less in Simsbury.

seven times as much personal wealth as the average citizen. Of course they sometimes failed in business, but most of them held at least £1,000 worth of property, their mean estate including £1,862 in the case of merchants and £1,288 for traders and shop-keepers.[9] Most men in colonial Connecticut except for the young acquired more land than personal wealth, but commercial men reversed that priority because they possessed much trading stock, money, and debts receivable. Indeed, in Hartford County, although they constituted only 3.5 percent of the men leaving inventories, they held over three-fifths of these forms of inventoried property and nearly 25 percent of the total personal estate.

Next in the economic rank order came the manufacturers, primarily ironmasters, fullers, distillers, maltsters, millers, and tanners. They held only a third as much personal property as did the men in trade, but that was more than any other occupational group except ministers and some public officials. In real estate they surpassed everyone but the merchants. About half owned total properties of £500 or more. The distribution of their inventoried estates in the accompanying table shows the relative absence of poor men among them.

Ranking with these entrepreneurs were the professional men, especially ministers, higher public officials, and lawyers. Of the first we may simply state that almost no poor minister appeared among the inventories until the late colonial period.[10] On the other hand, with few exceptions they did not accumulate large properties, so that their estates fell within fairly narrow limits. The richest 10 percent among them owned only one-fourth of their total wealth, a more even distribution than characterized any other occupational group except farmers. Professional men held a little more land than personal property, but the distinguishing feature of their wealth was the possession of extensive household goods, including, of course, libraries. Most men invested under half of their wealth in consumption goods, but the

[9] This is based on the estates of forty-eight of the former and forty-four of the latter in inventories of Hartford County, 1650–1719, and of the entire colony circa 1700 and 1750 as described. It does not include debts owed, which would reduce some estates. A supplementary study of inventories in Hartford district, 1754–1774, confirms these and other figures, at least as to basic differences.

[10] Tax lists do not indicate minister's wealth because they did not pay poll taxes and some towns exempted them entirely. Their economic position seems to have declined dramatically after 1755, if not before; see the addendum to Table IV.

ministers who left estates in Hartford County before 1720 held 75 percent of all their personal wealth in that form, 10 percent in books alone. Doctors ranked considerably lower on the scale of wealth. None acquired large estates, while some remained poor, at least during the colony's first century.

One other occupational group held more than the average share of property: the farmers. To some extent this higher rank results from the definition of a farmer. As used here, it excludes some very large landowners—some merchants and professionals, for example—who were only secondarily farmers. Adding them would have raised the mean wealth, but that is counteracted by two major exclusions: farm laborers at one extreme and at the other retired men in their seventies and eighties, no longer active them-selves, whose sons had inherited the property. A farmer by this narrowed definition owned livestock and almost always land, though tenantry did exist. Farmers invested less in consumption products than did most other men, and perhaps led as a result somewhat less comfortable lives. Their personal estates averaged £166 against the general £150. They clustered closely around the £134 median, rarely falling below £50 and usually between £75 and £300, so that the distribution of this property among their inventories was comparatively equal, the top 10 percent owning only 25 percent. Much of this sum was in the form of livestock, the norm being a couple of oxen, five other cows, two horses, and half a dozen pigs, worth collectively £25 or £30. To this sum must be added, as characteristic of farmers, agricultural imple-ments (£5 or more) and grains averaging £9.

The farmers' real estate exceeded the general average by 40 per-cent. Characteristically they occupied a home lot of about three acres, with a house, barn, and sometimes other small buildings, an orchard, a garden, and some pasture. This homestead averaged £50 to £100 in value. Adjoining they would own meadow and pasture land, a woodlot, often swamp or marsh land, and a few acres of plowed fields for grain. In addition they shared in "divi-sions" as the towns allotted their ungranted land, and invested in more when they could. The most valuable blocks of real estate belonged not so much to men engaged in farming as a primary occupation as to men with a nonfarm occupation, especially

TABLE III
Distribution of Total Wealth in Inventories, 1650–1753
(percentages, country pay)

	£ 1–49	50–99	100–199	200–299	300–399	400–499	500–999	1000+	Med. Age
Merchants	2	2	4	2	6	6	17	60	51
Traders/shopkeepers	0	0	7	7	7	7	28	45	48
Manufacturers	0	10	0	10	10	10	35	25	55?
Millers	2	5	13	10	6	12	32	20	52
Ministers	0	0	0	9	18	23	27	23	57?
All professionals	7	5	10	8	10	12	27	21	59
Tanners	0	5	5	14	18	9	36	14	49?
Farmers	1½	4½	14	11½	12	12	30	15	52½
Blacksmiths	11	17	19	11	9	11	17	5	46
Doctors		too few							
Joiners and turners	15	11	29	12	15	6	9	3	45
Coopers	9	13	29	18	11	2	16	2	46
Sailors	36	14	27	5	5	9	5	0	32
Weavers	19	23	23	21	11	2	2	0	41
Shoemakers	17	41	8	19	8	3	0	3	37?
Carpenters	33	21	23	14	7	0	2	0	43
Tailors	35	35	13	9	4	0	4	0	32?
Laborers	65	35	0	0	0	0	0	0	
Hartford Co., 1650–1719	12	15	20	15	11	7	13	7	49
Rest of Conn., 1700	9	10	17	18	16	7	17	5	
Hartford Co., 1750–1753	12	12	16	13	10	7	20	10	49½
All Conn., 1750	12	11	17	12	9	8	20	10	

TABLE IV
Inventory Wealth of Occupations (country pay)

		Personal				Real				Total		
	No.	Mean	Trim'd Mean	Median	Top 10%	Mean	Trim'd Mean	Median	Top 10%	Mean	Trim'd Mean	Median	Top 10%
Merchants	48	1041	927	631	32	785	623	418	39	1826	1579	1378	39
Traders/shopkeepers	44	753	630	514	37	535	407	343	45	1288	1107	900	32
Manufacturers	20	312	280	260	29	545	411	349	46	857	692	592	40
Millers	40	163	141	122	28	486	414	381	31	649	564	535	30
Ministers	22	318	291	297	23	403	342	290	32	721	640	526	25
All professionals	60	296	239	213	32	466	380	242	40	750	635	480	34
Tanners	22	227	152	146	41	349	300	306	30	570	500	460	30
Farmers	569	166	146	134	25	443	370	326	33½	608	528	471	30½
Blacksmiths	57	135	119	102	31	219	167	105	42	354	290	231	36
Doctors	17	130				201				331			
Joiners and turners	81	92	73	75	32	190	148	146	39	282	225	219	37
Coopers	46	127	96	78	39	184	154	120	35	312	250	199	40
Sailors	22	55	48	45	29	100	81	46	38	155	132	108	31
Weavers	57	65	59	49	27	96	80	68	33	161	140	117	30
Shoemakers	36	76	63	51	34	70	61	40	33	146	129	83	29
Carpenters	43	61	48	48	36	66	55	38	38	127	107	93	34
Tailors	23	66	53	37	40	54	42	31	42	120	99	87	36
Laborers	43	28	25	25	25	13	10	0	47	42	38	39	22
Hartford County, 1650–1719	1174	150	110	82	47	225	193	145	40	375	303	227	44
Rest of Conn., 1700	349	167	133	102	36	220	185	160	35	386	318	275	34
Hartford County, 1750–1753	255	132	100	91	42	331	240	190	42	444	356	280	41
All Conn., 1750	1233	134	107	92	35	319	246	187	41	445	357	280	39

Addendum: Hartford Area, 1754–1774 (unadjusted personal)

	No.	Mean	Median		No.	Mean	Median		No.	Mean	Median
Merchants	8	2017	1600	Doctors	16	254	130	Joiners/turners	45	66	50
Traders/shopkeepers	27	443	370	Misc. mfgrs.	13	211	215	Carpenters	14	46	50
Lawyers and officials	12	317	300	Ministers	17	176	125	Misc. Artisans	34	70	51
Millers	14	335	270	Farmers	402	143	120	Sailors	13	81	35
Tanners	12	244	210	Blacksmiths	44	129	105	Shoemakers	14	47	40
Ships' captains	20	270	140	Coopers	46	81	75	Soldiers	57	32	20
				Weavers	34	70	51	Laborers	38	19	18

traders.[11] The farmers' land was divided among them somewhat less equally than was the case with personal wealth, the top 10 percent owning 30 to 33 percent of the total, but this compares favorably with the general concentration.

At this point on the scale of occupations a sharp drop occurs, beginning just below the farmers and some of the manufacturers (tanners and blacksmiths). Falling well under the general mean or median wealth were the artisans who owned small shops, notably coopers, joiners, turners, carpenters, shoemakers, tailors, and weavers. Even the more prosperous—the first three—held property 25 percent below the norm, while the others owned less than half the average wealth. Their trades did not require a large initial investment and their modest incomes seldom permitted the accumulation of property. The exceptions occurred mainly among the coopers and the joiners, especially after 1700, who occasionally acquired substantial real estate. But even of these most did not accumulate over £100 in personal wealth, while the entire estates of carpenters, tailors, and shoemakers fell short of that sum. Sailors were about on the same level except that a few, dabbling in trade, managed to buy some land and end their lives in comfort. Soldiers, who almost always were young sons or transients, had still less property (see the addendum to Table IV).

The distribution of property among the men of various occupations was therefore as follows. Farmers, the most numerous group, owned half of Connecticut's personal property and at least three-fourths of the real estate. Laborers, despite the fact that they made up 30 percent of the men, held scarcely 5 percent of the personal and one percent of the real property. Artisans owned 7 percent of each type. Despite their small numbers the merchants, traders, and shopkeepers held 16 percent of the personal and 7 percent of the real wealth. Professionals owned around 5 percent—more than their share—and the remaining 3 percent belonged to miscellaneous individuals. The exceptional wealth of the men in trade and the above-average properties of the professionals contrasted with the poverty of the laborers and helped to create a concentration of wealth. On the other hand the equal distribution of property among farmers and artisans partly counteracted that effect and contributed to the relative equality so characteristic of colonial Connecticut.

[11] Of twenty-five men in Hartford County leaving over £1,000 in real estate during 1650–1719, at least eighteen were not primarily farmers.

Variable 4: Location

Men of prestige lived in every town, just as did men of various ages, marital statuses, and occupations; but they were distributed unequally from place to place, and the distribution of property also differed with location. During the seventeenth century four counties divided the colony into geographical areas: New London in the southeast, Fairfield at the other end toward New York, New Haven between them, and Hartford in the north. More importantly, each county contained towns of various types: trading centers, farming communities with ample supplies of good land, others with little such, and newly established frontier villages.

The distribution of property differed little from county to county. Geographically they were much alike, each possessing good harbors, rivers, land of varying quality, and similar resources; and none developed a city on the scale of Boston or plantations as in the South. The Hartford area got off to a head start because in the first migration an unusually large number of families brought substantial estates with them—nothing like the truly rich immigrants of, say, Maryland or South Carolina, but prosperous for Connecticut: the Chesters, Hayneses, Hookers, Lords, Talcotts, Welleses, Whitings, and Wolcotts furnished considerable capital. But by 1700, when estate inventories permit a satisfactory cross section, the ability of the southern towns to profit from external trade enabled them to overtake the more distant northern communities except for the town of Hartford itself. New London, Saybrook, New Haven, and Fairfield all were in the process of developing maritime commerce, but their prosperity at this point still lay in agriculture. In that pursuit they enjoyed an advantage over most northern towns, which contained proportionately more hills and less usable farm land. Besides, the north included most of the colony's frontier, a circumstance which naturally dragged down the average wealth in that region.

At the turn of the century the mean inventoried wealth of the colony's men was about £370, probably equal to £260 (country pay) for the living population. Of this sum a little over 40 percent was in personal property. New London County led the way by a considerable margin, not because of the property owned by the majority but because it contained more men with large estates. The accompanying tables (V–VIII) indicate the general situation, with the warning that the figures are approximate.[12] The greater mean wealth of New London shows clearly, but the medians indicate that most people owned about the same amount of property regardless of county, and the distribution of wealth, except for personal estates, differed little. Hartford district would show more property except for its larger number of new communities such as Haddam, Simsbury, Glastonbury, Waterbury, and Windham. New London's relative affluence derived more from the wealth of her traders than from any other circumstance, but her people also owned more farm animals than did farmers in other areas, notably cattle; Hartford County lagged considerably behind the other three in livestock.

The same districts fifty years later continued to show a fundamental resemblance although their relative rank had changed. Judging from the inventories, all contained about the same proportion of prosperous men, who among them everywhere held about the same percentage of the wealth. The Fairfield area had more personal wealth than the general norm, but fell short in large landed estates, New Haven leading the way. The Hartford district ranked third and New London fell from first to last (see Table VI).[13]

The distribution of livestock, in which New London had earlier ranked first and Hartford last, now reflected the increased wealth of the two western districts, Fairfield in particular outproducing Hartford by 50 percent. The inference that agricultural leadership had passed to the southwest is confirmed even more strikingly by an examination of the relative value of grains per estate, in which Fairfield led the way with £19, equal to New Haven and Hartford combined.

---

[12] New London evaluators ordinarily used "cash" money, which was worth about one-third less than "pay." Few inventories exist for that county until 1700, so those during 1700–1707 (reel A) were used (N = 106). We have fully as many inventories as we would expect from the population. The survey of Hartford inventories shows that the years around 1700 were not unusual, though the concentration of property was below the norm and fewer men died without land. I used 1695–1709 to obtain a large N.

[13] In 1750 the probate districts of New London, Plainfield, and Norwich composed New London County as it had existed in 1700; New Haven, Guilford, and the town of New Milford in Woodbury district equaled old New Haven County; 1700 Fairfield County comprehended the districts of Fairfield, Stamford, Danbury, and Litchfield, together with the town of Woodbury; while old Hartford County consisted of Hartford, Windham, and Colchester districts plus Waterbury town. Middletown district split off from Hartford in 1752.

TABLE V

GEOGRAPHICAL DISTRIBUTION OF PROPERTY, CA. 1700

(INVENTORIES, COUNTRY PAY)

	1700–1707 New London	1690–1699 New Haven	1690–1694 Fairfield	1695–1709 Hartford
	Percentages, Personal Wealth			
£ 1–49	20	25	25	33
50–99	31	23	23	27
100–199	19	28	31	28
200–299	16	14	10	6
300–499	8½	7	10	3½
500+	6	3½	1	3
Mean £	208	163	132	154
Trimmed Mean	150	133	115	95
Median	99	102½	104	82
10% own	45%	34%	30%	42%
	Percentages, Real Wealth			
£ none	9	11	10	7
1–49	4	10	15	12
50–99	15	15	13	17
100–199	31	27	21½	27
200–299	13	19	15	16
300–499	12	9	17	13
500+	16	9	9	8
Mean £	254	192	224	208
Trimmed Mean	213	165	179	161
Median	169	150	164	150
10% own	34%	33½%	36%	36%
	Percentages, Total Wealth			
£ 1–49	7½	10	7	9
50–99	8½	10	13	13
100–199	17½	16	17	21
200–299	23	15	19	18
300–499	17½	28	22	21
500+	26	20	22	18
Mean £	445	354	356	362
Trimmed Mean	354	305	294	260
Median	275	275	264	226
10% own	37%	34%	33½%	39%
N =	131	145	101	150

TABLE VI

Total Wealth for All Connecticut, ca. 1750

(adjusted to country pay as of 1700)

	Old New London Co.		Old New Haven Co.		Old Fairfield Co.		Old Hartford Co.		All of Connecticut	
	No.	%	No.	%	No.	%	No.	%	No.	%
£ 1–49	25	17	23	9	25	12	48	10	148	12
50–99	35	12	22	9	26	12½	55	12	138	11
100–199	55	18	45	18	37	18	75	16	212	17
200–299	27	9	31	12	26	12½	65	14	149	12
300–399	29	10	21	8	17	8	47	10	114	9
400–499	22	7	23	9	14	7	43	9	102	8
500–999	61	20	55	21	41	20	85	18	242	20
1000+	25	8	37	15	22	10½	44	10	128	10
Total	306		257		208		462		1233	
	£125,055		133,249		90,345		200,168		548,817	
Mean £	416		518		434		433		445	
Trimmed	324		427		354		340		357	
Median	242		333		263		267		280	
10% own	38%		35%		36%		38%		39%	

TABLE VII

Livestock Per Estate, ca. 1750

	Cattle		Horses		Sheep		Pigs		Total
	No.	£	No.	£	No.	£	No.	£	£
Fairfield	11	32	2½	8	27	6	5	3+	49
Hartford	6	17	1½	10	9	2	4	3	32
New London	8	20	1½	10	14	2½	4	2½	35
New Haven	10	30	2	11	12	3½	5	3+	48

TABLE VIII

Grains Per Estate, ca. 1750

	Wheat	Corn	Other	Total
Fairfield	£ 4+	£ 5	£ 9½	£ 19
Hartford	1	2+	5	8
New London	+	1	4+	5½
New Haven	2	2½	5½	10

These regional differences may have created satisfaction in the fortunate areas and discontent elsewhere, but they strike one as minor compared with the prevailing similarities, notably in the medians and the levels of concentration of wealth. Much more important were the contrasts between the types of towns: it did not matter nearly so much to the Connecticut family, in its economic capacity, whether it lived in the east or west, as whether it settled in a trading center or an agricultural village, an old town or a frontier settlement. For this analysis we must rely primarily upon estate inventories, since tax lists are too scarce to furnish more than illustrative evidence. The newest towns displayed the characteristics which we generally associate with the New England frontier. The men were comparatively young, as a rule 40 percent in their twenties and 25 percent in their thirties. Partly as a result, these contained few large estates and wealth was more evenly distributed than the norm for the colony, the top 10 percent among taxpayers owning 30 percent of the taxable wealth (exclusive of polls); inventories show a concentration only slightly higher. The mean wealth, regardless of age, fell consistently below that of the older communities. The frontier settlements differed from the older also in that they contained fewer farm laborers and more landowners (about 26 and 57 percent respectively).[14] These characteristics remained stable during the entire century under consideration.

Towns a generation older also shared certain features. The average age increased, and so did both the mean and median wealth. Land prices doubled, yet the proportion of landless men stayed small (less than one-fourth) because some undivided land still remained during the colony's first century. As on the frontier property was widely diffused, with the top decile owning only one-fourth of the taxable and one-third of the probate wealth; but exceptions occurred in the case of a few towns (such as Glastonbury) possessing some unusually good land which attracted well-to-do families.

As they became still older, Connecticut's towns divided into three types, depending upon the productivity of their soil and the

---

[14] See Charles S. Grant, *Democracy in the Connecticut Frontier Town of Kent* (New York, 1961), 95–99. For example in Bolton, 1731, almost 70 percent of the men were under forty years of age, and the town contained forty farmers, nineteen farm laborers, and ten with a nonfarm occupation. Fifteen men (22 percent) lacked improved land.

degree of commercial activity. The earliest immigrants had settled upon land of good quality and favorably located along the Sound or near major rivers. These afforded good opportunities for agricultural wealth, especially for men who inherited the best properties. The old Valley towns of Windsor and Wethersfield, for instance, showed a much higher average and median wealth than did the newer towns both in personal and real property. This increase reflected more prosperity among the rank and file but especially a larger proportion of men with big estates. In the case of real property the higher price of land accounted for this difference, and it had the additional effect of raising the proportion of landless men.[15] The share of wealth held by the top decile rose above one-third and after 1750 above 40 percent.

Third, a few towns became trading centers. These differed from the farming towns in several important respects. Crucial were the presence of traders and professional men at the top and of poor sailors and laborers at the bottom, with the resultant higher proportion of young, single men. In Connecticut, this latter class never rose to the levels of a Boston or a New York, being only slightly larger than the equivalent class of rural laborers. Nor did their presence depress the median wealth, for the towns' commercial activity created enough profits to benefit not only the merchants and shopkeepers but everybody else. The distribution of real estate resembled that of the most prosperous farming towns, because although the holdings in trading centers were smaller, land prices were higher. The effect of the rich men appears primarily in the very high level of personal wealth and the degree of its concentration, which greatly exceeded that of the farm towns. The distinguishing features of the trading centers were the broad gap between the mean and median (a strong indication of inequality), the high level of concentration, and the number of men with large personal estates.

Clearly the distribution of property differed from place to place. Wealth in the newly settled communities was equally distributed because both poor and rich men were fewer and the people owned less property than elsewhere. They might indeed possess consider-

---

[15] The number of poor, landless men in the farm towns began to increase during the eighteenth century as the undivided land disappeared. Fortunately the frontier remained open, and not until after 1750 did the proportion of such men rise significantly.

able amounts of land, but it was worth less than £1 per acre. In the older farming towns men with large estates remained (unless the community stagnated), while the young and poor often left. The general level of wealth there increased. Land values doubled, more than compensating for a tendency toward smaller holdings. Property became more concentrated, a process which reached a climax, especially in the distribution of personal estates, in the trading centers. Proportionately more men of substantial wealth resided there and until after 1750 they also contained more poor than did the farm towns. Despite these differences among the various types of town, all of Connecticut belonged to the same basic species, for the range of difference was narrow and became, if anything, even less pronounced over time.

Variable 5: Changes Over Time

The distribution of property varied, in colonial Connecticut, with the age structure, occupation, and place of residence. It changed also over time, but not in any simple way. Instead of a steady progression from the inequality characteristic of Europe to an economic democracy, or from a frontier-style equality toward the European species, we find in Connecticut a series of changes lacking any single clear direction until, perhaps, the very end of the colonial period.

Estate inventories from 1650 to 1669 show a high level of personal wealth among the men who immigrated in the early years. This personal property consisted not so much of consumption goods, which the people probably could not bring with them and which they only slowly acquired, but of valuable livestock and grains. A team of oxen, for instance, was worth £15 in the sixties, half again the usual cost in later decades. This prosperity affected most of the people except the young, for we find rather few small estates and both the trimmed mean[16] and median figures were high. The price of land on the other hand remained quite low during these years; even good meadow land sold for not over £3 to £5 an acre. Therefore the mean value of real wealth, for the

---

[16] The trimmed mean, as explained in the methodological note, eliminates the largest estates in order to focus on the average wealth of the people generally.

TABLE IX

ESTATE INVENTORIES, CA. 1700

	Trading Towns		Oldest Farming		Newer Farming		Frontier		General	
	No.	%	No.	%	No.	%	No.	%	No.	%
Personal property										
£ 1–49	56	30	68	25	52	26	18	37	194	28
50–99	35	19	67	25	65	33	14	28	181	26
100–199	60	32	74	27	47	24	13	26	194	28
200–299	15	8	35	13	19	10	3	6	72	10
300–499	11	6	22	8	11	6	0	0	44	6
500+	12	6	8	3	2	1	1	2	23	3
	189		274		196		49		708	
Total £	38,866		43,335		23,252		4,626		110,079	
Mean	206		158		118		94		157	
Median	108		104		85		75		94	
10% own	55.5%		37.9%		32.8%		31.5%		43.3%	
Real property										
£ none	24	13	29	11	11	6	7	11	71	10
1–49	26	14	25	9	22	11	14	22	87	12
50–99	19	10	39	14	28	14	17	27	103	15
100–199	44	24	55	20	63	33	10	16	172	24
200–299	24	13	52	19	37	19	7	11	120	17
300–399	17	9	22	8	13	7	5	8	57	8
400–499	8	4	15	6	7	4	2	3	32	4
500+	24	13	35	13	11	6	2	3	72	10
	186		272		192		64		714	
Total £	41,846		63,287		37,088		8,788		151,009	
Mean	225		233		193		137		211	
Median	154		177		158		82		155	
10% own	35.8%		39.7%		31.4%		34.6%		36.2%	

only time in the colony's history, was less than that of personal estates.

During the 1670's, however, personal property began a decline which reached a nadir in the 1680's, affecting everyone except the very young. The wealthy suffered the greatest losses. Thus the proportion of men with over £200 in personal property fell from 22 percent to only 7 percent—probably the lowest point during

TABLE X

ESTATE INVENTORIES, PERSONAL PROPERTY, CA. 1750

	Trading Towns		Oldest Farming		Newer Farming		Frontier		General	
	No.	%	No.	%	No.	%	No.	%	No.	%
£ 1–49	98	28	100	24	68	24	49	30	315	26
50–99	97	27	103	24	77	28	47	29	324	27
100–199	91	26	106	25	82	29	43	26	322	27
200–299	26	7	49	12	27	10	15	9	117	9
300–499	27	8	43	11	17	6	6	4	93	8
500+	14	4	16	4	7	3	3	2	40	3
	353		417		278		163		1211	
Total £	53,330		65,912		36,562		18,585		174,389	
Mean £	151		158		131		114		145	
Median £	92		106		96		86		95	
10% own	40.2%		35.1%		33.3%		32.8%		37.0%	

the colonial period. Real estate did rise because of the increasing price of good land in the older towns, but not enough to counteract the fall in personal wealth; moreover it dropped back during the later 1680's, almost duplicating the early low levels.

Various external and internal factors created the doldrums of the 1680's. First, an Atlantic-wide depression deprived the colonists of a market, affecting not only Connecticut men but people in all the British settlements. Second, whereas before 1660 many immigrants brought with them considerable wealth, now far fewer newcomers arrived. Therefore the population growth came from the New Englanders themselves, so that each year the available wealth, though increasing, had to be divided among more people, leaving a lower average. Apparently the new generation extracted more than it contributed. Thus we find a rise in the proportion of men owning less than £50 in personal wealth from 36 percent up to 55 percent—the highest of the entire colonial period—and until 1685 we also find a comparable increase in the landless class.[17] Finally, King Philip's War caused considerable damage to livestock, crops, and buildings and for some years the vacated land

[17] A high (unadjusted) mean for real estate evaluated in the inventories during the 1680's resulted from the death of many old settlers, rather than from a general prosperity.

lay idle. In Connecticut few towns originated during the 1670's and 1680's, and not until almost 1700 did a major advance resume.

After 1690 the colony experienced a partial recovery, enjoyed more by the younger men than the older. Few accumulated large personal estates, but the proportion with moderate properties rose considerably. Prices of livestock and grains stabilized, though at a lower level than the pre-1670 years. The value of land continued its earlier advance and largely accounts for a rise in the general mean. Of particular importance to the young men was the availability of frontier farms, reflected in a rising proportion of landowners. The value of capital and production goods in the inventories, which had dropped steeply until the 1680's began a slow recovery.

This upturn was temporarily arrested for some years after 1700, but recommenced around 1710, and the next decade witnessed considerable prosperity. Part of it was inflationary, accompanying an increase in the money supply, but when adjusted for inflation the inventories show a substantial increase in wealth of almost every sort except grain, affecting every kind of person, even the poorest. To some extent it reflected the temporary prosperity of "Queene Anne's War." Land prices jumped, especially in the older towns, creating a substantial rise in the real wealth (see graphs).

This happy situation did not last long. After the war ended in 1714, the value of inventoried estates began to slide back toward earlier levels. After adjusting for price changes, the personal wealth of the people (not just of the probate population) gradually declined, except for a brief period of recovery around 1730. Trends in real property are more difficult to determine because of price fluctuations, but there, too, after one peak in the late 1720's, wealth dropped sharply to a low in the mid-1740's. In 1750 a slight recovery in both types of property brought the levels back to about where they had been fifty years before. Not until the ten years preceding independence did the colony experience a real boom which, in personal wealth, finally returned the people to the days before King Philip's War, and even then real wealth rose only because of increasing land values: if we adjust these to the 1700 standard, real property fell, so that in total wealth the fifth generation about equaled the first.

These estimates come from Hartford County, where informa-

tion concerning the ages of the decedents and the living population permits generalizations from inventories to life. What about
the rest of the colony? Table XI, based upon inventories, indicates
that Hartford's experience followed the general pattern. Three of
the four counties suffered a decline in personal wealth between
1700 and 1750, due not to a reduction in the medians but in the
means, reflecting fewer large estates.[18] Fairfield district registered
a gain in personal wealth, evidently due to more large properties.
In real estate New Haven (which lacked an extensive frontier)
led a general advance attributable to increased prices. In sum, per
capita wealth in Connecticut neither increased nor decreased over
time, but fluctuated depending upon a variety of internal and
external circumstances.

What of the distribution of wealth among the people and the
degree of concentration? Here too one encounters fluctuation
rather than a consistent trend. In Hartford district the proportion
of poor men, with personal estates of less than £50 and, characteristically, no land, at first was under 40 percent (see Table XIII).
At that time the top 10 percent of wealth holders owned fully
half of the total property. The depression in its first phase increased the inequality in landholding, the share of the top decile
rising to 60 percent as the proportion of landless males rose. Subsequently land became more accessible and 80 or 90 percent of the
men had at least a little land by 1700, and the wealthiest group
held only 40 percent of the real property (of probated estates,
about 36 percent for the living men). The depression of the 1680's
also reduced the value of personal estates belonging to poor and
rich alike, properties worth over £500 almost disappearing. The
proportion of personal wealth owned by the top 10 percent, however, fluctuated only slightly during Connecticut's early decades,
averaging 45 percent.

After 1700 the distribution of personal property in Connecticut
continued to fluctuate. The share of the top 10 percent gradually
declined, reaching low points in the late 1730's and the 1750's,
the general level being under 40 percent. The proportion of poor
people remained about the same. Really large estates failed to

---

[18] The decline in New London's personal wealth is a bit misleading because the
town of that name contained more property than the inventories of 1750–1753 indicate, but the general tendency is correct. All figures as usual in 1700 country pay.

Real Wealth Over Time, Hartford District*

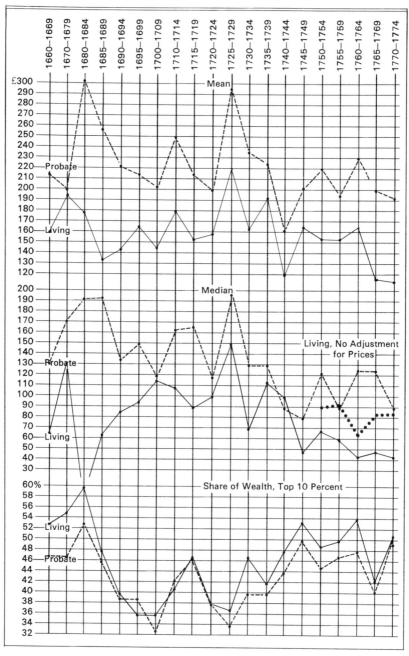

Personal Wealth Over Time, Hartford District

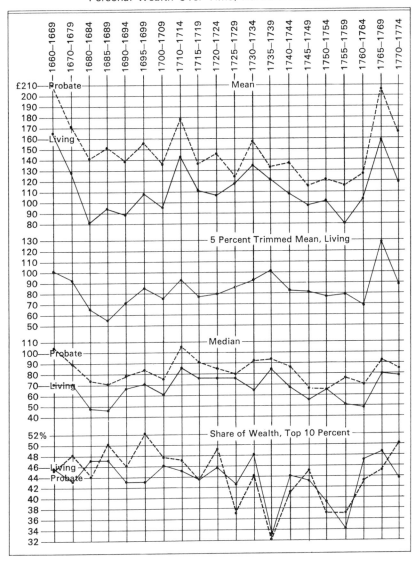

Personal Wealth, Men 30–59, Hartford Inventories

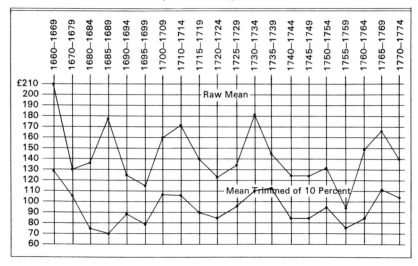

TABLE XI

PERSONAL WEALTH OVER TIME, HARTFORD DISTRICT INVENTORIES

(BY TOTALS AND AGE GROUPS)

	N*	All Estates	21–29	30–39	40–49	50–59	60+
			Raw Mean Wealth				
1650–1669	105	209	32	150	221	428	201
1670–1679	94	170	27	139	179	136	321
1680–1689	203	145	47	75	83	270	151
1690–1699	217	146	46	108	105	143	283
1700–1709	150	134	40	90	119	221	137
1710–1714	265	176	60	131	272	234	158
1715–1719	108	159	89	139	117	248	173
1750-1754	357	120	46	92	145	161	143
1755–1759	296	107	60	101	115	123	133
1760–1764	327	125	34	94	102	275	144
1765–1769	189	203	24	135	214	212	206
1770–1774	247	163	56	108	196	147	186

* Except during the period 1710–1714 and after 1750 the number of estates is too small for accuracy, especially for the age groups 21–29 and 30–39. Figures are not adjusted for changes in prices except after 1750, as follows: 1750–1754 divide by 7 for inventories in old tenor; 1755–1759 and 1765–1769 add one-fifth; 1770–1774 add one-tenth.

Trimmed Mean (of £500)

1650–1669	94	124	32	108	158	126	161
1670–1679	88	108	27	90	153	136	210
1680–1689	197	103	47	75	83	137	117
1690–1699	212	112	46	82	105	143	128
1700–1709	147	98	40	90	119	135	126
1710–1714	259	134	60	109	144	153	168
1715–1719	103	116	89	98	117	139	124
1750–1754	346	102	35	83	115	142	121
1755–1759		81	60	101	82	123	111
1760–1764		99	34	79	102	132	134
1765–1769		139	125	96	127	130	143
1770–1774		118	62	108	100	147	115

Raw Median

1650–1669	103		94	171	155	168
1670–1679	89	29	85	154	128	124
1680–1689	71	32	48	57	132	111
1690–1699	80	38	69	107	120	115
1700–1709	74	37	68	75	105	128
1710–1714	91	55	87	120	132	143
1715–1719	104	76	84	95	129	130
1750–1754	84	22	72	90	137	100
1755–1759	84	55	79	90	84	84
1760–1764	70	20	50	56	135	114
1765–1769	109	80	83	128	124	101
1770–1774	100	40	118	106	123	89

Living Population

	Mean	Trimmed Mean**	Median	%£1–49	%£50–199	%£200+
1650–1669	167	100	70	36	42	22
1670–1679	126	91	70	39	45	16
1680–1689	87	59	47	55	38	7
1690–1699	109	77	68	40	51	9
1700–1709	109	74	60	44	48	8
1710–1714	140	97	85	38	52	10
1715–1719	131	90	89	33	59	8
1750–1754	98	76	64	43	45	12
1755–1759	94	78	60	49	45	6
1760–1764	99	68	48	52	38	10
1765–1769	174	128	90	43	42	15
1770–1774	132	88	86	36	55	9

** Trimmed of top 5 percent.

TABLE XII

PERSONAL WEALTH OF MEN 30–59

(HARTFORD INVENTORIES, 10 PERCENT TRIMMED MEAN)

	N	£		N	£
1650–1669	39	129	1725–1729	97	96
1670–1679	51	106	1730–1734	103	110
1680–1684	54	75	1735–1739	83	112
1685–1689	40	70	1740–1744	92	83
1690–1694	63	89	1745–1749	105	83
1695–1699	72	79	1750–1754	203	94
1700–1709	82	108	1755–1759	153	76
1710–1714	152	107	1760–1764	183	83
1715–1719	62	90	1765–1769	84	111
1720–1724	52	84	1770–1774	102	103

appear, presumably due to the lack of commercial opportunity. On the other hand the percentage of large landowners did increase and the proportion of landless men in the probate population reached one-fourth by 1720, where it stayed; tax records correct this to one-third. The concentration of real estate, unlike that of personal property, began to rise steadily after the 1720's. In the colony as a whole, the share of the top 10 percent increased from 34 percent about 1700 to 41 percent fifty years later. In Hartford 10 percent of the men owned half of the land during the period 1745–1765, dropping below that level only in the final prosperous years.

Rising land prices, which began almost at once in the older towns, lead one to expect a deteriorating economic position among the young and single men. No such trend occurred in the Hartford district until after 1720, and probably not until after 1750.[19] This stability probably resulted from the availability of cheap land, allowing the towns to expand geographically in proportion to the increase in population until late in the colonial period.

In some societies the distribution of property was changing during these years because of shifts in the people's economic activities. Maryland and Virginia, for example, vastly increased the size of their propertyless labor force, while the great planters concen-

[19] Figures for real wealth are adjusted for price increases. The small number of single men in the records permits only tentative generalizations.

TABLE XIII

Changes in Inventory Wealth, 1700–1750

	New London Area		New Haven Area		Fairfield Area		Hartford Area		Total	
	1700	1750	1700	1750	1700	1750	1700	1750	1700	1750
Mean personal	208	116	163	146	132	154	150	120	163	134
Trimmed mean	150	94	133	115	115	120	95	95	123	107
Median	88	92	102½	114	104	109	80	84	98	92
Share top 10%	45%	34½%	34%	35½%	30%	38%	49%	37%	40%	35%
Share 2d decile	16	16½	16	19	18	22	13	17	16	19
Share 3d decile	11	13	12	13	13	10	10	11	12	12
Share mid-40%	23	29	32	28	33	24	23	29	27	28
Share lowest 30%	5	7	6	4½	6	6	5	6	5	6
Mean real	254	307	192	357	224	272	203	295	217	319
Trimmed mean	213	234	165	276	179	211	168	220	180	246
Median	169	173	150	230	164	150	150	162	157	187
Share top 10%	34%	40%	33½%	40%	36%	41%	36%	44½%	34%	41%
Share 2d decile	21	20	18	20	17	19	18	18	18	18½
Share 3d decile	12½	15	13	16	13	16	13	13	13	13½
Share mid-40%	27	25	31½	23	31	22	29	23	30	26
Share lowest 30%	5½	0	4	1	3	2	4	1	5	1

TABLE XIV

Share of Personal Wealth by Deciles in Hartford County

	Unadjusted Inventories					Living Population				
	Top 10%	Second 10%	Third 10%	Middle 40%	Bottom 30%	Top	Second	Third	Middle	Lowest
1650–1669	45	17	11	23	4	45½	17	12½	21	4
1670–1679	48	15	12	21	4	43	16	9	28	4
1680–1689	47	15	11	22	5	47	16	10	22½	4½
1690–1699	49	13	10	23	5	43	17	11	24	5
1700–1709	47½	14	11	22½	5	46	16	10	23½	4½
1710–1714	47	13½	10	24½	5	45	15	10	25	5
1715–1719	43½	13	10	27	6½	43½	13	11	27½	5
1720–1724	49	13	9	22	7	45½	13	10	24½	7
1725–1729	37	16	12	27	8	42½	16	11	25	5½
1730–1734	44	16	10	25	5	48	16	10	21½	4½
1735–1739	32	17	13	32	6	33	18	14	29½	5½
1740–1744	41	15	12	26	6	44	16	10	25	5
1745–1749	45	14	11	26	4	43	16	13	22	6
1750–1754	39	17	11	27	6	39	19	10	26	6
1755–1759	35	19	14	25	7	34	19	12	28	7
1760–1764	43½	16½	10	25	5	47	16	11	20	6
1765–1769	45	15	9½	25½	5	48½	18½	10	18½	4½
1770–1774	50	12	9	24	5	45½	13½	10	26	5

TABLE XV

WEALTH OF YOUNG MEN

(HARTFORD INVENTORIES)

	Personal	Real		Personal	Real
1650–1669	32	4	1730–1734	55	29
1670–1679	27	32	1735–1739	48	87
1680–1689	47	57	1740–1744	55	51
1690–1699	46	59	1745–1749	34	55
1700–1709	40	68	1750–1754	46	66
1710–1714	60	74	1755–1759	60	40
1715–1719	59	45	1760–1764	34	33
1720–1724	81	135	1765–1769	204	65
1725–1729	102	110	1770–1774	56	55

trated wealth in their own hands. The development of important commercial towns led to a comparable result. Nothing of the sort occurred in Connecticut. Neither slaves nor indentured servants existed in significant numbers until well into the eighteenth century. Our survey of 1700 turned up twenty such men, about 2 percent of the inventory population and less of the living. A census in 1756 indicated that blacks formed 3 percent of the population, including free Negroes. This number is not large enough to alter the distribution of wealth. The ratio of inventories belonging to traders and professional men stayed about the same throughout. Farmers, however, declined in relative numbers from over 60 percent in the seventeenth century to about 57 percent in 1700, just over half at mid-century, and (at least in Hartford) even fewer thereafter. Replacing them in part were artisans, whose numbers rose steadily from 10 percent of the inventory population to 25 percent. In the living population all of these figures were lower and that of laborers were much higher, but the trends remained unchanged. The shift toward more manufacturing is well known and economically important, but the process appears not to have affected the distribution of wealth, because those involved held about the same property as did farmers.

Changes in men's place of residence had only local effects on the distribution of wealth. The most obvious trend was decentralization. In 1676 Hartford town alone paid one-tenth of the colony's tax, and together with Wethersfield, Windsor, New London, New Haven, and Fairfield accounted for nearly half of the total. By

1700 that half-dozen paid 40 percent and in 1756, only 20 percent. Second, wealth shifted toward the southwest, both the Hartford and New London districts losing ground relatively while the areas of Fairfield, starting at just an average level, and New Haven, once at the bottom, ended as the richest in the colony. Third, the distribution of property in the several types of towns differed somewhat over time. In personal property trading towns began with a high level of wealth and a very high concentration, and then experienced a decline in both, with a revival during the last two decades. The oldest farming towns about held their own. During the early decades personal wealth tended to become more concentrated (at least in the Hartford County towns) but that leveled off later, and the principal shift was toward a concentration in land, especially after 1750. Connecticut stayed fundamentally rural, and on the whole no major economic change occurred.

We conclude that the distribution of property changed little during the colonial period. One might, indeed, point to the high level of concentration of real estate during the final decades as symptomatic of a growing rigidity, threatening a decline in opportunity for the young men. But we perceive no decrease in their property, and the general size of farms, in Hartford district at least, remained constant at about 100 acres. The continued formation of frontier villages, with their economic equality, counteracted the shift toward a higher level of wealth in the older towns and resulted in the absence of any universal long-term trend. Perhaps had Connecticut's people been confined to their own colony their situation might have worsened, but Pennsylvania, New York, Massachusetts, and Vermont all served as safety valves, permitting the colony to avoid any serious economic or social crisis.

Conclusion

This lengthy examination of the variables affecting the distribution of property in colonial Connecticut has revealed certain important generalizations, both about the wealth of the men considered collectively and of individuals. The colony contained only a small percentage of men owning more than £1,000 in total wealth and practically no one with £5,000—only three in Hartford district during the seventy years before 1720, nor did this tiny fraction increase. The poor, if this be defined as men with less than

£50 in property, usually formed one-third of the people. But for most of these men poverty was temporary, not permanent. Estate inventories at the turn of the century show but 10 percent dying with as little as £50 and one-fourth with under £100 (country pay), a proportion which remained unchanged until after 1750. Furthermore, we ought to exclude from these figures those who died before the age of thirty, which would reduce the percentages to 8 and 20. Obviously an overwhelming majority of men accumulated estates ranging from £100 to £500. Given the high birth rate one might have expected a decline in the mean or in the median, but no such general trend occurred. From 1690 until 1775 Connecticut managed to absorb a tenfold increase in population (at the least) with no decline in wealth per person and little rise in the proportion of the poor.

This property was not divided equally among the people but was concentrated in various ways. Certain components of wealth belonged almost entirely to a few individuals, such as slaves and servants, debts receivable, stocks in trade, ships, and money. Other forms of wealth were more widely dispersed. The wealthiest 10 percent, for example, owned just 30 percent of the inventoried clothing and one-third of the livestock. Overall this top decile, among the living men, possessed during the early decades (1650–1684) better than half of the total wealth, real property being more concentrated than personal. At this period one-third of the men lacked land entirely. Thereafter the share of this wealthiest group declined dramatically to a low of 39 percent around 1700, primarily because of a wider ownership of land. During the eighteenth century the figure rose to about 45 percent. This surely represents an equitable distribution compared with western Europe and nineteenth-century America.

The amount of property owned by a given individual in colonial Connecticut varied with a number of circumstances, among them his place of residence, the particular time, age and marital status, and occupation. The time factor proves comparatively minor. The general mean for all estates in Hartford district 1650–1719 and 1750–1754 was about £410.[20] Over time we have the following variations, expressed in percentages, between this general mean and means at particular periods:

[20] Unadjusted for age bias, country pay as of 1700. 1750–1754 inventories deflated one-seventh or one-eighth, "cash" inventories of 1710–1714 adjusted to pay. Intervening years omitted to minimize errors deriving from the changing value of money.

1650–1669	1670–1679	1680–1689	1690–1699
—10	—22	+5	—10

1700–1709	1710–1719	1750–1754
—18	+11	+10

TABLE XVI

INVENTORY WEALTH BY AGE AND PLACE

Age	21–29	30–39	40–49	50–59	60+	Totals
			Hartford Town			
£ 1–49	19	8	7	3	4	41
50–99	4	7	5	5	4	25
100–199	9	6	9	8	11	43
200–299	2	7	9	13	10	41
300–399	3	2	8	6	5	24
400–499	2	3	4	3	9	21
500–599		8	8	12	21	49
1000 +		6	8	14	17	45
Total	39	47	58	64	81	289
Total £	4,303	20,884	34,455	49,709	57,262	166,613
Mean £	110	444	594	777	707	580
			Old Farm Towns			
£ 1–49	21	18	7	1	10	57
50–99	10	11	12	8	11	52
100–199	19	25	13	11	24	92
200–299	9	12	15	13	13	62
300–399	1	4	10	12	21	48
400–499	1	5	10	8	9	33
500–999		6	12	19	26	63
1000 +		3	6	12	13	34
Total	61	84	85	84	127	441
Total £	6,739	18,848	32,511	50,074	58,559	166,731
Mean £	110	224	382	596	461	378
			Newer Farm Towns			
£ 1–49	8	2	3	5	2	21
50–99	8	10	5	2	4	29
100–199	15	13	11	9	12	60
200–299	1	6	12	14	17	50
300–399	1	4	7	5	13	30
400–499	1	2	5	10	15	33
500–599		3	3	8	15	29
1000 +				2	7	9
Total	34	40	47	55	85	261
Total £	3,813	8,119	11,569	18,593	38,178	80,272
Mean £	112	203	246	338	449	308

Frontier

£						
1–49	6	7			1	14
50–99	5	4	3	4	5	21
100–199	4	7	8	5	8	32
200–299		8	9	2	4	23
300–399		2	5	3	5	15
400–499		2	5	2	4	13
500–599			3	1	4	8
1000 +			1		1	2
Total	15	30	33	17	33	128
Total £	988	5,209	12,267	4,046	10,813	33,323
Mean £	66	173	371	238	327	260

Total, All Towns

£						
1–49	54	35	18	9	17	133
50–99	27	32	25	19	24	127
100–199	47	51	41	33	55	227
200–299	12	33	45	42	44	176
300–399	5	12	30	26	44	117
400–499	4	12	23	23	38	100
500–999		17	26	40	66	149
1000 +		9	15	28	38	90
Total	149	201	223	220	326	1119
Total £	15,843	53,060	90,802	122,422	164,812	446,939
Mean £	106	265	407	556	506	400

Or, if we adjust for age bias, the general mean becomes £280 and the variations are, in sequence, +3, −2, −14, −7, −7, +17, and +18. Thus at any given time the individual might expect his wealth to vary 10 percent from the norm, up or down.

If our Connecticut Yankee lived in a trading town, he might be far better off than if he resided elsewhere. In 1700 the general raw mean for the colony was £368. That in the commercial centers was £431, in the older farming towns £391, in the newer communities £311, and in the frontier settlements £231, a variation respectively of +17, +6, −15½, and −37 percent, averaging 19 percent. Lack of age information prevents an adjustment for age-bias except in the Hartford district. Here however we can compare the raw means and the age-adjusted means for Hartford itself, the old towns of Windsor and Wethersfield, the newer ones (Farmington, Middletown, Haddam), and all the rest. Ignoring time, and using all the inventories through 1719, we find that the deviations from the general are, in order, +39½, +10, −23, and −35 percent, averaging 27 percent, a figure more than twice as large as that measuring variations over time.

The connection between occupation and wealth offers no such difficulty. In this case we can draw upon all of our samples of Connecticut inventories (through 1753), producing Table XVII. The general mean remained £400, but that of merchants exceeded £1800 while laborers averaged only £48. Obviously these variations surpassed any of those just reviewed, reaching 87 percent overall,

TABLE XVII

INVENTORY TOTAL WEALTH

(BY OCCUPATION AND AGE)

Age group	21–29	30–39	40–49	50–59	60+	Total
			Farmers			
Number	66	121	165	172	281	805
Total £	11,525	35,030	63,914	85,474	132,116	328,059
Mean £	175	290	387	497	471	410
Dispersion	81	188	225	223	288	228
			Laborers			
Number	52	31	10	7	3	103
Total £	2,250	1,475	650	400	125	4,900
Mean £	43	48	65	57	42	48
Dispersion	29	29	40?	37?	22?	32
			Lesser artisans			
Number	39	46	48	26	46	207
Total £	3,525	7,075	9,167	5,700	15,964	41,131
Mean £	90	154	190	220	347	200
Dispersion	53	76	116	115	233	180
			Manufacturers			
Number	1	6	6	12	15	40
Total £	150	2,000	4,413	11,648	18,755	37,166
Mean £		333	735	971	1250	929
Dispersion				494	750	590
			Men in trade			
Number	5	11	12	18	19	65
Total £	975	8,645	22,035	39,739	30,432	101,826
Mean £	195	786	1939	2208	1602	1567
Dispersion	93?	463	1606	1911	1090	1302
			Professionals			
Number		7	6	6	16	35
Total £		6,139	5,280	4,690	13,348	29,457
Mean £		877	880	782	834	842
Dispersion					657	603

or if we correct for the difference in the number of men in each occupational group, 74 percent. An adjustment from inventory data to the living population is also necessary, for inventories include four times the actual proportion of men in trade, the professions, and large manufacturing, but only one-tenth the true percentage of laborers. Tax lists suggest the following proportions, generalizing without reference to time or place, to which we append the means and deviations:

TABLE XVIII

DEVIATIONS, MEANS OF OCCUPATIONAL GROUPS

	% of Population	Estate Mean	Deviation
Farmers	52	608	+52
Small artisans	10	210	−47½
Manufacturers	4	570	+42½
Professionals	2	750	+87½
Men in trade	2	1560	+290
Laborers	30	42	−89½

Appropriately weighted these yield a deviation of about 63 percent, far greater than that for time or place. However inaccurate the calculation of variance, it clearly has exposed a variable of major significance.

The variables of age and marital status seem more important than any except occupation. Table XIX displays both of these and

TABLE XIX

RAW MEANS OF TOTAL WEALTH

(BY AGE AND MARITAL STATUS)

	21–29	30–39	40–49	50–59	60+	Total	N	Variation
Single men	91	195	111	197	189	122	157	−71
Married men								
No children	125	156	258	329	432	209	91	−52
Young children	171	298	319	556	213	290	220	−32
Teen-aged children		312	500	810	652	551	189	+29
Grown children			563	579	536	560	316	+31
Grandchildren			434	598	565	568	240	+33
							Tot.	41
Total Mean	113	260	434	592	549	428		
N	157	213	234	236	373		1,213	
Variation	−74	−39	0	+38	+28			36

shows also the relationship between them. Adjusting for the living population yields a general deviation figure of 47 for age and 48½ for marital status. The table demonstrates that the two factors, though obviously related, were not identical, since regardless of age one's wealth jumped upon marriage and the birth of children, continued to rise as the children entered the teens, and then leveled off; and also, to trace the other variable, regardless of marital status wealth increased with age until one passed sixty, except for single men.

We now perceive a hierarchy of relationships between the level of wealth and a set of objective circumstances affecting wealth, about as follows:

Deviation from mean

Time	10
Place	25
Age	47
Marital status	48½?
Occupation	63

The question arises, to what extent have we accounted for the distribution of wealth? Let us take another course. If everyone owned an equal amount of wealth, instead of a distribution, each person would leave at his death £400, and every 10 percent of the men would possess 10 percent of the property.[21] Actually we have a general figure of concentration of 40 percent for the top decile and another 17 percent for the second decile. Can we reduce these to ten percent by utilizing all the variables thus far discussed? Let us begin by constructing a table which eliminates the age factor as a variable (Table XX). It shows that irrespective of age, property was unequally distributed among these occupational groups, and it emphasizes the importance of occupation, since the differences are greater as one reads down the columns, from occupation to occupation, than across. We have succeeded in reducing the percentage of concentration somewhat, but have still some distance to go.

---

[21] An alternative measure of concentration takes the difference between the wealth of every person and the mean for everybody, the process being repeated for each category. Thus fifty-two laborers in their twenties left property totaling £43 each. The total sum by which the property of each man varied from the mean was £1480, giving an average of £29. Sixty-six farmers of the same age, whose mean wealth was £175, varied by £5370, or £81 each. There are still other methods, but that adopted here is simple in concept and execution.

TABLE XX

PERCENT SHARE OF WEALTH, TOP TWO DECILES

	21–29	30–39	40–49	50–59	60+	Total	N
			Richest 10%				
Laborers	35	27				32	103
Farmers	26	26	31	27	31	31	805
Lesser artisans	27	30	25	21	35	34	207
Manufacturers				27?	28½?	31	40
Professionals					30?	32	35
Men in trade		23?	35?	33?	29?	39	65
			Richest 20%				
Laborers	44	42	46	45		49	
Farmers	43	42	47	44	48	48	
Lesser artisans	46	51	44	39	52	49	
Manufacturers				44	46	48	
Professionals					54	53	
Men in trade		42	59	55	51	60	

We can now eliminate the effect of another variable, that of location, by asking whether these contrasts are due to place of residence, or exist apart from geographical circumstance. For this purpose we can examine farmers and the lesser artisans aged forty to fifty-nine, which furnish two large groups with the age factor minor, and men in trade over age forty for supporting data. The analysis shows that farmers living at the same time, in the same sorts of places, and of the same age group, nevertheless held different amounts of wealth, 10 percent owning about 27½ percent; 20 percent of the farmers held 45 percent of the total. The property of artisans in a given place remained at a nearly constant level of concentration over time, at about 23½ percent for the top decile and 40 percent for the top 20 percent.[22] The traders, though too few in number to permit more than crude approximations, varied greatly in property from town to town. Yet place of residence exercised little effect on the level of concentration. There remains among the traders a concentration of 27 percent for the top decile and for the richest 20 percent of 46 percent. Thus farmers, artisans, and merchants all confirm the existence of some factors not considered thus far and which create, instead of an equal distribution of wealth, a situation in which (among decedents)

[22] The means differed little from town to town, but the share of the two highest deciles was somewhat greater in Hartford than in the oldest towns, and the newer communities were at the bottom.

one-fifth of the men owned about 46 percent of the wealth and one-tenth, 27 percent.

The residual inequalities in the distribution of property presumably result from the advantages or handicaps of the individual's family background and from his own unique capacities. The relative influence of these variables may very well lie beyond the capacity of our data to measure, but we can advance one more step by an hypothesis: if every man owned the same property as his father, inheritance counted for everything and individual ability nothing. Perhaps less emphatically, if the son always followed his father's occupation, inheritance supplies the primary explanation for the so far unexplained differences.

Testing this hypothesis requires a definition of when the son's property differs significantly from his father's. A difference of two times or one-half seems reasonable; that is, if a parental estate totaled £200, a son held his own with property between £100 and £400, perhaps allowing for a little leeway. Applying this principle to Hartford district from 1680 to 1719, of 371 known cases, 14 percent of the sons improved upon their fathers' economic rank, 30 percent fell short, and 56 percent stayed even.[23] Granted the several assumptions, the evidence indicates that previous unexplained inequalities in the distribution of property arise both from inheritance and individual capacity, the former exercising more influence than the latter.

These analyses of our data permit some tentative generalizations concerning the distribution of wealth in colonial Connecticut. Several qualitative variables created an unequal division of property. They included, first, the individual's family background, such as his father's wealth and social status, together with his education (broadly defined) and in addition his own personal attributes. Second, one's occupation exerted an influence fully as great and perhaps even more important, though of course occupation was itself a dependent variable of family background. Third, age and marital status also affected the distribution of

[23] The surprising downward trend reflects partly the superior capital of the original settlers, partly the depression of the late seventeenth century, and partly the failure of the area to maintain an economic level, a deficiency made up by immigrants with capital. The cases examined exclude sons who died in their twenties, before they could acquire property, and both fathers and sons who died when they were old, unless other information (such as a will which mentioned property given away) disclosed their economic status.

property, primarily because of the young and single men. After the man had married and entered middle age, however, these factors became minor. Fourth, place of residence made some difference, though less than one might expect. Residents of the newest towns owned less property than those of the older, and the concentration was also lower due to the age structure and to a dissimilar occupational makeup. The trading centers contained higher levels of wealth and a greater concentration due largely to the presence there of more traders.

Finally, changes over time had surprisingly little effect. A long decline before 1690, a partial recovery, another decline after 1715, a rise again twenty years later followed by still another reversal, with a final recovery after 1760 show a cyclical movement rather than a consistent trend. This resulted from the absence of those influences which in other colonies did cause a long-term change: no important urbanization, no influx of servants or slaves, no class of great landowners, no major shifts in economic opportunity until, perhaps, at the very end.

This stability, so often observed as a characteristic of Connecticut's society, is certainly an outstanding feature of her distribution of wealth. A second is the predominance of small property holders. Excluding the young men, whom one does not expect to accumulate wealth, not over one-fourth at the very most fell short of acquiring estates worth £100 (country pay), a sum which probably sufficed for a decent standard of living. On the other hand even fewer owned £500 worth or more. Inequalities certainly existed, measured by a concentration of wealth and symbolized by titles, but the titles gradually lost their significance and the concentration did not increase until the very end of the colonial period. By 1763, on the eve of the Revolution, two major statements describe the distribution of property: the people had enjoyed no major economic advance in over a hundred years, but they had faced neither a rising inequality of fortune nor a growing class of propertyless. This pleasant situation depended, however, on the availability of new land. The final years of the colonial period would bring to an end this long era of economic stability.

Note on Sources

This study utilized, first, the colony-wide assessments, which

give number of polls and the total evaluation for each town for
1654–1655, 1669, 1676–1709, and 1756, as printed in the *Colonial
Records*. The key assessment lists were from Hartford, 1655; Middletown, 1670, 1673, and 1679; Norwalk, 1671 and 1687; Windsor,
1675, 1686, and 1702; Lyme, 1688; Stamford, 1701; Derby, 1718;
Haddam, 1719; Waterbury, 1730; Wethersfield, 1730 and 1771–
1773; Glastonbury, 1730; Bolton, 1731; Groton, 1735; Goshen,
1751; and Milford, 1768. Other lists just contain the taxpayer's
name and his tax. The most valuable source was the series of over
1,100 estate inventories from Hartford district between 1650 and
1720 and nearly 1,400 during the years 1750 to 1775. The initial,
major analysis covered the period through 1753, and later research
on the final period added detail concerning those years. The 1,000-
odd inventories between 1720 and 1749 are less useful because of
the rapid and uneven inflation, but are incorporated into certain
tables. Hartford district contained a variety of towns, from the
trading center of Hartford and old Connecticut River Valley
towns like Windsor, to frontier settlements, at first near the original centers (Simsbury), later in more remote hills. In using the
Hartford inventories one has the advantage of the publication by
Charles William Manwaring, comp., *A Digest of the Early Connecticut Probate Records 1635–1750* (3 vols., Hartford, 1904–1906).
These print the wills and the total figure for almost every inventory; each volume is indexed, a great asset when one is trying to
discover the age of every individual. The full inventories and the
valuable accounts of administration are in the Connecticut State
Library.

   In 1700 the four probate districts coincided with the four counties, but beginning in 1719 additional districts cut across county
lines, so that the two terms can no longer be used synonymously.
After 1750 this study used not only Hartford district records but
those of Middletown, Farmington, and Simsbury districts, all
originally part of Hartford. In addition to the Hartford material,
research included a cross section of all the inventories from the
rest of the colony during two time periods, one circa 1700, the
other 1750–1753, totaling about 1,200. These served to test the
reliability of the Hartford series. One deficiency in this study is
the absence, so far, of other cross sections, especially at the end of
the colonial period. Also, lack of information prevents adjust-
ments for age bias except in Hartford.

Note on Prices

Until after 1700, Connecticut's citizens used as their standard of value "country pay"—the price articles commonly sold for. At that time an ounce of silver was worth about 8 shillings, a bushel of wheat cost 4 shillings, corn 2 shillings, a yoke of oxen £10 or so, and a cow, £3.10. Then for a few years—depending on the probate district—the people used either "country pay" or "cash" (or "money"), in which the value of silver was legally fixed at 6 shillings 8 pence and the Spanish dollar at 6 shillings. After 1710 issues of paper money created a price inflation at first gradual until the mid-1730's, then steep. During the 1750's the colony abandoned its inflated "old tenor" currency, reverting to the earlier "cash" standard, now called "lawful" or "proclamation" money. The price of most articles of personal property fluctuated roughly in proportion to these changes (but the price of horses rose, of sheep fell). The cost of land, however, rose more rapidly than did the inflation generally and continued to increase until the end of the colonial period. In order to trace changes in the level of wealth over time, one must adjust the inventory values according to a price index derived from the inventories themselves (we cannot simply use the price of silver because other prices lagged behind). In the text, all figures are in country pay as of 1700 unless otherwise noted. The following table shows the change in value of key items and the deflator or inflator used for personal and real property. Figures are in pounds £, shillings (2/) and pence.

Date		Yoke of oxen	Cow	Bushel of corn	Acre of meadow	Adjustment for Personal	Real
1660–1679	pay	£15	£5.14	3/3	£5		add ⅓
1680–1689		10.8	3.10	2/6	7		
1690–1699		10.8	3.10	2/6	7.10		
1700–1709		10.10	3.16	2/6	7.10		
1710–1714	pay	10	3.10	2/9	8		sub. 10%
	cash	8	2.12	2/	6	add ⅕	add 10%
1715–1719	pay	10	3.5	2/6	8+	sub. 10%	sub. 20%
	cash	8	3	2/	?	add 10%	
1720-1724		9	3	2/6	10		sub. ¼
1725–1729		11	4	4/	11	sub. 10%	sub. ⅓
1730–1734		15	5	4/	12	sub. ⅓	sub. 40%
1735–1739		17.10	6	5/	15	sub. 40%	sub. 60%
1740–1744		26	10	7/	24	sub. 60%	take ¼

1745–1749		37	12	8/6	32	take 2/7	take 2/9
1750–1754		65+	22.10	20/	54	take 1/7	take 1/8+
1755–1759	lawful	8	2.10	1/10	11	add 20%	sub. 1/3
1760–1764		11	3.4	2/6	11.10		sub. 1/3
1765–1769		9	3	2/	12	add 1/5	sub. 1/3
1770–1774		10.6	3.5	2/	15	add 10%	sub. 1/2

Methodological Note

Correct interpretation of estate inventories requires information on the age structures of the probate and living populations.
This is difficult even in Connecticut. For many individuals the
exact year of birth remains unknown, and the following assumptions fixed approximate dates: age at marriage, 25 (23 by ca.
1750), first child at 26, married but no children ±25, young children in thirties, teen-agers in forties, grown children in fifties,
grandchildren over sixty. Age structure of the living population
was derived primarily from assessment lists which specified the
polls. The great migration to Connecticut consisted primarily of
family groups, most of the men being in their thirties and forties,
so that the age structure soon became relatively stable. Moreover,
no subsequent influx of young single men occurred. We do find
a slight increase in the number of older men, and demographic
fluctuations follow certain events such as King Philip's War. The
particular age structure of the probate population at any given
time also differed, for example with a serious epidemic or a military disaster. In addition, the newest towns contained more young
men—as many as two-thirds in their twenties and thirties—than
the older. The overall age structure was approximately as follows:

Age	% of Adults
21–29	35–36
30–39	23–27
40–49	16–17
50–59	11–15
60 and up	9–11

Sources for determining men's ages included the probate records
themselves, vital records (especially those in the Connecticut State
Library), town histories, and genealogies.

Space prohibits a full description of the method for adjusting for age bias. In brief, one first determines the distribution of wealth for each age group in the probate records and then reproduces that distribution as it would exist in the living. During the years 1690–1709 in Hartford County, men aged twenty-one to twenty-nine supplied 14.8 percent of the inventories, but formed 36 percent of the living. The distribution of their probate wealth, shown in the left-hand column, therefore changes to that of the right-hand column, showing the distribution among the living:

£			
£ 1–49	3.5%	8%
50–99	2.7	7
100–199	7.0	17
200–299	1.2	3
300–399	0.4	1
Total	14.8	36

If we suspect a wealth bias, in which the inventories understate the proportion of landless poor men even after the above adjustment, we can change the distribution of wealth in the right-hand column: thus probably half of the 36 percent owned less than £50 worth of property. Practically all such changes would occur in this youngest age-group, the wealth bias consisting primarily of the omission of dependents and young, single men. The effect of adjusting for this bias, which is fairly constant over time, is to lower the mean by about 10 percent and to raise the share of wealth held by the top 10 percent of the men by about 2 percent. The addition of adult male slaves would have no substantial effect on these figures in Connecticut.

A further difficulty in the interpretation of probate records results from the effect on the mean wealth, at any given time, of an exceptionally large estate. If during a five-year period 100 men leave £12,000 worth of property, the mean is £120, but if one man worth £2,000 died then rather than a few years later, the mean jumps to £139. In studying changes over time we need to adjust for this, perhaps by averaging out the large estates over a longer period, or by eliminating all above a certain value, or trimming a certain proportion off the top, in order to study general trends without such eccentric distortions. We cannot rely upon the inventories of a limited time period for any general statements, partly because of such fortuitous deaths, partly because of price changes, and also because of business cycles and the varying age structures of the decedents. At best we must admit an error of 10 percent.

Estate inventories here include debts receivable, but debts payable are not subtracted.

James Wright and the Origins of the Revolution in Georgia

Kenneth Coleman

I EVER MEANT to discharge my duty as a Faithful Servant of the Crown, and can with the greatest truth declare I also meant at the same time to promote to the utmost of my power and Abilities the true Interest of the People."[1] James Wright's 1773 views of his position as governor of Georgia sum up well the man and his regard for the empire and for Georgia. To Wright each was part of a unified whole. True, London was the central control post, but colonials were allowed sufficient leeway for their own development under a benevolent system of law and government. This, ideally, was the way the British Empire should and could operate. Wright was a loyal servant of the King who would invariably carry out his orders from Whitehall, but he saw no reason for conflict between London and Savannah. This concept of empire and the colony's place in it is essential to any understanding of James Wright's role in Georgia's developing Revolutionary crisis.

Wright was born in London during 1716 and came to South Carolina with his father, Robert Wright, who was chief justice

---

[1] Reply of James Wright to Upper House of Assembly in reply to address of congratulations upon return to Georgia from England, February 15, 1773, in Allen D. Candler and Lucian Lamar Knight, eds., *The Colonial Records of the State of Georgia* [*CRG*] (26 vols., Atlanta, 1904–1916), XVII, 688–690. (Volumes 27–39 [MsCRG] exist in manuscript in the Georgia Department of Archives and History, Atlanta.)

of that colony from 1731 to 1739. James held various legal positions and practiced law in Charles Town from early manhood. He was acting attorney general before he entered Gray's Inn in London, where he was called to the bar. He was attorney general of South Carolina from 1742 to 1757, when he became South Carolina's agent in London. He returned to America as lieutenant governor of Georgia in 1760 and became governor the next year.[2] With his residence in London and his steady advancement in colonial government, it is not surprising that he came to have admiration for the British Empire as he knew it. As governor of Georgia he would have a chance to promote that empire in both America and Britain.

James Wright was a true conservative who believed in slow and orderly change. He was reserved in his personal relationships and kept his ideas on many topics to himself. He was not a very extroverted person who could charm people into doing what he wanted. Because of his phlegmatic personality he has suffered in comparisons with his predecessor in Georgia, Henry Ellis, who was noted for charming almost everybody he met. Wright soon became an efficient governor who showed Georgians that he had their welfare at heart by working doggedly for their benefit.

Wright possessed a legalistic mind and always insisted upon meticulous obedience to laws or orders which he received or issued. He was a persistent administrator who sent detailed reports of his activities to his superiors in London. He did his part and expected those he worked with to do theirs. There was little levity or give and take in his nature, though he realized the limitations of most people. He came from a respectable, but not wealthy, family and possessed great desire and determination to succeed in life. He expected to achieve this success through his innate ability and his devotion to work, not through influence or doubtful practices.

Wright arrived in Georgia at a propitious time so far as the colony's development was concerned. Population growth during

---

[2] Biographical information on Wright is found in an article by E. Irving Carlyle in the *Dictionary of National Biography* (63 vols., New York, 1888–1900), LXIII, 107–109. Information on his governorship in Georgia may be found in Kenneth Coleman, "James Wright," in Horace Montgomery, ed., *Georgians in Profile* (Athens, 1958), 40–60; Kenneth Coleman, *The American Revolution in Georgia* (Athens, 1958); and W. W. Abbot, *The Royal Governors of Georgia* (Chapel Hill, 1959).

Georgia's first two decades had been agonizingly slow because of the rigid social and economic controls of the Trustees and the danger of Spanish and French aggression from the south and west. About 1750, just as Georgia was becoming a royal colony, settlers began coming in from the Carolinas and Virginia, now that slavery and larger landholdings were allowed. After gradual growth in the 1750's Georgia was set for much more rapid development once the Spanish and French dangers were removed by the Treaty of Paris of 1763. The only remaining menace was the Creek Indians, and Wright was able to continue good relations with them.[3]

That same year the first major land cession made by the Creeks since 1739 was completed, and Georgia now offered the best land available to settlers in the Southern Piedmont. Naturally there would be a great influx of new inhabitants, mainly from the Carolinas and Virginia with some settlers coming directly from Europe. Georgia was now in the best position in her entire history to grow and prosper. And James Wright was the ideal governor to preside over this development. From his South Carolina residence he knew what made for success in the area. Unlike many other colonial governors, he was not in Georgia only until he could get a better appointment. His personal economic base came more and more to be in Georgia so that he had a great interest in the colony's success. Moreover, it was his desire to succeed as governor and to receive the approval of the London authorities. With this personal investment in the colony and his knowledge of the area, Wright worked harder and met with more success in helping to build up his province than did some other colonial governors.

Soon after he came to Savannah, Wright sold his South Carolina lands and began to buy Georgia acreage. Beginning in 1766, he usually received annual grants of 2,000 to 3,000 acres of land under the headright system, based upon his growing number of slaves. By 1775 he owned some 26,000 acres divided into ten to twelve plantations, worked by 525 slaves, and bringing in an estimated £5,000 to £6,000 sterling a year income.[4] He always had a

---

[3] On Indian relations see Abbot, *Royal Governors, passim.*

[4] Conveyances, Book U, in the Ga. Dept. of Archives and History, *passim*; *CRG.,* VIII, 511, 595–596; IX, 606, 695–696; X, 80–81, 160, 278, 393, 539, 563, 607–609, 670, 728, 729, 751, 854, 880, 982; claims of Sir James Wright for loyalist losses, in Public Record Office [PRO], Audit Office, 13: 37.

reputation for being an excellent planter and owning good land.

As governor, Wright transferred his personal loyalties as well as his economic interests from South Carolina to Georgia. This first became obvious in 1763 when the Treaty of Paris put Florida under British sovereignty. The land between the Altamaha and the St. Marys Rivers, just south of Georgia, now for the first time became desirable to British colonists. This land had been granted to Carolina in her original charter, but it had never been occupied because of its proximity to Spanish Florida. In April, May, and June, 1763, Governor Thomas Boone of South Carolina issued warrants of survey to 400 important Carolinians for 500,000 acres between the Altamaha and St. Marys. Boone's haste evidently arose from his fear that this area might be taken away from South Carolina. Georgians objected strenuously. Wright immediately rushed a protest to Charles Town, but Governor Boone refused to acknowledge it. Georgians and Wright felt that the area should be added to their colony, as it was by the royal proclamation of October, 1763. Wright feared that the South Carolina grants would be held for speculation rather than for quick settlement, thus retarding economic development and the creation of a defensive perimeter on Georgia's southern frontier. Wright attempted, unsuccessfully, to get officials in London to disallow the grants.[5] By leaping to the defense of Georgia against South Carolina, the governor endeared himself to many Georgians who disliked South Carolina and were glad to have a governor who would exert himself for their colony.

Wright also tried, without much success, to increase Georgia's direct trade with Britain and reduce her trade through Charles Town, for which that port secured credit in London.[6] Improved port facilities at Savannah were necessary, and merchants there built better wharves and warehouses. Neither the merchants nor their governor could change the nature of the Savannah River enough to make Savannah a port which the largest ocean-going

[5] *CRG*, IX, 29–44; XIV, 59; XVII, 50–52; *Georgia Gazette*, April 21, August 25, 1763; Charles C. Jones, Jr., *History of Georgia* (2 vols., Boston, 1883), II, 28–35; Abbot, *Royal Governors*, 100–102.

[6] *CRG*, XIII, 682; Percy Scott Flippin, "The Royal Government in Georgia, 1752–1776," in the *Georgia Historical Quarterly* [*GHQ*], 9 (1925), 224–225; Jones, *History of Georgia*, II, 74.

vessels of the day could use easily. Wright established Sunbury in 1762 as a port of entry for the Midway area. He also attempted unsuccessfully in the 1770's to develop ports at Brunswick and at St. Marys, farther south.[7]

In everything that Wright tried to do for the colony's economy, he remained within the precepts of the mercantilistic thinking of the day. He sought to build up production in agriculture, lumbering, and naval stores but showed no interest in developing manufacturing. He tried in 1768 to dissuade the British government from discontinuing the bounty on raw silk because of the realization that financial encouragement was necessary for silk production. However, the home government dropped the bounty, and silk production declined.[8] In his economic activities Wright demonstrated his concern for the colony and his loyalty to the concept of empire current in London—a recurring theme during his Georgia years.

Wright worked diligently to secure more settlers. Only with increased population could the frontier be made safe and economic growth secured. Despite the more than 3,000 people who came under the trustees, a report in 1751, the year before the colony became royal, showed only 1,700 whites and 400 blacks in Georgia. When Governor Henry Ellis arrived in 1757, he reported 4,000 to 5,000 whites and 2,000 blacks. Three years later Wright found 6,000 whites and 3,000 blacks. Much more rapid growth is shown by 10,000 whites and 8,000 blacks in 1766 and in 18,000 whites and 15,000 blacks in 1773. Wright certainly did all that he could to help entice new population to Georgia, and the colony expanded at a more rapid rate during his tenure than did any other southern colony.

After both the Indian cession of 1763 and that of 1773, the governor issued proclamations setting forth the terms upon which the land could be had by settlers. After the 1773 cession he made an extended tour of the newly acquired land to investigate the fertility of the soil, the timber and mineral resources, the streams and mill sites, and anything else which might aid in its settlement

---

[7] *CRG*, VIII, 671–673; XV, 502; MsCRG, XVIII, Part I, 649, 824–877; XXXVII, 75–76; PRO, Treasury I: 415, f 5–8; Georgia Historical Society *Collections*, 3 (1873), 162–163.

[8] Ga. Hist. Soc. *Colls.* (1873), 166–167; Jones, *History of Georgia*, II, 24–25, 75–76.

and use. Such information must have been helpful to prospective settlers who had not seen the area themselves.[9]

Wright worked closely with the assembly to pay the travel and initial equipment expenses for new settlers from Europe, especially for the Scotch-Irish who were coming to America in large numbers but who frequently were very poor. When a 1768 act to make such payments was dropped because of British opposition, the governor nevertheless approved payments out of public funds under it to people who had left their homes thinking the law would be enacted.[10]

To make for more contiguous settlement and thus a safer frontier, Wright tried to restrict the size of land grants to the amount that individuals were entitled to under the headright system—one hundred acres for the head of the family and fifty acres for each other member, free or slave. Larger grants, which would likely be held for speculative purposes, got in the way of attracting new settlers and creating an unbroken line of settlement.[11]

Besides population, another indicator of economic development was Georgia's export trade. The year after Wright arrived at least £15,870 worth of local produce was exported. This increased to £99,483 by 1770 and £121,677 by 1773. All Georgia trade figures must be considered in relative terms. They are inexact because so much trade went to Charles Town via the inland passage, and there are no extant records of this trade.

Wright sought to provide the effective political leadership necessary for growth and prosperity in Georgia through open actions rather than through political bargains. He lacked the charisma and popularity of Henry Ellis, his predecessor, but he was a much more competent and efficient governor than Ellis had been.[12] He always took the initiative with his council and invariably gained its full backing. His relations with the Commons House of Assembly were, of course, harder to control; but if the matter did not concern the growing American rights movement

---

[9] MsCRG, XXXVIII, Part I, 85–86, 138–160; Jones, *History of Georgia*, II, 130–132.

[10] *CRG*, X, 671–672; XV, 40, 271–272; XVII, 401–407; XVIII, 743–748; XIX, Part I, 182, 191; *Georgia Gazette*, February 23, March 9, 23, 1774.

[11] Land Grants are in *CRG*, VII–XII, *passim*; Wright's statements are in Wright to Hillsborough, March 8, 1769, in MsCRG, XXXVII, 400–401; Wright to Board of Trade, December 27, 1771, in the *Journal of Board of Trade, 1768–1775* (London, 1938), 294.

[12] On Ellis as governor see Abbot, *Royal Governors*, 57–83.

after 1764, the governor was able to do business easily with the commons house and to lead it in legislating for many matters which were considered for the benefit of the colony. He often wrote or modified bills to meet objections from London. He tried to influence assemblymen through private conversations rather than through public arguments. He signed most bills passed by the assembly if they did not violate his instructions, regardless of his personal feelings about them.[13] In short, he was an assiduous administrator, but not as good a politician, as events after 1764 demonstrate.

Wright always worked to prevent trouble by taking action before problems reached an impasse. For instance, at the time of the Regulator uprisings in the Carolinas, he and his council established a circuit court at Augusta for the convenience of the upper parishes and to prevent troubles like those in South Carolina.[14] In 1769 and 1770 the governor and the commons house engaged in heated arguments over representation in the commons house for the four parishes created south of the Altamaha River in 1765. Wright agreed that they should be represented, but he refused to issue writs of election because he had not received permission to do so from London, despite his requests. The objectors attacked Wright for adhering to his private instructions from the King rather than to the rights of British subjects in America and the objectors' incorrect interpretation of the Proclamation of 1763. But the Georgia argument against the royal prerogative did not go as far in 1770 as it did in some other colonies. Early in 1771 Wright received the desired instructions and settled the matter, although the delay had created bad feelings between himself and the commons house. To prevent such a problem arising again, immediately after the 1773 Indian cession Wright asked for and gained permission to allow representation in the new area as soon as its population justified it.[15]

---

[13] For Wright's relations with his council see *CRG*, VII–XII. For his relations with the commons house see *ibid.*, XIII–XV, and Flippin, "Royal Government in Georgia," in *GHQ*, 8 (1924), 266–277.

[14] *CRG*, X, 397–399; XIV, 524, 535.

[15] Wright to Hillsborough, December 26, 1768, cited in Flippin, "Royal Government in Georgia," 8: 245; May 11, December 11, 1770, MsCRG, XXXVII, 450–451, 489; Wright to Dartmouth, August 10, 1773, *ibid.*, XXXVIII, Part I, 83–84; Dartmouth to Wright, October 23, 1773, *ibid.*, 92–93; *CRG*, X, 945–946; XV, 46–49, 86–87, 127–128, 153, 159–160, 202, 206–207, 298–299; XIX, Part I, 170; *Georgia Gazette*, March 14, 1770.

Good Indian relations were essential to population and economic growth in Georgia. Wright had inherited peace with Georgia's Indians, and the removal of the Spanish and French in 1763 made this easier to maintain. Wright felt that both Indians and whites should live up to their treaty agreements. He tried to prevent whites from settling upon Indian lands which had not been ceded and to keep traders from cheating the Indians—the two things most likely to cause Indian troubles. The governor cooperated with Indian Superintendent John Stuart in his attempts to secure uniform trade regulations in all southern colonies, but this was never possible.[16]

The 1763 Indian cession resulted from the Treaty of Paris of that year, and Wright had little specifically to do with it. The 1773 cession was much more the direct result of his work. By 1768 the good lands of the 1763 cession had been granted and settlers were beginning to press against the frontier again. Thus Wright favored a new land cession to continue the development of the colony and to maintain peace with the Indians. The governor's views were reinforced by traders who had sold the Indians more than they could pay for. While Wright was in England from 1771 to 1773 he secured approval for the cession. Upon his return to Georgia in 1773, he and Superintendent Stuart conferred with the Creeks and Cherokees at Augusta and obtained the desired land.[17]

Wright was a competent governor who was truly concerned about the welfare and development of his colony and who led his government with considerable success. He belonged to Georgia fully and came to believe more and more that Georgia belonged to himself to guide and to show to London at its best advantage. Perhaps Wright became too possessive in his feelings about the colony and took growing differences of opinion by colonists too much as a personal affront. No doubt many of the colonists respected Wright because he worked hard at his job. Certainly much of Georgia's advancement during his governorship was tied

[16] On Wright's Indian policy see *CRG*, VII–XV, *passim*; specifically VIII, 522–524, 697; XVIII, 594–595, 703–705; MsCRG, XXXVII, 100–175; XXXVIII, Part II, 114–116; Flippin, "Royal Government in Georgia," 8: 87–88, 275; 13: 139; *Georgia Gazette*, June 30, December 16, 1763.

[17] John R. Alden, *John Stuart and the Southern Colonial Frontier* (Ann Arbor, 1944), 301–308; MsCRG, XXXVII, 547–555; XXXVIII, Part I, 15–37, 83; Stuart to Gage, April 22, 1773, in the Gage Papers, Am. Ser., Clements Library [CL].

to and aided by his actions. This was Wright's greatest success as governor, and, ironically, his greatest contribution to Georgia's participation in the dawning revolt.

Besides aiding Georgia's advancement between 1764 and 1775, Wright also sought to keep ahead of the developing American rights group and thus hopefully to prevent rebellious actions. As the spirit of resistance to imperial policy grew, Wright sometimes thought British actions ill-advised. He knew that officials in London often failed to consider American viewpoints or desires. Wright was an American who understood the colonists considerably better than did distant officials in England. Hoping to prevent trouble, he sometimes sent advice to London, but it was usually ignored except for specific Georgia problems.

When the Georgia assembly objected to the economic effects of the Sugar Act of 1764 and the proposed Stamp Act, the governor took no action. To him, this was an orderly and respectful protest made by a legal body.[18] But when he was requested to call the assembly into session to consider sending delegates to the Stamp Act Congress, Wright refused.[19] Unified intercolonial protest was too much for him to countenance.

As November 1, 1765, the date that the Stamp Act was to go into effect, approached, the Sons of Liberty organized in Savannah and made it clear that the sale of stamps would be opposed. The arrival of the proceedings of the Stamp Act Congress in late November reinforced popular opposition. The Commons House of Assembly on December 14 adopted and dispatched to the King, Lords, and Commons the petitions of the Stamp Act Congress.[20] Wright made no effort to stop such a regular and legal protest, which he probably could not have prevented anyway.

On November 1 there were no stamps, stamp distributor, nor even a copy of the Stamp Act in Georgia. The governor and council stopped land grants, but allowed ship clearances, which required stamps under the law, to continue. Certainly Wright approved this decision and probably suggested it. The governor, seeing what had happened in other colonies, issued a proclama-

---

[18] *CRG*, XIV, 142–144, 252–253; XVII, 199–200; Ga. Hist. Soc. *Colls.*, 6 (1904), 30–33.
[19] *CRG*, XIV, 270–274.
[20] Wright to Conway, January 31, 1766, in Jones, *History of Georgia*, II, 60–65; *Georgia Gazette*, October 31, November 7, 14, 1765; *CRG*, IX, 438–439; XIV, 300–301, 304–306, 315–317.

tion against riots and got council approval for protection of stamps and the stamp agent when they appeared. The stamps arrived in December, but there was still no distributor. On December 16 Wright and his council agreed that the Stamp Act was now fully in effect in Georgia, but a majority of the council opposed the appointment of a temporary distributor and the ports of Savannah and Sunbury were effectively closed. Vessels in port were detained for a month awaiting the distributor's arrival.[21]

On January 2, 1766, Wright faced down a mob at his gate which inquired what he intended to do about the stamps. He sent the crowd away without giving in to their threats. Then, hearing that 200 Liberty Boys had gathered in Savannah to destroy the stamps, the governor collected about fifty guards and moved the stamps to a safer place. Special guards were posted, and the governor did not have his clothes off for four days. When the stamp distributor finally arrived on January 3, 1766, Wright protected him while he sold enough stamps to clear the vessels ready to depart.[22]

After this sale of stamps—the only stamps to be issued in any of the colonies which later rebelled—more vociferous and threatening objections from Georgians resulted in a cessation of sales and the departure of the distributor. In February the governor was glad to have the chance to send the stamps out of the colony.[23]

Wright's successful defense of the Stamp Act showed a good bit about the kind of person he was and the way he could outmaneuver his opponents. Even though he probably thought the act unwise, once it was the law he did all that he could to enforce it. He could have allowed himself to be intimidated by the mob, or he could have permitted the distributor to resign and let business be conducted without stamps. Popular fury resulted in such actions in other colonies. Instead he enforced the act against all objections at considerable personal danger to himself. But by February, 1766, it was obvious that the act was a failure and that any further attempt to enforce it would probably increase popular turmoil to far too dangerous a level. Throughout the stamp

[21] CRG, IX, 454–458, 460; Wright to Conway, January 31, 1766, in Jones, History of Georgia, II, 60–65.

[22] Wright to Conway, January 31, 1766, in Jones, History of Georgia, II, 60–65; The Newport Mercury, February 10, 1766; South Carolina Gazette, January 21, February 25, 1766; James Habersham to George Whitefield, January 27, 1766, in Ga. Hist. Soc. Colls. (1904), 54–55; MsCRG, XXXVII, 112, 121–122.

[23] See sources cited in footnote 22 above.

troubles Wright fought to keep the initiative in his own hands and to prevent his opponents from getting ahead of him. In this he achieved considerable success.

Once the troubles were over, the governor tried—successfully he said—to convince influential colonists of the error of mob action. But he appealed only to the old leaders in the colony. He was incapable of understanding popular leadership in such a crisis. There was still a "knot of rebellious turbulent spirits" in Savannah that Wright knew he could not change. As always, he was repairing his bridges and trying to prevent similar troubles in the future. Some indication of his success can be seen in his statement in late January, 1766, before the trouble was over, that "there is still a possibility of restoring the peace and tranquility of the Province." Yet if peace and tranquility did not come, Wright was quite willing to call on General Gage for military assistance in imposing peace upon Georgia. This proved unnecessary. The success of his firm stand was reflected in the address of the Commons House of the Assembly to Wright upon the repeal of the Stamp Act: "We cannot indeed but felicitate ourselves in that we have no injuries or damages either of a public or a private nature, nor any votes or resolutions derogatory to the honor of his Majesty's government or tending to destroy the true constitutional dependence of the Colonies on the Imperial Crown and Parliament of Great Britain to reconsider."[24]

Regardless of how unwise Wright considered the Stamp Act, he thought its repeal under mob pressure worse. Forced repeal would undermine the authority of the British government, demonstrate to the colonists the success of their tactics, and end any future hopes of controlling the colonies. Wright's strong stand in 1765 and 1766 may have convinced him of his superior abilities and perhaps made it more difficult for him to work with the American rights groups thereafter. His actions certainly increased the number of persons in Georgia who would stand against him in future crises.

Wright and the assembly were thankful that there had not been really serious trouble in Georgia,[25] but the flow of imperial events prevented a full relaxation of tensions. In the next year, 1767,

---

[24] Wright to Conway, January 31, March 10, 1766, in MsCRG, XXXVII, 116–117; Jones, *History of Georgia*, II, 60–71.
[25] *CRG*, XIV, 370–381.

Parliament passed the Townshend Revenue Acts, and the colonial opposition ended the short truce which repeal of the Stamp Act had brought. When the assembly met in November of 1768, Wright informed it that the King did not approve of the circular letter opposing the Townshend Acts sent out by the Massachusetts House of Representatives and had instructed him to dissolve the assembly if it took up this circular. The commons house first considered its most pressing business; then on December 24 it determined that the Massachusetts circular was a proper exercise of the right of petition. It adopted a "dutiful and loyal" address to the King on the subject. Wright immediately dissolved the assembly, ignoring the right of subjects to petition the Crown.[26]

It was September, 1769, before real opposition to the Townshend Acts surfaced in Georgia. At least three protest meetings were held in Savannah during that month, and the last adopted a nonimportation agreement that contained no enforcement machinery. A small group from Savannah apparently led the objectors, and they got little backing elsewhere in the colony. Wright worked privately to prevent the securing of signatures, but his efforts may not have been necessary. No more was heard of the nonimportation agreement, and most Georgians must have been lukewarm about it at best.

After the excitement over the Townshend Acts there was no further trouble in Georgia until April of 1771. The commons house then unanimously elected as speaker Noble Wimberly Jones, the former speaker who had become one of the leading opponents of British action. Wright, exercising a power never used before in Georgia, disapproved Jones's selection. The commons house then elected Archibald Bulloch, who was just as anti-British as Jones. The next day the house resolved that the refusal by the governor to accept a speaker elected by a unanimous vote was a "high Breach of the Privilege of the House, and tends to subvert the most valuable Rights and Liberties of the People."[28]

Wright and his council agreed that such a denial of royal

[26] *CRG*, XIV, 592–596, 643–659; XVII, 454; Wright to Hillsborough, December 23, 1768, in MsCRG, XXXVII, 380; *Georgia Gazette*, December 28, 1768.

[27] *Georgia Gazette*, September 20, 1769; Allen D. Candler, ed., *The Revolutionary Records of the State of Georgia [RRG]* (3 vols., Atlanta, 1908), I, 8–11; Wright to Hillsborough, November 8, 1769, March 1, May 10, 1770, in MsCRG, XXXVII, 423, 436, 444–452.

[28] *CRG*, XV, 305–306, 311–314; XI, 335–336; Wright to Hillsborough, April 30, 1771, in MsCRG, XXXVII, 535–538.

authority made it impossible to do business with the assembly. After a fruitless private attempt to get the resolution rescinded, Wright dissolved the assembly before it had transacted any business. British officials approved his action, and they issued instructions to disapprove whoever was chosen as speaker by the next assembly. By the time of the next assembly meeting, Wright was in England on leave; but the argument was continued with James Habersham, the acting governor.[29]

Wright returned to Georgia in February, 1773, now Sir James Wright, Bart., an honor which had been conferred upon him as a reward for his stable leadership in Georgia. There was no further trouble until July and August of 1774, when Savannahians held two protest meetings denouncing the Intolerable Acts. Petitions circulated in the colony attacking both of these meetings and their resolutions, obviously with the approval of if not with the support of the governor. The August meeting debated the sending of delegates to the First Continental Congress but took no action. This time, unlike the Stamp Act Congress, Wright could not be blamed for Georgia not being represented.[30]

On January 17 and 18, 1775, the assembly and the first Georgia Provincial Congress met in Savannah, with some overlapping membership.[31] The Congress adopted the Continental Association of the First Continental Congress with amendments, elected delegates to the Second Continental Congress, and took other actions which placed Georgia in concert with the other colonies. However, since this congress represented only five of the twelve parishes in Georgia, it did not feel that it could speak for the entire colony. It hoped that the assembly would approve its actions and make them official. To prevent this, Wright prorogued the assembly on February 10.[32] A scheduled meeting of this assembly in May could not secure a quorum, an indication of the spread of rebellious feeling in the colony.[33]

---

[29] *CRG*, XI, 429; XV, 320–325, 329–334; XVII 655–658; Hillsborough to Habersham, December 4, 1771, in MsCRG, XXXVII, 552–553; Habersham to Hillsborough, April 30, 1772, in Ga. Hist. Soc. *Colls.* (1904), 174–180.

[30] Wright to Dartmouth, July 25, August 18, 24, 1775, in MsCRG, XXXVIII, Part I, 293–294, 298, 302–311; Wright to Thomas Gage, August 19, November 4, December 24, 1774, in the Gage Papers, Am. Ser., CL; *Georgia Gazette*, August 3, September 7, 21, 28, October 12, November 24, 1774.

[31] *Georgia Gazette*, January 25, 1775.

[32] *RRG*, I, 63–66; Ga. Hist. Soc. *Colls.*, 10 (1952), 11–12.

[33] Ga. Hist. Soc. *Colls.* (1952), 21–22.

As late as June, 1775, Wright showed his determination not to give in to his opponents, who certainly did not dominate Georgia yet. On the night of June 2 local agitators spiked the cannon on the battery at Savannah and threw them over the bluff to prevent their being used in the celebration of the King's birthday on June 4. Wright had some of the cannon recovered, drilled out, and fired for the birthday. Moreover, he gave his usual entertainment for the public officials. The whigs countered the next day with a celebration at the newly erected liberty pole and an elegant dinner at Tondee's long room.[34]

In the summer two provincial congresses met, more and more taking over de facto control of Georgia. The provincial congress became Georgia's first revolutionary government. Wright remained in Savannah until February of 1776, when he finally left for England. He realized increasingly during his last six months that he had little if any power to control what was happening.[35] Revolution was at hand, despite all the governor could do, to a degree because of what he had done.

Wright's actions and attitudes did several things to affect the climate of revolution in Georgia. It certainly took the self-confidence that came from recent economic and political developments in order for Georgians to be able and willing to join the other colonists in rebellion. Georgians had to be convinced that they were able to take care of themselves politically, economically, and militarily. The maturing process of the last fifteen years, over which Wright had presided and which he had abetted to a considerable degree, had created this conviction of self-sufficiency. A comparison of revolutionary activities in Georgia with those in East Florida illustrates this. Florida, a British province only since 1763, had a population and economy too small to support open revolt; the government was too new. But unparalleled population and economic growth in Georgia became a base for the successful political challenge to British authority there. Georgia had really shot up from an uncertain infancy to a feeling of maturity in the last fifteen to twenty years.

[34] *Georgia Gazette*, June 7, 1775.
[35] Wright to Dartmouth, several June and July letters, in Ga. Hist. Soc. *Colls.* (1873), 183–195.

Wright refused to yield to colonial objections and did what he could to uphold royal authority. He also strove to keep ahead of the objectors and to convince Georgians that they would be better off by not challenging Britain's authority. Wright's personal and official progress and that of many others in Georgia convinced him that similar successes were possible for many colonists. Rebellion, as he saw it, could only harm Georgia and her inhabitants. His belief in the British political system reinforced his innate conservatism, and the success of Georgia in her rapid development as a part of the benevolent British Empire all reinforced his belief that there could be no liberty except under law nor real progress except within the empire.

Yet Wright's hard line and unshakeable insistence upon living up to the letter of his instructions from London made enemies for him and hurt his cause. In considering his continuing refusal to countenance colonial opposition, two explanations are possible. The first is that he did not understand his opponents adequately and believed that any compromise would aid the plans of those not fully committed to the empire. The other possibility is that Wright understood what the results of his actions would be, but that his nature made it impossible for him to give in for the sake of expediency. He would obey his orders from London, regardless of the consequences, because that was his duty and the right thing to do. From what is known of Wright's abilities, his knowledge of colonials, and his set of mind, the latter is probably the correct view. It is very hard to know Wright's true beliefs on important topics, for he was given neither to baring his soul to London nor to arguing with his superiors there.

From what Wright did and wrote, there is no indication that he felt that colonial rights were being violated between 1765 and 1775. He felt that much done in London was unwise, but not necessarily constitutionally wrong. He certainly believed strongly in the precedence of the government in London over that in the colonies. The colonial constitutional argument seems not to have affected him at all. He talked about colonists with a "strange idea of Liberty" that only local representatives could levy taxes. In an analysis of the causes of revolt written in 1777 he only mentioned the argument over parliamentary taxation as the reason Americans rebelled. He did not say if he considered such taxation constitutional or not.[36] It seems very probable that he did not consider it unconstitutional.

Wright, like most Loyalists, did not want to have to choose between England and America. He did not see why the problems were beyond a reconciliation of differences allowing for much of the old relationship to continue. That is what reasonable people would like, and Wright would certainly have believed himself a reasonable person. Yet by 1775 a choice between the two was necessary. That was the tragedy of Loyalists during the Revolutionary era. Wright by the end of 1775 must have realized that many of his actions in Georgia had helped to bring about the "wrong" results and that nothing he could then do would make any difference. He was caught in the vise of history.

[36] Robert G. Mitchell, ed., "Sir James Wright Looks at the American Revolution," in *GHQ*, 53 (1969), 509–518; Jones, *History of Georgia*, II, 71–72.

The Role of the Courts in the Making of the Revolution in Virginia

George M. Curtis III

EARLY in 1774, most observers would have viewed the prospect of a political revolution in Virginia as unlikely. The colony's real and personal wealth, the maturity of its institutions, and the growing diversification of its economy all dictated against radical political change. Divisive internal issues of long standing which gave energy and focus to opposition politics in Massachusetts, New York, and Pennsylvania were absent in Virginia. The scandal surrounding Speaker Robinson's fiscal maladministration, if not settled, commanded little public attention in 1774, and the issue of sectional political representation in the House of Burgesses had subsided. Economic and political dissatisfactions with the empire, although increasingly volatile after 1760, had not galvanized Virginians into revolution. Furthermore, cultural and emotional ties to England remained strong, posing formidable barriers to any explicit declaration of Virginia's constitutional, political, and economic autonomy. By the end of 1774, however, Virginia had changed from a constitutionally obedient colony into a community in open revolt.

Certain Virginians, as they became convinced of the futility of any further compromises with the British government, intensified their criticism of virtually every act of imperial authority. Specific factors aided the thrust of opposition. Politically and administratively, Virginians had achieved extensive control over local affairs.

Conversely, royal authority had become increasingly undermined by the dependence on co-operation from the Council, House of Burgesses, and gentry. Most importantly, the colony's political leadership was both secure and mature. Lawyer, planter, and essayist Richard Bland was still active in 1774; the great legal thinkers, George Mason, Edmund Pendleton, and Thomas Jefferson were ready to inherit and extend Bland's considerable influence. Such men as Patrick Henry, George Washington, Peyton Randolph, and Richard Henry Lee were proven political organizers of exceptional skill. This nucleus encompassed a blend of youth and age, enthusiasm and deliberateness, tenacity and patience. Until the spring of 1774, the missing link was the presence of a local issue to give substance to the nascent patriot cause.

The mounting irritations with the Scottish and English commercial system, exacerbated by the financial crisis which struck Great Britain and Virginia between 1772 and 1774, aroused broad-based popular criticism of imperial administration. Virginia radicals, exploiting the Committee of Correspondence as one more means of sustaining colonial opposition, succeeded in channeling and focusing this criticism. Few were more designing and energetic than Richard Henry Lee. As a principal member of the Committee of Correspondence, Lee exchanged a lively correspondence with Samuel Adams to gather and disseminate information and tactics. Poised to exploit every possible situation, Lee informed Adams early in May, 1774, that he expected the current session of the burgesses to support Massachusetts in "repelling the revenue act with the Tea ships." Furthermore he assured Adams that the legislators would certainly "animadvert on some other tyrannic proceedings of Administration."[1] Lee did not inform his Massachusetts coconspirator that he and Thomas Jefferson had already initiated a move to obstruct royal government by dislocating the operations of the Virginia court system. Well before the news of the Boston Port Act burst upon Williamsburg on May 19, the radical leaders had commenced specific plans that would lead Virginia to independence.

As the nerve center for a society which was still rural in nature,

---

[1] Oliver P. Chitwood, *Richard Henry Lee: Statesman of the Revolution* (Morgantown, 1967), 53–57; Lee to Samuel Adams, May 8, 1774, in James C. Ballagh, ed., *The Letters of Richard Henry Lee* (2 vols., New York, 1911–1914), I, 110.

the court system was the most conspicuous institution in Virginia. Independent from direct control of the governor and yet having an immediate impact on every aspect of Virginia life, the courts were an obvious target for political manipulation designed to obstruct royal government and build popular support. For generations the courts had provided a public arena for settling problems involving local political power and imperial economic interests. It was also in the courts that British creditors had to sue to collect the most troublesome colonial debts. Virginia leaders realized that the judiciary was a critical part in both the empire's economic machinery and the colony's political order. Stopping Virginia's courts would necessarily cause the imperial economic system to falter. Obstructing the use of the court system would gain many adherents, because this technique avoided what was to Virginians the deplorable violence in the politics that so often characterized radical opposition in other colonies. Prior to 1774 Virginians had twice turned to economic boycott as a means of opposing imperial policy. The experience had been difficult for agricultural producers unable to sell surplus crops while they remained vulnerable to litigation brought by British creditors. Closing the courts would protect both large and small exporters in the event of another boycott by removing the nagging possibility of debt suits in a situation where the producers were restrained from exploiting customary British markets. Finally, if the radicals could stop only that portion of judicial administration pertaining to the imperial economy while managing to keep certain courts open for local business, they would have established their political credibility in a revolutionary crisis.

In April, 1774, a normally insignificant administrative act, the Fee Act, expired. The radicals, particularly Jefferson and Lee, instantly realized that the timing of the expiration had far-reaching implications. This regulatory act established the schedule of payments of officers of the courts, including the General Court. On the surface, the Fee Act did not compare to major bills which established economic and political policies; nevertheless, it was critical to the functioning of government. Fees as part of costs in law suits had become so inextricably linked with judgments that the courts required legislative regulation in order to operate. Disproportionate governmental disruption would be the inevitable consequence if such a statute became void. The Fee

Act became an Achilles heel for the entire governmental system, and hence the best instrument for precipitating revolution in Virginia.[2]

The Fee Act, a temporary statute requiring repeated legislative action, had been renewed by the House of Burgesses in 1765, 1766, 1769, and 1772. The 1772 statute was scheduled to expire on April 12, 1774, the very moment when the General Court was to convene for its spring session. Unfortunately, the commencement of the House of Burgesses was still three weeks away. The semi-annual session of the General Court was therefore jeopardized because there was no enabling legislation for court fees. Faced with the undesirable prospect of an early recess, the justices immediately sought advice from two members of the General Court bar—Thomas Jefferson and Edmund Pendleton.[3]

Edmund Pendleton wrote an opinion for the General Court supporting the constitutionality of a temporary order to allow the court to remain open, charging the usual fees until the legislature could act. His arguments for keeping the courts open in 1774 resembled those he had used during the Stamp Act crisis. Although framed in neutral legal language, Pendleton's opinion included a strong indictment of those who, wanting the court closed again, exploited the rhetoric of constitutional separation of powers to gain their political ends. In continuing the schedule

---

[2] Such studies as Charles Lingley's *The Transition in Virginia from Colony to Commonwealth* (New York, 1910); H. J. Eckenrode's *The Revolution in Virginia* (Hamden, 1964); Thad Tate's "The Coming of the Revolution in Virginia: Britain's Challenge to Virginia's Ruling Class, 1763–1766," in the *William and Mary Quarterly* [*WMQ*], 3rd Ser., 19 (1962), 323–343; and Terrance L. Mahan's "Virginia Reaction to British Policy, 1763–1776" (doctoral dissertation, University of Wisconsin, 1960) do not stress the manipulation of the court system as a central device for hastening the Revolution. Most historians have emphasized the events which occurred after Virginians learned about the Boston Port Act on May 19, 1774. The fee bill controversy in both the General Court and the House of Burgesses, however, preceded the useful political news from the North by a substantial margin in time. Alert as the patriots were in exploiting the fee bill, their counterparts in Maryland had politicized the issue even earlier. See Charles A. Barker, *The Background of the Revolution in Maryland* (New Haven, 1940), 344–358, and Ronald Hoffman, *A Spirit of Dissension: Economics, Politics, and the Revolution in Maryland* (Baltimore, 1973), 92–125.

[3] W. W. Hening, ed., *The Statutes at Large, being a Collection of all the Laws of Virginia from the First Session of the Legislature in the Year 1619* (13 vols., Richmond, 1809–1823), VIII, 186, 266, 299, 515; David Mays, *Edmund Pendleton, 1721–1803: A Biography* (2 vols., Cambridge, 1952), 244–248; and David J. Mays, ed., *The Letters and Papers of Edmund Pendleton, 1734–1803* (2 vols., Charlottesville, 1967), I, 84–85.

of fees that had become traditional, the court could justify its action in two ways. First, it was maintaining, not changing, a schedule which the burgesses had reaffirmed over the years, thereby investing it with all the properties of a well-established tradition. Second, in the absence of a statute, the order was "a reasonable direction to their [the court's] officers what fees to charge." In doing this the Virginia General Court would also follow English precedent scrupulously. The cumulative effect of Virginia tradition and English precedent even enabled a party to request a jury to adjust the fees if the suitor objected to the court's opinion.[4]

Pendleton argued that a court order to remain in session was not only fair under the circumstances but also helped provide "a remedy against the litigious and unjust opponent." Precedent also supported the court's intervention in determining costs. "Costs were not recovered at Common Law." According to British statutory history, juries and courts co-operated in establishing costs. "When juries have fixed the costs by their verdict courts have examined and enlarged them as 'costs de incremento' and at length it has long prevailed for the jury to assess the damages only to so much besides costs which are left wholly to the court to regulate." By taking such history and practice into consideration, Pendleton believed that the General Court would be above criticism.[5]

Pendleton predicted judicial anarchy if Virginians refused to honor such an order. Any party to a winning suit faced the possibility that his costs might be lost or indefinitely suspended if the court waited for the legislature to pass a new fee bill. "Or must the courts of justice stop all proceedings on account of doubts about the quantum of their officers fees?" Such a prospect was outrageous in Pendleton's estimation. "To make fees the primary consideration" of the court's continued operation debased the very "purpose of their institution." Pendleton concluded on a note mixed with foreboding and despair. "I consider the stopping of courts of justice (except in cases of invasion) as fixing an indelible mark of infamy on a country. I hope it will never take place here."[6]

---

[4] Mays, ed., *Pendleton Papers*, I, 84–85.

[5] *Ibid.*, 85.

[6] *Idem.* Pendleton made these same arguments almost three months later. Just days before the August convention convened, he reasserted his belief that all courts

Jefferson, on the other hand, opposed any preemptive action by the General Court. Having conducted his own research into the common law and statutory history of the fee acts, his conclusions were diametrically opposed to those of Pendleton. For Jefferson, common law offered no precedent for the General Court's action. Furthermore, he contended that Pendleton had failed to distinguish properly between temporary and perpetual statutes establishing fees. Since the founding of the colony the burgesses had passed fourteen acts regulating court fees. During the eighteenth century, all fee regulations had been temporary, and Jefferson stressed that the legislature's decisions to limit the life of these statutes was explicit and therefore a clear injunction against any judicial action. Nor was he worried about the welfare of the judicial institution. On the contrary, Jefferson interpreted a General Court order of this kind as an act of judicial usurpation, an unwarranted encroachment upon the traditional powers and prerogatives of the legislature. Jefferson believed that such policy clearly violated constitutional safeguards that Virginians must never compromise.

Responding to Pendleton's contention that a long series of such acts established a right to continue assessing fees in the absence of enabling legislation, Jefferson retorted:

> If therefore it be supposed that this passage gives to fees, which have for some time subsisted under a temporary act of legislature the authority of custom, it must be answered that the situation is as false as its doctrine is absurd. To say that a regulation introduced by a temporary law, shall when the law expires, continue a law under that temporary usage or custom, is to make no difference between temporary and perpetual acts.[7]

---

should remain open regardless of the political situation. See Pendleton to Ralph Wormeley, Jr., July 28, 1774, *ibid.*, 96–98.

[7] Jefferson's opinion for the General Court, May [?], 1774, Papers of Thomas Jefferson, Library of Congress [LC]. David Mays dated these opinions to correspond with the date of the General Court order to continue the assessment of fees. I have assumed that they were submitted prior to the court's decision and that they were not published either at that time or afterward. Mays claims that Jefferson's opinion was in Pendleton's handwriting. See Mays, ed., *Pendleton Papers*, I, 85n. The only comment Mays made concerning the two opinions was that "Jefferson was in hearty agreement with Pendleton, and wrote a memorandum of law in support of his position." On both technical and conceptual grounds the two were diametrically opposed. See Mays, *Pendleton*, I, 247.

To reach his conclusion pressing the court to remain open, Pendleton was forced to define judicial power broadly. In contrast, Jefferson, by restricting himself to a narrow construction of common law and Virginia statutory precedent, fashioned a view of judicial deference to the legislature. The court should assiduously avoid any hint of legislative policy making according to Jefferson. To comply with Jefferson's view, the court would have to halt proceedings until a new law regulating fees became effective. Pendleton forthrightly predicted that court closure would lead to judicial anarchy, terms which for him were synonymous with political anarchy. Jefferson chose not to dispute Pendleton's prediction. His silence on this crucial political consideration implied his agreement that disruption would be the inevitable consequence of closing the General Court. The silence also carried the implication that Jefferson actively favored just such consequences.[8]

Having seen the opinions, the General Court elected to remain open in the manner that Pendleton suggested. From a practical standpoint, the justices could assume, like Pendleton, that the legislature would soon pass the requisite enabling statute, thereby making the entire issue moot. Within the historical context of the court's constitutional development, the decision was almost inevitable. The General Court, as an increasingly assertive and independent institution, was quite capable of disregarding Jefferson's warnings about judicial usurpation of the legislative function. Many leaders defended publicly the self-consciousness and self-reliance of the General Court and the Virginia court system as a whole. Most experienced attorneys fully understood the Virginia tradition of judicial independence as enunciated by Attorney General Sir William Jones in 1681 and expanded by Sir John Randolph during the first third of the eighteenth century. According to this judicial philosophy, the General Court, when treating British statutes and imperial instructions, was vested with the

---

[8] For the public debate over the constitutional and political implications of the fee bill in Maryland see Peter S. Onuf, ed., *Maryland and the Empire, 1773: The Antilon-First Citizen Letters*, (Baltimore, 1974). There is a remarkable similarity in the arguments and citations used by Jefferson and Antilon's (Daniel Dulany, Jr.) Fourth Letter (pp. 154–191). Unfortunately, neither Jefferson nor Pendleton acknowledged their Maryland counterparts whose exchange in the *Maryland Gazette* examined the legal and constitutional points at length.

responsibility of interpreting English practice so that it would conform to Virginia's local interests. The General Court thus assumed more than a caretaker or middleman role in an appellate system reaching from Virginia county courts to the privy council in Great Britain. It became an institution for the affirmation of the uniqueness of Virginia's laws and customs or, to use the contemporary term, the Virginia constitution.[9]

After 1760 there was increasing political acceptance of an activist judiciary. The burgesses, in their appeal to the home government for the right to control emissions of paper currency during 1762, recognized the Virginia judiciary as the most compatible administrative and judicial arbiter in statutory and equity cases arising from disputes between British creditors and Virginia debtors.[10] Throughout the Two Penny Act controversy in the 1760's, the Virginia court system served as the stage for each succeeding act of the constitutional and political drama. Most significantly, the General Court on several occasions during these years upheld legislative policies which further exacerbated litigation or were patently contrary to royal instructions regarding the suspending clause. Just when the disputes over the Two Penny Acts subsided, the General Court agreed to hear an appeal involving fundamental questions about ecclesiastical jurisdiction. In so doing, the court first had to rule that the dispute was properly before it rather than that the dispute was a question for legislative determination, as the king's attorney had recommended. The attorneys who persuaded the court that it did indeed have general ecclesiastical jurisdiction were George Wythe and Thomas Jefferson.[11] At the same time, the arrival of William Blackstone's pro-

[9] R. T. Barton, ed., *Virginia Colonial Decisions . . . Reports by Sir John Randolph and by Edward Barradall of Decisions of the General Court of Virginia, 1728–1741* (2 vols., Boston, 1909), 160–161, B1; and Joseph Smith, *Appeals to the Privy Council from the American Plantations* (New York, 1965), 485. The *Reports* of Randolph and Barradall as well as Thomas Jefferson, ed., *Reports of Cases Determined in the General Court of Virginia, from 1730 to 1740 and from 1768 to 1772* (Charlottesville, 1829) comprise a relatively unmined resource for understanding precisely how Virginians distinguished their constitutional and legal order from that of Great Britain.

[10] "Address and Representation of the House of Burgesses to Lt. Governor Fauquier in Defense of Issuing Paper Money," May 28, 1763, in William J. Van Schreeven, comp., and Robert L. Scribner, ed., *Revolutionary Virginia: The Road to Independence, A Documentary Record*, Vol. I, "Forming Thunderclouds and the First Convention, 1763–1774," (Charlottesville, 1973), 6–7.

[11] The fullest treatment of the judicial aspects of litigation issuing from the Two

vocative *Commentaries,* paradoxically advocating parliamentary supremacy and extensive discretion for the judiciary in the interpretation of statutes, brought mixed reaction in Virginia. Few endorsed Blackstone's political deference to Parliament. Yet many Virginians realized that the colony's courts on both the county and appellate levels had already evolved the judicial philosophy Blackstone espoused.[12]

Aside from the judiciary's involvement in public policy issues, the court system itself underwent extensive examination in the decade before 1774. Specifically, criticism was mounting concerning the efficiency of criminal and debt litigation. Concerned burgesses sought to alleviate the growing problems by reforming procedures and jurisdictions. By March, 1772, the supporters of court reform, with Richard Bland as their spokesman, had proceeded far enough in the legislative process for their bill to be printed. The stated purpose urged an alteration of the existing court structure to prevent further "delays in recovering debts" and to encourage "speedy determination of [criminal] suits." To achieve these ends the adherents of reform were prepared to change the existing system markedly by creating an independent General Court and a circuit system for criminal adjudication.

The justices of the General Court, although selected by the governor, would serve the governor only in a judicial capacity, thereby eliminating the traditional three-hat affair of council members sitting as upper house, executive council, and General Court. Furthermore, each justice would preside over one of the new circuits designed to function like the English courts of assize. The jurisdiction of the county courts was to remain the same. But criminal appeals and adjudication of capital crimes, formerly the responsibility of the General Court meeting semiannually for that

---

Penny Act controversy can be found in Smith, *Appeals to the Privy Council,* 606–626. The General Court asserted its jurisdiction in ecclesiastical matters in *Godwin et al. v. Lunan,* October, 1771, in Jefferson, ed., *Reports,* 96–97, for which Jefferson appended a detailed and scholarly argument (pp. 137–142).

[12] "Undated Entries 1774," in Jack P. Greene, ed., *The Diary of Colonel Landon Carter of Sabine Hall, 1752–1788* (2 vols., Charlottesville, 1965), II, 910, and Julius Waterman, "Thomas Jefferson and Blackstone's Commentaries," in David Flaherty, ed., *Essays in the History of Early American Law* (Chapel Hill, 1969), 451–487. Critical questions remain concerning the patriots' political and intellectual appropriation of both Edward Coke and William Blackstone in a manner comparable to the way Bernard Bailyn has suggested Massachusetts leaders relied upon seventeenth-century Whig writers.

purpose, now would be reserved for the circuit courts, limiting the General Court exclusively to civil appeals. The implications of the bill were momentous. The governor would no longer take a direct part in the judicial process; it was a separation of governmental functions which anticipated changes often considered as products of the American Revolution. The technical changes mirrored a growing sensitivity to Virginia's new counties and growing population. Docket considerations for the General Court acknowledged the existence of an overburdened case load, a predictable result of such growth.[13]

Governor Dunmore believed that these reforms were both sensible and acceptable to the majority. He was wrong; the bill failed final passage. Among other things, Dunmore underestimated the influence of the county judges. Much of Virginia's judicial independence and political stability stemmed from the county courts, led for generations by men who controlled politics, governmental administration, and everyday justice on the local level. The House of Burgesses became an extension of this local leadership both in personnel and outlook. Burgesses may well have seen the advantages of time and expense in modernizing the criminal courts, but reflecting county interests, they balked at any reforms which appeared to threaten their control over local matters. The 1772 reorganization might permit the long arm of imperial policy to reach into the Virginia counties to erode hard-earned autonomy, a prospect which moved local judges to oppose reform of the court system not only in 1772 but also for many years thereafter.[14]

Even the special session of the house in March, 1773, was highlighted by a dispute over judicial procedure. Governor Dunmore agreed to the session, responding to an outbreak of counterfeiting which many feared had already reached emergency proportions. Just prior to the beginning of the session, Dunmore, without adequate explanation, permitted authorities to transfer

[13] "A bill for the More Easy and Speedy Administration of Justice," March 28, 1772; enclosure in Dunmore to Hillsborough, May 20, 1772; Public Record Office [PRO] C.O. 5/1350, ff. 77–79, Colonial Records Project, Colonial Williamsburg Foundation.

[14] For postwar circuit reform problems see Charles T. Cullen, "St. George Tucker and Law in Virginia, 1772–1804" (doctoral dissertation, University of Virginia, 1971). Charles Cullen's knowledge of the postwar court system has greatly clarified my understanding of the prewar situation. Dunmore to Hillsborough, May 20, 1772, PRO C.O. 5/1350, ff. 74–76.

several notorious counterfeiters from their home county to the examining court in York County. The burgesses reacted immediately, accusing the governor of judicial impropriety, and insisting that the ends of public safety never warranted an illegal manipulation of criminal procedures. The rebuked governor apologized, but later puzzled over the vehemence of the house remonstrance.[15] However, the attempts to protect and at the same time streamline an overburdened judiciary underscored the trust Virginians had in the court system as a clearing house for questions of law and public policy. When the General Court resolved to continue the lapsed Fee Act in April, 1774, the justices endorsed Pendleton's insistence upon guarding against any assault which might compromise the institution's fundamental capacity to do justice. On his part, Pendleton supported the emerging institutional independence of the court. Jefferson, despite his earlier defense of the court's assuming general ecclesiastical jurisdiction, chose in 1774 to defer to the legislature for reasons which extended beyond considerations of judicial philosophy.

When the burgesses returned to Williamsburg during the first week in May, 1774, they immediately began the task of selecting members for standing committees, little suspecting that the committee for courts of justice would attempt to obstruct normal legislative business. Richard Henry Lee was chairman of the committee, which was undistinguished in its membership and, significantly, lacked Pendleton and others who were seeking to protect the General Court by quick passage of the expired act. Just why Pendleton and others failed to press for membership on the committee remains unclear. The committee was to investigate expired statutes and all other unfinished business from the previous legislative sessions and make recommendations for house action. Like other standing committees, it had general subpoena powers to "send for Persons, Papers and Records for their Information." Instead of turning immediately to expired statutes, though, Lee's committee collected all the unfinished business from the March, 1773, session and reported on twenty unresolved petitions. In each instance, the petitions dealt with particular local

[15] John P. Kennedy, ed., *Journal of the House of Burgesses [JHB], 1773–1776* (Richmond, 1905), March 4–12, 1773, pp. 10–33; Dunmore to Dartmouth, March 31, 1773, PRO C.O. 5/1351, ff. 26–31.

disputes concerning county administration, courthouse location, and church matters—nothing as politically pressing as the Fee Act. It was only after completing this clerical obligation that Lee announced the status of the Fee Act: it "ought not to be revived."[16]

Nothing in the opinions of either Pendleton or Jefferson made even the slightest allusion to prior attempts to transform the Fee Act into a political issue. On the contrary, the court closure during the Stamp Act controversy had been a clearly separate and unique situation, and there had been no fights over passage of the fee bills after 1765. Lee was consciously breaking new ground. The house immediately refused the Lee committee's recommendation, however, and ordered a favorable resolution as well as a new fee bill. The ten-man committee reported the bill the very next day. After its second reading, the bill went to the committee of propositions and grievances. Under normal circumstances this committee, which numbered about thirty-six men, would have prepared the bill for final reading and engrossment at the end of the legislative session.[17]

Before the full house had the opportunity to act on the fee bill, news of the Boston Port Act arrived in Williamsburg, and the political atmosphere changed drastically. Jefferson, Lee, and others, understanding the new options open to them, acted quickly. They fixed upon the device of having the house call for a day of fasting and prayer in sympathy for Boston. As soon as the burgesses voted favorably on this proposal, Governor Dunmore dissolved the legislature for overstepping its constitutional prerogatives. The disbanded burgesses regrouped, signed an association which criticized the governor's prorogation, recommended a voluntary boycott of the East India Company, and called for a general colonial congress. Three days later, the few burgesses remaining in Williamsburg agreed to summon delegates from Virginia counties to attend an August convention in Williams-

[16] David Mays argued that Lee's tactics were obstructionist in the eyes of such proponents of the bill's passage as Pendleton. See Mays, *Pendleton*, I, 244–248. Examination of the committee's presentation priorities bears out Mays. See *JHB*, May 6–9, 1774, pp. 76–84. The question remains, however, as to why Pendleton and his allies did not make any attempt to control or influence the committee.

[17] *JHB*, May 6 and 11, 1774, pp. 73–77, 88–91. For a discussion of court closure during the Stamp Act controversy, see Edmund S. and Helen M. Morgan, *The Stamp Act Crisis: Prologue to Revolution* (Chapel Hill, 1953), 168–179.

burg to consider "the Preservation of the Common Rights and Liberty of British America."[18] Within the space of three short weeks, politics in Virginia changed from piecemeal opposition to imperial policies and obstruction of royal authority to extra-legalism pointing directly toward revolution and independence.

Dunmore's dissolution of the house had a profound effect on the course of politics. Few burgesses had expected the May session to become anything extraordinary; still fewer anticipated either the news of the Boston Port Act or its impact on Virginians. Almost overnight the colony became engulfed in an outpouring of popular support for Boston. The emotional atmosphere inevitably influenced and shaped the manner in which the radicals conducted their assault on the courts. Earlier, the efforts of Jefferson and Lee had been directed toward the comparatively small yet close fraternity of General Court attorneys and members of the house. Outwardly, these arguments concerning the General Court and fees were confined to narrow procedural questions. In a single stroke, Dunmore's dissolution eliminated the fee bill as an exploitable political issue in the house. If opposition to the fee bill had been merely legalistic, the governor's action would have signaled a final radical victory. On the contrary, the radicals utilized the dissolution to step up plans for enlisting popular support. Anticipating that the upcoming county meetings would endorse some expression of economic retaliation, radicals realized that court closure remained a critical issue.[19]

As soon as the house ceased to provide a forum for the radicals, they turned to the newspapers as a medium to broadcast their political intentions for Virginia's courts. On June 2 both Williamsburg papers published a letter to "the Lawyers" from "Querist" which raised pointed questions about the General

---

[18] Jefferson's autobiography in Paul Leicester Ford, ed., *The Writings of Thomas Jefferson* (New York, 1892–1899), I, 9–10. For details of dissolution see Julian P. Boyd, ed., *The Papers of Thomas Jefferson* (Princeton, 1950 to date), I, 105–110; *JHB*, May 24, 1774, pp. 130–132; and Rind and Purdie and Dixon, *Virginia Gazette*, May 26, 1774. Landon Carter described Dunmore's actions in some detail. See Greene, ed., *Diary of Landon Carter*, June 3, 1774, II, 818.

[19] For Washington's response to dissolution see Washington to George William Fairfax, June 10, 1774, in John C. Fitzpatrick, ed., *The Writings of George Washington* (39 vols., Washington, 1931–1944), III, 221–226. For Mason's reaction see Mason to Martin Cockburn, May 26, 1774, in Robert A. Rutland, ed., *The Papers of George Mason, 1725–1792* (3 vols., Chapel Hill, 1970), I, 190–191.

Court's order, questions very similar to Jefferson's earlier opinion. "Querist" criticized the James City court for issuing "an ordinance in the same words" as the General Court. If such ordinances proved effective, the Virginia court system might continue to operate in near normal fashion. "Querist" denied the authority of any court, General Court or county court, to make legislative decisions, claiming the delegation of this power to the legislature was a fundamental element of the constitution. If any court assumed that the judiciary could set fees, the abrogation became an unconstitutional exercise. "Querist" concluded with the thinly disguised warning that any lawyer who appeared in any court relying upon judicial fiat to stay open would automatically be suspected himself.[20] At a meeting the following day, June 3, the Chesterfield county court, with Archibald Cary presiding, sustained the "Querist." In a unanimous opinion, the justices affirmed "that they have not any power to order the Fees" until the legislature acted.[21] By the end of the first week in June, the opinions and policies of Jefferson and Lee had begun to spread through the colony. The Chesterfield court was the first county bench to transform Jefferson's opinion into operational policy. Soon other counties followed Chesterfield's lead. "Querist," as spokesman for the Virginia bar, initiated what was to become a series of newspaper announcements intended to guide the political behavior of Virginia lawyers.[22]

During June and July, debates over court closure continued to command broad attention. The future of the court system figured centrally in the pamphlets of John Randolph, Robert C. Nicholas, and Thomson Mason. The resolutions of county meetings that preceded the August convention also added a significant dimen-

---

[20] Rind and Purdie and Dixon, *Virgina Gazette*, June 2, 1774.

[21] "Notes and Queries," in the *Virginia Magazine of History and Biography* [*VMHB*], 14 (1906), 90–91.

[22] For an analysis of the development of the Virginia bar see Alan M. Smith, "Virginia Lawyers, 1680–1776: The Birth of an American Profession" (doctoral dissertation, Johns Hopkins University, 1967). A more general survey is Charles Warren, *A History of the American Bar* (New York, 1966). The role of the courts in the coming of the Revolution varied widely from colony to colony. Two studies of Massachusetts illuminate the contrasts. See John D. Cushing, "The Judiciary and Public Opinion in Revolutionary Massachusetts," in George A. Billias, ed., *Selected Essays: Law and Authority in Colonial America*, (Barre, 1965), 168–186, and John M. Murrin, "The Legal Transformation: The Bench and Bar of Eighteenth-Century Massachusetts," in Stanley N. Katz, ed., *Colonial America* (Boston, 1971), 415–449.

sion to popularizing the issue of court closure. The meetings themselves were unprecedented—with few exceptions, they were open to the public, not restricted to the freeholders. Of the thirty-one counties whose resolutions were printed, only four restricted the meetings to freeholders. The remaining counties welcomed any others interested in the proceedings, sometimes, as was the case in the Norfolk County and Borough meeting, even taking pride in the attendance of "Freeholders, Merchants, Tradesmen, and other Inhabitants."[23] The atmosphere of these meetings was electric with news of the dissolution of the burgesses, wild rumors about British squadrons closing the port of Boston, differing claims about American rights, and divergent opinions regarding the need for united American opposition. Using the newspaper as the circulating medium, the resolutions of these popular, extra-legal meetings reached a colony-wide audience. Only Middlesex County remained soured on the propriety of radical opposition to British policy, a stand which later inspired some bawdy satire in the *Virginia Gazette*.[24] With one voice, other counties proclaimed their allegiance to Boston and urged the upcoming August convention to adopt a variety of measures to toughen American opposition, especially by the tested means of intercolonial congresses and economic boycott.

As county after county published instructions to their delegates, several central themes emerged, in part because some counties copied freely from neighbors. Several counties kept their instructions brief, granting both their delegates and the August convention broad latitude to adopt whatever policies proved to be necessary. Most, however, insisted that Virginia must deny Britain's right to tax Americans without colonial consent. In general, these resolutions radiated an optimism which resulted from the widespread conviction that Virginians were on solid constitutional and political ground. The assertion of Virginia's legislative independence was neither new nor unique—Richard Bland had used similar arguments during the fight against the Reverend John Camm, and by 1774 Bland's position had become part of the political vernacular. But Virginia counties went further during the summer of 1774 when they sought to bind their destiny with

[23] Rind, *Virginia Gazette*, August 11, 25, 1774.
[24] Van Schreeven, comp., *Revolutionary Virginia*, 111–169.

that of Massachusetts. They declared explicitly that Virginia must become an inextricable part of a continental whole. By inference, then, the resolves of the counties were fundamental expressions of popular will and, at the same time, statements of portentous political and constitutional meaning.[25]

Reinforcing the constitutional firmness was the determination of many counties to supplement resolutions for economic boycott with mandates for court closure. One-third of the counties made specific proposals, the most inclusive being those of Norfolk and Spotsylvania counties urging the convention "to break off all commercial Connexions with Great Britain" until American demands were met. Eight counties, seven of which were in the northern neck, made explicit suggestions regarding the operations of the colony's courts. With George Mason providing pen and direction, the meeting of "the freeholders, merchants, and other inhabitants" of Prince William County and the town of Dumfries, held on the early date of June 6, declared simply that "the courts of justice in this colony ought to decline trying any civil causes until the said [Coercive] acts are repealed." Later, the Stafford and Essex meetings reiterated Prince William's initial salvo.[26] Between June 22 and July 14, Westmoreland, Richmond, and Gloucester counties, also in open meetings, added conditions to their pleas for closure. "Immediately upon the non-exportation plan taking place," no person ought to attempt "to recover any debt." The citizens defended their position claiming it would be "utterly inconsistent with such a scheme [nonexportation] for any man to be compelled to pay without the means wherewith he may pay."[27]

Of all the counties commenting upon court closure, only Fauquier, meeting on July 9, adhered to the traditional election process which restricted participation to freeholders. An openly

[25] The most recent publication of Bland's *Inquiry* appears *ibid.*, 27–46. The cultural and institutional impact of the political and constitutional controversies surrounding the established church is explored in Rhys Isaac, "Religion and Authority: Problems of the Anglican Establishment in Virginia in the Era of the Great Awakening and the Parson's Cause," in *WMQ*, 3rd Ser., 30 (1973) 3–36. On the county meetings see Van Schreeven, comp., *Revolutionary Virginia*, 111–169 *passim*.

[26] "Prince William County," June 6, 1774, p. 153; "Essex County," July 9, 1774, p. 126; and "Stafford County," July 28, 1774, p. 161, all in Van Schreeven, comp., *Revolutionary Virginia*.

[27] "Westmoreland County," June 22, 1774, p. 164; "Richmond County," June 29, 1774, p. 156; and "Gloucester County," July 14, 1774, p. 137, *ibid.*

belligerent attitude colored its disposition toward court closure in a manner not generally present in other county resolves. The freeholders insisted upon a total economic boycott "till the said act [Boston Port Act] of Parliament shall be repealed, and till the ships of war and troops be withdrawn from the said town and port of Boston, and the rights and freedom of same be restored." Until Great Britain complied, "the courts of justice ought to decline the trial of civil causes, except attachments, where the attached goods are perishable, and motions against the collectors and sheriffs for money actually in their hands." This clarification meant that strictly local civil and criminal issues could be settled by the county court which should remain open to do local legal business.[28]

As soon as Mason had finished with the Prince William County resolutions, he joined George Washington for the Fairfax County meeting on July 18. Skeptical of American willingness to sustain economic boycotts, Mason and Washington persuaded Fairfax citizens to establish stringent conditions for the county's participation. The resolves carefully stipulated that Fairfax would only join in a nonexportation agreement that was continental in scope. Furthermore, the county would endorse a cessation of tobacco production only in conjunction with other tobacco-growing colonies. Finally, if an American congress could achieve unanimous compliance with these conditions, then, at that time and not sooner, Fairfax County would join all American courts, not just those in Virginia, in refusing to render any judgments "for any Debt."[29] The political skepticism of the Fairfax framers reflected their awareness of both the tenuousness of intercolonial co-operation and the gravity of the immediate political situation. However,

[28] "Fauquier County," July 9, 1774, p. 134, *ibid.*

[29] "Fairfax County," July 18, 1774, p. 132, *ibid.* With the exception of Gloucester, all the counties giving explicit directions regarding court closure were in the northern neck. The proximity to Maryland and its fee bill controversy must have been influential, but nowhere in either the Virginia newspapers or the correspondence of Washington, Lee, or Mason are there references to the Antilon-First Citizen letters. In analyzing Maryland neither Barker nor Onuf indicate that the controversy spilled over into Virginia. Ronald Hoffman does stress how the fee question became a means for radicals to win popular support. See *A Spirit of Dissension*, 112–124. Even if Lee and others were familiar with the situation in Maryland, the fee bill controversy as a political and economic issue in Virginia developed quite differently, primarily because Virginia's radicals succeeded in enlarging the initial controversy to include closure of the courts.

Fairfax County, having steadfastly counseled against all rash resolutions which often evaporated in the heat of economic and political pressure, promised to adopt sweeping measures of opposition.

For all the different phrases, stresses, and conditions, all these counties subscribed to the positive manipulation of the court system as a crucial tool for Virginia's opposition. Overtly, these resolutions did not order local courts to stop debt litigation of British creditors as a means of exerting political pressure in England and Scotland. Such explicitly provocative pronouncements were superfluous in a colony that had already leveled a public attack on foreign merchants.[30] What these resolutions did emphasize was a practical concern for protecting local economic interests. If Virginia was determined to adopt nonexportation, a policy some still thought dubious, these counties wanted to anticipate the economic hardships sure to come. Judges must not allow creditors to descend upon planters who were unable to export their principal money crop. A court which refused to proceed with any debt suits would protect Virginians economically in the dispute with Great Britain. In other words, if the political situation continued to deteriorate after the summer of 1774 and culminated in a mercantilistic strike before the end of 1775, the colonial producers would not be vulnerable to litigation arising from unsettled foreign transactions. During earlier boycotts, Virginia's economic flanks had not been protected. The radicals grasped the political and economic necessity of making Virginia's interests secure in 1774. Washington, Jefferson, Lee, and many Virginia counties argued the position that it was inequitable to assume that local producers, large and small, could, on the one hand, suspend production and, on the other hand, allow foreign creditors freedom to sue in Virginia courts. Conscientious Virginians would have sufficient time before nonexportation went into effect to clear foreign debts. Thereafter, court closure would only benefit those few debtors traditionally reluctant to pay. Or, as merchant Charles Yates pointed out, "it is in vain to suppose those who have delayed and

---

[30] For published attacks on Scots merchants see Rind, *Virginia Gazette*, January 31, October 31, 1771, May 12, 1774, July 21, 1774; and Purdie and Dixon, *Virginia Gazette*, November 25, 1773, December 16, 1773. For public pronouncements against Scots see Landon Carter's advice from the Richmond county court bench in Greene, ed., *Diary of Landon Carter*, June 8, 1774, II, 821.

evaded for ten years, will under such circumstances be prevailed on to pay."[31]

As the county resolves found their way into print they fueled the mounting public debate. The disputes over the moral and economic justifications for nonimportation and nonexportation included significant but disparate commentary on the role of the court system. Thomson Mason, for instance, who published a series of essays during the summer of 1774 under the signature of "A British American," denounced all plans for economic boycott. In its place Mason substituted a novel scheme for manipulating the courts. Mason urged his countrymen to "punish any judge who shall dare to enforce" any act of Parliament, "made since the settlement of America." A more effective measure than "entering into associations to starve twenty thousand of your innocent manufacturing fellow subjects in Great Britain," according to Mason, would be the conscious willingness "to sacrifice to your just resentment three or four, or even three or four dozen, unconstitutional or corrupt judges in each colony." Labeling judges who retained any vestige of allegiance to British statutory precedent "trespassers," Mason believed that private criminal prosecutions

---

[31] Most historians have overlooked this 1774 argument. Instead of looking to the conventions and the subsequent county court transactions, historians have attached themselves to thematic reiterations of Thomas Jefferson's postwar estimate of the size of the prewar debt. From Jefferson's statement historians have miraculously extracted the Virginia debt as a primary cause of the Revolution. Disregarding the size, geographic distribution, and age of individual debts, as well as neglecting to assay the size and scope of fixed and durable assets of the colony, historians have committed some gratuitous errors of economic interpretation. Emory Evans, "Planter Indebtedness and the Coming of the Revolution in Virginia," capped the interpretation when he claimed that as indebtedness became "a political weapon to secure a change in British policy," it created a climate conducive to radical pleas for revolution. See *WMQ*, 3rd Ser., 19 (1962). Jacob Price's "British-Chesapeake Trade, 1750–1775," in Virginia Platt and David Skaggs, ed., *Of Mother Country and Plantations: Proceedings of the Twenty-Seventh Conference in Early American History* (Bowling Green, 1971), 7–41, and Mark Egnal and Joseph Ernst's "An Economic Interpretation of the American Revolution," in *WMQ*, 3rd Ser., 29 (1972), 3–32, have brought a new understanding to eighteenth-century economic history, and together they comprise a promising beginning for a re-evaluation of the realities of the Virginia economy on the eve of independence. Charles Yates to John Lowthwaite, December 5, 1774, in the Charles Yates Letterbook, 1773–1783, 123–124, Alderman Library, University of Virginia [AL–UV]. I am indebted to Stuart Butler, Edward Ayres, and Harold Gill for introducing me to the ideas, practices, and accomplishments of Virginia and foreign merchants before and after the war.

against errant judges and public nullification of their judgments represented the most promising constitutional course for his countrymen who were bent upon using the court system for political purposes.[32] Such an eccentric proposition from someone opposed to political manipulation of the economy only served to emphasize the practicality of those schemes for court closure already publicized.

Vexed by all the pronouncements dragging the court system into the political arena, the king's attorney general, John Randolph, broke gentlemanly silence to chide his fellow colonists. Randolph granted time-honored methods of petition for redress of legitimate grievances. But the current intemperate appeals to emotion could only lead to disgrace; or worse, a once cherished social order might pass, irretrievably, into chaos and oblivion. Randolph predicted a loss of "Honor and Integrity" if Virginians closed their courts. Considering the practicalities, he emphasized that severe economic dislocation would be the inevitable consequence of such irrational politics. He concluded with the dire criticism that "to stop the Avenues of Justice, and by that Means put it out of the Power of an honest Creditor to recover his Demand, a Creditor who may be ruined by such an Impediment thrown in his Way, cannot be justified by the greatest Libertine in Politicks."[33]

Privately, Edmund Pendleton agreed with Randolph but resisted any temptation to broadcast his convictions. Arriving in Williamsburg a week before the opening of the convention, Pendleton wrote Ralph Wormeley, Jr., reaffirming the opinion he had composed for the General Court in May. "The Order of the General Court is right," he insisted, and further, "I sincerely wish the County Courts had followed the example." He concluded in a vein similar to Randolph's. Court closure "if persevered in will fix an eternal Stigma on the Country, introduce Anarchy and disorder and render life and property here precarious." But Pendleton implored Wormeley to keep this "Judgment" confidential since Pendleton had found "a great Majority" in Williamsburg opposed to his position, thereby persuading him that it had

---

[32] "The British American," no. 9 (published in Rind, *Virginia Gazette*, July 28, 1774), in Van Schreeven, comp., *Revolutionary Virginia*, 193–203.

[33] Earl G. Swem, ed., *Considerations on the Present State of Virginia, Attributed to John Randolph, Attorney General, and Considerations on the Present State of Virginia Examined by Robert Carter Nicholas* (New York, 1919), 19–20, 29–33.

become his "duty Not to publish it further." Thoroughly distressed with all radical politics, Wormeley had little respect and no understanding for Pendleton's hedging. As soon as he received the letter, Wormeley added an acid postscript claiming that "this paragraph plainly points out the game that this complacent casuist means to play."[34] Wormeley never joined the patriot ranks. Pendleton, despite initial misgivings about politicizing the courts, very soon became one of the most important of Virginia's revolutionary leaders, serving as president of the Virginia Committee of Safety before becoming the first speaker of the Commonwealth's House of Delegates.

Randolph presumed, as did many others, that all the courts ceased operations during the summer of 1774. Responding publicly to Randolph's essay, Robert Carter Nicholas accused the king's attorney of gratuitous exaggeration. Noting that Randolph's multiple offices included "a Seat in one or more Courts of Justice," Nicholas asked rhetorically why Randolph had not prevented the misfortune he bemoaned. Having set the barb, Nicholas introduced the ubiquitous theme of emergency as justification for extreme action. Granting that he disliked closing the courts, "in Cases of the last Necessity" such measures were bound to occur. Reverting to the popular theme, Nicholas blamed the governor for having caused the trouble by dissolving the legislature before the passage of the fee bill. Without it, "Magistrates, who act on Oath, think they cannot proceed in Business." Vested with responsibility for preserving law and order, Virginia's judges according to Nicholas were "universally resolved" that they were constitutionally forbidden from acting without legislative sanction. As Nicholas echoed Jefferson's April opinion for the General Court, he added another dimension to the June demands of the "Querist" that was strikingly similar to the opinion of the Chesterfield court. Asking the attorneys to stay away from the General Court was one thing, but suggesting that every judge had a constitutional duty not to act was tenuous logic indeed.[35]

---

[34] Pendleton to Ralph Wormeley, Jr., July 28, 1774, in Mays, ed., *Pendleton Papers,* I, 97–98. Wormeley's note is on the original in Papers of the Wormeley Family of Rosegill, 1773–1802, AL–UV.

[35] Swem, ed., *Considerations on the Present State of Virginia,* 41–52, 70–76. Robert C. Nicholas was a member of the James City county court which had accepted the General Court order. See Edward Ingle, ed., "Justices of the Peace of Colonial Virginia, 1757–1775," in the *Bulletin of the Virginia State Library,* 14 (1921) 47, 72, 73, 88, 117.

Virginians never went to the extremes suggested by Nicholas. In fact, the August convention made no explicit comment about the court system at all. The delegates seemingly expended all their energies on establishing the Virginia Association and selecting delegates for the first Continental Congress. The convention's silence was in stark contrast to all the heated debate during the summer on the subject of court closure. The situation remained in limbo for a month, with the General Court due to meet in October for the fall term. Then on September 8, the *Virginia Gazette* published a report that shed bright light on the unpublicized convention deliberations. In an announcement designed to keep attorneys, their clients, and any witnesses away from the General Court session, the report stated that the convention delegates had indeed considered the Fee Act. The delegates disagreed with the General Court's determination to continue. "Officers fees, since the expiration of the act, . . . cannot be legally taxed." The announcement contended that attorneys, giving proper consideration to unsettled conditions in the colony, should determine that it was impossible to attend court. This decision would not put a halt to all judicial business, however. "It is therefore presumable there will be no trials at the next general court, except in criminal cases, in which all the justices in the colony are determined to proceed, in preserving that good order so necessary at this critical period."[36]

The culmination of public and private recommendations for court closure produced the effect the radicals sought—the highest court in Virginia ceased. The General Court did convene for its regular session in October. But according to reports from Rind's *Virginia Gazette,* the justices, "after mature deliberation," decided to recess all civil proceedings. The editor explained this critical decision by stressing that the court had no real alternative, given the "suspension" of the Fee Act.[37] Merchant Thomas Adams interpreted the events in more practical terms, claiming that the court "could not proceed to Business for want of two of our Principal Counsel." Other lawyers, "out of Respect to them [Continental Congress delegates Edmund Pendleton and Patrick Henry],"

[36] Rind, *Virginia Gazette,* September 8, 1774.
[37] Rind and Purdie and Dixon, *Virginia Gazette,* October 13, 1774.

decided not to appear either.[38] Later, however, when Dunmore commented about the lawyers' boycott, he claimed that deference to Pendleton and Henry was never foremost in the lawyers' minds. Fear of popular reprisal caused nonattendance according to the governor. The "people" did not "allow them to attend or evidence to appear."[39] The General Court, with no practical choice, turned to criminal cases which did not require counsel. In an abbreviated session of four days, the court dispatched twenty indicted persons, five of whom received the death sentence.[40]

The General Court, now exposed to a formidable combination of political and social pressures, was powerless. The judges had ordered the court to remain open, but they could not force the Virginia attorneys to co-operate. Those on the committee for courts of justice who had counseled against renewal of the Fee bill achieved their victory after all. The Virginia General Court, against its own declared intention, went into hibernation. As the colony's highest appellate court, it would not survive the winter.

Richard Henry Lee anticipated victory well before the fateful October session and began to co-ordinate his business affairs accordingly. Other planters and merchants quickly began to adjust their affairs also. With surprising swiftness, the traditional credit structure dependent upon civil law sank into disarray, and by the end of 1774, according to all accounts, the system was in shambles. County courts refused to hear debt cases, precisely as had been recommended by the 1774 county meetings. The county courts, unlike the General Court, continued to meet but on a restricted basis. Local courts probated wills, cared for orphans, prosecuted criminals, and continued to administer the counties, but all judicial accommodation of the empire's commerce stopped. At year's end, Charles Yates described the situation precisely: "All our inferior or County Courts have been as good as shut since last June. It is true they are held at the stated times for the purposes of Probates, Records and Criminal affairs. No

---

[38] Thomas Adams to T. Hill, November, 1774, in *VMHB*, 23 (1925), 178.

[39] Dunmore to Dartmouth, December 24, 1774, PRO C.O. 5/1353, ff. 7–39.

[40] Pinkney, *Virginia Gazette*, October 20, 1774. Also see Hugh Rankin, *Criminal Trial Proceedings in the General Court of Colonial Virginia* (Williamsburg, 1965), 89–90, and Felix Rackow, "The Right to Counsel: English and American Precedents," *WMQ*, 3rd Ser., 11 (1954), 3–27.

Dockett business is done. It has been refused to let Judgements be entered by consent of Parties, so that you see all collections must cease in that mode."[41]

Merchants, no longer able to resort to litigation as their final economic and legal recourse, revamped old ideas to collect troublesome debts. Richard Henry Lee advised his brother, William, to return to Virginia from London. "You have many debts that none so well as yourself can settle," urged the elder brother, knowing that the pressures of personal presence might be the only persuasive substitute for judicial rulings.[42] Virginia merchants, perceiving the economic ramifications of court closure, adopted measures similar to Lee's. But few were optimistic about their prospects and many expressed profound fear for the future, sensing that the deep constitutional rift would necessarily be a long time in healing.[43]

The local and imperial issues in Virginia were thus joined, and few had either the will or the way to stem the onrushing tide of revolution. Charles Yates noticed the intimidating "determination of leading and warm men" and cautioned that it was "in vain, nay in some cases dangerous to reason" with those so committed. Upon returning from a frontier Indian war later consecrated in his name, Governor Dunmore also realized that politics in Virginia had undergone a radical transformation during the second half

[41] Examples of county courts continuing to meet include Caroline, Spotsylvania, Augusta, Fairfax, and York. The order books for these counties are on deposit at the Virginia State Library. I chose these particular counties for their political, economic, and geographic importance. See Charles Yates to John Lowthwaite, December 5, 1774, in the Charles Yates Letterbook, 1773–1783, pp. 123–124, AL–UV. See also Yates to Samuel Martin, July 5, 1774, and Yates to John Hardy, December, 1774, in the Yates Letterbook, 82–84; 111–119, for an earlier analysis of court closure and its impact.

[42] Richard H. Lee to William Lee, June 29, 1774, Ballagh, ed., *Letters of Richard Henry Lee,* I, 118–122.

[43] Indications of distress and foreboding can be seen in Harry Piper to Messrs. Dixon and Littledale, June 9, 1774, in the Harry Piper Letterbook, 1767–1775, AL–UV; John H. Norton to George W. Fairfax, June 31, 1774, in the Fairfax of Cameron Manuscripts, Gays House; Charles Yates to Samuel Martin, July 5, 1774, Charles Yates to John Hardy, August 26, 1774, Charles Yates to Samuel and William Vernon, October 5, 1774, Charles Yates to Samuel Martin, September 28, 1774, and Charles Yates to Henry Fletcher, February 16, 1775, all in the Yates Letterbook, AL–UV; Benjamin Toler to Samuel Gist, April 15, 1775, in Loyalist Claims, Ser. II— Virginia Claims, 1782–1790, PRO A.O. 13/30, folder G; Alexander Watson to Alexander Watson, November 10, 1775, in Intercepted Letters, Virginia State Library; and Robert Honeyman Diary, January 2, 1776, LC, 2.

of 1774. He viewed "the Power of Government" being "entirely disregarded, if not wholly overturned." Dunmore knew precisely what had precipitated the crisis. "The abolishing the Courts of Justice was the first step taken, in which men of fortune and preeminence joined equally with the lowest and meanest."[44]

During the years just prior to his death in 1813, Edmund Randolph, in composing his history of Virginia, echoed Dunmore's earlier assessment. Referring to the Fee Act controversy, Randolph cautioned his readers to remember the context of the times, for "in times of General sensibility, almost every public event is tortured into an affinity with the predominent passions." By utilizing every available scrap of constitutional terminology, the radicals shifted the blame for court closure on Dunmore's decision to dissolve the legislature. Having so "tortured" events, they "proclaimed a derangement in the machine of government which was immediately converted into the misrule of the King." In short, the radicals staged a political event and then carefully exploited the broader controversy to achieve a practical political end.[45]

The radicals' manipulation of the Virginia courts succeeded far beyond any of their expectations. By the end of 1774 they had set in motion the process that eventually carried Virginia to independence. Thereafter, in quick succession, county committees of safety organized to enforce the association, and Virginia conventions assumed increasing governmental powers. Even Dunmore conceded radical ascendency when he called the burgesses into session on June 1, 1775. Forced to eschew the habit of punitive prorogation, Dunmore, realizing that the closed courts had caused critical dislocation, pleaded for a resumption of normal judicial operations. For the first time, the burgesses denied Dunmore's request outright. Emphasizing that since the dissolution of May, 1774, "our Situation has undergone a total Change," the members declared themselves beyond appeasement. The house refused even to discuss court closure until after the governor and Parliament reversed ten years of imperial policy. Cynically reminding Dun-

---

[44] Yates to Lowthwaite, December 5, 1774, Yates Letterbook, AL–UV; Dunmore to Dartmouth, December 24, 1774, PRO C.O. 5/1353, ff. 7–39.

[45] Edmund Randolph, *History of Virginia*, ed. with an intro. by Arthur H. Shaffer (Charlottesville, 1970), 199.

more that "Money is not a plant of the native Growth of this Country," the burgesses repeated every economic and constitutional reason which had been used earlier to close the courts.[46] And so what had started out as informal pressure had become formalized policy for house and convention alike. Having "deposed" His Majesty in the courthouse, it only remained for Virginians to render the coup de grace on the battlefield.

[46] *JHB,* June 5, 1775, p. 188.

Daniel Claus: A Personal History of Militant Loyalism in New York

Jonathan G. Rossie

DANIEL CLAUS was born on September 13, 1727, in a small German town near Heilbronn in the present south German state of Baden, Württemberg. His father was the town's prefect, and as a member of the lesser landed gentry, Daniel enjoyed the benefits of economic security and a classical education, gaining a proficiency in Greek as well as German, French, and English. With his family background and education, Daniel Claus could have looked forward to a comfortable if, perhaps, unexciting future. Instead, at the age of twenty-two, he was drawn by the lure of commercial opportunity to the British American colonies. Although disappointed in commerce, he prospered in America and achieved a position of status he could never have attained had he remained in Germany. However, within fifty years of his birth, Daniel Claus risked and lost virtually all his worldly possessions in the struggle to preserve England's sovereignty over her rebellious colonies. In this respect, Claus suffered the same fate as many thousands of other American Loyalists; but in many ways he had both more to offer the Loyalist cause and, in the end, more to lose.

The purpose of this essay is not to find in Claus's experience any general conclusions concerning the nature of Loyalism, except, perhaps, to indicate that the reasons for remaining loyal to the crown were as various and numerous as those who chose to do so. Rather, an attempt will be made to understand the factors which led one man to oppose revolution and to examine the effectiveness of Claus's opposition.

Daniel Claus came to America in 1749, arriving during the autumn of that year in Philadelphia. He came to explore the possibilities of involving himself in the colonial silk and tobacco trade. Quickly discouraged by the prospects of such a venture, he attempted to find passage back to Germany. But the earliest he could have departed would have been late in the following year, and this arbitrarily imposed delay decisively changed his life.

During that winter of 1749–1750, Claus, quite by chance, made the acquaintance of Conrad Weiser. Physically the two men made a strange pair. Young Daniel with his slight build, delicate features, and large eyes, which gave his face an almost feminine appearance, contrasted dramatically with the older man's burly, woods-toughened physique. Weiser, fifty-three years old, was chief Indian agent for Pennsylvania. He had been born in Herrenberg, Germany, had migrated to New York with his father in 1710, and had spent his early years in Schoharie, where he became fluent in the Iroquois language. When Claus met him, Weiser was completing plans for a diplomatic mission to the political center of the Iroquois Confederacy at Onondaga. Befriending his young countryman, Weiser invited Claus to join the expedition.

To Claus, stranded in a strange land far from friends and family, Weiser's offer was irresistible. In addition to Weiser's friendship, the prospect of traveling through the wilderness to the Iroquois country naturally appealed to a young man looking for opportunity. Thus in May, 1750, Weiser and Claus set off for central New York, stopping briefly at Weiser's former home at Schoharie, then proceeding up the Mohawk River and visiting the villages of the Lower Mohawks (among whom Weiser had many friends) before arriving in Onondaga during September. There they spent a month before returning to Philadelphia, several weeks later than planned. Claus had again missed the ship returning to Germany, but it no longer mattered. His future lay in America with the Indians he had just visited.

Daniel Claus left little in his diary to indicate what his reactions were to the startlingly new world to which Weiser introduced him—except his initial revulsion toward the food offered by his Indian hosts. The experience must have made a deep impression, and his behavior apparently commended itself to Weiser, for the Indian agent introduced Claus to Governor James Hamilton in Philadelphia and secured the latter's approval to send Claus back to Fort Hunter, "at government expence, to learn the Iroquois language."[1] At Fort Hunter, Claus lived at the home of the young Joseph Brant and began a lifelong friendship which was of great importance. His tutor in Indian language and custom was the influential Mohawk sachem, King Hendrick. Claus quickly proved himself a willing and adept student. Here, too, he met the dynamic William Johnson, the man who would play the major role in shaping Claus's future career.

In 1752, when Claus first met William Johnson, the latter's influence among the Iroquois and allied tribes was rising rapidly. Indeed, Johnson had already displaced Claus's friend and mentor Conrad Weiser as the most influential white man in the Iroquois councils. His position was greatly enhanced by his adoption by the Mohawks, and the privilege he enjoyed, as a sachem of that tribe, of attending the league's councils at Onondaga—not merely as a guest, but as an active participant. Johnson, like Weiser before him, recognized in Claus promising material for future Indian service; in the spring of 1752 he convinced the young man that he could continue his study of Indian languages equally as well at Fort Johnson, where he could also be gainfully employed as a bookkeeper.

For three years Claus tried to serve the diverging and rival interests of the Pennsylvania government, which looked upon him as a possible successor to the aging Weiser, and William Johnson, under whose powerful personality both he and the Iroquois were falling. Finally, with the outbreak of the French and Indian War in the spring of 1755, Claus made his decision. He entered the Indian service as a lieutenant, interpreter, and deputy secretary of William Johnson. During the course of the war Claus saw active service along the New York frontier from Lake George to Niagara and bore an increasingly heavy burden of the responsibility for treating with the Indians and raising and directing

---

[1] All information concerning Daniel Claus's early experiences in America is drawn from his memoranda contained in volume XXIII of the Claus Papers in the Public Archives of Canada [PAC].

Indian auxiliaries. With the financial backing and influence of William Johnson, moreover, he secured a lieutenancy in the 60th or Royal American Regiment in 1756.

Johnson also rose to greater power as a result of the war. As a major general commanding provincial forces and Indians, he defeated the French at the Battle of Lake George in September, 1755; the following year he was made a baronet and superintendent of the newly created Northern Indian Department.[2] With the reduction of Canada in 1760 and the end of the war in America, Sir William Johnson had enough confidence in Daniel Claus's abilities to secure for him appointment as deputy superintendent of Indian affairs in Canada.

As Sir William's deputy in Canada, Daniel Claus had the difficult task of winning the friendship of Indian tribes long allied with the French against the British. It was a task made all the more difficult by the continuation of the war in Europe and the possibility that Canada would be returned to French control when a peace was finally negotiated. As one participant noted:

> From the conquest of Canada to the conclusion of a general peace . . . , the Canada Indians were kept in a continual state of restlessness and alarm. . . . Every now and then a report was spread among them of a French and Spanish fleet and army being in the river St. Lawrence to retake Canada. . . . During this interval Mr. Claus had much trouble making frequent visits to the Indian settlements, discoursing with them, and convincing them of the absurdity and falsehood of these reports . . . by which means he often quieted them until the country was ceded by the peace of 1763.[3]

Following the Peace of Paris, Claus and Sir William kept themselves busy through a series of conferences with the various northern Indian nations to secure treaties which would assure the Indians that their lands would be protected from encroachment by white settlers and unscrupulous traders. In return they asked only the Indians' pledge to remain peaceful and recognize the sovereignty of the British crown. The end result, they hoped, would be a permanent boundary between the white settlements

[2] The most complete record of Claus's service during the French and Indian War is found in a document he wrote during the 1780's entitled "A General Outline of the Services of Daniel Claus, from his entry into the Indian Service until 1783," in the Claus Papers, PAC, XIV, 17–25.

[3] *Ibid.,* 20–21.

and the Indian land that would usher in an era of peaceful coexistence. Needless to say, this policy was not welcomed by colonial land speculators and settlers who saw the end of French rule as the opening of a new period of expansion. But for a time and with the support of the British army, the leaders of the Indian service had the upper hand.

Now in his mid-thirties, Daniel Claus had gained a position with extensive authority and great responsibility in shaping and implementing the new British Indian policy. His innate intelligence, his facility with languages, and his seemingly boundless energy had earned him the respect and trust of his superiors. He further enhanced his future prospects by marrying Sir William Johnson's eldest daughter, Nancy, in 1762, and as Sir William's senior deputy *and* son-in-law, it was not beyond the realm of possibility that Daniel Claus might someday advance to the superintendency.

With Canadian Indian affairs becoming more tranquil, from 1765 on Claus spent more time at his new home, Claus Manor, between Guy Park and Mt. Johnson in New York, and less in Canada. Sir William's new mansion, Johnson Hall, had become the center for Indian affairs in the Northern Department, and Claus, as his father-in-law's health began to fail, became more heavily involved in the problems of departmental management. Although he still made annual trips to Canada to transact necessary business, the management of the Canadian Indians was left largely to trusted assistants. The Mohawk Valley was now his home, and it was there that Claus expected to live out his life in peace and relative prosperity.

Superficially at least, Daniel Claus was an American by 1775. For a quarter of a century he had lived and labored in the colonies, he had secured a high position in the Indian service, and he was now comfortably established at Claus Manor with his wife and young son, William. In the voluminous correspondence he conducted during this period, in his diary and memoranda, Claus rarely spoke of Germany or the family he left behind. His home was in the Mohawk Valley, and his family was the Johnsons.

Nevertheless, there is an odd sense of disassociation about Claus's attachment to America. One searches in vain in his writings for commentary, or even awareness, of the traumatic political upheavals of the 1760's and 1770's which led inexorably toward revolution. There is neither condemnation nor praise for those supporting or attacking Parliamentary rule of the colonies. He certainly must have been aware of those debates. Indeed, both Sir William and Guy Johnson, with whom Claus had intimate contact, were deeply entwined with the issues being debated in Parliament and the American assemblies. But until the question of allegiance was forced upon him in 1775, Daniel Claus apparently remained neutral in his opinions. Part of the solution to this puzzle may lie in the basic lack of interest in politics per se, or he may have been overconfident that the troubles between the colonies and the mother country would soon pass. Also, devotion to his work may have provided a baffle which screened him from the intensifying political crisis. One cannot escape the feeling, however, that the basic cause for Claus's general silence was a deep, unquestioning loyalty to Sir William Johnson. Put quite simply, whatever the magnetic Sir William thought was correct would be accepted by his German son-in-law.

If so, his faith in Sir William was put to the test in 1774. In March of that year, aware of his approaching death, Sir William Johnson decided that the time had come to choose his successor to the superintendency of the Northern Indian Department. Sir William himself claimed that he was prompted to do so by the expressed concern of the leaders of the Iroquois Confederacy. "They had reason to fear," he wrote the Secretary for Colonial Affairs, Lord Dartmouth, "that in case of my death their affairs might fall into some of those channels which gave them their first prejudice against the English, or into the hands of some person unacquainted with the nature and politics of the people, and the duties of my office. . . ."[4] Undoubtedly the Iroquois were concerned lest their management fall into unsympathetic hands. Sir William, however, had other, compelling reasons to choose his successor with care. Through his influence with the Iroquois, Sir William had amassed vast property holdings over the years, and a new superintendent, inimical to the Johnsons' interests, might well pose a threat to the family's prosperity. Since much of the Johnson landholdings were based solely on Indian cessions,

---

[4] Sir William Johnson to Earl of Dartmouth, April 17, 1774, in E. B. O'Callaghan, ed., *Documents Relative to the Colonial History of the State of New York* [*NYCD*] (15 vols., Albany, 1853–1887), VIII, 419.

their security depended upon the continued good will not only of the Indians, but also of the department that supervised them. Thus, for Sir William it was essential that a trusted kinsman should succeed to the superintendency.

The natural choice for the position would have been his son, John Johnson, now thirty-two and connected by marriage to the powerful Watts family of New York City. However, John made it clear that he was not interested in the superintendency. Sir William was thus left with a difficult choice between his two sons-in-law, Daniel Claus and Guy Johnson.

Guy Johnson, born in Ireland in 1740, had come to New York in the 1750's and served his uncle as secretary through most of the French and Indian War. He was rewarded for his service by being appointed deputy to the Six Nations in 1762, and he continued to act occasionally as secretary for the department. In 1763 Guy married Sir William's second daughter, Mary, thus strengthening his kinship ties. As Sir William's health failed, Guy Johnson assumed the greater share of the administrative detail and correspondence of the Indian department. Unlike Claus, though, he never gained much proficiency in Indian languages or extensive knowledge of their customs.

Daniel Claus's qualifications rested on his long, meritorious service, and acknowledged rapport with the Indians and, of course, his marriage to Sir William's daughter Nancy. In addition, he was the senior deputy superintendent in the department, having secured his appointment two years before Guy received his. Claus's major liability was his apparent lack of interest in political affairs, at a time when imperial politics might well be crucial to the survival of the Indian department after Sir William's death.

Torn by the dilemma of choosing between men for whom he had the highest regard and fearful of creating jealousy between his two sons-in-law, Sir William equivocated. In early April, 1774, he called Claus into his office at Johnson Hall and with a great show of secrecy locked the door. In some detail he outlined his predicament. By right of seniority, Claus should receive nomination to succeed to the superintendency, but Guy Johnson was better known to the officials who would have to approve the nomination. Rather unfairly, Johnson left it to Claus's "serious and mature consideration" to decide whether he or Guy Johnson should be put forward in nomination. "The affair would sooner succeed," Sir William commented, "if Col. Johnson's name was mentioned in the letters of recommendation." Sir William urged Claus to take a few days to think the matter over, but promised that if Claus agreed to Guy's nomination he would arrange matters in such a way so that Claus would receive half the superintendent's salary, and that "there should be no difference in rank or superiority observed" between the two men. Technically Guy would gain the title of superintendent while Daniel would retain that of deputy superintendent,[5] but they would work as equals.

Claus discussed the issue with his wife, but there was really no doubt what his decision would be. Sir William was not only his father-in-law, but also "the best friend I had in America" and "I could not hesitate in adopting his opinion and advice. . . ." Thus Claus told Sir William that he accepted the plan to nominate Guy Johnson and to divide the emoluments and direction of the department between the two brothers-in-law.[6]

Satisfied with this resolution of the thorny problem, Sir William wrote the Earl of Dartmouth recommending Guy Johnson as his successor and dispatched another letter to General Thomas Gage urging him to support the nomination.[7] Shortly thereafter, on July 11, 1774, while conducting a Six Nations' conference at Johnson Hall, Sir William collapsed and died. Acting under his authority as commander-in-chief in America, General Gage directed Guy Johnson to assume authority in Indian affairs as acting superintendent. At the same time, Gage informed Dartmouth of his action and urged confirmation of Guy Johnson's appointment as superintendent, commenting that he "had for some time transacted most of the Indian business, and I believe him to be both capable, and fit for the employment."[8]

Guy Johnson and Daniel Claus took on the task of directing Indian affairs for the northern department at a most impropitious time. Fanned by the ideology of liberty and ministerial tyranny, popular reaction to the Intolerable Acts was sweeping through the American colonies and starting a chain reaction which culminated in armed rebellion during 1775. The authority of the crown in

---

[5] "Memorandum," in the Claus Papers, PAC, XIV.

[6] *Idem.*

[7] Sir William Johnson to Earl of Dartmouth, April 17, 1774, in *NYCD*, VIII, 419–421.

[8] Thomas Gage to Earl of Dartmouth, July 18, 1774, in A. C. Flick et al., eds., *William Johnson Papers [WJP]* (11 vols., Albany, 1921–1953), VIII, 1185–1186.

America, on which the Indian superintendency so squarely rested, was suddenly in jeopardy.

The outbreak of hostilities between the British army and the colonists and the subsequent events which led to the Declaration of Independence created a sharp division in American society. As the conflict turned to overt rebellion, hopes for a peaceful reconciliation with Great Britain diminished, and the question of allegiance became a matter of uppermost importance. Those who refused to shift their allegiance from crown to revolutionary congresses were labeled "Tories" (although they thought of themselves as "Loyalists") and declared enemies of liberty. As is so often the case in such upheavals, neutrality could not be tolerated by the revolutionary leadership—if one did not actively pledge support to the Revolution, he became an enemy from within.

Much has been written over the past two hundred years about the Loyalists of the American Revolution, but little light has been shed on why they chose to remain loyal, except, of course, in the relatively few, well-documented cases where individuals stated their reasons for adhering to the crown. It is clear, however, that the view long held that the Loyalists consisted for the most part of wealthy landowners and merchants or royal placemen is erroneous. The nearly half-million men and women who steadfastly maintained their loyalty to the crown represented a cross section of American society—small farmers, artisans, mechanics, as well as members of the propertied class. Economic status, social position, religion, and national origin provide no adequate key to unlock the mystery of the Loyalist phenomenon. One must conclude in the end that loyalty, whether to crown or the emerging United States, was a matter of individual conscience.

Of course, as the American Revolution progressed, the relative strength of the contending parties determined the political complexion of given areas. Those sections of the colonies firmly controlled by Patriot civil and military organizations gradually forced out (or imprisoned) die-hard Loyalists, while they won the tacit support of those waverers (perhaps a majority of the population) who did not strongly support either side. The reverse was true in those few areas controlled by the British military. In both types of areas, a certain political stability was imposed, to be disrupted only briefly as the fortunes of war shifted the control of the area from one party to the other.

At the same time there were extensive areas where neither side could exert sufficient force to make its power completely dominant. In these contested zones the struggle between Patriot and Loyalist became nasty civil wars which pitted neighbors and kinsmen against one another in struggles increasingly marked by savage brutality. The infamous "neutral ground" in Westchester County was one such area. The Mohawk Valley and adjacent territory in central New York was another.

Loyalists in the Mohawk Valley were numerous and occupied key positions of authority in 1775. Sir John Johnson, who had inherited not only his father's baronetcy and vast landholdings, but also his father's influence over large numbers of tenants, dependents, and settlers long accustomed to look to Johnson Hall for leadership, had a strong position from which to rally Loyalist support. In addition, officers with Loyalist sympathies dominated the Tryon County militia. Sir John was major general commanding the militia, and both Daniel Claus and Guy Johnson held commissions as colonels; they could reasonably expect a sizable percentage of the rank and file to rally in support of the King's cause. Further strengthening the position of the King's friends in the valley was the influence exercised by Guy Johnson and Daniel Claus over the powerful Iroquois Confederacy through their control of the Northern Indian Department. This could and did raise local fears that the Indians would be turned loose against those who dared openly to support the Patriots.

In fact, however, Guy Johnson and Daniel Claus, far from inciting the Indians to take up the hatchet, desperately attempted to avoid a general Indian war. Enraged by the influx of white settlers into the Ohio Valley in violation of treaty commitments, the Shawnees had gone on the warpath in 1774. As dependents of the Iroquois, they called upon the powerful confederacy and its allies to join them in a general war against the whites. In October, 1774, after months of negotiation, the Grand Council of the Iroquois at Onondaga declared its intention to remain at peace and use its influence to persuade the Shawnees to seek an amicable settlement of their grievances.

Guy Johnson, with some justice, believed that few men outside the Indian department appreciated the magnitude of the disaster so narrowly averted. "The Six Nations alone," he informed the British commander-in-chief in America, "have now above 2000 fighting men, and very powerful friends ready to espouse any part they take...." If the Iroquois had decided to go to war, the minor outbreak in the Ohio country would have escalated into a general conflagration engulfing the entire American frontier.[9] With rebellion stirring in the provinces the British ministry could little afford a major Indian war.

Johnson and Claus had little time to congratulate themselves on the success of their diplomacy. By the end of 1774 a new and far more menacing threat to the crown's Indian relations emerged. While Sir William held the dominant influence over the Iroquois during his lifetime, dissenting New England missionaries, most notably Samuel Kirkland, were challenging that dominance. A firm supporter of the Patriot cause, Kirkland by early 1775 was successfully transforming his religious influence among the Oneidas and Tuscaroras into political agitation designed to break the Iroquois' allegiance to the crown.[10]

Superficially it would appear that Kirkland's goal was the same as that of Johnson and Claus: to convince the Iroquois to remain neutral in the growing rupture between England and her colonies. The critical difference lay in the insistence by the leaders of the Indian department that neutrality must not alter the Iroquois alliance with the crown and Kirkland's efforts to secure the Indians' disavowal of that allegiance. Whether either party at this stage contemplated a more active future role for the Iroquois is a moot question. What is clear is that both suspected the other of doing so, prompting Johnson to order the removal of all New England missionaries from the Indian country in May, 1775. At the same time, rumors were assiduously spread that Johnson was inciting the Indians to fall upon the settlements.[11]

In the small, widely scattered settlements of Tryon County the threat of an Indian war would have been alarming even during normal times. But given the increasing division between Patriot and Loyalist in the county, and the fear of the former that, far from joining in the common defense, the latter would act in concert with the Indians, apprehension gave way to panic in the spring of 1775 and precipitated the first major confrontation between the two factions.

In August of 1774, under the leadership of Christopher Yates

[9] Guy Johnson to Thomas Gage, November 24, 1774, in *WJP*, XIII, 694–695.

[10] Barbara Graymont, *The Iroquois in the American Revolution* (Syracuse, 1972), 42 *passim*. Graymont's excellent book is the only reliable secondary work dealing with the role played by the Iroquois and the Indian department during the Revolution.

[11] *Ibid.*, 62–63.

and John Frey,[12] the Tryon Committee of Correspondence had been organized to "give whatever relief it is in our power to the poor distressed Inhabitants of Boston, and . . . join and unite with our Brethren of the rest of this Colony in anything tending to support and defend our Rights and Liberties."[13] Acting for the considerable segment of Tryon's population which opposed Parliamentary actions threatening their "Rights and Liberties," the committee professed its unswerving loyalty to King George and confined itself to raising subscriptions for the support of "the suffering poor of Boston." It also kept its constituents informed of the proceedings of the New York Provincial Congress and the Continental Congress, and sent information concerning the activities of those suspected of being inimical to the American cause to the more powerful Albany committee. While tension mounted between the committee and its supporters and those who viewed its activities as potentially treasonous, overt action was avoided by both groups until May, 1775. The outbreak of hostilities in Massachusetts and the support pledged by the Continental Congress for the colonial forces besieging the British army in Boston brought matters to a head in Tryon County.

The Johnsons made the first move by having the county grand jury and most of the magistrates sign a declaration denouncing the actions of the Continental Congress.[14] Assuring the Albany committee that the declaration by the grand jury did not reflect the opinion of the majority of the county's inhabitants, Yates and his colleagues organized a public demonstration in support of the Congress. In the act of erecting a liberty pole the demonstrators were confronted by Sir John and Colonel Guy Johnson at the head of a sizable body of armed men. Although no shots were fired, the Patriots were quickly, but not altogether gently, dispersed.[15] During the remaining weeks of May the situation in the

[12] Christopher P. Yates, a lawyer, was a delegate to the New York Provincial Congress and, at this time, a captain in the Tryon County militia. In 1776 he received a major's commission in the First New York Regiment. John Frey was descended from a Swiss family which settled in the Palatine district of what became Tryon County in 1689. A prominent Patriot, although most of his family were Loyalists, he held the rank of major in the militia and succeeded the Loyalist Alexander White as sheriff of the county.

[13] *The Minute Book of the Committee of Safety of Tryon County* (New York, 1905), 1–3.

[14] *Ibid.*, 4–5.

[15] *Ibid.*, 7.

county quickly deteriorated as two armed camps sprang into existence. Initially at a disadvantage because of the Johnsons' control of militia stores and the powder magazine, the committee managed to arm its supporters with assistance from Schenectady and Albany and by early June felt secure enough to offer the Johnsons a peaceful settlement of their differences. In a letter to Guy Johnson, the committee apologized for its earlier suspicions that he was encouraging hostilities by the Indians, thanked him for his continuing efforts to keep the Iroquois peaceful, and pledged its support for his activities as superintendent of the Northern Indian Department.

The committee also assured Johnson that its members were loyal subjects of the crown. Their disagreement was with Parliament, which the committee members argued was violating the rights guaranteed to them by "the Laws and Constitution of England . . . ," not with the King. Therefore, the committeemen observed, "we cannot think, that as you and your family possess very large estates in this county, you are unfavorable to American freedom, altho' you may differ with us, in the mode of obtaining a redress of grievances." Having thus assured Johnson that the committee meant him no harm, the members called on him to disperse the armed force he commanded, which was "extremely unnecessary and greatly inflames the minds of the people. . . ."[16]

It was obviously worth every effort on the committee's part to neutralize the opposition of the Johnson family and bring them and the family's considerable following to accept passively, if they could not support, the measures the committee deemed necessary to protect American liberties. For the same reasons a similar offer of protection and support was made to Daniel Claus.[17]

It is essential for an understanding of the tragedy which was fast overtaking the valley to recognize the sincerity of the committee's offer and the extent to which it would have gone to heal the inflamed feelings between friends and family. If the Johnson family and its numerous dependents were the only parties in opposition to the Patriot faction, one could view the offer as a matter of political expedience—although even here there were close ties of friendship between them and the various members of

[16] *Ibid.*, 18–24.
[17] Daniel Claus to H. T. Cramahé, Lt. Governor of Quebec, March 30, 1778, in the Claus Papers, PAC, II, 5–10.

the committee. But the division over loyalty had struck much deeper. Most, if not all, of the committee members had close family ties with men decidedly opposed to the Patriot cause. The family allegiances of the three men (John Frey, Christopher Yates, and Nicholas Herkimer) who chaired the committee from 1774 to 1776 as the acknowledged leaders of the Patriot faction in Tryon County amply demonstrate the personal dilemmas facing the valley residents. John Frey's father, Colonel Henry Frey, an influential county leader and member of the New York Assembly, steadfastly refused to recognize the authority of the extralegal Patriot governments and was jailed as a Loyalist in 1776.[18] John's brother, Hendrick Frey, eventually was arrested with his father and imprisoned as a Loyalist in Hartford, Connecticut. He subsequently escaped and became an officer in the Indian service, directing raids against his former friends and kin. Another brother, Bernard, also joined the Indian department and took part in the 1780 raid which destroyed the homes of his Patriot relatives at Frybush.[19] Christopher Yates was involved in this family tragedy by his marriage to the Frey brothers' sister. Nicholas Herkimer faced a similar division within his family. His brother, Hans Yost Herkimer, left for Canada with Guy Johnson and Daniel Claus in the summer of 1775 and played an active role in the Indian department until his death in the 1780's. Other kinsmen, Joseph and Nicholas Herkimer, espoused the Loyalist cause; they too joined the Indian department. When General Nicholas Herkimer led the Tryon County militia toward Oriskany in 1777, his brother, brother-in-law, and nephew were among those who laid the fatal ambush that would take the life of the general and hundreds of his compatriots.[20]

The highly personal nature of the growing political division in Tryon County at first inhibited the actions of both the Patriot and Loyalist factions. Ultimately the continued intransigence of Parliament, the spread of the war outside of Massachusetts and, finally, the Declaration of Independence forced men to act as their con-

---

[18] Abbot Collection, New York State Library, item 612; Ernest Cruikshank, *The Story of Butler's Rangers* (Ontario, 1893), 30–31.

[19] Jeptha Root Simms, *Frontiersmen of New York* (2 vols., Albany, 1882), II, 378, 585n; Lorenzo Sabine, *Biographical Sketches of Loyalists of the American Revolution* (2 vols., Boston, 1864), I, 448.

[20] Simms, *Frontiersmen*, II, 517–519, 533; Cruikshank, *Butler's Rangers*, 25, 36.

sciences dictated. The result in the Mohawk Valley, as both sides had long feared, was a brutal civil war.

While many of the valley Loyalists would avoid making their final commitment until 1776, Daniel Claus, Guy Johnson, and others directly associated with the management of the Indian department took decisive, irrevocable action in 1775. At the end of May, Claus, Johnson, and John Butler,[21] along with 120 whites and 90 Mohawks, left for an Indian congress. They judged the site between German Flats and Fort Stanwix, originally selected for the meeting, unsuitable because of the hostility of the disaffected Oneidas. Johnson and Claus finally convened the congress of more than one thousand Iroquois men, women, and children at Oswego in mid-June.[22] At the congress Johnson and Claus secured a pledge that the Indians would assist the British troops in keeping open communications along the St. Lawrence River and the Great Lakes. The Iroquois were also encouraged to spurn overtures from the Continental Congress, but they were not encouraged to take any offensive action against the rebellious colonists. Their business concluded, Johnson, Claus, and their party of Indian officers and Mohawks proceeded to Montreal to secure the same pledge from the Canadian Indians.[23]

So far, despite rumors to the contrary, Johnson and Claus had made no attempt to engage the support of the Indians in suppressing the rebellion. This was about to change. On July 24 the Earl of Dartmouth drafted new instructions for the Indian department. Citing information that the Americans had already talked some Indians into fighting for them, the Colonial Secretary declared that the moment had arrived to secure the active assistance of the Six Nations. "It is . . . His Majesty's pleasure," he informed Guy Johnson, "that you do lose no time in taking such steps as may induce them to take up the hatchet against his Majesty's rebellious subjects in America. . . ."[24]

Long before Dartmouth's letter reached New York, Guy John-

---

[21] John Butler, at this time an interpreter in the Indian department, would be appointed a deputy superintendent in 1776. At the end of 1777 he began to organize the detachment of Loyalist irregulars known as Butler's Rangers which he commanded for the remainder of the war.

[22] Graymont, *Iroquois*, 64.

[23] "Journal of Col. Guy Johnson from May to November, 1775," in *NYCD*, VIII, 658–659.

[24] Earl of Dartmouth to Guy Johnson, July 24, 1775, *ibid.*, VIII, 596.

son and Daniel Claus found themselves compelled by circumstances to urge the Iroquois to war. In doing so, they themselves took the final irrevocable step of armed opposition to the spreading rebellion. Canada, unlike western New York, was now a theater of war. A large American force under the command of General Philip Schuyler was gathering on Lake Champlain for invasion and the reduction of the British posts on the St. Lawrence. The goal was to lure the Canadian provinces, by force if necessary, into following the Patriot cause. Heavily outnumbered, Governor-General Guy Carleton required the active support of the Canadian Indians if he was to repel the American offensive. In addition, the Indian department, with the Hudson River denied to it, now depended exclusively on the St. Lawrence River to transport the presents and trade goods needed to maintain the allegiance of the Indian nations. The passive pledge secured at Oswego to leave communications open would not suffice in Canada. The Iroquois would have to fight to keep the lines open to the western posts.

In fact, Claus and Johnson if they were to retain control of the Northern Indian Department in the name of the crown, had no choice but to declare their unequivocal opposition to the Continental Congress and its policies, for on July 12 and 13, 1775, Congress created its own Indian departments for the northern, middle, and southern districts, appointed commissioners to superintend them, and empowered its agents to treat with the Indians "in the name, and on behalf of the United Colonies, in order to preserve peace and friendship with the said Indians. . . ." Further, the commissioners were instructed to seize and have imprisoned the crown's superintendents and agents if they attempted to thwart congressional efforts.[25] With Congress's Northern Indian Department encompassing the same region as the crown's, Claus and Johnson could either retire from the Indian service or fight to retain their control. There was never any question which they would choose to do.

To some extent the decision made by Johnson, Claus, and most of their agents to oppose the American rebellion actively was dictated by their duty to support the King whose commissions they

---

[25] Worthington C. Ford et al., eds., *The Journals of the Continental Congress, 1774–1789* (34 vols., Washington, 1904–1937), II, 174–183.

held. But by itself this was an insufficient cause. Many civil and military officers of the crown chose to resign their commissions and cast their lot with the colonies. A better reason was their strong attachment to the department and the policies established by Sir William Johnson. Sir William and his successors firmly believed that the department alone stood between the Indians and rapacious colonists who, with the support of their local governments, were intent upon driving the Indians from their lands. Strongly colored though the policy was by paternalism, the crown's Indian officers remained convinced that they alone could protect the interests of their charges. The Indian policies pursued by the American government after 1783 amply vindicated this conviction. Guy Johnson and Daniel Claus thus were determined to retain the management of the northern Indians in the crown's interest, but their ability to do so was severely jeopardized by the autumn of 1775. Whoever succeeded in managing Indian affairs in the north could do so only with the co-operation of the Iroquois, and the Continental Congress, seeking only their neutrality in the dispute between the colonies and England, was in a better position to achieve its goal than Johnson and Claus who were now seeking the Indians' active assistance against the rebels.

For more than half a century the League of the Iroquois had pursued a policy of neutrality toward the white man's wars. Even Sir William Johnson, at the height of his powers, had failed to bring the full league into combat against the French. In 1775 continued neutrality seemed even more essential to the strength and influence of the Iroquois Confederacy. As belligerents many of their warriors inevitably would be slain, their villages would be destroyed by the enemy, and should they choose the losing side, their lands would be forfeitable. On the other hand, if they stood aside in the present conflict, husbanded their strength, then the victor—England or the United Colonies—would be compelled to deal with them respectfully and with honor.

Neutrality was also essential to the very survival of the confederacy. The Mohawks, their land completely surrounded by white settlements and disappearing under steady encroachment, realized from the first that their only hope for a future lay in the protection of the crown. Conversely, Samuel Kirkland and other New England missionaries had disposed the Oneidas and Tuscaroras to side with the American rebels. Thus any policy other than neutrality would have had the devastating effect of pitting members of the league against one another and signal the end of the centuries old confederacy.

With little difficulty, then, the commissioners appointed by Congress to superintend Indian affairs in the northern department secured a satisfactory treaty from the Iroquois. In return for congressional pledges of good will, the sachems of the Six Nations, meeting in Albany during August, 1775, declared the league's intention to remain at peace. Succinctly summarizing their position, the Oneida sachem Senghnagenrat informed the commissioners: "We shan't take notice of any hostile propositions that may be made to us, for we bear an equal proportion of love to you, and the others over the great waters, in the present dispute; we shall remain at peace and smoke our pipes. . . ."[26] Barring an overt act of bad faith on the part of the Americans, Johnson's and Claus's chances of persuading the Six Nations to fight for the crown seemed slim.

Hard on the heels of the news of the Albany treaty came another blow to Johnson's and Claus's control of the northern department. In early 1774 Sir William Johnson had received information that Captain John Campbell of the 27th Regiment had been appointed agent for Indian affairs for the Province of Quebec. Sir William was somewhat startled to find that the management of the Canadian Indians thus had been removed from his control and, more directly, from that of his deputy superintendent, Daniel Claus. To make matters worse, Campbell was granted a salary of £300 a year, £100 more than Claus or other deputy superintendents. His informant disclosed that the appointment had been secured in London by Sir Guy Carleton, who was returning to Canada as its governor. Even more alarming was the speculation that Campbell would only act as a front for his father-in-law, La Corne St. Luc, the former head of Indian affairs under the French regime.[27]

---

[26] "Proceedings of the Commissioners of the Twelve United Colonies with the Six Nations," in *NYCD*, VIII, 612. The six Iroquois nations which constituted the League of the Iroquois or Ircquois Confederacy, were, from east to west: the Mohawks, Oneidas, Tuscaroras, Onondagas, Cayugas, and Senecas.

[27] James Stevenson to Sir William Johnson, March 31, 1774, and April 1, 1774, in *WJP*, VIII, 1103, 1109. In commenting on the appointment of Campbell, Stevenson wryly referred to the Scriptures, Matthew, 25:29: "For unto every one that hath shall be given, and he shall have abundance: but from him that hath not shall be taken away even that which he hath."

Sir William died before he could clarify Campbell's relationship to his department, but Guy Johnson took the matter up with General Gage in November, 1774, inquiring about the nature and extent of Campbell's authority and, specifically, whether he was responsible to the superintendent for the northern department, or, as his actions indicated, solely to Governor Carleton. Gage replied that so far as he knew Campbell's agency was "confined to the Indians in the neighborhood of Canada, and was to be under the general guidance of the Superintendent of the Northern District." He could not, however, enlighten Johnson concerning Campbell's precise duties nor even as to the boundaries of the newly created Province of Quebec.[28] These questions were still unanswered when Johnson and Claus arrived in Montreal in July, 1775, but it was not long before they discovered which way the wind blew.

Campbell was unavailable for questioning, having returned to England in the spring, but Carleton made it clear that he, not Johnson, now directed Indian affairs in the Province of Quebec. Carleton apparently had been vexed by the autonomy enjoyed by Claus under the old organization of the Northern Indian Department and had secured Campbell's appointment as a deputy superintendent, directly responsible to the governor, to put matters under his jurisdiction. Furthermore, Carleton stated that in his military capacity as commander of British forces in Canada, he expected Johnson and Claus to place themselves under his supervision. While he applauded the two men's success in inculcating a warlike spirit in the Indians who attended the large conference at La Chine on July 26, he informed Johnson that Indian war parties could be employed only within the boundaries of the Province of Quebec, and then at the discretion of the governor-general.[29]

General Carleton, faced with the imminence of an American invasion, could reasonably insist upon control of Indian military

[28] Guy Johnson to Thomas Gage, November 10, 1774, in *WJP*, XIII, 691; Thomas Gage to Guy Johnson, November 28, 1774, *ibid.*, 698. Although neither Gage nor Johnson had apparently seen as yet the text of the Quebec Act, it contained provisions of the highest importance for the latter. In addition to establishing a civil government, the Province of Quebec, for those areas of French Canada until then under military rule, it extended the borders of the new province to include the area north of the Ohio River between the Appalachians and the Mississippi. It thus extended the authority of the new government deep into the territory controlled by the Iroquois and their dependents south of the Great Lakes.

[29] "Journal of Col. Guy Johnson," in *NYCD*, VIII, 659–660.

operations undertaken within his area of command. However, he could not legally interfere with Johnson's superintendency, which included the deployment of Indian war parties outside of Canada. Technically, Guy Johnson's only superior in America was the British commander-in-chief, Thomas Gage, and, so far as Johnson knew, he was still responsible for the management of all Indian tribes north of the Ohio River (including those of Canada). Throughout August Johnson vainly attempted to get Carleton's approval for raids against the Americans' line of supply on Lake Champlain. (The general's control of the military supplies necessary for such raids made it impossible for the superintendent to act independently.) Then, on September 10, the final, crippling blow to his and Claus's authority fell with the return from England of John Campbell, bearing a royal commission appointing him superintendent of Indian affairs for Canada.[30]

It was now uncertain what, if any, position Johnson and Claus had in the Indian service. With the management of the Canadian Indians removed from the northern department, and the Iroquois professing neutrality, the brothers-in-law decided to take their case directly to the ministry in London and find out precisely where they stood. Upon their arrival in England in early December, 1775, Johnson and Claus found that Lord George Germain had succeeded Dartmouth as head of the American department and, while he agreed that his predecessor's appointment of Campbell had been unwise, there was nothing he could (or would) do about the matter. Guy Johnson received as compensation a new commission as superintendent of the Six Nations and their confederates. The best Johnson could do was offer a deputy superintendency to his brother-in-law. Claus refused to accept Johnson's favor, since it would make him subordinate to his relative with inferior pay, a significant change from the arrangement made by Sir William. Instead, Claus took half the superintendent's salary from the time of Sir William's death to March 26, 1776, and decided to wait in England to secure some post in Canada where he believed his services would be most valuable. Guy Johnson reluctantly parted from his brother-in-law and sailed for New York City to join the army under Sir William Howe.[31]

[30] *Ibid.*, 662.
[31] "Memorandum," in the Claus Papers, PAC, XIV.

In the absence of the two senior officers of the Indian department, General Guy Carleton appointed John Butler to the post of deputy superintendent and directed him to act for Superintendent Johnson until the latter returned from England. Carleton's selection of Butler was to lead to bitter recriminations from Daniel Claus and would add to the department's growing problems because of the divisive feud between the two men.

John Butler was born in Connecticut during 1728, but his father, Captain Walter Butler, commandant at Fort Hunter, moved the family to the Mohawk Valley in 1742. John Butler served in numerous campaigns—mostly under Sir William—throughout the French and Indian War and rose to the provincial rank of lieutenant colonel. Following the war he was associated with the Indian department, principally as an interpreter, and he carried on a lucrative trade with the Indians. While no one could doubt his experience in dealing with the Indians, some could and did question his qualifications for the high, responsible post in the department to which Carleton had appointed him.

Of critical importance to the crown's management of Indian affairs was the fact that during the crucial year of 1776, responsibility for that task in the North rested with a man who lacked the stature and experience to command the complete respect of the Indians. In councils with representatives of the Six Nations and other tribes, Butler vigorously pleaded the King's cause and urged their support. However, with the exception of the Mohawks (who needed no convincing) and some wavering on the part of the Senecas and Cayugas, he failed to budge the Iroquois from their official policy of neutrality. Indeed, according to his major critic, Daniel Claus, the modest success in stirring some of the Indians to action in 1776 was due to the efforts of Joseph Brant, who had returned with Guy Johnson and made his way to Niagara, and not Butler, whom Claus bitterly criticized for his "backwardness and inactivity. . . ."[32]

There is some evidence that Butler was jealous of Brant's success, and had greeted the latter upon his return to Niagara with marked coolness, even contempt. Brant was later to complain that Butler took every opportunity to obstruct his operations by refus-

[32] Daniel Claus to Captain Watts, September 14, 1779, *ibid.*, XXV, 124–127; Graymont, *Iroquois*, 86, 94–101.

ing to grant his raiding parties sufficient gun powder and supplies. Claus, always quick to ascribe the worst motives to Butler, claimed his actions were prompted by envy of the younger man's spirit and success. Whatever the true reasons, the enmity between Butler and the department's most active Indian leader constituted another factor which inhibited the effectiveness of the department during the war.[33]

Meanwhile, the two men most qualified to direct the department's affairs were far removed from the council fires of the Iroquois. Guy Johnson, who arrived in Staten Island in late July, 1776, remained in New York City for the next two and a half years, expecting to accompany a victorious British army in its march up the Hudson to Albany. He therefore did not assume direct, effective leadership of the department he headed until late 1779, and many of the problems that plagued British leadership with the Iroquois during those critical years were exacerbated by his long absence. For his part Daniel Claus continued his discussions with the ministry in an effort to become joint superintendent with Johnson in the Six Nations department in keeping with Sir William's intentions, or, failing that, to grasp the superintendency of the Canadian department. With dimming prospects of gaining either appointment, Claus, after learning about plans for a northern campaign in 1777, accepted a commission as superintendent for the Indians accompanying Barry St. Leger's expedition to the Mohawk Valley.[34]

Although it was clear that Claus's commission gave him authority over the Indians and agents of the Six Nations department who would take part in the campaign (the Canadian Indians under Campbell already having been earmarked to support Burgoyne), Claus's status in the department once the campaign was concluded was ambiguous. To make matters worse, Sir Guy Carleton, under whom Claus would have to work, was a bitter enemy of Lord George Germain and viewed Claus's appointment as gratuitous interference by the Secretary of State. Claus sensed Carleton's hostility as soon as he returned to Canada in June, 1777. The general spurned his request for specific orders and refused to grant him military rank, although Claus, like all senior officers in the

---

[33] "Anecdotes of Brant," in the Claus Papers, PAC, II, 38–50.
[34] "Memorandum," *ibid.*, XIV.

Indian department, had a courtesy rank of colonel and had held the rank of captain in the 60th Regiment. Carleton also refused to authorize the purchase of Indian goods (tomahawks, knives, kettles, blankets, and paint) which Claus insisted would be necessary for the campaign. The general assured him that Colonel Butler would provide such items.[35]

More disturbing to Claus was the failure of the Canadian commander to obtain accurate information about the strength of the principal obstacle to the expedition, Fort Stanwix. Commanding as it did the carrying place between the Mohawk River and Wood Creek, Fort Stanwix was the key to the water route over which trade and military convoys moved from Lake Ontario to the Hudson River. As long as it remained in American hands, no major, sustained invasion of the Mohawk Valley by the British was possible. The gathering of intelligence was one task the Indian officers with small groups of Indians were eminently suited for, but Carleton feared such parties might commit atrocities against innocent settlers. He was reluctant to authorize the necessary scouting parties. As a result, he, and initially St. Leger, depended on a dated report from Colonel Butler to the effect that the fort was in a weak state with a garrison of sixty men and a wooden palisade which could be easily breached by the expedition's two six- and two three-pound cannons. Not satisfied, Claus immediately dispatched an experienced department officer, John Hare, with a band of Mohawks under John Odiserundy to reconnoiter the fort and bring back prisoners for interrogation. This party returned at the end of June with five prisoners, four scalps, and disturbing news that Stanwix was being strengthened with earth implacements. Further, the garrison had been increased to nearly 600 men. St. Leger, for unexplained reasons, refused to believe the prisoners' statements (which proved to be quite accurate), and the expedition proceeded with a comforting but inaccurate estimate of the enemy's strength.

On August 2, the main British force laid siege to Fort Stanwix. Lacking adequate artillery support, St. Leger could not take the fortress by storm. The garrison would have to be starved into submission. For their part, the American troops under the command of twenty-eight-year-old Colonel Peter Gansevoort realized that

---

[35] Daniel Claus to Secretary Knox, October 16, 1777, in *NYCD*, VIII, 718.

unless a strong American relief force could lift the siege, they were doomed. By August 5 that relief seemed at hand. General Nicholas Herkimer, who had nearly 1,000 Tryon County militia, dispatched messengers to Colonel Gansevoort requesting the garrison to make a sortie the next day to clear a path for the militia column. Accordingly, in the early afternoon of the sixth Lieutenant Colonel Marinus Willett with 250 men sallied forth, unaware that Herkimer's men were already desperately fighting for their lives. However, instead of marching to the aid of their beleaguered comrades, Willett's men contented themselves with looting the camps of the Loyalists and Indians and then returned to the fort with their booty.

Alerted to the approach of Herkimer's force, St. Leger had dispatched Sir John Johnson with fifty of his Royal New Yorkers and an Indian department contingent of fifty rangers and nearly 400 Indians to intercept the relief column. Barely five miles from the fort an ambush was laid in a steep ravine near Oriskany Creek, and at approximately 10 A.M. the militia obligingly walked into the trap. The battle which ensued was a desperate affair, one of the bloodiest of the war. Fighting from heavy cover, often hand-to-hand, the battle raged until late afternoon when the surviving militiamen began their retreat. Estimates by both sides placed the American casualties at about five hundred killed, wounded, and captured, while only eight Loyalists and thirty-three Indians were slain. Nearly the entire membership of the Tryon County Committee of Safety perished in the battle or died of wounds, including Nicholas Herkimer. Adding to the bitterness of defeat was the role played by Loyalist kinsmen and neighbors of the militiamen which added fratricide to the other horrors of the day.[36]

In the end, despite the success at Oriskany, the St. Leger expedition failed. The Fort Stanwix garrison, contemptuous of the ineffective efforts of the British six- and three-pounders to breach the sod-covered walls, steadfastly refused to surrender. At the same time, morale in the British camp was ebbing. The Indians mourned their losses at Oriskany, and the Loyalists and British

---

[36] Christopher Ward, *The War of the Revolution* (2 vols., New York, 1952), II, 491; *Minute Book of the Committee of Safety of Tryon County*, 146; Graymont, *Iroquois*, 132–136; Claus to Knox, October 16, 1777, in *NYCD*, VIII, 721. Claus put the number of Tryon militiamen killed at five hundred, and he reported only eight Loyalists and thirty-two Indians killed.

regulars realized, as the momentum of the expedition foundered, that each day wasted before Fort Stanwix increased the likelihood that a second, larger relief force would fall upon them. Thus, when news arrived that General Benedict Arnold with a powerful force of Continentals and militia was only two days march from the fort, Indians and whites alike precipitously ended the siege, and on August 22 began the long retreat westward.

In assessing the causes for the expedition's failure, St. Leger blamed lack of aggressiveness of the Indians and their white officers after the Oriskany ambush and their precipitous retreat when they learned of Arnold's approach. Daniel Claus, as the man responsible for the Indians, quite naturally found other reasons for the failure. "Thus has an expedition miscarried," he reported, "merely for want of timely and good intelligence. For it is impossible to believe that had the Brigadier St. Leger known the real state of the fort and garrison of Fort Stanwix, he could possibly have proceeded from Montreal without a sufficient train of artillary [*sic*] and his full compliment [*sic*] of troops." He singled out for particular blame John Butler's handling of Indian affairs at Niagara, and his spending of large sums of money on the Indians over the past two years at the same time he had kept them inactive.[37]

While the causes for St. Leger's failure were undoubtedly more complex than either he or Claus perceived, Claus did his best during the remaining years of the war to see that the commanding general in Canada was supplied with a constant flow of reliable intelligence concerning developments in northern and central New York. To accomplish this, he would send scouting parties of mixed Indians and whites into the valley regularly. He also created a network of informants from Albany to Fort Stanwix.

In the wake of the failure of the St. Leger expedition and the defeat of Burgoyne at Saratoga, several factors made all but inevitable the future course of the war in the Mohawk Valley. From the start a substantial percentage of the valley's population was inclined toward Loyalism. During the first two years of the Revolution, under increasing pressure to sign documents attesting to their support of the American cause, hundreds, perhaps thousands, refused and were either imprisoned or sought sanctuary in

---

[37] Claus to Knox, October 16, 1777, in *NYCD*, VIII, 720–722.

Canada. Many others took the simpler, if less principled course, of swearing allegiance to the new government while harboring loyalty to the old.[38] For those Loyalists, like Claus, who fled to Canada, nothing could be more natural than a fixed resolve to return and reclaim what was theirs, or, failing that, wreak vengeance on their Patriot persecutors. In either case, the continued presence in the region of *secret* Loyalists would facilitate their efforts.

Another factor was the military importance of the Mohawk Valley as a supplier of grain, livestock, and other commodities for the Continental Army and the state militia. Having failed in 1777 to secure the area under British control, the destruction of the region's productivity became an integral part of British strategy. In the execution of this strategy, the role played by former valley residents attached to either the Indian department, Sir John Johnson's Royal New Yorkers, or Butler's Rangers would deepen the hatred already firmly implanted at Oriskany.

The final factor controlling the fate of the Mohawk Valley was the Iroquois Confederacy. Thus far the Americans had succeeded in holding the majority of the Iroquois neutral, giving a modicum of security to the frontier. As long as this situation persisted, Loyalist border raids could never be truly effective. Not only did the raiders need logistical support in Indian territory, which separated by hundreds of miles the Loyalist bases and the intended target area, but neutral Indians also posed a danger. They could detect and report to the American military the approach of raiding parties. Indeed, the Americans were already employing Oneidas and Tuscaroras as far ranging scouts for that purpose.

The task facing Daniel Claus and other Indian officers at the end of 1777 was somehow to woo the Iroquois from neutrality to a pro-British alliance, but the prospects for doing so were anything but encouraging. Several hundred Iroquois warriors had joined the St. Leger expedition, yet this did not indicate a general departure from the league's official stance of neutrality. The steadiest, most reliably pro-British component of that Indian force

---

[38] A rough idea of the magnitude of the Loyalist problem in central New York can be gained by referring to the previously cited Tryon County committee of safety minutes and the *Minutes of the Albany Committee of Correspondence, 1775–1778* (2 vols., Albany, 1923–1925), the second volume of which contains the minutes of the Schenectady committee.

was the 300 warriors (mostly Mohawks) led by Joseph Brant. Claus also relocated some 150 Six Nation and Missisauga Indians from Canada whose loyalty could be counted upon. However, the only large contingent of warriors from the remaining tribes of the confederacy were Senecas, whom John Butler, with great difficulty, had persuaded to join St. Leger.[39]

The energy and skill that John Butler displayed in convincing the Senecas to forsake neutrality for the warpath belies Claus's oft-voiced criticism of his inactivity. In any event, Butler's success was in the end offset by St. Leger's failure and the fact that a majority of the Indians killed or wounded at Oriskany were Senecas. All of this tended once more to make peaceful neutrality more appealing than the warpath.

Another obstacle to winning the full support of the Six Nations was the continuing disorganization of the Indian department. Of all the ways in which the valley Loyalists could advance the British cause, active employment in the Indian service should have been the most productive. Many were familiar with the language and customs of the Iroquois, and a substantial number had been associated with the department for some years prior to the Revolution. Given proper direction and vigorous leadership, the Six Nations department could have utilized this potential to forge the Iroquois into an effective and deadly weapon for the crown. Instead, with Guy Johnson lingering in New York City, the department for all intents and purposes lacked a head, and the direction of department affairs fell to his deputies, Claus and Butler, who could not, or would not, set aside their personal differences to work for the good of the service.

Of the two, Claus, with his many years of experience and broader knowledge of Indian administration, could have rendered the more valuable service to the crown. Unfortunately, Sir Guy Carleton bore a strong personal animosity toward Claus; at the end of the 1777 campaign he summarily informed Claus that he no longer had a position in the Indian department. Technically, Carleton was correct. The commission Claus obtained in London gave him "the sole Superintendency of the Indian Nations"

---

[39] Graymont, *Iroquois*, 118–125; Claus to Knox, October 16, 1777, in *NYCD*, VIII, 720; "A General Outline of the Services of Daniel Claus," in the Claus Papers, PAC, XIV, 30.

co-operating with St. Leger;[40] the end of the campaign also ended his command.

There was a desperate need in Montreal for a man of Claus's qualifications and influence to co-ordinate activities between the Six Nations department and British military headquarters. The British needed a knowledgeable administrator who could expedite the movement of goods and military supplies to Britain's Indian allies and at the same time assume over-all direction of the numerous scouting parties sent into enemy territory to secure intelligence upon which to base military operations. General Frederick Haldimand, when he succeeded Carleton in the summer of 1778, was quick to utilize Claus for this purpose, but in the meantime Carleton did his best to ignore Claus; he even refused to honor payment of the accounts Claus rendered for the St. Leger campaign.[41]

In the matter of the accounts, Carleton was simply petty. He approved without question the claims presented by John Butler, when legally those accounts should have been rendered to Claus for approval, and forced Claus to appeal to London to secure money to appease his creditors. Besides causing Claus some embarrassment, this action served to exacerbate further the strained relations between Claus and John Butler. Bitterly remarking that in his fifteen years as chief Indian agent in Canada he had not spent one-fourth what Butler had in two years, Claus began to harbor dark suspicions concerning Butler's misuse of public monies.[42]

Also of immediate concern to Claus was Carleton's prompt approval of John Butler's request to form and command a corps of rangers at Niagara. Butler's avowed purpose was to form a corps of woods-wise Loyalists, most of whom were former residents of the Mohawk region, who could serve as screening and intelligence gathering units for future military operations, and, in the interim between major campaigns, carry the war to the American frontier in small unit raids on exposed settlements.

Whatever value such an organization might have had, Butler's means of creating it raised serious problems for the Indian department. Most of the officers and many of the men in the new ranger

---

[40] "Memorandum," in the Claus Papers, PAC, XIV.

[41] Claus to Knox, October 16, 1777, in *NYCD*, VIII, 722–723; Sir John Johnson to Claus, July 2, 1778, in the Claus Papers, PAC, II, 35–38.

[42] Claus to Knox, November 6, 1777, in *NYCD*, VIII, 723–724; Claus to John Blackburn, October 21, 1779, in the Claus Papers, PAC, XXV, 145–156.

corps were recruited from the Indian department, thus depriving that administrative unit of some of its most experienced and valuable men. This also interrupted existing department policy, established by Sir William Johnson, to intermix rangers and Indians while on service. Also, Johnson's rule that all rangers had to be acquainted with the Indians and their language, was not consistently maintained by Butler,[43] a fact which in future operations led to numerous problems when Butler's Rangers, as they most frequently did, acted in conjunction with the Indians. A further complication was added by Butler's retention of his position as deputy superintendent in the Six Nations department which made him directly responsible to two superiors—one in the military and the other in the Indian department. Inevitably, his critics claimed that Butler became ever more concerned with the success and glorification of his Rangers (which he soon expanded to two corps) and less attentive to his responsibilities in the Indian department. Besides baffling future historians, who would find it all but impossible to distinguish between actions by Butler's Rangers and the rangers of the Indian Department, the development of Butler's corps created a spirit of competition between the two which did little to promote the Loyalists' cause.

There was yet another basis for Claus's hostility about the formation of Butler's Rangers. While he could justify the operational necessity for employing Indians against the rebels, he thought it no "great Merit" for white men to vie with the Indians in the "killing, burning, and destroying" that inevitably would occur.[44]

Yet Claus's concern over Butler's military style was secondary to the mounting problem of securing the full support of the Iroquois and employing the Indians more effectively. For this purpose, without official standing in the eyes of Carleton, Claus dispatched agents to the Iroquois country.[45] One of the side effects of the battle of Oriskany had been an open rupture within the Iroquois Confederacy. Oneidas had fought with the rebels in that engagement. In retribution other Six Nations Indians under Claus had burned a nearby Oneida settlement, destroyed their crops, and killed or driven off their cattle. The Oneidas countered

[43] Claus to Knox, October 16, 1777, in *NYCD*, VIII, 722.

[44] Claus to Frederick Haldimand, October 12, 1778, in the Claus Papers, PAC, XXV, 54–58.

[45] Claus to Knox, October 16, 1777, in *NYCD*, VIII, 723.

by forcing Mary Brant and her family and the pro-British Mohawks from their homes in the Upper and Lower Mohawk towns. More than a hundred were forced to seek sanctuary in Canada.[46]

Thus in addition to the department's continuing attempt to convince the League of the Six Nations that its future security depended on an active allegiance to Great Britain, efforts now had to be exerted to reunify the Longhouse. For so long as the Oneidas, Tuscaroras, and some of the Onondagas co-operated with the Americans they would constitute a serious threat to British efforts to win the unqualified support of the remaining Iroquois. The so-called "Rebel Iroquois" frequently sent emissaries to other Iroquois villages in western New York and even Canada, urging their brethren to desert the British and make peace with the Americans. Counteracting this propaganda was an arduous and often frustrating task for the Indian department. The program was not entirely successful until 1780 when, in the aftermath of the Clinton-Sullivan campaign, the enraged Mohawks, Senecas, Cayugas, and Onondagas firmly pledged themselves to the King's cause and coerced most of their errant Oneida and Tuscarora brothers to join them on the warpath.

The problem of the proper employment of the Indians was also one which the department only partially solved. "Indians with small bodies of troops are often exposed to what appears to them as very discouraging difficulties," commented Guy Johnson in 1778, "in which cases they cannot be expected to keep together like British troops. . . . They do not adopt the same ideas of bravery, neither can they feel so much interest in our cause as Britons do. . . ." Still, he saw great utility in employing them as security and intelligence gathering scouts, and "to strike terror into the enemy."[47] Johnson also claimed that reports of Indian cruelty were exaggerated, rather naively claiming "that the tomahawk which is so much talked of, is seldom used but to smoke through, or to cut wood with, and that they are very rarely guilty of any cruelty more, than scalping the dead, in which article, even, they may be restrained."[48]

Claus agreed with Johnson's assessment of the proper means of using the Indians, and he did his best to implement those ideas.

---

[46] Claus to Knox, November 6, 1777, *ibid.*, 725–726.
[47] Guy Johnson to Lord George Germain, March 12, 1778, *ibid.*, 740–741.
[48] *Ibid.*, 741.

However, he could not share his brother-in-law's optimism about the behavior of Indians on such missions. Based upon his own experience in two wars, Claus knew that it was impossible to impose European codes of conduct on Indian war parties. At best, department officers accompanying such parties could prevent the molestation of women, children, and unarmed men. However, they could not prevent their being taken captive, nor could they halt the scalping of enemy dead. Indeed, the department condoned the latter practice as useful in maintaining morale. For instance, Claus, while complaining that the Indians refused to take any man alive who was found in arms against them—"for fear they say they should come again when released"—observed with approbation that Captain Frye's party gave ten scalps to the Canadian Indians to "keep up their martial spirit."[49] Nevertheless, as Claus and others continued to emphasize the need for prisoners to provide intelligence, more prisoners and fewer scalps resulted—particularly if the Indians did not experience losses which called for revenge. Consequently, most tales of Indian atrocities against defenseless settlers were the product of Patriot propaganda or postwar elaboration by fireside talespinners.

Senior officers in the department continued to be sensitive about the conduct of the Indians and lost no opportunity to report what they considered evidences of humanity shown by the raiding parties they sent out. One example involved a party of twenty-two Mohawks and three rangers who were dispatched from St. Johns in July, 1779, to gather information near Lake George. The party surprised the commanding officer at Fort George, Major Hopkins, several officers and enlisted men, and three women having a picnic and picking huckleberries on a small island near the fort. In the fighting that followed Major Hopkins refused to surrender, and he, a captain, a corporal, and five privates were killed and scalped. The remaining eight soldiers were taken prisoner. Unfortunately two of the women were "unluckily" killed, but they were not scalped; the third was left on the island unmolested. Obviously, the surviving woman, surrounded by her dead and mutilated friends, was not as impressed with the humanity of the raiders as were department officials.[50]

Despite the department's continuing concern that their raiding

---

[49] Claus to Haldimand, November 18, 1778, in the Claus Papers, PAC, XXV, 54–58.
[50] P. Langan to Claus, July 22, 1779, *ibid.*, XXVI, 104–107.

parties should act in a humane fashion, the shift in emphasis from intelligence gathering to destruction of the Mohawk region's productivity dramatically increased the horror and hatred with which the settlers viewed their red and white tormentors. This change in emphasis was forced upon the Indian department by the British command's decision not to mount another major northern offensive after the twin disasters of 1777. This precluded the use of the Indians as a screening force for a major invasion and substantially reduced the usefulness of the intelligence they gathered about American defenses in western and northern New York. With military operations in the north shifting to southern New York, New Jersey, and Pennsylvania, the only significant military role the Indians could play was the destruction of crops and farm animals raised in the region and destined for the support of Washington's army. Increasingly after 1777 the department recorded the achievements of its raiding parties in numbers of farms burned, crops and cattle destroyed, and farmers killed or carried off to captivity in Canada.

Purely from a military standpoint, the new tactics adopted by the Indian department and Butler's Rangers seemed justified. The raids destroyed vast quantities of provisions, and, according to reliable sources, forced nearly half of the valley's population to abandon their land. They also forced the diversion of troops from Washington's hard-pressed army to protect the frontier. Unfortunately, the prominent role played by Loyalist rangers in laying waste to the farms of their kin and former neighbors transformed the border war into an emotionally charged blood feud. Under such conditions atrocities became not only possible but probable. In this respect, the war on the frontier reached a turning point in 1778.

Except for the blood bath at Oriskany, border settlers had not suffered greatly during more than three years of war. But in the summer of 1778 attacks by Loyalists and Indians began on a new scale. In late June Colonel John Butler with a mixed force of rangers and Indians struck the prosperous settlements in the Wyoming Valley and, although there was no massacre of noncombatants as later alleged, the militia unit which attempted to defend the valley was bloodily defeated with more than 300 killed, and the settlements were destroyed.

During the same month Joseph Brant with a force composed

principally of rangers and Mohawks began a major campaign of destruction against the settlements in central New York. They started at the head of Otsego Lake, swept through the Schoharie Valley and culminated at German Flats in September. The most devastating blow was that struck at German Flats on September 17, during which Brant with 300 whites and 150 Indians burned 63 houses, 57 barns (with grain and fodder), 3 grist mills, 1 saw mill, and drove off 235 horses, 229 horned cattle, and 269 sheep. They also destroyed a great number of hogs which they obviously did not relish driving through the woods.[51] Brant's men accomplished the sacking of German Flats without the death of a single noncombatant; however, this may have been due less to restraint by the raiders than the fact that the forewarned populace sought refuge in nearby blockhouses and forts.

In the final major raid of the season, at Cherry Valley, the people were not so fortunate. The Cherry Valley massacre, with its indiscriminate slaughter of women and children, did more than all the other incidents of the border war to blacken the image of the Loyalist rangers and their Indian allies. Although it became associated in most people's minds with what they considered to be the typical bloodthirstiness of those "incarnate fiends," it was in truth atypical behavior.

Although no one may ever know for certain why the massacre took place or who was responsible, the general causes were clear from the first. They consituted for Daniel Claus a vindication of his warnings about the formation of Butler's Rangers. The attack was conceived and executed by Captain Walter Butler, Major Butler's son, who with little previous experience with either Indians or military operations, was exercising his first independent command over a detachment of some 150 Rangers, 50 men of Sir John Johnson's regiment, and 321 Indians.[52] Following the practice of Butler's Rangers—and contrary to that of the Indian department—the Rangers were to attack the fort as a separate group. Butler expected the Indians as a separate force to assist in the attack. Had the Indians been under the direction of a strong leader, and had Walter Butler been more experienced, the foray

[51] "Colonel Bellinger's Report to Governor Clinton," September 19, 1778, in Hugh Hastings and J. A. Holden, eds., *Public Papers of George Clinton* (10 vols., Albany, 1899–1914), IV, 47–49.

[52] Graymont, *Iroquois*, 184.

might have succeeded in its primary objective, the capture of the fort. Unfortunately, neither was the case.

Instead of a single, strong leader, the Indians, mostly Senecas, were led by a number of head warriors who were more inclined to compete with one another than to co-operate. The Indians also had little respect for Butler, who nearly lost their support altogether by his harsh treatment of Joseph Brant. Brant with his own party rendezvoused with Butler's force before the attack, and Butler asserted his right to command both parties. Brant, who was senior to Butler, denied his authority and threatened to lead his followers back to Niagara. The Indians with Butler's party then expressed their doubts concerning Butler's experience and indicated that they would quit the expedition if Brant did. Thus, as he put it, against his better judgment but for the good of the service, Brant agreed to go along and endure Butler's supercilious behavior. However, ninety of the white rangers who had served with Brant all summer refused to accept Butler's command and, ignoring his threats to treat all as rebels, went back to the settlements to hide themselves until spring.

On November 11 Butler attacked the fort as planned. He had the support of Brant and his small band of Mohawks, but the rest of the Indians, leaderless and disgruntled, proceeded to loot the small settlement and slaughter the inhabitants instead of striking at the fort. Without the Indians' support the assault on the fort failed. Before order could be restored thirty-two civilians, mostly women and children, and sixteen soldiers had been killed.[53]

Claus, Brant, and other Indian department officers were shocked and outraged by what had happened. They made clear their opinion that responsibility for the tragedy rested squarely with Walter Butler. Adding to their bitterness was the fact that a large percentage of the dead civilians were well-known Loyalists. Consequently, the Cherry Valley massacre widened the breach between the Indian department and Butler's Rangers. Daniel Claus from this point on increased his efforts to discredit John Butler and the corps he commanded.

Another result of the Cherry Valley massacre and the raids preceding it was the decision by the Continental Congress to mount

---

[53] Taylor and Duffin to Claus, November 11, 1778, in the Claus Papers, PAC, XXV, 46–48; Claus to Haldimand, November 20, 1778, *ibid.*, 59–62; Taylor and Duffin to Claus, December 1, 1778, *ibid.*, 70–73; Claus to Haldimand, March 17, 1779, *ibid.*, 82–84.

a major offensive campaign against the Indian country in 1779, to destroy the Iroquois capacity to wage war, and, hopefully, to capture the posts—Niagara, Carleton Island, and Oswegatchie—from which the raiding parties were supplied and dispatched. The ensuing campaign, however, led by Generals John Sullivan and James Clinton, was only partially successful. It laid waste to the Cayuga and Seneca country (while an auxiliary expedition destroyed the Onondaga villages) and defeated Butler's force of Loyalists and Indians at Newtown. But it failed to push on and capture Niagara or the other British posts. The campaign's success rested mostly on the destruction of the Seneca, Cayuga, and Onondaga villages, their crops, orchards, granaries, and livestock, forcing thousands of Indians to pour into Niagara and become a drain on the British army, which had to feed them. But the campaign did not secure the New York frontier, for instead of destroying the Indians' will to fight, it united the Iroquois in the common cause of avenging their losses. Consequently, Daniel Claus predicted that "if the Rebels don't settle matters with England this winter, [the] next campaign will be the most bloody and barbarous ever heard of in the world."[54]

Guy Johnson, having at long last reached Niagara in late autumn, 1779, found himself overwhelmed by the problem posed by the refugee Iroquois, initially some 3,500 strong. The new spirit of the Indians, though, encouraged Johnson. He agreed that the warriors would be eager to retaliate in the coming year, and even hoped "to be able to amuse them a little on the frontiers during the winter."[55] With Johnson energetically organizing and dispatching raiding parties, Claus's prediction for 1780 was largely realized. Between February 11 and July 1 nearly 500 Indians and whites from the Indian department made forays into the frontier. From July through October large parties of 300 and 400 attacked the settlements and, supported by Sir John Johnson and his Royal New Yorkers, desolated the Schoharie and Mohawk valleys.[56]

However, the intensified activity of the Indians and the destruc-

---

[54] Claus to John Blackburn, November 4, 1779, *ibid.*, 142–144.

[55] Guy Johnson to Claus, November 21, 1779, *ibid.*, 152–155.

[56] Graymont, *Iroquois*, 229. Details of many of these raids can be found in Claus's reports to Haldimand in volumes II and XXV of the Claus Papers, PAC, and the Haldimand Papers, PAC, particularly the correspondence between his headquarters and the officers commanding at Oswegatchie, Carleton Island, and Niagara, the bases from which most of the raids against the New York frontier were launched.

tion wrought upon the frontiers in 1780 and 1781 could not alter the course of the war, which was rapidly approaching its end. Some might wonder what effect the Indians would have had if the Indian department had succeeded in mustering the strength in 1776 that they were able to gather after 1779. Daniel Claus, drawing upon his long years of experience with the Indians, had no doubts: "The Six Nations have a ridiculous notion that the balance of power on the American continent is in their hands. The French last war with immense expence had almost every Indian on the Continent in their interest, but savage faith is so precarious in war that all expence & bribery is thrown away upon them for they join neither party heartily until they are sure which will prevail, and then they join when not wanted & fall upon the loosing party . . . ; the only means to make them act any ways hearty is to endeavour to draw them on to loose blood when revenge will undo all bribery."[57]

While there may be a trace of cynicism in Claus's evaluation, it does place in perspective the role played by the Indian department in the war for American independence. It was a supporting role for the main theater of British operations in the North. The incessant raids directed by the department against the frontier region destroyed large quantities of grain and livestock which were desperately needed for the American war effort. The department also forced a diversion of American troops to guard the exposed frontiers and thereby significantly weakened Washington's army. And, finally, largely through the efforts of Daniel Claus, small scouting parties provided a constant flow of intelligence which made it possible for the British command in Canada to anticipate by several weeks any major American operation in New York.

In executing these functions, the Indian department was constantly harassed by internal division, most importantly the rivalry between Claus, Butler, and Campbell, which certainly lessened the department's effectiveness. In addition, the British command never provided adequate financial or military support for the department's operations. This failure made it impossible for Claus and Butler to secure the full, active support of the Iroquois during the first four years of the war. It is reasonable to

[57] Claus to Haldimand, May 15, 1780, in the Claus Papers, PAC, XXV, 184–187.

suppose that had the department solved its internal problems and secured the support it needed from the British army, it could have rendered untenable American control of the Mohawk Valley region, and thereby greatly increased its contribution to the British war effort. Nevertheless, the department's activities could not, and did not, play a decisive role in the outcome of the Revolution.

Indeed, that outcome, and its personal implications, had been long foreseen by Claus and his associates. As early as June, 1778, Sir John Johnson confided to Claus that France's entry into the war meant England would be forced to negotiate a settlement with the United States. "I fear," he accurately forecasted, "the terms will prove unfavorable to us, who have lost all we could lose."[58] Claus had already come to similar conclusions. His activities since he left his home in June, 1775, assured the forfeiture of his real and personal estate, and he could expect "confinement and ill usuage" should he dare to return.[59] Occasionally, Daniel Claus would still hope that somehow he might "once more enjoy . . . that peace of mind and rural happiness" he had known before the Revolution, "and live content upon the banks of the Mohawk under our own vine and fig tree. . . ."[60]

But it was not to be. The conclusion of peace in 1783 left him, with tens of thousands of other Loyalists, a debt-ridden exile. Claus's estate and most of his personal property were irretrievably lost. In addition he was deeply in debt. He had borrowed heavily during the war, not only to support his family, but also to pay out of his own pocket many of the Indian department's expenses. Thus, Daniel Claus, nearing sixty, faced a grim and uncertain future with little to show for more than thirty years of dedicated service to the crown. To satisfy his creditors and secure his family's well-being, he returned to Great Britain, and in 1787 died while futilely seeking remuneration for his losses from the government he served so long and so well.

[58] Sir John Johnson to Claus, June 18, 1778, *ibid.*, II, 25–26.
[59] Claus to Cramahé, March 30, 1778, *ibid.*, 5–10.
[60] Claus to Captain Watts, September 14, 1779, *ibid.*, XXV, 124.

Political Change in Revolutionary America:
A Sectional Reinterpretation

Joseph L. Davis

I . . . wish the distinctions Southern and Northern were
lost in the glorious Name of American.

JOSEPH WARD[1]

THE ADOPTION of a constitution which erected a national
government in 1789 brought the United States full circle to the
type of centralized authority which Great Britain had in theory
exerted prior to the Revolution. This change from the revolutionary ideology contained in America's first constitution, the
Articles of Confederation, is crucial to an understanding of the
American Revolution. During the Revolutionary Era two major
factions, one supporting a weak and the other a strong central government, engaged in a series of confrontations for control of the
new nation. Most of the men who supported independence (the
federalists) perceived the Revolution as a struggle against those
who wanted a powerful central government in America. They
wanted central government limited and controlled to keep it a servant of rather than a dictator over the states and the people.
Generally those who were reconciliationists or who had opposed
independence (the nationalists) did not reject the institution of
central government. They believed that a central government had
to be formulated with power enough to impose its will and
enforce its dictates upon the states, if it was to prevent profound

AUTHOR'S NOTE: I want to express my gratitude to the National Endowment for the
Humanities, whose support of a broader study enabled this article to be written.
   [1] Joseph Ward to John Adams, December 3, 1775, in the Adams Mss. Trust, Massachusetts Historical Society [MHS].

political and social upheaval after separation from Great Britain. It is this conflict between federalists and nationalists which began as early as 1774 to which we must look for a deeper comprehension of the developments which led to the Constitution of 1787.

There was, however, more to revolutionary politics than the relatively narrow limits of ideological dispute. Political differences among the members of Congress were also affected by state and especially sectional interests which, at times, assumed a higher priority than ideological commitment or factional solidarity.[2] The American Revolution has been variously discussed as an intellectual, ideological, economic, and social movement, but though the sectional nature of American politics has, in some form or other, long been acknowledged, sectional conflict has been given at best a secondary place in most studies of the American Revolution. Inasmuch as the theme of the Revolution, and especially the creation of a national government, is supposed to be unity, little attention has been paid to the continuous impact of sectional conflict on the political changes in eighteenth-century America. This essay is intended to demonstrate how sectional conflict affected the struggle between federalists and nationalists throughout the Revolutionary Era, and, in particular, how it prevented the federalists, at critical junctures, from defending their ideology and the Articles of Confederation against nationalist attack.

Some historians have largely ignored the implications of sectional or any other forms of internal conflict, and instead have described how a consensus and the slow process of political maturation resulted in the formulation of the Constitution of 1787.[3]

[2] This study is, by its very nature, limited to those men who wielded power. The thoughts and positions of the men who were in Congress or who held state office, or who were in other ways important did not necessarily represent all the people in their particular state or section. When state and/or sectional attitudes are labeled, the intent is to represent only the viewpoint of that particular segment of the elite which is under discussion and should not be interpreted as a blanket generalization. For example, when a specific stance is identified as southern or New England, no implication is intended that the interest of a group like New England merchants or southern planters should stand for entire regions. This essay is based on Joseph L. Davis, "Sections, Factions, and Political Centralism in the Confederation Period: 1774–1787" (doctoral dissertation, University of Wisconsin, 1972).

[3] Richard B. Morris, "The Confederation Period and the American Historians," in the *William and Mary Quarterly* [*WMQ*], 3rd Ser., 19 (1962); Cecelia M. Kenyon, "Republicanism and Radicalism in the American Revolution: An Old Fashioned Interpretation," in *WMQ*, 3rd Ser., 19 (1962); Bernard Bailyn, "Political Experience and Enlightenment Ideas in Eighteenth Century America," in the *American Histor-*

Others have primarily focused on the ideological struggle between federalists and nationalists to delineate the steps which led to the Philadelphia Convention. This is not to say that sectional conflicts have been ignored. On the contrary, the sectionally divisive problems of western lands, the navigation of the Mississippi River, and centralized commerce have been discussed. But the effect of those issues on the factional struggle between federalists and nationalists is usually overlooked in favor of citing the importance of other nonideological conflicts such as that concerning the federal debt. While sectional interest is often cited in the discussion of the formulation of the Articles of Confederation, the role of sectional conflict is given considerably less weight, if any at all, in describing the continuing story of constitutional change.[4] A few historians have demonstrated the existence of sectional awarenesses and analyzed sectional identities in far greater detail than any other group. Although some historians have been in tune with the sectional forces at play in the many conflicts in Congress in the 1770's and 1780's, they have failed to connect that conflict to the usually simultaneous federalist-nationalist confrontations. Ideological and sectional conflicts did not take place in isolation from one another; they affected each other in significant ways and this interaction must be understood in order to explain the politics of Revolutionary America.[5]

We can use the terms "federalist" and "nationalist," as they are above defined, to label certain broad groupings of men, but we

ical Review, 68 (1961); Clinton Rossiter, "The Political Theory of the American Revolution," in John P. Roche, ed., *Origins of American Political Thought* (New York, 1967), 97–113; Edmund S. Morgan, *The Birth of the Republic* (Chicago, 1956); Gordon Wood, *The Creation of the American Republic, 1776–1787* (New York, 1969); Charles F. Warren, *The Making of the Constitution* (Boston, 1928); George Bancroft, *History of the Formation of the Constitution of the United States of America* (2 vols., New York, 1882).

[4] Merrill Jensen, *The Articles of Confederation* (Madison, 1940); *The New Nation* (New York, 1950); Jackson T. Main, *The Antifederalists* (Chapel Hill, 1961); E. James Ferguson, *The Power of the Purse* (Chapel Hill, 1961); Ferguson, "The Nationalists of 1781–1783, and the Economic Interpretation of the Constitution," in the *Journal of American History*, 56 (1969); J. Allen Smith, *The Spirit of American Government* (Cambridge, 1907).

[5] John R. Alden, *The First South* (Baton Rouge, 1961); *The South in the Revolution, 1763–1789* (Baton Rouge, 1957); Fulmer Mood, "The Origin, Evolution, and Application of the Sectional Concept, 1750–1790," in Merrill Jensen, ed., *Regionalism in America* (Madison, 1951). Some provocative essays may be found in Staughton Lynd, *Class Conflict, Slavery, and the United States Constitution* (Indianapolis, 1967).

must guard against giving those imprecise terms too much weight and ascribing to each faction a homogeneity which did not exist. Both factional and sectional labels must be qualified with the understanding that many factors (both ideology and interest) affected the various groupings and often blurred the major divisions. Although quantitative methods have recently provided us with a more rigorous description of the various voting alignments in the Confederation Congress, it is dangerous to rely solely on them to describe the political scene. Because the political scene was complicated by ideological subgroups within factions and by sectional, subsectional, and state interests, which can easily escape the static eye of the computer, analyses of congressional voting behavior can provide useful information, but not a final answer to the many questions arising out of a discussion of eighteenth-century politics.[6]

Throughout the Revolutionary Era the sections vied with each other for power and because the stakes were so very high, sectional competition spread jealousy and mistrust to issues which, on the surface, had very little to do with sectional interests. While the clash of interests between New England, the Middle States, and the South became more intense later on, the impact of sectional conflict was no less significant in 1775 and 1776 than it was ten years later. Sectional interests were so strongly defended that only at those infrequent times when extraordinary pressures forced the elite, or a part of it, to stand together against a common threat to its position and power did co-operation replace conflict. Nevertheless, whether defending their interests against Great Britain in

[6] See H. James Henderson, "The Structure of Politics in the Continental Congress," in Stephen G. Kurtz and James H. Hutson, eds., *Essays on the American Revolution* (Chapel Hill, 1973); Henderson, *Party Politics in the Continental Congress* (New York, 1974). Henderson's sound account of the voting behavior in Congress is limited by a reliance upon rather standard interpretations of many of the issues and by the additional support of only the most easily accessible contemporary correspondence. The evidence in his book does not support his statement that roll-call analysis must be used "in association with other sources and methods of inquiry." (xiv) A series of congressional voting blocs, upon which Henderson bases so much of his thesis, are derived from unspecified votes. In many instances, especially after 1782, he seems to be justifying the results of his computations instead of trying to elucidate reasons for behavior. While Henderson admits that the disagreement over the relationship between national government and state power affected partisan politics, he emphasizes the regional basis of partisan politics to such an extent that the equally fundamental issue of ideological conflict is shunted much too far into the background.

1777 or against the people in 1787, the political leaders were still motivated by interests which threatened to engulf them all in a sectional conflagration. The disabling effects of sectional conflict were especially damaging to the federalists, whose factional superiority in Congress depended upon intersectional accord between New England and the South. The factional blocs in Congress reflected the influence of sectionalism; federalists were concentrated in New England, nationalists were in the Middle States, and both were trying to secure southern support. Despite the fact that both factions were internally bound together by a more or less common ideology and their respective memberships extended across sectional lines, the alignment and realignment of sectional blocs had a direct impact on factional superiority in Congress.[7] Although in the early years of the Revolution the federalists were able to control Congress because of the degree to which the Lee-Adams Junto cemented New England and the South, the differences between those sections, which demanded "the utmost caution on both sides and the most considerate forebearance with one another," were not easily resolved.

Southerners, for example, seemed to fear that New England aimed not only at independence from Great Britain "but of the other colonies too." They think, wrote Joseph Hawley, that Massachusetts men "affect to dictate and take the lead in Continental Measures; that we are apt from an inward vanity and self-conceit to assume big and haughty airs." Hawley thus advised his friend John Adams to avoid any conduct which might upset the southerners and hence jeopardize their support for New England's acts of resistance.[8] Adams did not face an easy task. Soon after arriving in Congress he nervously reported an alarming "diversity of religions, educations, manners, interests, such as it would seem almost impossible to unite on one plan of conduct." This diversity led some conservatives to venture the logical predic-

[7] See Henderson, "The Structure of Politics," 165–166.
[8] John Adams to Joseph Hawley, November 25, 1775, in Edmund C. Burnett, ed., *Letters of Members of the Continental Congress* [*LMCC*] (8 vols., Washington, 1921–1936), I, 259–260; Samuel Adams to James Warren, September 25, 1774, in Harry A. Cushing, ed., *The Writings of Samuel Adams* [*WSA*] (4 vols., New York, 1911–1914), III, 156–157; Joseph Hawley to John Adams, July 25, 1774, in C. F. Adams, *Life and Works of John Adams* (10 vols., Boston, 1850–1856), IX, 344–345.

tion that once political separation from Great Britain occurred "commercial interests will interfere; there will be no supreme power to interpose, and discord and animosity must ensue."[9] Even in the face of British invasion and British attempts to split the colonies North and South, sectional fears abounded and threatened to destroy the modicum of intercolonial co-operation which had been spurred by British transgressions and to undo the beneficial realization, particularly common among federalists, that union was the only way to defeat the British.

The second Continental Congress was much "like the first," with sectional prejudice running from North to South as well as from South to North. While John Adams castigated the southerners for their fear of New England's "Designs of Independency—An American Republic—Presbyterian Principles—and twenty other things," he nevertheless admitted his own "local Attachment . . . hardness . . . Prejudice in favour of New England . . . [where] the People are purer English Blood less mixed with Scotch, Irish, Dutch, French, Swedish than any other."[10] Southern fears of a northern domination were strengthened by suggestions that Congress move north from Philadelphia. The distrust ran so deep in 1775 that some at least considered the creation of "two grand Republics" by Congress—one northern and one southern—as a real possibility.[11] Some of the most serious conflicts occurred in the Continental army. In order to mollify southern fears that New England might eventually use its "Veteran Soldiers" to the other colonies' disadvantage, New England, in June, 1775, agreed to appoint George Washington as commander-in-chief. Washington's appointment did not allay sectionally inspired fears and jealousies to the extent that has often been assumed. The United States faced

[9] John Adams to William Tudor, September 24, 1774, in C. F. Adams, ed., *Works*, IX, 346; Samuel Seabury, "A View of the Controversy Between Great Britain and Her Colonies," December 14, 1774, in Alpheus T. Mason, *Free Government in the Making* (New York, 1965), 118.

[10] Silas Deane to Mrs. Deane, June 3, 1775, in *LMCC*, I, 111; John Adams to Abigail Adams, June 17, 1775, *ibid.*, 130; to Abigail Adams, October 29, 1775, in the Adams Mss. Trust, MHS.

[11] Titus Hosmer to Silas Deane, May 28, 1775, in the Connecticut Historical Society *Collections*, 2 (1870), 235; John McKesson to Gov. George Clinton, June 10, 1775, in the *Public Papers of George Clinton* (10 vols., Albany, 1899–1914), I, 199–200; George Clinton to John McKesson, June 15, 1775, in *LMCC*, I, 125.

a common enemy, but only three of the fourteen senior officers in the Continental army were southerners.[12] Even Nathanael Greene thought that the New England states would have to recall some of their officers "to remove any unfavourable impressions that might arise in the Southern Colonies." Apparently the only recourse to balance the inequity was to ignore the rules of seniority, so Congress promoted southern officers over New Englanders. The promotions outraged many New Englanders in and out of Congress and further strained the already tense intersectional relations.[13] While southerners snipped at New Englanders as "not like the Children of the South" in either valor or expertise, the New Englanders claimed that the promotions confirmed the observation "which some have had the impudence to make—'The Massachusetts men make good soldiers, but we must send to the Southward for our officers'."[14]

There were other early signs of sectional tension. There were reports of hostilities between New England and Pennsylvania troops; some New Yorkers were unwilling to have New England troops stationed in New York City; and southerners objected to the high pay and bonuses New England troops were receiving. These clashes—the removal of General Wooster and the conflicts between Generals Gates and Schuyler and their supporters—did little to foster the intercolonial co-operation necessary for a vigorous prosecution of the war or a successful revolution.[15]

[12] John Adams to James Warren, June 6, 1775, in the *Warren-Adams Letters,* Massachusetts Historical Society *Collections,* 72, 73 (2 vols., 1917–1925), I, 25; See Jonathan G. Rossie, "The Politics of Command: The Continental Congress and Its Generals" (doctoral dissertation, University of Wisconsin, 1966), 29; Samuel W. Patterson, *Horatio Gates, Defender of American Liberties* (New York, 1966), 49; Alden, *The First South,* 25; Henderson, *Party Politics,* 53.

[13] Nathanael Greene to Gov. Cooke, August 9, 1775, in "Revolutionary Correspondence from 1775–1782," Rhode Island Historical Society *Collections,* 6 (1867), 117–118; Thomas Jefferson to Patrick Henry, July 16, 1776, in *LMCC,* II, 14.

[14] John Haslett to Caesar Rodney, October 10, 1775, in George H. Ryden, ed., *Letters To and From Caesar Rodney, 1756–1784* (Philadelphia, 1933), 138; Joseph Ward to John Adams, August 8, 1776, in the Adams Mss. Trust, MHS.

[15] James Sullivan to John Sullivan, December 6, 1775, in Otis G. Hammond, ed., *Letters and Papers of Major-General John Sullivan,* New Hampshire Historical Society *Collections,* 13–15 (3 vols., 1939), I, 138. See Samuel H. Parsons to John Adams, [September, 1775], in the Adams Mss. Trust, MHS; Alexander Hamilton to John Jay, November 26, 1775, in Harold C. Syrett et al., eds., *The Papers of Alexander Hamilton* (New York, 1961 to date), I, 177; William Hooper to James Iredell, January 6, 1776, in Griffith J. McRee, *Life and Correspondence of James Iredell* (2 vols., New York, 1858), I, 269; John Adams, *Autobiography,* August 12, 1776, in Lyman H. Butterfield,

The sectional differences which plagued the Continental army also retarded the movement for independence. The New Englanders, who had no guarantee that the southerners would follow them to revolution, were afraid that they might "make their Terms of Peace and forsake us." Federalist plans for the Revolution did little to smooth the road to independence. Heavily influenced by New England's radicalism, the federalists wanted to establish a continental government to protect the fledgling union. They also wanted to use Congress to prepare the nation for independence and union by first having state governments established "under the authority of the People."[16] This projected political change, though hardly alien to New England, was, John Adams said, accepted in the South only by men "of free Spirits and liberal Minds, who are very few." The rest, which included "the Barons of the South and the Proprietary Interests in the Middle Colonies" had what he called a "reluctance to Republican Government." These cautious men were afraid of the people; afraid of the degree to which republicanism might instill in them expectations of further change. It was the belief that political upheaval was too easy on the local and state levels, that the creation of state governments would be "attended with the greatest anarchy," which predisposed the skeptical and conservative nationalists to question the wisdom of placing the balance of power in the states and to advocate the creation of a central government able to exert control over them.[17]

Although some southerners—Adams's men of liberal minds—were outspoken federalists, the faction, at least from an observer's perspective, bore the unmistakable stamp of an unwelcome and dangerous New England radicalism. The Lee-Adams Junto was a strange alliance of men with a common ideology who had fun-

---

ed., *The Adams Papers* [*AP*], Sers. I: *Diary and Autobiography of John Adams* (4 vols., Boston, 1961), III, 405–406; William Williams to Joseph Trumbull, September 26, 1776, in *LMCC*, II, 104.

[16] Samuel Osgood to John Adams, December 4, 1775, in the Adams Mss. Trust, MHS; Samuel Adams to Samuel Cooper, April 30, 1776, in *WSA*, III, 241. See Thomas Paine, "Common Sense," in Moncure D. Conway, ed., *Writings of Thomas Paine* (4 vols., New York, 1894–1896), I, 95; John Adams to Abigail Adams, May 17, 1776, and to Zabiel Adams, June 21, 1776, in the Adams Mss. Trust, MHS.

[17] John Adams to Abigail Adams, February 18, 1776, in the Adams Mss. Trust, MHS; to Horatio Gates, March 23, 1776, in *LMCC*, I, 406; James Sullivan to John Adams, May 9, 1776, in the Adams Mss. Trust, MHS.

damentally different and antithetical sectional interests. This flaw undercut the federalists throughout the period. As late as May, 1776, it was reported that the Tories were certain that the southern states would never support independence. Some southern reconciliationists attacked southern federalists like the Lees for blindly following "those wise men of the East." It was even charged that a "Tiptoe Gentleman," possibly John Hancock (who John Adams later said "had courted Mr. Duane, Mr. Dickinson and their party"), had, in 1776, gone "tripping around Congress, indefatigable in insinuating distrusts of the New England States . . . to make us [i.e. the southerners] look upon the New England States with a Kind of Horror."[18]

Because it was well understood that a central government could, very easily, be used to further sectional goals, each section was reluctant to undermine its own interests for fear that the others might be unduly benefited. It was, for example, reported that one of the reasons for New England's objection to Benjamin Franklin's Albany Plan in 1754 was the "great sway which the Southern Colonies . . . would have in all the determinations of the Grand Council." Edward Rutledge's first reaction to the Articles of Confederation was strikingly similar. He feared that it would subject the southern states to "the Government of the Eastern Provinces." Before a plan of union was formulated there seemed to be a distinct possibility that competing state and sectional interests would produce "intestine Wars and Convulsions" after separation, or, at the very least, prevent the establishment of a central government which would "be agreed to by all the colonies."[19]

Reflecting on the possibility that certain issues would block co-operation, Patrick Henry warned John Adams and Richard Henry Lee to confine an intercolonial union "to Objects of Offensive & Defensive Nature . . . [for] if a Minute Arrangement of

[18] Joseph Hawley to Elbridge Gerry, May 1, 1776, in James T. Austin, *The Life of Elbridge Gerry, with Contemporary Letters* (Boston, 1828), 175–176; Carter Braxton to Landon Carter, May 17, 1776, in *LMCC*, I, 454; John Adams, *Autobiography*, May 15, 1776, in *AP*, III, 34, 335; Christopher Gadsden to Samuel Adams, April 4, 1779, in Richard Walsh, ed., *The Writings of Christopher Gadsden* [*WCG*] (Columbia, 1966), 163.

[19] Willard, Secretary of the Province, to Bollan, Agent in London, December 31, 1754, in Albert B. Hart, *Commonwealth History of Massachusetts* (5 vols., New York, 1828), II, 461; Edward Rutledge to John Jay, June 29, 1776, in *LMCC*, I, 517; Carter Braxton to Landon Carter, April 14, 1776, *ibid.*, 420–423; Joseph Hewes to Samuel Johnston, July 28, 1776, *ibid.*, II, 28.

things is attempted . . . you may split & divide." Congress did not dissolve; it declared independence; and by late 1777 formulated a confederation. The need to meet a common enemy somewhat balanced the countervailing forces of state and sectional interests. But completion of the Confederation in Congress did not signal the end of either ideological or sectional disputes. Held together by little more than a common fear, the states and sections only reluctantly sacrificed their own interests. That they established a binding union was not so much a testament to their willing accord and self-sacrifice as it was a reflection of the realization that in the face of war even "an imperfect and somewhat unequal Confederacy . . . [was] better than none."[20] The sectionally divisive problems of revenue, commerce, and western lands, which were decided in Congress by October, 1777, were sidestepped by a compromise born of necessity; they were not solved. They remained troublesome throughout the Revolutionary Era: they slowed progress of the Articles of Confederation in Congress, stalled their ratification by the states, and caused major clashes in Congress in the 1780's and in the Philadelphia Convention in 1787.

Particularly irksome, and fundamental to the sectional conflict in the nation, was the clash between northern commercial and southern staple interests. The North, with its ships and seamen, poised itself to enter the world economy, while much of the South relied upon merchants, whether American or foreign, to carry its produce to market. The end of British rule gave northern merchants and southern land barons the promise of future wealth and power. At issue, from a sectional standpoint, was the kind of policies to pursue and the direction to be taken by the United States. At stake for the federalists was the intersectional concert and congeniality so vital to their strength. The New England merchants, who admittedly hoped to control the nation's carrying trade, wanted Congress to have a regulatory power over commerce.[21] The southerners so feared northern commercial superi-

[20] Patrick Henry to Richard Henry Lee, to John Adams, May 20, 1776, in William W. Henry, *Patrick Henry, Life, Correspondence & Speeches* (3 vols., New York, 1891), I, 410–413; Charles Carroll of Carrollton to Charles Carroll of Annapolis, June 26, 1777, in the Carroll Papers, Maryland Historical Society [MdHS].

[21] Joseph Plamer to John Adams, February 19, 1776, Cotton Tufts to John Adams, April 24, 1777, both in the Adams Mss. Trust, MHS. It is important to bear in mind that there were conflicts in the North between New England and Middle States farmers, manufacturers, and merchants, and in the South between planters and merchants.

ority that they refused to support the creation of a powerful navy in 1775 and complained that if New England privateering continued they would "become a devoted prey to their more formidable Eastern neighbours." They were worried that if Congress were given a power over commerce a commercial monopoly might easily "be given away by those, which have no staple, as the price of commercial privelage to them."[22]

Even after some major concessions allayed many of Edward Rutledge's fears, some southerners were still very concerned with the unfavorable sectional balance in Congress, by the prospect that Congress could set policy "contrary to the united opposition of Virginia, the two Carolinas, and Georgia: States possessing more than one half of the whole territory of the confederacy." Because of this unfavorable sectional balance, many southerners, throughout the period, looked to the western lands to insure a degree of sectional independence. They believed that the new states which would arise in the West could more than balance northern commercial superiority by shifting the sectional balance of power south. Thus they defended the right of individual states to determine the question of claims in the western lands, supported America's right to the free navigation of the Mississippi River, pushed for the early and easy admittance of new states into the union, and tried to prevent their vast unimproved holdings from being included in national revenue schemes. Although their own commercial interest dictated otherwise, most New Englanders in Congress acceded to southern demands; for example, Congress was not given jurisdiction over the western lands and state quotas for federal requisitions were to be decided by the value of improved lands only. While the New Englanders might have had little choice in 1776 and 1777 since they were so dependent upon southern support in Congress, there was still a fear that the South might become "too great and powerful So as to become dangerous to the rest."[23] These fundamental differences continued to

---

[22] William Hooper to Joseph Hewes, January 1, 1777, in *LMCC*, II, 200; Thomas Jefferson to John Adams, December 17, 1777, in Julian P. Boyd, ed., *The Papers of Thomas Jefferson* [*PTJ*] (Princeton, 1950 to date), II, 120.

[23] William H. Drayton, Speech to the South Carolina Assembly, January 20, 1778, in Hezekiah Niles, *Principles and Acts of the Revolution in America* (Baltimore, 1822), 363; John Adams to Abigail Adams, May 17, 1776, in the Adams Mss. Trust, MHS. See also Jensen, *The Articles of Confederation*, 145–160.

generate jealousies which set the sections at odds. Southerners still complained about the large bonuses New England gave to its soldiers, and northerners criticized the southerners for not sending enough troops north and for using more than their fair share of continental supplies. Philip Schuyler was removed from command of the Northern Army, owing, he thought, to his "not being a New England man in principle," and attacks on George Washington were ascribed to New England resentment.[24] The strain on the federalists of these unabated sectional tensions was compounded by a number of new developments that cost them their control of Congress.

By 1779 the war was going badly; finances were in a disarray; the army faced serious supply problems; and different men were seizing political offices in some of the states. In addition there was the effect of increased southern support for the nationalists and French entry into the war. Although most Americans had long desired French assistance, the conflict in Europe between Arthur Lee and Silas Deane and the subsequent Lee-Deane fight in Congress cooled the French toward the Lee-Adams Junto. This had grave repercussions for the federalists in light of close French connections with Robert Morris's Middle States politico-mercantile network. The federalists opposed the practices and feared the growing power of the Morris faction and the French. Despite the need for military and financial assistance, many federalists were reluctant to establish too close relations with the French: those "specious half friends . . . who played off our commissioners and ambassadors like puppets." Although the original model treaty passed in 1776 had been designed to prevent a political connection with the French, the exigencies of war, French designs, and the duplicitous behavior of Silas Deane and Benjamin Franklin produced an alliance with the French in early 1778 that was much more binding than the federalists wanted. During the discussion of Silas Deane's recall and peace demands in 1778 and 1779, the

[24] Gov. Trumbull to George Washington, February 21, 1777, in Jared Sparks, ed., *Correspondence of the American Revolution, Being Letters of Eminent Men to George Washington* (4 vols., Boston, 1853), I, 343–346; Nathan Hale and others to Congress, June 7, 1777, in the Papers of Continental Congress, Item 78, XI, ff. 169–170; Philip Schuyler to Gouverneur Morris, September 7, 1777, in Jared Sparks, *The Life of Gouverneur Morris, With Selections From His Correspondence* (3 vols., Boston, 1832), I, 143. See also Rossie, "Politics of Command," 395–421; Patterson, *Horatio Gates*, 200–250.

nationalists, with strong French support, tried to unseat the Lee-Adams Junto. The sectional overtones of the struggle were especially damaging to the federalists. Deane was supported by his Middle States allies and by many of the southern delegates, who were reluctant to support Arthur Lee and New England's war aims for fear of antagonizing the French. The French, in order to further their own interests, wanted to limit the federalists', more specifically New England's, influence in America's foreign affairs and, among other things, prevent the United States from gaining entry into the northern fisheries.[25]

The French interfered directly during Congress's formulation of peace demands. The New Englanders, especially those interested in furthering their section's commercial influence, argued that America needed a navy, that "the Source of Seamen is the Fishery" which was "as Valueable [sic] to America and more so to Old Massachusetts than the Tobacco Fields of the middle states or the Rice Swamps of the South." In an effort to throw New England's demands into disrepute the French, through Conrad Gérard, strongly implied that their continued support was contingent upon a renunciation of the fisheries demand. Not content with arguing the merits of the case the French accused the Lee-Adams Junto of favoring the British. It was even whispered in Congress that France could engineer a peace "unless G[reat] B[ritain] should be encouraged by a faction in Congress to continue the war, in hopes, that that faction may at last, on the condition of Britain's acknowledging our Independence, prevail on the States to enter into offensive & defensive treaties with her." Thus, in some southern eyes New England's obdurate stance on the peace demands was seen as threatening the French Alliance

[25] Henry Laurens to Gov. William Livingston, January 27, 1778, in David D. Wallace, *Life of Henry Laurens* (New York, 1915), 276–277. Neil Storch, "Congressional Politics and Diplomacy, 1775–1783" (doctoral dissertation, University of Wisconsin, 1969); William C. Stinchcombe, *The American Revolution and the French Alliance* (Syracuse, 1969). For an interesting comparison between the model treaty and the French Alliance see John Adams to James Warren, May 20, 1783, in the *Warren-Adams Letters*, II, 192–193. John R. Alden describes the conflict over peace demands as being solely a sectional fight. He ignores the pressures on the South, namely French and nationalist politicking, and instead concentrates on southern fears that New England would gain entry into the fisheries. Although this sectional jealousy was important, its real significance lies in the uses to which the nationalists and French put it. See Alden, *The First South*, 54–57.

and lengthening a pattern of warfare which was growing more and more desperate in the South. Most southerners had little difficulty making a choice between supporting New England and supporting the French. The fisheries were, in any event, not important to the southern states, and it was soon evident that Richard Henry Lee and Henry Laurens were viewed as "two Monsters . . . who pursue points in which the southern states have no interests."[26]

The friction between the sections did damage the federalists' fragile intersectional coalition. The right of entry into the fisheries was not included in America's peace demands, and in September, 1779, Arthur Lee was replaced as commissioner to Spain by a minister plenipotentiary, John Jay—the price New England had to pay for John Adams's appointment as peace commissioner. Although Adams went to Europe armed with instructions to negotiate a commercial treaty with the British, which he and others hoped would establish America's right of entry into the fisheries, congressional control had already slipped from the federalists' grasp. Before he left America Adams remarked that Congress "resemble[d] a picture in the gallery of the C[ount] de Vergennes." William Lee, writing from Germany, wondered if the only way to secure independence was to become "the Voluntary Slaves of France." He told his brother of plots against the United States from that quarter and warned that "Your Salvation in my opinion must arise from an Union more strict than ever with New England." Swept by the exigencies of war, most southerners ignored Lee's warning.[27]

By 1780 the same conditions which had precipitated Congress's departure from federalist foreign policies—the pressures of war,

[26] Samuel Adams to Samuel Cooper, April 29, 1779, in *LMCC*, IV, 185; Charles Carroll of Carrollton to Charles Carroll of Annapolis, May 8, 1779, in the Carroll Papers, MdHS; James Lovell to John Adams, June 19, 1779, in the Adams Mss. Trust, MHS. See James Fallon to Thomas Burke, April 1, 1779, in the Thomas Burke Papers, Southern Historical Collections, University of North Carolina Library.

[27] John Adams to Henry Laurens, October 25, 1779, in the Adams Mss. Trust, MHS; William Lee to Richard Henry Lee, October 14, 1779, in the Lee Family Papers, University of Virginia Library. For evidence of the increasing military pressure on the southern states see Christopher Gadsden to Samuel Adams, April 4, 1779, in *WCG*, 161–162; Richard Henry Lee to Arthur Lee, May 23, 1779, in *LMCC*, IV, 227–228.

a change in southern factional loyalties, an apparent lack of national co-ordination and congressional authority, and the fact that the Articles of Confederation had not been ratified—set the stage for a nationalist takeover. The nationalists increased their demands for strengthening Congress's power and some even called for a convention of the states to write a new constitution. Within a few months the worsening state of warfare in the South and increased factional strength in Congress obviated the nationalists' need for extracongressional reform. Furthermore, southern support for the nationalists continued until the victory at Yorktown turned the war in America's favor during late 1781. Earlier in that year, in the opening salvo of their movement to strengthen Congress, the nationalists revised America's peace commission. The federalists were as sure as ever that the French wanted to continue "the war, in order to weaken America as well as Great Britain, and thereby leave us at the end of it, as dependent as possible upon themselves." Yet, they were in no position to strike back or even defend themselves. Their warnings, even more so than in 1778, fell on deaf ears. In attacking the French, Robert Morris, and Benjamin Franklin, they simply opened themselves to renewed charges that they were enemies to the French alliance and uncommitted to any but their own interests. Congress gave the French final control of peace negotiations; added John Jay and Benjamin Franklin to the commission; and revoked John Adams's commercial commission.[28]

By this time southern support for the nationalists was even stronger than it had been in 1779. A league of neutral European nations, lately formed, reportedly intended to force a peace *uti possidetis* on the warring parties in America. The French used this threat to further bind southern interests to their own. With Great Britain chalking up impressive victories in the southern states, and even seizing Charles Town, there was a distinct possibility that an imposed peace would result in a loss to America of parts of North Carolina, South Carolina, and Georgia. The southern delegates were so afraid of this that they even agreed to cede partial control over the Mississippi River to Spain in return for

---

[28] George Mason to George Mason, Jr., 1781, in Niles, *Principles and Acts*, 305; *Secret Journals of the Acts and Proceedings of Congress* (4 vols., Boston, 1821), II, 224–232, 463; Davis, "Sections, Factions," 23–29, 282–290.

Spanish assistance in the war.[29] The revision of America's peace instructions had far greater implications than only a further disavowal of New England war aims. The nationalists hoped to eliminate the threat of a strong New England voice in national politics by circumscribing New England's postwar economic resources. Their strategy was unchanged since James Warren had charged in 1779 that Robert Morris and his followers, who "neither like the political principles, or manner of N[ew] England, . . . [wanted] to reduce their trade, and consequently their power and influence. What could more effectually do that than by ceding all right and claim to the fishery to get a Peace rather than see us Flourish." The New Englanders had no doubt, at any time during the Revolutionary Era, that their "weight in the Union" depended upon their "naval strength."[30]

The revision of the peace instructions did more than demonstrate nationalist strength. The same conditions which helped the nationalists circumscribe New England interests in the area of foreign policy also enabled them to work within the structure of the recently ratified Articles of Confederation with the prospect of expanding congressional authority. Although the powers which the nationalists wanted Congress to possess would have restructured the Confederation, they did not confine themselves solely to constitutional reform. They also tried to strengthen Congress by extending those powers which Congress already possessed. The nationalists defended their proposed reforms on utilitarian grounds and advocated a congressionally controlled impost to create a national revenue and to tighten the bands of union and

[29] "The Plain Politician," in the *Maryland Gazette* (Baltimore), March 3, 1780; "An Anti-Anglican," in the *Maryland Gazette*, April 14, 1780; John Rutledge to South Carolina delegates, May 24, December 8, 1780, in *South Carolina Historical and Genealogical Magazine* (1916, 1917), XVII, 133, XVIII, 48; James Madison to Joseph Jones, November 25, 1780, in William T. Hutchinson et al., eds., *The Papers of James Madison* [*PJM*] (Chicago, 1962 to date), II, 702–704. Alden cites the conflict over the navigation of the Mississippi River as extending from 1779–1789. However, until well after 1783 many New Englanders, in and out of Congress, strongly supported America's right to the navigation. The move to cede control over the Mississippi was a southern reaction to war pressures, not a New England disavowal of southern interests This makes the Mississippi conflict in 1786 all the more important, because it clearly demonstrates the power of postwar sectional jealousies. See Alden, *The First South*, 54–57.

[30] James Warren to John Adams, June 13, 1779, in the Adams Mss. Trust, MHS; Stephen Higginson to Elbridge Gerry, April 28, 1784, in Miscellany, New-York Historical Society [NYHS].

cement their own factional superiority. They created and manned new executive posts with which they hoped to centralize and extend their own and congressional influence. Although many men in Congress and in the states supported reforms designed, in part, to bring about a modicum of congressional efficiency and authority, giving Congress, for example, an impost power, they were most unwilling to substantively revise the Articles of Confederation.[31]

The nationalists' meteoric rise to power was too dependent upon wartime exigency. Once the pressure of war began to ease, they lost the key to their success. America's victory at Yorktown, which lessened the threat of British victory or an imposed peace and eased the air of impending doom, subverted the nationalist movement. The abyss into which the United States had apparently fallen in 1779, which had vitalized the nationalist movement and accounted for much of its early success, seemed to have a bottom.

The collapse of the nationalist movement was drawing near in late 1782 when Rhode Island and Virginia federalists refused to ratify the impost amendment. Faced with the apparent demise of their movement, some nationalists schemed to strengthen Congress by using the public creditors and the Continental army stationed at Newburgh, New York, to press for the formulation of a second impost, designed, as had been the first, to build a revenue base upon which to extend both congressional and their own influence.[32] However, their gamble to force reform before peace not only failed, but also precipitated a storm of antinationalist sentiment. The federalists were very successful in 1783 and early 1784 in combatting and, in fact, stopping the nationalist threat. To a certain extent the nationalists replaced the British in binding northern and southern federalists against a common enemy. David Howell, for example, remarked that his "good friends Mr. A. Lee & Col. Bland received me with a smile [in Congress] & cooperate in every measure for maintaining the Sovereignty of the

[31] There were amendments proposed on May 2, August 22, and October 3, 1781. Sees Worthington Chauncy Ford et al., eds., *The Journals of the Continental Congress, 1774–1789* [*JCC*] (34 vols., Washington, 1904–1937), XIX, 236, XXI, 894–896; Allan Nevins, *The American States During and After the Revolution, 1775–1789* (New York, 1924), 629.

[32] Richard H. Kohn, "The Inside History of the Newburgh Conspiracy: America and the Coup d'Etat," in *WMQ*, 3rd Ser., 27 (1970); Davis, "Sections, Factions," 57–97.

Individual States." Yet the federalists still faced a dilemma. If they failed to reform the Articles of Confederation to meet the problems which the nation faced in the postwar years, the nationalists could continue to strive for their own brand of reform; if they did reform the Articles of Confederation, they ran the risk of "overleap[ing] the fences established by the Confederation to secure the liberties of the respective States."[33]

This ideological question was only part of the problem. The Confederation's stability depended as much upon the states supporting each other as their supporting Congress. In this regard interstate jealousy and squabbling was as potentially dangerous to the Confederation as were the nationalists, because there still were not workable solutions to the many sectionally divisive problems facing the nation. Northern and southern federalists' co-operation in attacking the nationalists did not mean that they were less committed to or less concerned about their own antithetical interests. On the contrary, northern and southern federalists did not exhibit a similar sense of accord and co-operation on those issues which were related not to the question of political balance in the constitutional system, but to the question of sectional balance. Although the end of the war provided the federalists with the opportunity to attack the nationalists and the French and reclaim control of the nation, it also produced a climate conducive to renewed conflicts of interest. With national defense no longer pressing the states and sections together, the old maladies began to rise slowly to the surface in an even more virulent form than in 1776 and 1777. In the end it was this conflict which prevented solutions to the many problems facing the nation in the postwar era. The failure to reform the Articles of Confederation, in turn, resulted in continued nationalist charges that the nation's problems were caused by an ineffective and powerless central government. At the same time that they were winning major victories against the nationalists, the federalists were being battered by the almost uncontrollable forces of sectional conflict.

For example, in 1783 when William Gordon of Massachusetts opposed the calling of a convention of the states to revise the Articles of Confederation because "a better band of Union than

---

[33] David Howell to Nicholas Brown, July 30, 1783, in the Brown Papers, John Carter Brown Library; Richard Henry Lee to William Whipple, July 1, 1783, in the William Whipple Papers, Force Transcripts, Library of Congress [LC].

the present I despair of seeing, considering the opposite cases of the people in the different states," he was not simply defending federalist ideology. Echoing the fears of 1775 and 1776, Gordon had told John Adams in September, 1782, that the United States had better "remain a collection of Republics, and not become an Empire," for

> if America becomes an Empire, the seat of government will be to the southward, and the Northern States will be insignificant provinces. Empire will suit the southern gentry; they are habituated to despotism by being the sovereigns of slaves: and it is only accident and interest that had made the body of them the temporary sons of liberty. The New Englanders should be resolute in retaining the Sovereignty of the several states, and should look out in time against all distant encroachments.[34]

The influence of this sort of sectional thinking was nowhere better evident than in the two-year struggle over the location of a capital city.

In mid-June, 1783, when soldiers from the Pennsylvania Line who were demanding a redress of grievances surrounded the Pennsylvania State House, Congress left Philadelphia. The removal increased the importance of the previously postponed debates on the location of a permanent residence for Congress. It was widely acknowledged that the residence would benefit the state in which it was situated and would also shift the sectional balance in the nation. Moreover, the location was a vital part of federalist efforts to diminish the nationalists' influence. They believed that there was a connection between the nationalists' influence upon Congress and the residence in Robert Morris's home city.[35]

---

[34] William Gordon to George Washington, August 13, 1783, and to John Adams, September 7, 1782, in "Letters of Reverend William Gordon, Historian of the American Revolution, 1770–1799," Massachusetts Historical Society *Proceedings*, 63 (1931), 499, 469. Henderson's discussion of post-1783 politics concentrates on what he calls the southern ascendency. He does not consider the implications of the antinationalist movement which accounted for the brief but significant re-emergence of the Lee-Adams Junto on such issues as opposition to the Society of the Cincinnati, the impost, and support for the creation of a Board of Treasury. He also does not investigate the dual-residence and the early debates on commerce, which were distinctly antinationalist. The spectacular but momentary rise of federalist fortunes makes the sectional conflict after 1784 even more dramatic. See Henderson, "The Structure of Politics," 186–187; Henderson, *Party Politics*, 350–430.

[35] William Gordon to Arthur Lee, April 2, 1783, Mass. Hist. Soc. *Proc.* (1931), 489–490; Arthur Lee to Francis Dana, July 6, 1782, in *LMCC*, VI, 379; Stephen Higginson

In their determination to keep Congress out of Philadelphia the New England federalists had to overcome a strong southern aversion to a northern site. The southerners wanted to balance northern commercial and numerical superiority with a southern capital. They believed that even a temporary residence in the North would defeat that aim and would make "a removal to a Southern position more difficult, than it would be from Philada [*sic*]." William Grayson of Virginia even argued that the New Englanders were attacking the nationalists so as "to dupe the Southern States by making Phila.ᵃ [*sic*] a bug-bear and so pull you further *North*." However, in late October, 1783, with New Jersey, Pennsylvania, and Maryland absent from Congress, the New England states rushed through a complex residence plan which provided Congress with two temporary and two permanent locations: the former at Trenton and Annapolis and the latter on the Delaware and the Potomac.[36]

Although the dual-residence compromise was an important federalist victory in terms of limiting nationalist influence in the immediate postwar years, too much cannot be made of its effect on intersectional relations. The term compromise may even be a misnomer, because New England and the South resolved nothing. The New Englanders, by their own admission, had no other alternative but to give the South a share in the federal residence in order "to prevent the return of Congress to Philadelphia, for a temporary residence." They were convinced that if Congress were to return to Philadelphia, a capital city would never be constructed, and Congress would never again make its escape from the nationalists' power center. Although Elbridge Gerry proposed the dual-residence resolves and was generally considered to be the father of the project, it was the southerners who were in the position to set terms. Their obvious willingness to return to Philadelphia in preference to a northern residence forced the New Englanders to make concessions—the South gave up nothing and stood to gain a lot. The North Carolina delegates optimistically reported that having gotten "Congress to the Southward for Six

---

to Elbridge Gerry, August 5, 1783, in *LMCC*, VII, 252. See also Varnum L. Collins, *The Continental Congress at Princeton* (Princeton, 1908).

[36] James Madison to Edmund Randolph, July 28, 1783, in *PJM*, VII, 263; William Grayson to _____, September 11, 1783, in The Etting Collection, Members of Old Congress, Historical Society of Pennsylvania; *JCC*, XXV, 654–655, 667–668, 706–715.

Months . . . some future Congress will prevent their return to this side [i.e. north] of the Waters of the Chesapeak."[37]

Southerners believed that the future lay with them, and their behavior during the whole of the residence issue and during the later Confederation Period attested to this. Although they did not have the votes and ability to set policy, they followed a strategy of obstructionism in relation to those matters which, from their viewpoint, could be better solved when their own and not northern interests predominated. The southerners were certain that the great migration to the Trans-Allegheny region in the 1770's and 1780's was inexorably tilting the weight of population and influence toward them. "A TRUE AMERICAN" noted that "it must be obvious to everyone, that emigration from abroad prevails much more in the Southern States than those of the eastward, especially in the back settlements; no one can therefore falsely venture to predict, which part of the Continent will be most consequential [in] a century." It was, moreover, easy to foresee a southern superiority much sooner than that. The southerners wanted a residence chosen when they could insure its location in the South, as Jefferson said in late 1783, to "cement us to our Western Friends when they shall be formed into separate states."[38]

The unstable foundation upon which the dual-residence solution rested was not lost on some observers. Edward Bancroft, the sagacious British agent, predicted that not only would the dual-

[37] Abiel Foster to Meshech Weare, October 23, 1783, in *LMCC*, VII, 348; North Carolina delegates to Gov. Martin, October 24, 1783, *ibid.*, 353–354. Alden's discussion of the dual-residence compromise falls short of a complete understanding of the interests at play. He does not consider the profound influence of the ideological conflict which disposed the New Englanders to agree to a half-time southern capital, and he neglects to work the capital fight of 1784 and 1785 into the broader context of sectional politics. See Alden, *The First South*, 66–69. H. James Henderson is equally vague about the meaning of the capital fight. Despite his intention to demonstrate the sectional nature of partisan politics in Congress, he glosses over the capital fight and the rich implications (both in terms of antinationalism and sectionalism) of the dual-residence compromise—despite an abundance of roll calls. See Henderson, *Party Politics*, 339–343.

[38] "A TRUE AMERICAN," in the *Baltimore Advertiser*, July 29, 1783; Thomas Jefferson to George Rogers Clark, December 4, 1783, in *PTJ*, VI, 371; Davis, "Sections, Factions," 120–159. Although Henderson maintains that from 1784 to 1787 the "southern delegates . . . achieved a level of cohesion sufficient to lead in the shaping of policy," the fact remains that the southern delegates did not so much set policy as prevent northern, and in most instances, majority policies from being implemented. See Henderson, "The Structure of Politics," 174.

residence compromise quickly disintegrate, but that the Union would surely dissolve and it was only a "question whether [to] have thirteen *separate* States in *alliance* or whether the New England, the middle & the Southern States will form three new Confederations." William Gordon, certainly not motivated by Bancroft's desire to see the Union collapse, was no less cheerless in his assertion that the Union "by not suiting the Northern climate however well adapted for the southern will after a time bring on fresh wars and fighting among ourselves, and make the whole one great [nation], or break us into smaller ones, instead of remaining separate states, united by a Confederation, under a Congress freely chosen by the powers of each state."[39] These dire predictions were balanced by a more optimistic though less realistic view. Stephen Higginson, for one, did not believe that sectional conflict was systemic. He instead argued that the nationalists had tried to take over the nation by keeping up "a jealousy between the Eastern and Southern States . . . calculated to subjugate both." He had every confidence that because they "now understand the Views of the Junto . . . in future the southern & eastern states will in general be united." Higginson's conspiratorial view of the nature of sectional conflict continued even in the face of increasing sectional tensions.

The nationalists might have sown some seeds of distrust, but increased sectional conflict had nothing to do with their behavior. By early 1784 the issues of commerce and western lands, which were as closely related to sectional dominance as was the location of a capital city, began to rupture the federalists' intersectional coalition in a revival of the "old partialities."[40] The continuing struggle over the location of a capital city was as much an effect as a cause of this sectional conflict.

In 1784 New England backed out of the dual-residence compromise and, with support from New York, New Jersey, and at times Pennsylvania, pushed Congress to locate in New York City and to

[39] Edward Bancroft to _____, November 8, 1783, in Public Record Office, Foreign Office 4, Vol. 3; William Gordon to John Adams, January 7, 1784, in the Adams Mss. Trust, MHS.

[40] Stephen Higginson to Elbridge Gerry, December/January, 1783–1784, in the Russell W. Knight Collection, MHS; Silas Deane to Beaumarchais, April 2, 1784, in *The Deane Papers,* New-York Historical Society *Collections,* 19–23 (1886–1890), V, 287.

appropriate $100,000 for the erection of a capital city on the Delaware. The southern states vociferously objected, and in mid-1785 William Grayson successfully engineered a revocation of the capital appropriation. The question of a permanent residence for Congress was not settled until the creation of another national government. Thus southern obstruction was successful in the long run; it was equally successful in blocking commercial reform of the Articles of Confederation.

The reluctance of foreign nations—and especially Great Britain—to enter into commercial treaties with the United States, led northern merchants to demand that Congress be given broader powers to regulate American commerce. Initially northern and southern federalists alike looked to commercial accord with Great Britain as another means to weaken nationalist and French influence. Henry Laurens, Ralph Izard, and the Lees agreed with New Englanders like John Adams in 1783 that the failure to establish an equitable Anglo-American trade resulted as much from earlier nationalist and French machinations, like revoking the commercial commission in 1781, as it did from America's overly anxious reception of British goods and merchants. There were other southerners, who cannot be counted in federalist ranks, who also supported the merchants' later argument that foreign nations could not be expected to negotiate with the United States until Congress was given the authority to compel state obedience to the stipulations in commercial treaties. These men, including James Monroe, Thomas Jefferson, George Washington, and James Madison, were partially motivated by their interest in navigating the Potomac River. Their intention to establish their own control over a vibrant Potomac River Valley commerce made them most amenable to, and in fact desirous of, uplifting the nation's sagging economy.

Many other southerners still feared, as they had in 1776, that a centralization of the American economy would destroy the South's ability "to buy cheap & sell at profitable rates." They wanted all merchants, whether American or foreign, to compete for their marketable goods, and they believed that giving Congress more authority over commerce would be handing control of the southern economy over to northern merchants. There was even a fear that because the northern states possessed much of the "paper money and other continental securities . . . [they] might be tempted by their naval superiority to pay themselves out of the rich commerce of the Southern States." Within a short time these sorts of fears polarized northern and southern federalists. Although the latter sympathized with the plight of the northern merchants, they were not about to sacrifice their own interests. For them the problem of America's commerce remained British recalcitrance and not a defect in the Articles of Confederation. By mid-1784 even Stephen Higginson was drawn to the inevitable conclusion that only if the southern states were as dependent upon the British trade as were the New England states would there be "less difficulty in settling commercial treaties and very much less ground to apprehend a disunion of the States."[41]

The differences between the sections were too great to be overcome even in the face of a severe commercial depression and continued foreign insults. A proposed embargo power for Congress, passed on April 30, 1784, was never accepted by the states. This act, limited to a fifteen-year term, called for the states to give Congress the power "to prohibit any foreign goods from being imported into any of the United States, except in vessels belonging to or navigated by citizens of the United States or the subjects of foreign powers with whom the United States may have treaties of commerce." Even before it became evident that this act would not pass, the northern merchants began calling for more comprehensive reform. This proposal, the commerce amendment of March 28, 1785, died on the floor of Congress. It was to give Congress the power to regulate "the trade of the United States, as well with foreign Nations, as with each other."[42]

Because of the rather widespread belief that "eight states were of a particular interest whose business it would be to combine and shackle and fetter the others," a few southerners were willing to accede to commercial reform if eleven and not the usual nine states were required to set policy. In this way they likely would have been able to prevent those eight states from picking up the additional support of Baltimore and Charlestown merchants to complete their domination. Some southerners refused to consider

---

[41] James Madison to Edmund Randolph, May [20], 1783, in *PJM*, VII, 59–60; "THE NORTH AMERICAN, No. 1," in the *Pennsylvania Journal* (Philadelphia), September 17, 1783; Stephen Higginson to Elbridge Gerry, April 28, 1784, in *Miscellany*, NYHS.

[42] *JCC*, XXVI, 322, XXVIII, 201–205.

any reform, and still others believed that a navigation act, limited in scope and to operate only for a given number of years, would stabilize the economy without running the risk of a northern monopoly. This alternative was, however, unacceptable to the northern merchants, who reportedly wanted "something more lasting." This the South would not accept. Richard Henry Lee, leading the antireform southern delegates, argued, as he might not have in 1776, that "giving Congress a power to legislate over the trade of the Union would be dangerous in the extreme to the 5 Southern or Staple States, whose want of Ships and Seamen would expose their freightage & their produce to a most pernicious and destructive monopoly." If Congress were given a power to regulate trade, the South would, Lee feared, "be at the Mercy of our East & North."[43]

Southern refusal to support commercial reform set off a chain of events which rocked the Confederation. In an effort to secure a commerce amendment the Massachusetts General Court in late June, 1785, instructed its delegates in Congress to recommend the calling of a convention of states to revise the Articles of Confederation. But there was no assurance that constitutional reform would take only that direction. The Massachusetts delegates in Congress—Rufus King, Elbridge Gerry, and Samuel Holten—refused to obey their instructions, because they feared that a convention would "produce thro-out the Union, an exertion of the friends of Aristocracy, to send Members who would promote a change of Government." The delegates' objections to calling a convention were much more complex than the obvious implications to the nationalist-federalist conflict. Their fear of a major revision of the Articles of Confederation was equally, if not primarily, determined by sectional fears, and their analysis of the situation and the possible dangers was remarkably similar to William Gordon's warning in 1782 that the New England states would be the principal sufferers if the Confederation were centralized. The fear that the nationalists and the southerners could and would unite against New England was not new either in 1782

---

[43] James Monroe to James Madison, July 26, 1785, in *LMCC*, VIII, 171; Richard Henry Lee to James Madison, August 11, 1785, in the Burnett Collection, Box 10, LC. See also William Grayson to George Washington, July 25, 1785, in the Washington Papers, LC.

or 1785. It was simply more deeply felt in light of the ever-increasing sectional tensions.[44]

The commerce fight widened the rift between the sections to such a degree that it even brought into question the very existence of the union. Silas Deane predicted that the lack of accord in commercial goals would soon separate "the Northern from the Southern States." Indeed, an agitated Rufus King suggested that in the event the southern states continued to oppose giving Congress commercial powers the eight northern states were "*competent* to form, & in the event must form, a sub-confederation." King's purpose was not necessarily directed toward disunion. He believed that the southern states would accede to commercial reform, if they found "a decided disposition in the Eastern States to combine for their own security."[45]

Although the threat of subconfederation was probably all that King and some other New Englanders had in mind, the suggestion of such a radical alternative evidenced the temperature to which sectional animosity was rising. While subconfederation might not have been really feasible, it had been discussed at various times since 1775. The talk and number of proposals increased as sectional conflict intensified in 1786 and 1787. It has been asserted that these proposals came from future supporters of the Constitution of 1787, the men who came to be known as Federalists.

Not all political behavior in the 1770's and 1780's can be traced to the particlar ideologies of the two major factions. It is even

[44] Massachusetts delegates to the Legislature, September 3, 1785, in the Burnett Collection, Box 10, LC. Henderson uses the delegates' refusal to support a convention as evidence that King, Gerry, and Holten opposed the movement led by Monroe and Jefferson to give Congress greater commerce powers. This is misleading. Certainly Monroe and Jefferson, until 1786, supported commercial reform, but they followed a northern lead; once the Mississippi issue clarified the sectional positions, they withdrew their support. Monroe, in fact, became an arch opponent of New England policies. Henderson's earlier statement that the Massachusetts delegation in 1778 "differed little from 1786" ignores the intricacies of the ideological and sectional facets of the commerce fight and exemplifies the degree to which a reliance on roll-call votes can cloud our understanding of Revolutionary politics. See Henderson, "The Structure of Politics," 189, 170; Henderson, *Party Politics*, 363–366.

[45] "OBSERVATIONS ON A NAVIGABLE CANAL FROM LAKE CHAMPLAIN TO THE ST. LAWRENCE, submitted to Lord Dorchester by Silas Deane," October 25, 1785, in N.Y. Hist. Soc. *Colls.* (1890), 465; Rufus King to John Adams, November 2, 1785, in Charles R. King, *The Life and Correspondence of Rufus King* (6 vols., New York, 1894–1900), I, 113; to Caleb Davis, November 3, in the Caleb Davis Papers, Vol. 12b, MHS.

more invalid to attempt to describe political behavior before 1787 in terms of post-1787 behavior. Disunion sentiments were primarily motivated by the frustration which came out of the attempt to operate a polarized Congress in a sectionally torn nation. The apparent inability and unwillingness of the delegates to disregard their various sectional interests and solve some pressing problems reinforced the long-standing doubt that a union made up of such varied and distinct sectional interests could long endure. Although it is difficult to explain the role of sectional pressures in the politics of a nation which shortly created a powerful national government, the disunion proposals and the ideas which produced them have an important place in the closing years of the Confederation, for sectional conflict was one of the primary reasons for the Confederation's demise.

The New Englanders, from whom many of the subconfederation proposals emanated, were opponents of a strong central government driven by powerful sectional commitments and heightened sectional fears. Looking down upon the southerners as men whose "minds and constitutions want the energy and habit of attention and perseverance of the North States" and who would not agree to necessary commercial reforms, subconfederation seemed to some New Englanders a means to get rid of their opponents or at least to scare them. Continued southern recalcitrance in early 1786 pushed Benjamin Lincoln toward the conclusion that the union would be more easily governed and more assured of permanence if "the United States extend[ed] from east to west, instead of their standing, as they now do from North to South."[46] With almost nothing holding the sections together the situation

[46] Nathan Dane to Edward Pulling, January 8, 1786, in the Burnett Collection, Box 11, LC; Benjamin Lincoln to Rufus King, February 11, 1786, in King, *Life and Correspondence*, I, 118. Jackson T. Main's attempt to demonstrate that Federalists rather than Antifederalsists advocated disunion seems to be beside the point. His desire to correlate disunion sentiments with a view of the ideological conflicts during the Revolutionary era has little relation to the reasons why subconfederation was suggested. Certainly King, Lincoln, and some of the others who proposed disunion were strong supporters of the Constitution, but before 1787 they were equally strong defenders of the Confederation. Our understanding of the Confederation Period has often been weakened by attempts to bridge the gap between 1786 and 1788. Because the later constitutional period, like the period when the Articles of Confederation were being written, was a special and even an atypical time which caused sectional conflict to fade to the background, it is much more useful to compare the sectional conflicts in the Confederation Congress to the wheeling and dealing in the First Federal Congress. See Main, *The Antifederalists*, 283–284.

got progressively worse. Although disunion was never attempted, in 1786 the South was threatened by a possible sectional dismemberment which would have led to a perpetual second-class status in the nation.

In early 1786 the northern delegates in Congress developed a strategy, or were presented with an opportunity, to secure greater commercial power for Congress, a plan which further worsened intersectional relations. Massachusetts and New York, with the support of five other northern states, tried to give Congress de facto authority over commerce by entering into a commercial treaty with Spain. They also sought to insure their own sectional needs by agreeing with Spanish demands that in exchange for a treaty the United States give up the use of the Mississippi River. The conflict over the navigation of the Mississippi was really a contest for the future control of America. Closure threatened the long-standing southern hope that western expansion would eventually give them control of the nation. William Grayson had argued in April, 1785, that some northerners were "apprehensive of the consequences which may result from the new states taking their positions in the confederacy. They perhaps wish that this event may be delayed as long as possible." Although the Land Ordinances of 1784 and 1785 seemed to have fulfilled southern expectations regarding western expansion, the northerners had no desire to foster a pattern of expansion which might give control of the nation to the South.

By the summer of 1786 James Monroe, no longer the defender of northern interests he had been in 1785, reported that the northern desire to make it a condition that states entering the union have "one 13th of the free inhabitants of the U.S. . . . evinced plainly the policy of these men to be to keep them out of the confederacy." He also believed that the intended closure of the Mississippi River was designed to "throw the weight of population eastwards and keep it there. . . . In short, it is a system of policy which has for its object the keeping the weight of govt. and population in this quarter." Guillaume Otto, the French foreign minister and a keen observer of the American scene, became convinced that "this discussion will cause a great coolness between the two parties, and may be the germ of a future separation of the southern states."[47]

[47] William Grayson to George Washington, April 15, 1785, in the Burnett Collec-

Although Otto's observation proved inaccurate, sectional conflict arising out of the Mississippi controversy split the federalists as never before and ended their efforts to revise the Articles of Confederation. In response to Charles Pinckney's motion on May 3, 1786, Congress created a "Grand Committee on Federal Powers" to formulate amendments to the Articles of Confederation. Sectional politics played a dramatic role in deciding the question. Late in May, a few days before the Mississippi issue reached the floor of Congress, William Grayson sent an enlightening, and often misinterpreted, letter to James Madison. He asserted that proper amendments would never be agreed upon because "the eastern people mean nothing more than to carry the commercial point." He also maintained that "Mr. Pinckney, who brought forward the motion, will be astounded when he meets with a proposition to prevent the states from importing any more of the seed of Cain . . . [and New York and Pennsylvania would] feel themselves indisposed when they hear it proposed that it shall become a compact that the sessions [of Congress] shall always be held in the centre of the empire [i.e. near the Potomac]." Thus, Grayson's understanding of conflicting sectional interests, and not, as many historians have asserted, only ideological objections, convinced him that there could not be "a reformation on proper principles."[48]

In early August, after the Mississippi issue reached the floor of Congress, the Grand Committee proposed seven amendments to the Articles of Confederation. Among them were recommendations for more commerce power, a national revenue, and coercive sanctions. In reaction the southerners made it clear that if the Mississippi River were "given up to obtain a trivial commercial advantage for their brethren in the East," they would not agree to any amendments no matter how vital to the Confederation. In the last week of August seven northern states consistently voted against five southern states to give John Jay the authority to relinquish America's use of the Mississippi River. The report of the

---

tion, Box 10, LC; James Monroe to Thomas Jefferson, July 16, 1786, in *PTJ*, X, 143; to Patrick Henry, August 12, 1786, in *LMCC*, VIII, 424–425; Guillaume Otto to Vergennes, September 10, 1786, in Bancroft, *Formation of the Constitution*, II, 391.

[48] Thomas Rodney's *Diary*, May 3, 1786, in *LMCC*, VIII, 350; William Grayson to James Madison, May 28, 1786, in the Burnett Collection, Box 11, LC.

Grand Committee was, in the interim, tabled. There it remained for the duration of the Confederation.[49]

The defeat of the amendment proposals and, more importantly, the reason for their defeat had a dramatic impact on the political scene. With Congress closed as an avenue for constitutional reform the extracongressional alternative—a convention of the states—which many nationalists had so long supported seemed the only way left to reform the Articles of Confederation. Moreover, the sectionally stalemated Congress strengthened the nationalists' hand by demonstrating anew Congress's impotence and bankruptcy. On another level the rigidly polarized Congress filled many southerners with fear and then rage that soon resulted in a major sectional shift which further aided the nationalists. During the Mississippi controversy James Monroe learned about a plan that was afoot for "a dismemberment of the states east of the Hudson from the union." Benjamin Rush also reported a secret proposal to form "an Eastern, Middle, and Southern Confederacy."[50] Whether or not the information was reliable, Monroe thought that the South had to take precautions. He advised James Madison, at the time en route to the Annapolis Convention, that the southern states should "act with great circumspection and to be prepar'd for every possible event—to stand well with the Middle States especially." They did just that. At the Annapolis Convention, called by Virginia in early 1786 to suggest commercial reforms, delegates from five southern and middle states asked for a convention of the states to revise the Articles of Confederation.[51]

The New Englanders, with some few exceptions, did not support the plea for a general convention. They had questioned

[49] *JCC*, XXXI, 494–501; William Grayson, August 16, 18, 1786, Charles Thomson, *Minutes of Proceedings*, in *LMCC*, VIII, 427-428, 438; *Secret Journals*, IV, 81–127; Timothy Bloodworth to Gov. Caswell, August 28, 1786, in *LMCC*, VIII, 455.

[50] James Monroe to Patrick Henry, August 12, 1786, in *LMCC*, VIII, 242; to Thomas Jefferson, August 19, 1786, in *PTJ*, X, 277; to James Madison, September 3, 1786, in *LMCC*, VIII, 461; Benjamin Rush to Richard Price, October 27, 1786, in Lyman H. Butterfield, ed., *Letters of Benjamin Rush* (2 vols., Princeton, 1951), I, 408.

[51] James Monroe to James Madison, September 12, 1786, in the Burnett Collection, Box 11, LC. Despite the dramatic impact of the Annapolis convention on the political scene, little work has been done concerning the background to the meeting or the activity at Annapolis. See Davis, "Sections, Factions," 312–347.

Virginia's motivations for wanting the Annapolis Convention even before it met; and they were still scared that the nationalists could easily secure southern support to restructure the Confederation to their own disadvantage. By this time the New Englanders had far broader reasons for fearing an independent convention than they had had in 1785.[52] It has often been asserted that the civil disturbances in 1786, especially Shays's Rebellion in Massachusetts, produced a climate favorable to a general convention and to a major revision of the Articles of Confederation. Although it is true that the disturbances rocked many federalists' faith in the Confederation, the initial anxiety quickly passed, and they were controlled by the states which still feared "the growing power of Congress." Federalist ideology doubtless accounted for some of that dread in early 1787, but the question of sectional equilibrium is equally important in explaining New England's reluctance to tamper with the Confederation.

By early 1787 the sectional balance in Congress had, once again, shifted as the southerners succeeded in detaching New Jersey and Republican-controlled Pennsylvania from the seven state pro-occlusion bloc of 1786. Rufus King, for example, noted that both those states were now under "a *southern influence.*" The attempt to overturn John Jay's pro-occlusion instructions was not in itself important, because Jay had already realized that the southern states would never ratify a Spanish treaty and had decided to forego further negotiations. However, the re-emergence of the sectional configuration which had fueled the nationalist movement threatened New England. Observing the fact that every state south of New York had appointed delegates to the Philadelphia Convention, King thought it wise for Massachusetts to attend the convention "from an Idea of prudence, or for the purpose of watching, than from any expectation, that much Good will come from it."[53] Within two months King was referring to the reappearance of "the injurious influence of 1783" as the southern states

---

[52] Rufus King to Jonathan Jackson, June 11, 1786, in *LMCC*, VIII, 389; Stephen Higginson to John Adams, July, 1786, in J. Franklin Jameson, ed., *Letters of Stephen Higginson, 1783–1804*, American Historical Association *Annual Report*, 1 (1896), 734; Theodore Sedgwick to Caleb Strong, August 6, 1786, in *LMCC*, VIII, 415. Sedgwick even advocated subconfederation.

[53] *Pennsylvania Journal*, Supplement, March 14, 1787; Rufus King to Elbridge Gerry, February 18, 1787, in *LMCC*, VIII, 541.

tried to get Congress to return to Philadelphia, as they said, "to pay Sundry Stat[es] their incivility which lay east of the North."[54] Although it has been ignored in terms of its relationship to the steps which led to the Philadelphia Convention, this spring capital fight put New England on the defensive and more than balanced the anxiety-generated procentralist reaction which resulted from the civil disturbances.

It is even possible that nothing would have happened in Philadelphia had not many New Englanders' (and probably most federalists' continued) faith in the Articles of Confederation been shattered when a final chapter of Shays's Rebellion was written in the Massachusetts state election in the late spring of 1787. In the largest voter turnout of the 1780's a reform faction headed by John Hancock swept into power. Citizens, in and out of Massachusetts, expected that because the "Revolution" changed the administration that "Measures will be changed also so far as to accord with the Vox Populia."[55] It was this political takeover, only weeks before the Philadelphia Convention met, which convinced many eastern leaders, among them some previously strong defenders of the Articles of Confederation, that their control of state governments was not strong enough to protect them from the people. Elbridge Gerry, a committed federalist and later an opponent of the Constitution, went to Philadelphia convinced that "unless a system of government is adopted by compact, force, I expect, will plant the standard; for such an anarchy as now exists cannot last long." George Mason of Virginia, also a future opponent, wrote that "the expectation and hopes of all the union centre in this convention. God grant that we may be able to concert effectual means of preserving our country from the evils which threaten us."[56]

Despite the seriousness of the situation, sectional interests were still very much in evidence. The delegates to the Philadelphia Convention fought over such old issues as commerce and

[54] Rufus King to Elbridge Gerry, April 10, 1787, in the Rufus King Papers, NYHS; William Blount to John Gray Blount, April 18, 1787, in *LMCC*, VIII, 585.

[55] Theodore Foster to Dwight Foster, April 6, 1787, in the Dwight Foster Papers, MHS. For the "Revolution of 1787" see Van Beck Hall, *Politics Without Parties: Massachusetts, 1780–1791* (Pittsburgh, 1972), 227–256. Hall, however, has ignored the effect of the spring capital fight on the eastern leaders.

[56] Elbridge Gerry to James Monroe, June 11, 1787, in Bancroft, *Formation of the Constitution*, II, 428; George Mason to George Mason, Jr., May 20, 1787, *ibid.*, 421.

revenue apportionment. There were even some suggestions that the nation would be better off if the delegates "distribute[d] the States into three Republics," rather than trying to amend the Articles of Confederation or erecting "one general government." There was also some feeling that if the convention was unable to accomplish anything then two or perhaps three confederacies should be established.[57] But the delegates had a more compelling concern than their special interests. The erosion of governmental authority aided the nationalists by placing the elite—federalist and nationalist, northern and southern—in essentially the same position it had been in in 1776. Although many federalists would be outraged by what happened at Philadelphia, by the creation of a constitution which "had few federal features, [and] is rather a system of national government," they had a difficult choice to make. As Elbridge Gerry noted, if the people adopted the Constitution "their liberties may be lost; or, should they reject it altogether, anarchy may ensue." The Constitution's opponents were hampered because they had previously supported constitutional reform. A warning James Madison had given to James Monroe with respect to southern concessions during the Mississippi controversy had, as it turned out, prophetic meaning for the federalists: they too had "to combat under the disadvantage of having foresaken . . . [the] first ground." The nationalists had been describing the failings of the Confederation ever since 1780, and by 1787 their arguments had been, in a sense, empirically validated. The Constitution's opponents, trapped by their own espousal of the need for more effective central government, could only react awkwardly and defensively to the nationalists. They could not retreat, as they previously had, to the security of the Articles of Confederation.[58]

Even more important than the nation's general malaise were

[57] "THOUGHTS for the DELEGATES to the CONVENTION . . .," by "CAUTION," from a late New York Paper, in the Connecticut Courant (Hartford), April 16, 1787; Temple to Marquis Carmarthen, April 5, 1787, in Bancroft, Formation of the Constitution, II, 416; David Ramsay to Thomas Jefferson, April 7, 1787, ibid., 417; Forest to Castries, June 9, 1787, in Abraham Nasatir and Gary Elwyn Monell, eds., French Consuls in the United States: A Calendar of their Correspondence in the Archives Nationales (Washington, 1967), 101.

[58] Journal of the Massachusetts Ratifying Convention (Boston, 1856), 25; James Madison to James Monroe, August 18, 1786, in Stanislaus M. Hamilton, ed., Writings of James Monroe (7 vols., New York, 1893–1903), I, 152–156. It can be argued that by

the implications of the Shaysites' political victory in Massachusetts. Faced with common internal threats, the leaders felt obliged to build upon their points of agreed interests, specifically economic and political powers, rather than permit their conflicting interests to destroy them. However, sectional interests were still evident as each side felt it had something to gain from a new government. Madison remarked that "it is recommended to the Eastern States by their actual superiority of their populousness, and to the Southern by their expected superiority." In 1789 Samuel Henshaw told Theodore Sedgwick, "in my opinion we never had a worse House of Representatives [in Massachusetts]. I thank God we have a federal government." It was the need for this sort of buffer between the rulers and the ruled which, for a time, lessened the importance of sectional differences and held sectional conflict in check. But once the new government was in operation the sections began to jockey for position and influence; the sectional conflicts which emerged again and again to threaten and then to destroy the intersectional compromise which created the Constitution of 1787 necessitated the compromises of 1790, 1820, and 1850.[59]

---

early 1787 many southerners were willing to support major revisions of the Articles of Confederation. They counted on Middle States support and on the new southern states which could emerge out of the West to insure future sectional superiority. Henderson focuses on the latter, which is valid; however, he does not look at the spring capital fight and the political "revolution" in Massachusetts which together demonstrates the intricate balance between sectional and other considerations in the later Confederation Period. See Henderson, "The Structure of Politics," 191–192; Henderson, *Party Politics*, 383–420.

[59] James Madison to Thomas Jefferson, March 19, 1787, in *PTJ*, XI, 210; Samuel Henshaw to Theodore Sedgwick, June 14, 1789, in the Sedgwick Papers, MHS. For a discussion of the hammering out of the compromises contained in the Constitution see Kenneth R. Bowling, "Politics in the First Congress" (doctoral dissertation, University of Wisconsin, 1968); Bowling, "Dinner at Jefferson's: A Note on Jacob E. Cooke's 'The Compromise of 1790'," in *WMQ*, 3rd Ser., 28 (1971), 629–640.

After Newburgh: The Struggle for the Impost in Massachusetts

Stephen E. Patterson

THERE is a statement of John Adams—one of Merrill Jensen's favorite and most frequently cited quotations—that perhaps better than any other remark sums up the hard-headed, realistic viewpoint that has characterized Jensen's work on the beginnings of the United States. Adams wrote in 1817 that "there is an overweening fondness for representing this country as a scene of liberty, equality, fraternity, union, harmony and benevolence. But let not your sons or mine deceive themselves. This country, like all others, has been a theatre of parties and feuds for near two hundred years."[1] That idea has needed regular repetition even in recent years, for despite the increasingly close scrutiny under which the political behavior of the Revolutionary generation has come, the tendency still persists among some historians to ignore the internal conflict, political organization, and manipulative genius that shaped events, and to imagine that principle and ideology by themselves represented reality. Fortunately, Jensen's work stands as a constant reminder that the ordinary imperatives of human nature were not suspended during the early life of the new nation.

There were, nonetheless—as both Jensen's work and the work

---

[1] Adams to William Tudor, February 4, 1817, in Charles F. Adams, ed., *The Works of John Adams* (10 vols., Boston, 1850–1856), IX, 241–242.

of others attest—characteristics in the political development of the 1780's that were unique. The peculiar nature of the Articles of Confederation dictated as much, since a national politics was beginning to emerge while real power—the power to raise revenues—was still vested in the states. The overlap that developed between state and national politics is an area that has received less attention than it deserves.[2] It is an area in which "parties and feuds" were the rule, while men's principles were frequently shaped by political necessity.

The contours of the politics of the 1780's began to emerge in the second Continental Congress. From the time discussions began on the Articles of Confederation, opinions were polarized on the question of the proper locus of authority: the republican or federalist (and ultimately successful) notion that power should reside in the states, as close to the people as possible, versus the conservative or nationalist viewpoint, influenced by the experience of the British Empire, that power should be vested in a central government at the expense of the states in the name of economic stability and efficiency. Well documented, also, is the dominance from 1780 to 1784 of a conservative or nationalist bloc in the Congress, constituted chiefly of the delegates of the middle states, and headed by such men as Robert Morris, the Philadelphia merchant.[3]

Morris and his colleagues used their years of pre-eminence in the Congress to push for a national economic program that would have given Congress independent means by providing it with a revenue, increased its power through a consolidation and assumption of state debts, and created an elite class of supporters among the holders of government securities. In a desperate bid for the state support that could make the program a reality, Morris and his colleagues entered into a carefully contrived plot among army officers encamped with General George Washington at Newburgh, New York, in an effort to link officer grievances with the interests

[2] Perhaps the only study to link national and state politics during the Confederation is the excellent analysis by Jackson Turner Main, *Political Parties Before the Constitution* (Chapel Hill, 1973).

[3] Merrill Jensen, *The Articles of Confederation* (Madison, 1940), esp. Chap. VII; Merrill Jensen, *The New Nation* (New York, 1950), 50–56, 59–61; H. James Henderson, "The Structure of Politics in the Continental Congress," in Stephen G. Kurtz and James H. Hutson, eds., *Essays on the American Revolution* (Chapel Hill, 1973), 157–196, esp. 174, 184–186.

of government creditors in what was meant as a demonstration of the need for a strengthened national government. The threatened coup was stymied by Washington's firm assertion of control over the army.[4] But Congress was sufficiently impressed to vote that the states (though Rhode Island alone had defeated a similar request in 1781) be urged to grant Congress a 5 percent impost, or tax on imported commodities. And it also voted that retiring army officers should receive a lump sum separation payment, or "commutation" of the previously promised half-pay pension for life. By the spring of 1783 Congress had gone as far as it could go in instituting the nationalist program.

The lesser known part of the story is what happened thereafter in the states. Massachusetts provides an excellent case study of what happened on that level, not only because it was a large and important state, but also because its congressional delegates were not among the nationalist bloc. Massachusetts delegates usually voted with the New England bloc in Congress. Still, their vote camouflaged the internal division that existed within the state itself, obscuring the fact that there was strong nationalist feeling there also. The story of the adoption of the impost plan of 1783 in Massachusetts shows that the interplay of national and state issues contributed to the emergence of a nationalist force in the state while antinationalist sentiment built up among an already existing localist party. In addition, the struggle over the impost cast the state's old leaders, such as Samuel Adams, in curious new roles, while the style of politics that had characterized the Newburgh conspiracy—the secrecy and the subterfuge—similarly colored events in Massachusetts.

* * * *

On February 7, 1781, Congress, desperately seeking to solve its financial dilemma, created the office of superintendent of finance and two weeks later unanimously elected Robert Morris to the post. The unanimity was obtained only because Samuel Adams and Artemas Ward, the Massachusetts delegates, refused to vote.[5]

---

[4] Richard H. Kohn, "The Inside History of the Newburgh Conspiracy: America and the Coup d'Etat," in the *William and Mary Quarterly*, 3rd Ser., 27 (1970), 187–220.

[5] Edmund C. Burnett, ed., *Letters of Members of the Continental Congress* [*LMCC*] (8 vols., Washington, 1921–1936), VII, xi–xii.

Their objections to placing so much power in the hands of one man and their personal distrust of Morris were shared by others both in Congress and back in Massachusetts. They were objections that tended to grow rather than diminish in response to the "Financier's" activities in office.

On the other hand, there were men in Massachusetts who supported Morris, some of whom benefited from his rather confusing admixture of public and private business. Nathaniel Appleton, the Continental Loan officer in Boston, was, like Morris, involved in a private capacity with the supply of French forces in America.[6] Appleton vigorously promoted Massachusetts' grant of the first impost for continental use in 1781, which coincidentally put more money and hence more power into the hands of his superior. In another case, according to Stephen Higginson, Morris directed the marine department, which was in his charge, to fit out two ships at great expense. He then advised Congress to sell them. Because an eight-day limit was placed on payment, bids were low and two agents of Morris in Boston, Thomas Russell and a Mr. D. Parker, were able to buy the vessels for less than the cost of their recent repairs and fittings. Higginson's personal investigation showed that, by limiting the terms of sale of prize vessels, Morris was able to prevent their purchase by private merchants, "by which means, Mr. Morris and his connexions have had them at their own price."[7] The name of Thomas Russell appeared frequently on drafts used in Continental payments and, whether or not his Morris connections made him so, he was one of the wealthiest merchants in Boston during the 1780's.[8]

Morris's favors, however, were scattered among a very limited group. It is therefore not surprising that merchants divided politically on issues which concerned the Financier, issues such as the imposts of 1781 and 1783. As one of Massachusetts' congressional delegates in 1783, merchant-politician Stephen Higginson denounced Morris and his connections as "already too influential

[6] Nathaniel Appleton to Samuel Adams, April 24, 1782, in the Samuel Adams Papers, New York Public Library [NYPL], microfilm copy courtesy of Merrill Jensen; Robert A. East, *Business Enterprise in the American Revolutionary Era* (New York, 1938), 57–58.

[7] Stephen Higginson to Arthur Lee, [October], 1783, in "Letters of Stephen Higginson, 1783–1804," American Historical Association *Annual Report*, 1 (1896), 704–841, esp. 712–713.

[8] East, *Business Enterprise*, 57.

by far" and fretted about "a party in Congress so thoroughly in the interest of France as to have preferred her interest to ours."[9] Higginson saw the impost entirely as a measure of Morris's personal aggrandizement. "The impost I always was opposed to," he wrote to Samuel Adams from Congress, because of "the danger of too great influence resulting from it to individuals." When Congress accepted the second impost plan in April, 1783, Higginson attributed its passage to the influence of Morris. "His friends in Congress are many and powerful." In urging a rejection of this "strange, though artful, plan of finance," Higginson warned his Massachusetts correspondents that "the Impost would very greatly increase his [Morris's] power, for all officers will be appointed by him in effect, which may be necessary to collect it. Let this weight be added to his scale and the balance will be decidedly in his favor."[10]

Other merchants in Massachusetts, however, were less concerned about Morris than they were with strengthening the power of Congress. An impost, even if it taxed trade, would promote economic stability and would give some sense of over-all control to an otherwise chaotic financial system. Perhaps even more important, it would enable Congress to pay the principal and interest on the national debt. Thus, when the Massachusetts legislature took up the matter in 1783, Boston's representatives, who were merchants as well as politicians, led the movement for the impost.

Significantly, the debate and legislative alignment on this national issue superimposed itself upon an already existing party system that had grown out of the Revolution and that, with minor shifts in the established pattern, characterized all of the roll calls in the legislative session of 1783–1784. Of the 196 representatives who voted on five major issues during this session, 124 formed a bloc largely from small, rural towns in inland or western areas. They tended to adopt an agrarian and often localist viewpoint. On the other hand, fifty-four others formed a bloc made up largely of the representatives from eastern or important inland trading towns. They were led by Boston's merchant-politicians and gener-

[9] Stephen Higginson to Samuel Adams, May 20, 1783, in *LMCC*, VII, 166–167; Higginson to Theophilus Parsons, Sr., April [7?], 1783, *ibid.*, 122–124.

[10] May 20, 1783, *ibid.*, 166–167; to Theophilus Parson, Sr., April [7?], 1783, *ibid.*, 122–124.

ally adopted cosmopolitan and economically conservative views.[11] The other eighteen representatives voted with no party regularity.

While there were important exceptions, the "western" and "eastern" orientation of the respective parties continued the division which had been apparent in the vote on the state constitution of 1780.[12] Worcester County presented a solid western phalanx without a single eastern supporter and only two inconsistent voters among its thirty-two representatives. Hampshire County was only slightly less partisan with twenty-six of its thirty-four representatives taking the western position. The six who voted with the eastern conservatives were all from river towns: Springfield, Deerfield, Hadley, and Brimfield. Two others were inconsistent. Middlesex and Bristol counties divided with clear majorities favoring the western, agrarian view: seventeen of twenty-five in Middlesex, nine of twelve in Bristol. Eastern strength came from the almost equally divided counties of Suffolk, Essex, Plymouth, Lincoln, and Cumberland, and from the unanimously conservative maritime counties of Nantucket, Dukes, and Barnstable. Only in Berkshire, aside from the river towns, did the eastern group find support in the west. Berkshire and to a greater extent York County, Maine, which now provided solid support for the westerners, represented significant shifts from the alignments on the 1780 constitution and represented, with their swiftly growing populations, politically volatile areas.

A barren recitation of voting statistics, however, does not explain the political struggle over the impost. Superficially, one would expect the western agrarians to carry all before them with

[11] See Stephen E. Patterson, *Political Parties in Revolutionary Massachusetts* (Madison, 1973), 248–255; Journals of the House of Representatives [House Journals], microfilm A.1b, in Records of the States of the United States of America, July 8, July 9, October 8, October 17, 1783, and March 3, 1784. See also Van Beck Hall, *Politics Without Parties* (Pittsburgh, 1972), 156–157; and Main, *Political Parties Before the Constitution*, 90, 110.

[12] Massachusetts political groupings of the 1780's have been variously labeled. Jackson Turner Main has designated them the "cosmopolitans" and the "localists." He has provided biographical sketches of some of the important leaders in each group in *Political Parties Before the Constitution*, 409–418. Van Beck Hall has divided Massachusetts towns into the "most commercial-cosmopolitan" and the "least commercial-cosmopolitan" in *Politics Without Parties, passim*. My own preference is to use terms that were frequently used at the time, "western" and "eastern." While there were towns in both east and west that supported the opposite party, geography seems to have been the major determinant of partisan behavior. See Patterson, *Political Parties*, 92n, 249–250, 269–280.

their numerical weight. But many of the westerners were newcomers whose political outlook was largely shaped by local economic conditions and concerns and whose very attendance was
frequently influenced by those same concerns. Statistics, furthermore, do not account for the political skill with which such men
as the Bostonians, numerically impotent, wielded power out of all
proportion to their numbers. Nor do voting records explain the
curious interplay of personalities, the lingering feuds, or the
power-seeking maneuvers that shape political history. Social and
economic considerations shaped the partisan battle over the
impost, but sentiment, patriotism, and the long arm of Robert
Morris played their part, too.

*   *   *   *

Economic grievances vied with other matters when the Massachusetts General Court began its new session on May 28, 1783. A
popular clamor had already denounced the excise tax passed the
previous November to pay the interest on government securities
and thereby to secure "the public credit and to do justice to the
individual possessor."[13] Many representatives wanted to tackle the
excise act first while others were concerned about the congressional request for an impost, the already accomplished commutation of officers' pensions, and the election of congressional
delegates. At least thirty-seven westerners had specific instructions
to oppose commutation.

Quite conscious of the pressures they would face, the Boston-led
easterners prepared to head off any challenge to the excise act. A
small committee of easterners, appointed by both the house and
senate ostensibly to consider a letter from an excise collector,[14]
took matters into its own hands by devising a bill "to repeal certain parts of an act passed the 8th day of Nov. 1782 laying certain
duties of excise on certain articles therein mentioned." From all
appearances the easterners hoped to revise the excise act to save
it from complete repeal. To catch opponents of the excise off
guard, the senate gave first reading to the bill on the morning of
June 3 and then rushed it down to the house where it was given

[13] November 8, 1782, *Acts and Laws of the Commonwealth of Massachusets, 1782–83* (Boston, 1890).

[14] House Journals, October 11, 1783.

first reading the same morning. Continuing to telescope procedure, the easterners got the bill through second reading the next
morning and then convinced the house that the rules should be
waived so that the third and final reading could be given in the
afternoon. The rapidity of the whole affair, to say nothing of the
fact that the bill itself had been presented by a committee not
chosen for the express purpose, was more than even the unorga-
nized westerners could take. They made sure that on third
reading the bill went down to defeat.[15]

Showing complete aplomb, however, the easterners promptly
had the house appoint another committee with express powers not
only to revise the old excise act, but to frame a bill that would levy
both impost and excise duties "upon such articles as might be
expedient." The easterners said nothing about providing that
such an impost should be awarded to Congress; they were content
to accomplish their purpose a step at a time. Westerners agreed to
the formation of the committee, and two of their adherents joined
two easterners as members. The addition of the conservative
Senator Choate swung control into eastern hands. Still, the committee had to draft a bill it thought would be acceptable to the
house. As guidance to the committee, the house voted on June 6
that duties would have to be paid by importers and distillers
rather than by the individual consumers. And again on the same
day, the house fixed the rate of duties at 2 percent, considerably
below the 5 percent requested by Congress.[16]

Clearly, however, it was a small group of easterners who
directed the affairs of the house and took the initiative in legislative matters. The westerners, while they could muster votes on
important issues, did not attempt to control the day-to-day affairs
of the house. They let committees slip into eastern hands time and
time again. Confronted with a Boston member who failed to meet
the residency requirement for election to the house, they allowed
themselves to be easily maneuvered into accepting him.[17]

Despite their inability to manage the house, the westerners saw
to it that the impost and excise bill which finally emerged placed

---

[15] *Ibid.*, June 2, 3, and 4, 1783.

[16] House Journals, June 4, 6, 1783.

[17] House Journals, June 10, 1783; Warren to John Adams, June 24, 1783, in
Worthington C. Ford, ed., *Warren-Adams Letters* (2 vols., Boston, 1917–1925), II,
219–230.

heavy taxes on luxury items that farmers, fishermen, or laborers would not be apt to buy or own. When easterners tried to get a reconsideration of the tax on "wheel carriages," a symbol of wealth in those days, they were promptly squelched. By June 20 the bill was ready for final reading and was passed "after long debate." In its final form the bill gave evidence of constant compromise. The easterners had won a token impost of 5 percent on a very few items, such as nails, looking glasses, and china, while all other foreign imports were to be taxed at 2½ percent. Specific duties were required on a list of enumerated articles, including distilled spirits and wine as well as tea, coffee, cocoa, tobacco, and beaver hats. Further, an annual tax was to be required of the owners of carriages, running from five pounds for a coach or chariot down to nine shillings for a sulky or riding chair. The expressed purpose of the act was to "satisfy the numerous creditors to government" and to establish confidence in the public credit.[18]

The senate was slow to take up the bill. When it did on July 4 and 5, it introduced some deft changes. Primarily the senate was unwilling to create an impost without assigning its use to Congress. It, therefore, proposed "An act for levying certain imposts and duties upon foreign goods imported into this state and for granting the same to congress for the purpose of paying the interest and principal of the debt of the United States." The house reacted by proposing the formation of a joint committee to discuss the senate's new draft and by naming five committeemen. Significantly, four of them, headed by the nationalist-minded Theodore Sedgwick, favored the impost.[19]

The next move of the easterners was carefully contrived to attract western support but in the end backfired, for it solidified the western opposition and underlined the social and economic split in the house. The easterners had already made use of the western opposition to the old excise act to get their consent to an impost of sorts. Now, they sought to offer the westerners some sort of guarantee that an impost granted to Congress would not be used to pay the commutation of officers' pensions.

Commutation had resulted from the pressures of Newburgh,

[18] House Journals, June 13, 18, 19, 20, 1783; *Acts and Laws*, 1783, chap. 12, July 10, 1783.

[19] Journals of the Senate [Senate Journals], in Records of the States of the United States of America, microfilm A.1a., July 4, 5, 1783.

and guaranteed Continental officers a separation allowance equal to five years' salary in lieu of an earlier promise of half pay for life. Congress's approval of commutation had set off a great uproar in the Massachusetts farming communities where veterans of the War for Independence had long before given up their nearly worthless notes-in-lieu-of-pay, and now felt that they had been cheated. Why, then, should officers be so well treated. Moreover, many towns saw commutation as a direct affront to Republican institutions: a measure calculated "to raise and exalt some citizens in wealth and in grandeur, to the injury and oppression of others." Particularly enraging to these Massachusetts men were their own delegates' votes for commutation, and word of the dissatisfaction quickly reached Philadelphia. "The commutation given to the officers for their half pay I find is disagreeable to many in Massachusetts," wrote Stephen Higginson from Congress, "the Governor has wrote or the Council, I do not recollect which, for the yeas and nays on that question. They will find that we were unanimous, and if the design is to punish those who voted for it, by dropping them, they must have an entire new delegation." Higginson's suspicions were well-founded for, when the General Court took up the matter of electing delegates to Congress, it chose an entirely new slate and ordered Higginson and his colleagues back to Massachusetts.[20]

Hoping that an anticommutation statement would carry an impost specifically assigned to Congress, the easterners offered an amendment to the senate's impost and excise bill on July 8. But in the recorded division of the house that followed, the westerners overwhelmingly rejected the sugar-coated pill. Only the Bostonians, some representatives from large eastern towns, and a handful of Berkshiremen linked politically with Theodore Sedgwick supported the measure.[21] In a second recorded vote on the senate's bill which followed the next day, the westerners defeated in similar fashion an attempt to insert a clause that would pledge the use of the impost "for the purpose of discharging the interest or principal of the debts contracted on the faith of the United States for supporting the war." Full of confidence and completely aware by

[20] James T. Austin, *The Life of Elbridge Gerry* (Boston, 1828), 395–396; Higginson to Adams, May 20, 1783, in *LMCC*, VII, 168; House Journals, June, 1783.
[21] *Ibid.*, July 8, 1783. The division was 93 to 32 in the agrarians' favor.

now of their strength, the westerners pressed the house to offer its old bill to the senate. Settling for the best it could get under the circumstances, the senate promptly concurred with the house. The impost and excise act, with no mention of Congress, became law.[22]

The next day, July 11, the General Court forwarded a letter to Congress explaining that it had refused to grant the impost, "because of those measures of Congress which are extremely opposite and irritating to the principles and feeling, which the people of some of the eastern states, and of this in particular, inherit from their ancestors." More specifically, the letter complained of the half pay granted to the officers, the commutation of that pay, and the salaries paid by Congress to civil officials. The General Court agreed that Congress had the power to make provision for the payment of the army and such civil officials as were needed to manage the affairs of the United States, but, it added, "in making such provisions, due regard ever ought to be had to the welfare and happiness of the people, the rules of equity and the spirit and design of the confederation." The commutation is "inconsistent with that equality which ought to subsist among citizens of free and republican states," said the letter, and "such a measure appears to be calculated to raise and exalt some citizens in wealth and grandeur, to the injury and oppression of others." While Congress could, and did, reply that half pay was a contractual obligation of the United States guaranteed by the twelfth article of the Articles of Confederation, there was no denying the essential class consciousness inherent in the protest of the General Court.[23]

After a poor beginning, the first round in the legislative session of 1783 belonged to the agrarian, small town, western party. The second round, however, went to the easterners, aided curiously by Samuel Adams and by Robert Morris himself.

The second round began in August with the appointment of a joint committee of the house and senate whose responsibility was to correspond with the Massachusetts congressional delegates, whether or not the legislature was in session. In many ways, the committee was reminiscent of the old Revolutionary committees of correspondence whose significance lay in their ability to manipulate the flow of incoming and outgoing information, thereby

---

[22] *Ibid.*, July 9, 10, 1783; *Acts and Laws*, 1783, chap. 12, July 10, 1783.
[23] Quoted in Austin, *Gerry*, 395–396, 397–398.

giving considerable power to the committee members themselves. One man who knew well the rules of this game was Samuel Adams. He was chosen as the representative of the senate. The other two men were the Boston representatives John Rowe and Nathaniel Appleton, both merchants and supporters of a continental impost. The appointments of these two men reflected the continuing ability of eastern partisans to control committees even in the face of the western numerical majority. Appleton, furthermore, was the Continental Loan officer in Massachusetts and a close associate of Robert Morris. These three became, in effect, middlemen in the exchange of information between Congress and the Massachusetts legislature. "The correspondence is to be very extensive," explained Samuel Adams to Congressman Elbridge Gerry, and may include, according to the resolution of the General Court, " any other matter which relates to the being and welfare of the United States."[24]

The first letter of the Massachusetts delegates to the new committee showed that they did not favor wholesale support for a congressional impost. Rather, the three delegates—Gerry, Holten, and Higginson (the latter about to return to Massachusetts)— argued that Congress's need for revenue should be met only if it were willing to satisfy Massachusetts in other respects. The bargain must include prompt action on the matter of paper money. As the delegates had pointed out to Congress, most states had failed to provide for the sinking of the old Continental bills of credit. As a result, Massachusetts, in being one of the few to honor its promise, had suffered greatly by the difference in exchange between it and other states. Until other states made provision for taking their share of the paper out of circulation, Massachusetts had a perfect right to withhold the granting of an impost. Coupling the paper money grievance with those of commutation and the salaries of civil officers, the Massachusetts delegates gave "as our opinion to Congress that no impost will be granted by our constituents neither will they continue to supply the public treasury, unless their grievances are redressed."[25] By linking together

---

[24] Samuel Adams to Elbridge Gerry, September 9, 1783, in Austin, *Gerry*, 408–410.
[25] September 11, 1783, in *LMCC*, VII, 294–297. The position of the Massachusetts delegates took into account their many attempts to get Congress to consider the matter of the old Continental currency. See letters of delegates, *ibid.*, 36, 171–172, 173–174, 183–184, 244.

these three grievances, the delegates had skillfully created a package that would appeal to both rural and commercial towns, both east and west, and would thus almost certainly, had it been submitted, have received legislative support in Massachusetts. The General Court, however, never saw its delegates' recommendations, that is until it was too late.

When Stephen Higginson arrived back in Massachusetts in late September, he found the legislature ready to begin its fall session with Congress's request for an impost high on its agenda. Called upon to appear before the legislature "for information as to our public affairs," Higginson devoted his whole time to his favorite subject, Robert Morris. Morris, in Higginson's view, was the most serious threat to the survival of the new nation. And yet, Higginson was not quite sure whether the danger was increasing or decreasing. Only a month before, he had ambivalently written to Nathaniel Gorham that "things seem to be working right, the great man and his agents are very uneasy; they see their influence daily declining." But in the same letter Higginson warned: "The spider web is so nearly finished, so many of our members have got entangled in it and so artful are the maneuvers made use of to draw others into it, that I see no way of getting rid of the danger, of shaking off the fetters, but that of destroying him who has the management and has placed it at his will."[26] The latter view seems to have been the one he presented to the legislators. As he explained to Theodorick Bland, he attended the legislature "when convened and gave them a general view of matters touching upon the designs of the aristocratic junto in Congress; they appeared well pleased with the information and will be, believe me, more upon their guard in future as to their plans and insinuations."

In Higginson's mind the matter of the impost was so interconnected with the power of the Financier that he could not in conscience support it. There were men in Massachusetts who thought as he did, but there were others who saw Congress's need for a revenue; the legislators Higginson spoke to seemed to fall into this category. "They appear disposed to make every exertion to support the federal government," he wrote, "and are thor-

[26] August 5, 1783, *ibid.*, 251–252.

oughly impressed with the necessity of supporting and connecting the union."[27]

But Higginson said nothing about the congressional delegates' proposal to use the impost as a lever to pry concessions from Congress on the matters of paper money, commutation, and official salaries. Instead, he left it to Samuel Adams, chairman of the General Court's committee, to pass on that information. Ironically, Adams later offered Higginson's appearance before the house as an excuse for not having communicated the letter. In any event, the letter was suppressed, and its suppression illustrates the rather ambiguous position that old republicans like Sam Adams had by now been forced into. On the one hand, the Continental Congress was the accomplishment of the Revolution and, as Adams wrote to Elbridge Gerry, it "is and must be the cement of the union of the states." Whatever his other thoughts on the question of sovereignty, Adams believed that the continued effectiveness of Congress depended on its being provided with a revenue, and that meant the states must grant its request for an impost.

On the other hand, Adams's republican suspicions were as aroused as Higginson's by the Financier and by the unbridled concentration of power he represented. "The war is now over," said Adams to Elbridge Gerry, "and the people turn their eyes to the disposition of their money, a subject which I hope Congress will always have so clear a knowledge of, as to be able at any time to satisfy the rational enquiries of the people. To prevent groundless jealousies, it seems necessary not only that the principal in that department should himself be immaculate, but that care should be taken that no person be admitted to his confidence but such as have the entire confidence of the people." Any suspicion of the "high treasurer," added Adams, would surely reflect on the fidelity of Congress itself.[28]

Adams resolved his dilemma, however, in favor of the impost, apparently with the belief that it was the need of the moment; Robert Morris could be disposed of in due course. His decision naturally put him in league with nationalists and supporters of Morris, most immediately in the person of Nathaniel Appleton. Adams handed the congressional delegates' letter—which would

---

[27] October 6, 1783, *ibid.*, 323.
[28] Adams to Gerry, September 9, 1783, in Austin, *Gerry*, 408–410.

clearly delay Massachusetts granting the impost—to Appleton and its progress toward the legislature ended there. The third member of the committee, so it was later revealed, never saw the letter at all. Adams weakly wrote to Elbridge Gerry much later that "your letter of 11th September, directed to the committee, was through mere forgetfulness omitted to be communicated in season."[29]

But the failure to communicate the letter was not alone responsible for the success of the impost forces. It was time for Robert Morris himself to get into the act. By October 7 a joint committee of the legislature was reporting the preliminary draft of a bill granting an impost to Congress. On that day the senate voted to delete the severe limitations the westerners had placed in the draft bill. As the committee reported it, a grant of an impost should be "subject in every respect in its regulation to this legislature, the whole revenue of which to be solely appropriated towards defraying this commonwealth's proportions of the debts of the United States with this proviso, that no part of said revenue shall be applied to discharge the half pay or commutation granted by Congress to the officers of the continental army." The next day, in going through the bill item by item, the house reaffirmed its willingness to grant an impost but only under severe restrictions and under the complete regulation of the legislature. But when it voted on the matter of commutation, the proviso to prevent the use of the impost for this purpose just squeaked by with a margin of five votes. By afternoon the easterners felt confident enough to ask for reconsideration, and this time the commutation proviso was rejected. But when the easterners dared to suggest that the house concur in the proceedings of the senate, the renegade westerners promptly returned to the fold and the senate's version of the impost was defeated.[30]

The Morris ploy followed at exactly the right moment. On October 9 Governor Hancock sent an address to the house urging that the legislature "provide Congress with the means of paying the interest on the continental debt." His address was strengthened by a letter from John Adams which, from all appearances, advised the same thing and, in fact, made a strong plea for

[29] For Appleton's position on the impost see his letter to Samuel Adams, April 24, 1782, in the Samuel Adams Papers, NYPL; Adams to Gerry, [late 1783 or early 1784], in Austin, Gerry, 415.
[30] House Journals, October 7, 8, 1783.

strengthening the public credit. "The Thirteen states in relation to the discharge of the debts of Congress, must consider themselves as one body animated by one soul. The stability of our Confederation at home, our reputation abroad, our power of defence, the confidence and affection of the people of one state towards those of another, all depends upon it."[31] To the unsuspecting members of the legislature, the letter of their respected countryman, writing from Paris, certainly sounded like vigorous support for the impost. What Hancock did not communicate was that the letter, as he transmitted it, was incomplete (something Hancock may not have known), that he had just received it from Robert Morris, and that Morris had omitted the sections of the letter which showed that Adams's chief concern was his dealings with French financial houses at that time. The letter had nothing to do with the impost.

John Adams's supposed endorsement, however, gave new strength to the impost forces. Higginson (who seems to have learned of Morris's deception very quickly) reported that "Mr. Morris no doubt very well knew, that no other part of the letters from Mr. Adams would answer his purpose, he also knew the high character of Mr. Adams in this state, and the influence which his opinion has usually had with our legislature." The extract of the letter as communicated by Governor Hancock, "and Mr. Morris's reasoning upon it, has made a very strong impression on the minds in both houses, and I now think it very uncertain," said Higginson, "whether it [the impost] will not yet be adopted upon the plan of Congress."[32] The very day after Hancock's address the house and senate met in joint conference to consider the principal points in dispute. The questions before them were three: whether the revenue from an impost used to discharge the national debt should be credited to Massachusetts or to the United States in general; whether the state legislature would regulate the impost; and whether an impost could be used to pay for commutation. After discussion the two houses separated.[33]

Up to this point in the session no count had ever been made of

[31] *Ibid.*, October 9, 1783; John Adams to Robert Morris, July 11, 1783, in Francis Wharton, ed., *The Revolutionary Diplomatic Correspondence of the United States* (Washington, 1889) VI, 536–537.
[32] To Samuel Holten, October 14, 1783, in *LMCC*, VII, 333–335.
[33] House Journals, October 10, 1783.

the number of representatives actually instructed to oppose commutation. Apparently the curiosity of the easterners prompted the
motion on the eleventh for those so instructed to make it known
to the house. Of the 105 members then present, 37 were bound by
their instructions to vote against any provisions for the payment
of the commutation.[34] By the thirteenth, however, only 87 members were present in the house, and so many representatives from
small, rural towns had returned home that, according to Stephen
Higginson, "the two parties appear to be now nearly equal in the
House."[35] On that day a committee of both houses was appointed
to draw up an impost act, this time with specific provision that the
revenues should be to discharge the debt of the United States. Of
the five appointed to the committee from the house, two had solid
records of support for the westerners, and one other voted with
the easterners only once. The other two were easterners. The
senate appointments guaranteed a report favorable to the impost
since "the Senate are all but two in favor of it." Dissatisfaction
with the composition of the committee was voiced in the house
the next day, but it was quickly defeated.[36] On the fifteenth, the
bill "for granting to the United States in Congress assembled an
impost upon goods brought into this commonwealth" received
first reading in the house.[37]

During the second reading the house voted on each paragraph
as it came up. In the only recorded division during this reading,
the easterners outvoted the westerners by the narrow margin of
five votes. Though they were now in the minority, a hard core of
westerners still consistently clung to their position. Even if they
were outvoted on the impost, they might still get a proviso forbid-
ding the use of the revenues for the payment of the commutation.
On the seventeenth such an amendment was moved. Logically, the
easterners who had pushed for just such a proviso back in July in
order to get an impost should now have supported the westerners.
But such political maneuvers were now unnecessary, and they thus
worked feverishly to suppress all opposition to commutation. As

[34] *Ibid.*, October 11, 1783.

[35] Higginson to Samuel Holten, October 14, 1783, in *LMCC*, VII, 333–335.

[36] The members of the committee were Cross, Ammidown, Sullivan, Danielson,
Hosmer. House Journals, October 13, 14, 1783.

[37] Higginson to Samuel Holten, October 14, 1783, in *LMCC*, VII, 333–335; House
Journals, October 15, 1783.

Stephen Higginson contemptuously noted, "having effected their purpose, the quacks who raised the fever are now using all their arts to reduce it." When the votes were counted, the westerners found they had lost, seventy-four to sixty-four. So effective had been the efforts of easterners to quell the opposition that several men who regularly voted with the westerners voted this time with the easterners. Most of these were from Suffolk, Essex, and Middlesex counties. The Worcester County men, however, almost unanimously supported the proviso opposing commutation.[38]

Their voting strength clearly established, the easterners now called for the main question: should the impost bill be passed. With nearly the same division as on the commutation proviso, the bill passed, seventy-two to sixty-five, and with the concurrence of the senate, became law on October 20. With the exception of a list of enumerated articles which were to be taxed after an allowance of 10 percent for wastage, all other imports were to pay an impost of 5 percent. The General Court would retain some powers of regulation by appointing the collectors of impost. The act would go into force as soon as Congress notified Massachusetts that all the states had passed similar acts.[39]

*   *   *   *

Though the passing of the impost act in Massachusetts was a victory for the easterners and Robert Morris, it was accompanied by considerable controversy about Morris himself, a subject upon which even easterners divided. The persistent Stephen Higginson, naturally, could be relied on for anti-Morris initiative. In a letter to Samuel Holten, Higginson explained his efforts to defeat the impost by starting a whispering campaign against Morris. Knowing how rumors get started, Higginson provided the senate with "information" which "has been by them retailed to the members of the house, and has produced, as I am informed, no small fermentation. Probably their own comments and colourings may

---

[38] *Ibid.,* October 16 and 17, 1783; Higginson to Samuel Holten, October 14, 1783, in *LMCC,* VII, 335. Propaganda immediately appeared in the newspapers to make commutation more palatable to its opponents. Such was the intent of "A Farmer," who wrote in the *Boston Gazette,* October 20, 1783. With a satiric jibe at rural speech, the writer concluded, "I begin to fear us folks in the country towns are all in the dark about this mutation, as they call it."

[39] House Journals, October 17, 1783; *Acts and Laws,* 1783, chap. 18, October 20, 1783.

have increased it, much beyond what my own relations would have produced. This effect I expected, and I thought it very probable that their communications would not exactly correspond with the information I gave them." As Higginson continued, his plan worked for awhile and opposition to the impost mounted. "But," he added, "the effect of my information has been much more than balanced, by the extracts from John Adams's letter, which Mr. Morris transmitted to the governor for the purpose no doubt, of urging the Court to a compliance with the recommendation."[40]

Higginson's plan only partly failed. The impost was awarded Congress, but Higginson could still report to his friend, Arthur Lee, that "the legislature of this state . . . are not however in a temper, favorable to the views of the great man or his party. Their jealousies and their fears are roused, and they seem in earnest to have determined upon more vigilance in future."[41] Only two days after the impost became law, a joint committee reported on its examination of an estimate made by Congress of the national debt and the accounts of expenditure received from the superintendent of finance. The committee's report, accepted by the house without division, was a scathing, detailed criticism of Morris's slipshod accounting, together with a recommendation that the delegates of Massachusetts in Congress "be instructed to use their endeavours, to obtain an abridgement of the powers intrusted to the office of Superintendent of Finance." The committee particularly denounced Morris's placing a large sum loosely under the heading "Contingences" without providing an itemized account of what the "contingences" were.[42] The committee's action delighted Stephen Higginson. "Our delegates are now instructed to urge for a new arrangement of that department [treasury]," he wrote, "and if two or three more states would give similar instructions, I should expect that Mr. Financier must give up the reins and retire."[43]

For those inclined to think so, the success of the impost bill in

[40] Higginson to Holten, October 14, 1783, in *LMCC*, VII, 333–335.

[41] Higginson to Lee, [end of October ?], 1783, in Am. Hist. Assn. *Report* (1896), 711–712.

[42] *Supplement to the Acts and Resolves of Massachusetts*, collected and arranged by Edwin M. Bacon, I: 1780–1784 (Boston, 1896), 191–192. The report is dated October 22, 1783.

[43] Higginson to Arthur Lee, [end of October ?], 1783, in Am. Hist. Assn. *Report* (1896), 711–712 and notes.

this session of the legislature had the earmarks of a giant conspiracy. And particularly as the facts of the suppressed letter and the editing of the Adams letter by Robert Morris became known, the grounds for a conspiratorial interpretation appeared all the more firmly based. James Warren, who considered an impost "injurious to commerce and dangerous to public liberty," wrote to John Adams that he greatly feared the existence of a "foreign influence" both in Philadelphia and Boston. "This influence," he said, "is greatly strengthened by an union with those who wish to establish an Oligarchy, and who have nearly effected it." His republican suspicions thoroughly aroused, Warren added: "Morris is a King, and more than a King. He has the keys of the treasury at his command, appropriates money as he pleases, and everybody must look up to him for justice and favor." The impost, thought Warren, was simply an instrument to advance the "system" of the Financier.[44]

Stephen Higginson, of course, needed no prodding to see conspiracy writ large across the whole impost controversy. Writing to Samuel Holten, he asked, "is it not scandalous practice for Congress or their servants, to send extracts of letters and mutilated information to the states, in order to hurry them into their measures? Is it dealing fairly with them, to give them a partial view only of this situation, and conceal from them one side, and perhaps the most important one of the picture?"[45]

Common gossip about the "conspiracy," however, did not reach its peak until February, 1784, when the house of representatives itself investigated the matter of the suppressed letter. On February 5, a committee of the house, which had been appointed to inquire into the causes of delay in communicating the letter, reported. Their information, they stated, was based on their questioning of Samuel Adams, the chairman of the committee. Adams pleaded ill health at the time of the receipt of the letter. Because of his feebleness, he said, he had given the letter to Nathaniel Appleton who had not returned it until much later and then only when Adams had sent for it. John Rowe, the third member of the

---

[44] Warren to Adams, October 27, 1783, Ford, ed., *Warren-Adams Letters*, II, 229–232.

[45] October 14, 1783, in *LMCC*, VII, 333–335. Higginson again discusses "the mutilated extracts of Mr. Adams's last letters" in his letter to Arthur Lee, October 23, 1783, *ibid.*, 334.

committee, had not seen the letter. Adams had not later communicated the letter, he claimed, because Stephen Higginson had reported much of its contents when he was questioned by the legislature.[46]

The wording of the committee's report implied that Nathaniel Appleton was most responsible for the suppression of the letter and, after a motion absolving John Rowe of any implication, the house called on Appleton to defend himself. When Appleton had finished, the house ordered him to prepare a written statement to be entered in the journals of the house. The next day, Appleton's letter was read. Since Adams had implied that Appleton was responsible for the suppression, Appleton passed the buck right back. It was not his responsibility to communicate the letter, he stated; it was the responsibility of the chairman of the committee. In the afternoon the house voted that Appleton's reasons were unsatisfactory. A second motion to reconsider was rejected, and the whole question was then ordered to subside.[47]

But the question subsided only in the legislature. On February 6, the *Boston Gazette* published the suppressed letter which, it said, "has been the topic of much conversation the week past." Naturally enough, the enemies of Samuel Adams, and particularly of Nathaniel Appleton, chose to make as much of the episode as possible. "The suppression of our letter has produced a great fermentation," wrote Stephen Higginson. "It has much hurt our friend Mr. S. Adams and ruined Mr. Appleton's public course." Both men, according to Higginson, had admitted that they had suppressed the letter because "they were afraid it would hurt their darling child, the continental impost bill." Many of the representatives, reported Higginson, now said that had the letter not been suppressed, "the act would not have passed."[48] Samuel Adams, however, did not appear the least disturbed. "I could not help diverting myself with the ebullition of apparent zeal for the public good on this occasion," he wrote to Elbridge Gerry in Congress, "and upon its being said by a gentleman in Senate that it was the subject of warm conversation among the people without doors, I observed that the clamour would undoubtedly subside in the

[46] House Journals, February 5, 1784.

[47] *Ibid.*, February 5, 6, 1784.

[48] *Boston Gazette*, February 16, 1784; Higginson to Elbridge Gerry, [undated], in Austin, *Gerry*, 414–415.

afternoon of the first Monday on April next."[49] On that day, as Adams predicted, he was safely returned to the senate.[50]

Nathaniel Appleton was not so fortunate. Prior to the election for representatives, the *Independent Chronicle* republished the suppressed letter, together with all pertinent material from the investigation that had taken place in the house. The writer, who signed himself "C," stated boldly that the letter had been withheld from the knowledge of the legislature "until a most consequential act had passed that body."[51] Thus reminded of Appleton's censure by the house, the voters of Boston dropped him altogether as a candidate for re-election.[52]

The growing campaign against Robert Morris gained impetus from the letter controversy in Boston. Cited everywhere as a conspiracy, the suppressed letter was published in newspapers in several states. David Howell, one of Rhode Island's delegates to Congress, a bitter foe of Morris, and a veteran of the war against the impost, wrote from Annapolis that he had read the letter in "some of our papers this way." Howell was convinced that Massachusetts would not have granted an impost had the letter been communicated. "But," he said, "this letter was suppressed, and mutilated paragraphs (as I am told) of some hasty procured letters from our ministers in Europe, were offered to the House, and the measure was carried." Outdoing even Stephen Higginson in invective against the Financier, Howell added: "I cannot find words strong enough to express my indignation at the base means, the intrigue, the chicanery, the deceit, the circumvention, the fetches, the side winds, the bye blows, the ambushes, the stratagems, the manoeuvering, the desultory attacks, the regular approaches, the canting and snivelling as well as swearing and lying, and, in short, the total prostitution of every power and faculty of body and mind and office, to carry a point, which I need not name."[53]

John Adams in France must have been rather confused by the reports which reached him of the impost battle, particularly since

[49] [Late 1783 or early 1784], *ibid.*, 415.

[50] *Boston Gazette*, April 12, June 7, 1784.

[51] *LMCC*, VII, 483–484, 484n.

[52] May 11, 1784, in Thirty-First Report, Boston Records Commissioners, *Boston Town Records, 1784–96* (Boston, 1903), 11.

[53] Howell to Deputy Gov. Bowen, April 19, 1784, in William R. Staples, *Rhode Island in the Continental Congress* (Providence, 1870), 489.

his own letters had played a part in it. From his friend James Warren he heard nothing but opposition to the impost and vilification of Robert Morris. From the President of Congress, on the other hand, he heard: "Your letter on the subject of our credit abroad and the strengthening and cementing the Union at home came at a happy moment and has had a very good effect. Your countrymen were running wild on this subject, but your observations and opinion has helped to check them, and the legislature of Massachusetts have passed the 5 pr C recommended by Congress."[54] Robert Morris, assuming his correspondent to be sympathetic, readily admitted to Adams that he had "taken the liberty to make some extracts" from the letters and had sent them to the governor of Massachusetts. "Permit me, sir," he continued, "to give my feeble approbation and applause for those sentiments of wisdom and integrity, which are as happily expressed as they are forcibly conceived."[55]

Robert Morris's satisfaction, however, was short-lived, for within a few months of his victory in Massachusetts mounting opposition to his operations led to the abolition of the office of superintendent of finance. The Massachusetts General Court's detailed criticism of Morris's accounts in October, 1783, the censure of Appleton in February, and the unbounded rumors of conspiracy that spread from Massachusetts throughout the continent contributed significantly to Morris's downfall. But while the repercussions of the suppressed letter controversy ironically undercut Morris and his associate, Appleton, it seems almost certain that the man most responsible for both the suppression and the success of the impost in Massachusetts was Samuel Adams.

Adams and to a lesser extent John Hancock pose interesting problems of interpretation. For while it is clear that Massachusetts was divided over the impost along lines that corresponded to internal political divisions, it is equally clear that Adams and Hancock fitted into neither of the divisions. Alexander Hamilton's comment about divisions in Congress had almost equal applicability in Massachusetts: "There are two classes of men Sir in Congress of very different views," he had written to Washing-

---

[54] James Warren to John Adams, February 26, 1784, in Ford, ed., *Warren-Adams Letters*, II, 236; President to John Adams, November 1, 1783, in *LMCC*, VII, 363.

[55] Morris to Adams, September 20, 1783, in Wharton, ed., *Revolutionary Diplomatic Correspondence*, VI, 703.

ton in 1783, "one attached to state, the other to Continental politics."[56] But in Massachusetts, Adams represented a third force pulling men together rather than accentuating their divisions. And whether it was pragmatism, patriotism, or the old republican desire for consensus that motivated him, Adams had a powerful influence on his Massachusetts colleagues. Tristram Dalton, for example, was an opponent of the impost on the grounds that taxation by any body other than the state legislature represented slavery. "How," he asked Elbridge Gerry, could Adams be "so warm an advocate for the Impost Act? His more than reverential regard for the liberties of his Country, no one, who knows him can doubt of. His Capacity and Knowledge in Politics all the world admires. I confess to you that I am hesitating in my opinion on this subject on no account so much as because Mr. Adams differs from me."[57]

Dalton's hesitancy on the impost, however, had other roots also, for he shared what was coming to be a common position of all factions: that steps were needed to strengthen the new nation. The eventual willingness of some westerners in the Massachusetts legislature to compromise on the impost issue attests to that. But beyond that point, the people of Massachusetts and their legislators were divided. Nationalists could agree with Robert Morris that "the necessity of strengthening our Confederation, providing for our debts, and forming some federal constitution begins to be most seriously felt. But unfortunately for America, the narrow and illiberal prejudices of some have taken such deep root, that it must be difficult and may prove impracticable to remove them."[58] Still others—the "narrow and illiberal" to Morris—saw the problem, but found the solution more elusive, committed as they were to government that was close to the people and responsive to local needs. Dalton spoke for them when he wrote: "I wish that the People at large could be more fully possessed of the importance of a National Character. Our views are too contracted for the field now open. What steps can be taken to unite all the

---

[56] Hamilton to George Washington, [April 8, 1783], in Harold C. Syrett et al., eds., *The Papers of Alexander Hamilton* (New York, 1961 to date), III, 318.

[57] Dalton to Gerry, April 13, 1784, in the Elbridge Gerry Papers, II, Box 1770–1848, Massachusetts Historical Society [MHS].

[58] Morris to Adams, September 20, 1783, in Wharton, ed., *Revolutionary Diplomatic Correspondence*, VI, 703.

states by bonds indissoluble, which may still leave a sufficient degree of freedom and Independence[?]"[59] That unanswered question, together with inexperience in managing the state legislature, left the agrarian, localist, western majority vulnerable to defeat on the impost issue of 1783. Similar factors would defeat them again on the crucial vote on the federal constitution in 1788. Their failures, however, coupled with the similar role played by Samuel Adams in each event, should not obscure the basic fact: in Massachusetts, political divisions on national issues grew out of already existing factions within the state. Despite the primitive nature of their organization, they familiarized the people of Massachusetts with two-party conflict well before the Federalists and Republicans emerged in the 1790's.

[59] Dalton to Elbridge Gerry, February 11, 1784, in the Elbridge Gerry Papers, II, Box 1770–1848, MHS.

Democracy Run Rampant:
Rhode Island in the Confederation

John P. Kaminski

RHODE ISLAND, during the last half of the Confederation Period, was the most democratic state in America. Once the democratic Country Party[1] won control of the assembly, the will of the people was left unchecked. With a government responsive to the people, Rhode Island was able to undertake one of the most successful programs of debtor relief and public finance during the American Revolutionary Era. In implementing this fiscal policy, however, the ruling party entertained some radical schemes which would have provided for the equal distribution of all property as well as the socialization of the state's mercantile system. Politicians, newspaper editors, clergymen, and the American public in general all condemned this "democratical Tyranny." Because of the democratic tendencies of the ruling party in Rhode Island, the conservative minority, with its strongholds in Newport and Provi-

[1] Throughout this essay the word "democracy" is used as it is defined by Austin Ranney and Willmore Kendall in their study, *Democracy and the American Party System* (New York, 1956), 23–37; "(a) popular sovereignty, (b) political equality, (c) popular consultation, and (d) majority rule." All of these factors were present in Rhode Island during the Confederation Period. Party labels are taken from the contemporary usage. The conservative forces in Rhode Island were referred to as the Mercantile Party or, after May, 1786, as the Minority. The democratic forces were known as the Country Party or, after May, 1786, as the Majority.

dence, threatened to secede from the state.[2] Serious thought was even given to the forcible dismemberment of Rhode Island between Massachusetts and Connecticut.[3] Yet, despite all the abusive rhetoric, the democratic Country Party, because it was sympathetic to the plight of the suffering and offered a program of relief, unswervingly maintained the confidence of most Rhode Island freemen during the Confederation years.

Rhode Island's responsiveness to the people during the Confederation can be attributed to colonial precedent, to a democratically oriented constitution, to state and local governmental institutions which could not be controlled by a ruling elite, and to the hard times which created a disgruntled populace willing to assert its dissatisfaction at the polls. Unlike most of the states, Rhode Island did not draft a new constitution immediately after independence was declared. The charter of 1663, which granted colonial Rhode Island virtual local autonomy, served as the state's constitution until 1842. This charter provided that the towns would elect deputies semiannually to a state assembly which for all practical matters was supreme. The upper house of the legislature and the primary state officers were elected annually directly by the people, while the judiciary and lesser state officers were appointed by the assembly for one-year terms. Property qualifications were extremely low so that almost all male taxpayers could qualify to vote.[4]

The mere physical size of the state—thirty square miles—also contributed to the democratic tendencies of the government. Nowhere else in the country could state legislatures meet so frequently and allow deputies to consult so readily with their constituents on all important and controversial issues. Between 1786 and 1790 the assembly convened an average of six times yearly, more than twice as often as most other state legislatures.

[2] Jabez Bowen to George Washington, December 15, 1789, in RG 360, PCC, Item 78, Vol. X, 613, National Archives [NA]; William Ellery to Benjamin Huntington, April 17, May 3, 1790, in the Ellery Letters, Rhode Island State Archives [RISA].

[3] Francis Dana to Elbridge Gerry, September 2, 1787, in the L. W. Smith Collection, Morristown National Historical Park [MNHP]; William Ellery to Benjamin Huntington, August 31, 1788, in the Hutington Autograph Collection, Jervis Library [JL]; William Ellery to Benjamin Huntington, July 20, 1787, in the Thomas C. Bright Papers, JL.

[4] Irwin H. Polishook, *Rhode Island and the Union, 1774–1795* (Evanston, 1969), 41–42.

Rhode Island's population, estimated at 59,670 in 1786, also favored democracy.[5] The two largest towns, Newport and Providence, each had fewer than 7,000 inhabitants; the remaining twenty-eight towns had an average population of fewer than 1,675. It was this limited population in the framework of the town meeting that contributed most to Rhode Island's democracy during the Confederation. Furthermore, the state's heterogeneous population, especially in religious matters, fostered an added incentive of tolerance in most phases of life.

The town meeting was the fulcrum of political power in Rhode Island. All important local, state, and national issues were debated and decided in that arena. The towns were required by the constitution to meet at least twice annually to elect deputies to the state assembly. Most towns, however, met much more frequently, averaging seven meetings during each of the Confederation years. The towns of Hopkinton and South Kingstown, both Country Party strongholds, led the way with eighty-four and eighty-one meetings respectively between 1784 and 1790.[6]

Democracy expressed itself in the town meeting in various ways. Most obvious, of course, was the direct election of state officers, councillors, and deputies to the assembly. Furthermore, the electorate exercised a high degree of control over their representatives and often instructed them on specific issues. If a deputy violated his instructions, the freemen were capable of defeating him at the next election, which was never more than six months away.

The initiative was also widely used in Rhode Island town meetings as freemen instructed their deputies to introduce proposals of various sorts into the state assembly. Moreover, state political leaders, before submitting new proposals to the assembly, often sounded them out with their own constituents in town meetings. Only if the response was favorable would the proposal be introduced into the assembly.[7]

The most unique application of democracy in Rhode Island,

[5] "Bostonian," in the *Pennsylvania Packet* (Philadelphia), December 11, 1786.

[6] All of these figures are based upon an examination of the town meeting records of twenty-six of Rhode Island's thirty towns.

[7] In a South Kingstown town meeting held in July, 1789, Country Party leader Samuel J. Potter moved that the tender provision on paper money be repealed. The meeting rejected the proposal, and Potter let the matter drop. William Ellery to Benjamin Huntington, July 13, 1789, in the Ellery Letters, RISA; Ellery to Huntington, July 21, 1789, in the Bright Papers, JL.

however, was the widespread use of the referendum. Party chieftains frequently submitted controversial policy decisions and legislative proposals to the freemen in town meetings. These referenda were not mere rubber stamps used by politicians. Legislators well knew the danger they faced if popular mandates were ignored. Between 1786 and 1789 the state assembly sent no fewer than nine major pieces of legislation to the towns for the consideration of the freemen. Six of these items dealt with state economic policy, one with legislative apportionment, and two with the federal Constitution. In the first of these referenda, in February, 1786, twenty-seven of the state's thirty towns endorsed a proposal to emit paper money; but the legislature, dominated by fiscal conservatives, rejected the mandate. Within two months a majority of these conservative deputies were defeated for re-election and new deputies, most of whom had pledged to vote for paper money, were elected.

The remaining issues were submitted to the towns for consideration between 1787 and 1789 when the legislature was dominated by the Country Party. On all eight issues the ruling party sustained the dictates of the freemen—five pieces of legislation approved by the towns were enacted, while three proposals which failed to get the endorsement of the freemen were rejected. The referendum, therefore, was used by the democratic forces in Rhode Island as a weather vane of public opinion on key issues. Rather than enacting controversial legislation which might become embarrassing or even impossible to defend at the next election, the Country Party submitted proposals to the towns and yielded to the will of the people. It was this kind of responsiveness that conservatives throughout the country feared. Yet it was this kind of responsiveness that produced an authentic democracy in Rhode Island during the Confederation.

Shortly after the War for Independence, the need for responsive state governments was most acute. An unfavorable balance of trade had developed, which combined with the damage suffered during the war and, more importantly, the lack of a circulating medium of exchange—paper or specie—contributed to a serious depression in 1784–1786.[8] Confronted with deflation, each state reacted individually to its own particular problems. Certain similarities, however, occurred.

[8] Merrill Jensen, *The New Nation* (New York, 1950), 187–193.

Immediately after the war, many of the state governments were dominated by fiscally conservative, mercantile-creditor factions. These fiscal conservatives believed that the state governments should take an active role in stimulating the economy; consequently, they endorsed state acts of incorporation, lotteries, bounties, and tariffs. These conservatives, however, bitterly opposed debtor-relief policies. They suggested that private individuals, through honesty, thrift, and industriousness, were responsible for their own economic well-being.[9] Government, they argued, should only interfere when one citizen transgressed the rights of another or when the state was endangered. Furthermore, state governments should also honor their own contractual obligations by paying their state debts with specie.

As the hard times continued, an opposition arose to those politicians who opposed debtor relief. The leaders of this opposition maintained that government should provide economic stability through both monetary and fiscal policies. Demands for tax relief, paper money, debtor legislation, and commercial restrictions mounted, much to the dismay of men in power. Paper money was demanded to provide both debtor relief and a means of funding state debts. The financially distressed petitioned assemblies for paper money "or even leather buttons" that would "answer for internal commerce as well as silver and gold."[10] The whole superstructure of credit wobbled and threatened to collapse as a few prominent debtors went bankrupt.[11] Sheriffs seized and sold the private property of debtors who, in turn, were often imprisoned if they could not meet all their creditors' demands.[12] As the depression deepened, the cleavage between those who opposed and those who favored government aid to debtors widened. Violence threatened in every quarter of the country, and open riot occurred in almost every state.[13] Conservatives feared that

---

[9] "A.Z.," in the *Providence Gazette*, February 26, 1786; *Freeman's Journal* (Philadelphia), August 29, 1787.

[10] "Crisis," in the *New Hampshire Gazette* (Portsmouth), July 20, 1786.

[11] Ebenezer Hazard to Jeremy Belknap, July 5, 18, November 6, 1784, in the Belknap Papers, Massachusetts Historical Society [MHS].

[12] *Northern Centinel* (Lansingburgh, New York), October 1, 1787; Nathaniel Durkee, Jr., to Abraham Ten Broeck, July 3, 1786, in the Ten Broeck Papers, Albany Institute of History and Art.

[13] For the July, 1785, riot in Camden, South Carolina, see David Ramsay, *History of South Carolina* (2 vols., Charleston, 1809), II, 428–429. For the Charles County,

"Everything hastens to another Revolution in America."[14] People wanted government action, not puritanical lectures from "flint-hearted misers" on how hard times could be cured.[15] Consequently, every state government reacted in some manner to the increased demand for relief, but none so radically as Rhode Island.

At the close of the Revolution, Rhode Island's economy was in serious straits. Added to the large-scale destruction inflicted by the British and the unfavorable balance of trade that soon developed, the state was saddled with a burdensome public debt, much of which had become concentrated in the hands of the state's merchants. After the war public and private creditors demanded payment of both interest and principal. The state, in order to meet its obligations, began levying heavier poll and real estate taxes and import duties.[16]

At the same time, the depression created a scarcity of specie and circulating paper currency, which made the increased tax load seem intolerable and ruinous.[17] As the months passed, the situation worsened, and many traders resorted to barter. Although farmers were unable to obtain hard money for their produce, the state and private creditors insisted on payment in specie.[18] "An universal

---

Maryland, riot, see the *Maryland Gazette* (Annapolis), July 20, September 21, and December 28, 1786. For a York County, Pennsylvania, riot, see the *Pennsylvania Mercury* (Philadelphia), June 8, 1787. For riots in Massachusetts, see any of various accounts of Shays's Rebellion and Van Beck Hall, *Politics Without Parties: Massachusetts, 1780–1791* (Pittsburgh, 1972), 184–189. For the Sharon, Connecticut, riot in May, 1787, see Richard D. Hershcopf, "The New England Farmer and Politics, 1785–1787" (master's thesis, University of Wisconsin, 1947), 169–172. For the Exeter, New Hampshire, riot in September, 1786, see the *American Museum* (Philadelphia), V (1789), 263–265. Richard Henry Lee wrote to his brother Henry, "The friends to American honor and happiness here all join in lamenting the riots and mobbish proceedings in Virginia" (September 13, 1787, in Misc. Papers, New York Public Library [NYPL]).

[14] William Smith to Evan Nepean, August 17, 1785, in America and England, Vol. I, 279, Bancroft Transcripts, NYPL.

[15] "A Freeman," in the *Newport Mercury*, February 26, 1785.

[16] Joseph Smith to Brown & Benson, December 20, 1785, in the Brown Papers, John Carter Brown Library [JCBL]; "A Freeman," in the *Newport Mercury*, February 12, 1785; *United States Chronicle*, March 31, 1785.

[17] Jabez Bowen, *To the Freemen of the State of Rhode-Island, Etc.* (Providence, April 13, 1786); William Chace to Edward Forbes, June 25, 1785, in the Nicholas Low Papers, Library of Congress [LC]; "Honestus," in the *Newport Mercury*, January 30, 1786; Cumberland Petition, February 25, 1786, in the Papers Relating to the Adoption of the Constitution, RISA.

[18] Polishook, *R.I. and the Union*, 104–106.

ill-humour and discontent" spread "amongst the oppressed."[19] The state appeared to be divided between two warring factions: a creditor faction, which advocated a policy of riding out the depression, and a farmer-debtor faction, many of whom were on the edge of bankruptcy, which advocated the enactment of public relief measures.

Rhode Island thus faced the dilemma of either repudiating its public debt, accelerating its tax program, or postponing the day of reckoning. In order to resolve this dilemma, and to relieve private debtors, appeals for paper money were voiced. The struggle began in February and April, 1784, when the towns of Westerly and Hopkinton petitioned the assembly for a state currency, but there was little support in the legislature.[20] Again in February, 1786, a proposal for paper money was introduced in the lower house and was rejected by a two to one majority.[21] But even in defeat the paper money forces gained something. The assembly, seeing that the inflationists' strength had grown, requested the towns to instruct their deputies on the paper money issue. If enough towns supported paper money and instructed their deputies accordingly, the assembly would be obliged to authorize it. The towns responded by overwhelmingly instructing their deputies to support paper money. Only three of thirty towns (Providence, Newport, and Portsmouth) instructed their deputies otherwise.[22] Nevertheless, in March, 1786, the pro-paper forces again failed to persuade the assembly to issue paper money.

Paper money men, however, led by Charlestown Assemblyman Jonathan J. Hazard, continued their struggle for debtor relief. Hazard and his cohorts believed that the solution to the state's postwar problems lay in the reincarnation of colonial fiscal meas-

---

[19] John Temple to Lord Carmathen, October 4, 1786, in George Bancroft, ed., *History of the Formation of the Constitution* (2 vols., New York, 1882), I, 398; "A.Z.," in the *United States Chronicle*, September 22, 1785. "A Real Friend to the Public" sketched the many sufferings of the unfortunate debtor yeomen and proposed a loan office to alleviate the hardships. See the *Newport Mercury*, February 5, 1785.

[20] Westerly Town Meeting, February 20, 1784, Westerly Town Hall; Hopkinton Town Meeting, April 24, 1784, Hopkinton Town Hall; *United States Chronicle*, March 10, 1785; *Newport Mercury*, March 12, 1785.

[21] Papers Relating to the Adoption of the Constitution, RISA.

[22] Samuel G. Arnold, *An Historical Sketch of Middletown, Rhode Island* (Newport, 1876), 33.

ures. The colonial records revealed, at least to Hazard and his friends, that paper money had been successfully loaned to Rhode Islanders on real estate collateral, thereby aiding agriculture and commerce, decreasing taxes, and creating extra revenue from interest payments on land bank loans.[23]

Even if the paper bills depreciated, Hazard theorized that the state would benefit. Taxes, payable in paper, could be increased to the level where the depreciation would halt because of the demand for paper money to pay the taxes. With the burgeoning revenue from higher taxes, the state would be able to retire its debt more expeditiously—perhaps within a year or two. It therefore mattered little whether the paper money depreciated or not. Rhode Island would in either case be transformed from a debtor into a creditor state, thus easing the tax burden on the state's freemen.[24]

Anti-paper money men, however, vehemently insisted that there was no need for relief legislation. Despite this assertion, the assembly, on the eve of the 1786 spring elections, enacted several relief measures.[25] Furthermore, state bounties were given to selected Rhode Island products—hemp, flax, and wool—while the state's tax program was enlarged to include an excise on certain items.[26] These acts aided the economy somewhat, but hard times continued, and most of the towns remained behind in tax payments.

This limited program failed to satisfy a majority of Rhode Islanders. The ruling party in the assembly had neither legislated quickly enough, nor, when it did legislate, was the program what

[23] "Beau Jonathan," an ardent patriot, was a member of the assembly most of the time from 1776 to 1790. He was elected to Congress in 1787 and 1788. According to Wilkins Updike, "Hazard was a politician of great tact and talent, and one of the most efficient leaders of the Paper Money party, in 1786, and their ablest debater. . . . He was a natural orator, with a ready command of language, subtle and ingenious in debate. . . . He was for a long time the idol of the country interests, manager of the State, leader of the Legislature, in fact, the political dictator in Rhode Island." See Updike, *History of the Episcopal Church in Naragansett, Rhode Island* (New York, 1847). 328–329. Updike, and his older brother Daniel, were personal friends of Hazard's. For articles on Rhode Island's colonial experience with paper money, see the *Newport Mercury*, February 6, 13, 20, 27, May 15, 1786.

[24] "A Friend to the Public," in the *Newport Mercury*, January 30, 1786.

[25] *Rhode Island Acts and Resolves*, March, 1786, pp. 14–19; John R. Bartlett, ed., *Records of the State of Rhode Island [RSRI]* (10 vols., Providence, 1856–1865), X, 87–88, 90, 106, 115, 180–182.

[26] *Acts and Resolves*, March, 1786, pp. 14–19; *Providence Gazette*, March 4, February 25, 1786; *United States Chronicle*, March 23, April 6, 1786.

the voters wanted. The polarization of parties therefore intensified. The town of Smithfield, seeing little chance of relief from the "several heavy and unjust taxes" levied by the assembly, condemned the state's policy of paying interest on its debt, interest that "was worth more than the principal was, when loaned."[27]

The cry for paper money continued. Many Rhode Islanders believed that merchants had purchased large portions of the public debt at depreciated prices and that it would be equitable to pay these men with a new issue of paper money.[28] The town of Cumberland petitioned the assembly that only paper bills could relieve its people.[29] Tiverton freemen stated that the economic "Calamitys" caused by the shortage of hard money made them "the prey of Sheriffs, Lawyers and Goalers [*sic*]." Pro-paper men argued that more people suffered from lawsuits and executions for debt at that time than would ever suffer from paper money, even if the bills depreciated. Other states, it was argued, had already emitted paper money and were experiencing the good times of old. Finally, paper advocates argued that a fiat currency was wanted not in preference to specie, but in preference to no medium of exchange whatever.[30]

The advocates of a state currency realized that there was little hope of getting paper money from a legislature they did not control. Consequently, a spirited election took place in the spring of 1786. Governor William Greene and Deputy-Governor Jabez Bowen led the Mercantile Party in opposition to John Collins and Daniel Owen, who headed a slate of candidates that included "almost an intire [*sic*] new set of Assistants."[31] The Country Party ran on the battle cry "To Relieve The Distressed," and all of its candidates specifically pledged themselves to vote for paper money and to attempt to solve the problem of the public debt.[32]

---

[27] Smithfield Town Meeting, February 24, April 19, 1786, in Papers Relating to the Adoption of the Constitution, RISA; "A Friend to the Public," in the *Newport Mercury*, January 30, 1786.

[28] William R. Staples, *Rhode Island in the Continental Congress, 1765–1790* (Providence, 1870), 688; "Q.Z.," in the *United States Chronicle*, February 23, 1786.

[29] Polishook, *R.I. and the Union*, 120.

[30] *Newport Mercury*, May 15, 1786.

[31] Greene was a rich merchant, and Bowen had alienated many freemen when, in 1784, he had quashed a move to delay the collection of taxes. William Ellery to Benjamin Huntington, April 11, 1786, in the Bright Papers, JL.

[32] Polishook, *R.I. and the Union*, 124–125.

The election was nothing less than a "revolution." The Country Party won an overwhelming victory. Forty-five new deputies were elected to the seventy-man assembly, while half of the ten-man upper house also won election for the first time. Although Newport, Providence, and Bristol returned their mercantile representatives who had opposed paper money, the character of the legislature had been drastically altered.[33] James Manning, the state's delegate to Congress, later reported that "A more infamous set of men under the character of a legislature, never, I believe, disgraced the annals of the world."[34] Collins and Owen also won impressive victories.[35] Conservative William Ellery of Newport lamented, "Paper money has carried all before it; down will go governors, departments, generals, assistants, deputies, judges, etc."[36] Rhode Island inflationists were at last in a position to enact the program they had advocated for over two years.

When the assembly met in early May it went to work immediately. The collection of the last tax and the recent excise law were suspended.[37] On May 5, 1786, a Warwick deputy proposed that paper money be issued to relieve the scarcity of specie that had caused distress throughout the land. After "a long and interesting Debate," a committee was appointed to draft a bill for the purpose. Before the end of the month the bill passed despite the strenuous opposition of the deputies from Providence, Newport, Westerly, and Bristol.[38]

The act, which authorized the emission of £100,000 of paper, provided that money be loaned on mortgage to any Rhode Islander who owned real estate worth double the value of the amount to be borrowed.[39] The money was to be apportioned

---

[33] Archibald Crary to George Washington, February 2, 1790, in the Washington Papers, Series 7, LC; Theodore Foster to Dwight Foster, August 7, 1788, in the Dwight Foster Papers, MHS.

[34] To the Rev. Dr. Hezekiah Smith, January 18, 1787, in the Manning Papers, Brown University Library.

[35] Polishook, *R.I. and the Union*, 125n.

[36] William Ellery to Benjamin Huntington, April 25, 1786, in the Huntington Autograph Collection, JL.

[37] Samuel G. Arnold, *History of the State of Rhode Island* (2 vols., Providence, 1894), II, 520.

[38] *Providence Gazette*, May 13, 1786. The Country Party crowned its efforts by repealing the relief legislation passed by the previous legislature. See *RSRI*, X, 205, 251; Moses Brown to Nicholas Brown, August 30, 1786, in the Brown Papers, JCBL.

[39] *Acts and Resolves*, May, 1786, pp. 13–17. The provision allowing every qualified

among the towns in the same manner as the last state tax.[40] In each town the bills were to be delivered to two trustees appointed by the assembly. These trustees would grant the loans.

The act declared paper money legal tender. If a creditor refused to accept payment in paper, he was liable to forfeit his entire claim to the state. Never before had such a radical legal tender provision been introduced.[41]

Almost immediately after the paper money act was passed, insults and ridicule were hurled upon the state. A correspondent from Hartford styled the act "the most extraordinary that ever disgraced the annals of democratical tyranny." The writer lamented "the depravity of human nature" that could "sanctify such palpable fraud and dishonesty, by a solemn Act of legislation."[42] Another writer questioned whether the act was a breach of the Articles of Confederation.[43] "Rogue Island" was charged with committing a crime against its people and the other states, while a Bostonian maintained that "Fool-Island" had demonstrated that it was incapable of governing itself "and therefore one of the Sister States must take them into her care and protection."[44]

After listening to such criticism for a month, the Country Party decided to act. At its June session, the legislature passed a penalty

---

Rhode Islander to share equally in the proposed paper money was explained in detail in June, 1786. A three-man committee ruled that "no Freeholder [shall] have more than One Right [to borrow paper money], and that to be apportioned to him in the Town where he lives. . . . If a Freeholder has not sufficient Estate to give double Security for his Share, he may have liberty to sell or dispose of the Whole of his Share, or the Residue." To qualify for a share of the town's quota of paper money, freeholders had to apply to the trustees within three weeks after notice was given of the availability of loans. After that time anyone could receive any amount on loan so long as the necessary security was given. See *Acts and Resolves*, June, 1786, p. 15; December, 1788, pp. 4–6.

[40] The August, 1785, state tax levied a total of £20,000 on the towns. Each town therefore received, in paper money, exactly five times the amount of its tax assessment in August, 1785. See *Acts and Resolves*, August, 1785, pp. 15–16.

[41] *Acts and Resolves*, May, 1786, pp. 13–17; *Newport Mercury*, May 15, 1786. When a creditor refused payment in paper, the debtor could deposit his money with a judge in his district. The judge would then issue a citation informing the creditor of the lodgment. If the creditor failed to accept the money in payment within ten days, the judge would advertise the lodgment in the state's newspapers for three weeks. If, after three months, the creditor failed to claim his money, the debt would be forever canceled and the lodgment, minus the judge's fees and expenses, would be forfeited to the state.

[42] *United States Chronicle*, June 1, 1786.

[43] *Ibid.*, July 6, 1786; "Monitor," in the *Newport Mercury*, August 7, 1786.

[44] "Jonathan," in the *United States Chronicle*, May 25, 1786.

act aimed at maintaining the integrity of the new currency. The act provided that anyone convicted of depreciating the paper money would be fined £100 for the first offense, half of which would go to "the Person who shall inform" and half to the state. Anyone convicted a second time was subject to the same fine along with disenfranchisement.[45] Naturally the Minority denounced this novel measure. It was an act, they said, that would have disgraced the Algerian courts.[46]

The only way to avoid prosecution under the penalty act seemed to be to refrain from all commercial activity. It was asserted that business in both Newport and Providence came to a virtual standstill.[47] However, total work stoppage never occurred; most shops closed for only a brief period. Judge Ebenezer Thompson, of the court of common pleas for Providence County, promised not to prosecute anyone accused of discriminating between paper and coin. When the inevitable informer pressed charges against a shopkeeper, the judge remained true to his word and conveniently managed to be out of town chasing his runaway cow when the case came before his court.[48]

Country Party leaders condemned the daily transgressions of the penalty act[49] and urged farmers to withhold their produce from the two major towns. This policy was apparently effective. During the last week in June the uneasiness in Newport turned into open riot. Several merchants were intimidated and their stores rifled. Only the timely intervention of Governor Collins, the council, and some leading citizens prevented major violence.[50]

Minority leaders in Providence were alarmed. "Scarcity and want [were] beginning to be felt" and violence was anticipated unless the town took action. Consequently, a town meeting was

---

[45] *Acts and Resolves*, June, 1786, pp. 8–9; *Providence Gazette*, July 8, 1786.

[46] *Ibid.*; "A Farmer," in the *Providence Gazette*, August 19, 1786. "A Whig" commented on the effect the penalty act had. "Some of the partisans of a fraudulent paper money have had the audacity lately to pimp around circles of honest citizens . . . in order to find some pretext for informing against them."

[47] *United States Chronicle*, July 13, 1786; "A Mechanic," in the *Newport Herald*, March 13, 1788; "M," in the *Newport Mercury*, August 7, 1786.

[48] Edwin Stone, ed., *The Life and Recollections of John Howland* (Providence, 1857), 101–103.

[49] *Pennsylvania Packet* (Philadelphia), August 22, 1786.

[50] "Extract of a letter from a gentleman in Providence, R.I., to his friend at the southward, dated July 1, 1786," in the *New Jersey Gazette* (Trenton), August 28, 1786; John Brown, *Providence Gazette*, July 8, 1786; *Newport Mercury*, August 7, 1786.

called to discuss means to supply provisions. On July 24, 1786, three hundred freemen assembled and overwhelmingly adopted resolutions that provided that merchants, shopkeepers, and traders should carry on business as usual, that farmers bringing in their produce be treated fairly, and that the town borrow $500 specie to purchase food for the needy.[51]

Country leaders interpreted the Providence resolutions as an attack on the paper money system.[52] To counter the Minority's actions, Providence County farmers gathered at Scituate on August 10 and at East Greenwich on August 22 where they considered measures to support the paper money.[53] Less than a week after the Scituate meeting, Governor Collins, because of "the great Uneasiness now prevailing among the good People of this State," called a special session of the legislature.[54] The Minority, because of the danger of more drastic actions from the East Greenwich meeting and the special session of the legislature, pushed for a compromise plan, which was summarily rejected by the Majority.[55]

On August 22, 1786, deputies from sixteen towns assembled at East Greenwich and appointed a committee to draft resolutions which were accepted a little before midnight. The resolutions more than justified the fears of the Minority. They asked the legislature to support the original paper money act and pass any necessary amendments to enforce the penalty act. The convention also recommended that all produce be withheld from anyone who discriminated against paper money. Furthermore, the assembly was requested to consider three other proposals, all of which were aimed at the Minority: equal representation of the towns in the legislature; the re-evaluation of public securities; and the restriction of private negotiable notes of hand.[56] The Providence delegation and two or three other delegates opposed these resolutions

---

[51] *Providence Gazette*, July 29, 1786; *Newport Mercury*, August 7, 1786.

[52] South Kingstown Town Meeting, July 31, 1786, in the *Providence Gazette*, August 5, 1786; *Newport Mercury*, August 7, 1786.

[53] *Newport Mercury*, August 14, 1786; *Providence Gazette*, August 19, 1786.

[54] *United States Chronicle*, August 17, 1786.

[55] *Ibid.*, July 13, 20, 1786. These compromise measures were proposed again at the East Greenwich convention; *Providence Gazette*, August 26, 1786.

[56] *Ibid.* The equal representation resolve was considered in earnest by the legislature in February and April, 1787. The resolves dealing with private negotiable notes and the public securities were considered in the December, 1786, session.

and, in vain, offered conciliatory measures.[57] The convention's proceedings were immediately sent to the assembly which had convened that day in Newport.

Governor Collins opened the special session of the legislature on August 23. He condemned the machinations of "a Combination of influential Men" who were attempting to defeat the intent of the state's laws. Collins warned the legislators that

> if their [sic] is no check to the present Combination against the Laws, your Lives are unsafe,—your Property is unsecure,—and your Liberties are at a fatal—a final—and a melancholy End.—so avert this impending Catastrophe, party Spirit and private Interest must be laid aside,—the public Good must be the Pole Star,—the Legislature must be wise—and the Executive decisive.[58]

The legislature responded with an amendment to the penalty act which was aimed at producing swift and final judgment. The most odious provisions of the act, according to the Minority, provided that cases were to be tried in special courts without juries and without the right of appeal "according to the laws of the land."[59] The deputies from Providence, Newport, New Shoreham, Bristol, and Warren protested, stating that the new penalty act violated the Articles of Confederation, the Treaty of Peace of 1783, and the constitutional and natural rights of the citizens of Rhode Island. Furthermore, the state would be unable to pay its congressional requisitions with paper money, while the act would destroy all remaining credit.[60] The Country Party rejected the protest and voted to keep it off the records.

Seemingly in response to the Minority protest, the Country Party passed an act which allowed the state to use its paper money to pay Congress the arrears of continental taxes.[61] Since the state was already using its paper money to pay the interest on some national securities owned by Rhode Islanders, Country Party leaders believed it only just that Rhode Island's congressional requisitions also be payable in paper money.[62] Congress, however, disagreed and on September 18 adopted a resolution prohibiting

---

[57] Arnold, *Hist. of R.I.*, II, 522–523.

[58] *United States Chronicle*, September 7, 1786.

[59] *RSRI*, X, 212–213; *Providence Gazette*, September 2, 1786.

[60] *Providence Gazette*, September 2, 1786.

[61] *RSRI*, X, 212–213.

[62] William Ellery to Governor John Collins, June 28, 1786, in Staples, *R.I. in the Cont. Cong.*, 563.

the payment of congressional requisitions in state paper money.[63] Country Party leaders swallowed this bitter pill, but remembered this action when more important fiscal matters concerning the state debt later arose.

Despite the two penalty acts, the Minority maintained its opposition and paper money continued to depreciate. The Providence County towns, therefore, held another convention at Smithfield on September 13, 1786. The convention blamed the Minority for the "truly alarming" situation of the state. To counteract the subversive tendencies "of the mercantile Interest," it proposed that the assembly consider several anti-Minority provisions, one of which called for a state trade system which would have effectively destroyed the merchants as a class.[64]

This radical, socialistic state trade system was fleshed out in an article signed "W.B." in the *United States Chronicle*, the Majority's semiofficial newspaper.[65]

> The people at large, as a State, to provide stores, wharves, shipyards, &c, and order taxes to be paid in money, timber, lumber, labour, or any kind of produce; appropriate the same to the use of building vessels, setting up manufactories, and encouraging agriculture—the raising of sheep, hemp, flax, &c. As fast as vessels are fitted for the sea, let them with all convenient speed be sent away, some on fishing voyages, and some on merchant voyages, as may be thought best. Encourage every mechanical business in the State as well as husbandry. Import no superfluities, nails, hats, shoes, boots, paper, &c. &c. but have every necessary as much as possible manufactured within the State. By these ways and means our stores will soon be furnished with almost every necessary article, both foreign and domestic; our wharves will be lined with lumber, and our shipyards with timber.—The Honorable the General Assembly will take the lead in this business, and will order it carried on in such manner, and under such regulations, as they in their wisdom shall think most convenient for the welfare, advantage, and well-being of the State.—A small sketch of the effects and consequences of this business is as follows, viz.
>
> •   •   •   •
>
> . . . We will take care and not import any more into the State than what our exports from the State will purchase, and all we take

[63] *United States Chronicle*, October 12, 1786; James Manning and Nathan Miller to Governor Collins, September 28, 1786, in Staples, *R.I. in the Cont. Cong.*, 564–565.

[64] *Providence Gazette*, September 30, 1786.

[65] *United States Chronicle*, September 21, 1786.

from the sea, such as whales, cod, and other fish, we will turn into hard money, at other ports, and introduce it into this State;—by these means we shall soon establish a fund adequate to the foreign demand against us; and then we will add riches to the state in the same way. The domestic debt will be easily paid, for when we have it in our power, as a State, to emit as much money as we please, and keep it good, it cannot be a hard matter to establish a fund to answer domestic purposes.

. . . it will set the wheels of industry to running;—here will be employ for the poor, and others, both in town and country, and such pay as they want; not only so, but it will give a fatal stab to the pernicious business of speculation, sharping and hawking, and the dealers in the same must then have recourse to some more honest calling of livelihood; in short, I dare say, it would increase the quantity of labour in this State at least 100,000 days work in a year, which being reckoned at three shillings per day, would amount to a valuable sum of money. Indeed the advantages flowing from this business are almost innumerable; and when it is adopted and carried into execution, it will be obtaining our independence in good earnest.

The Smithfield convention made its recommendations to Governor Collins and requested that he call a special session of the legislature to consider the proposals. A week later, "at the request of" the convention, Collins called the legislature to meet on October 2.[66]

One week after the Smithfield convention met, the superior court considered an immensely important test case involving the second penalty act. In the case of *Trevett v. Weeden*, the plaintiff stated that on September 13 paper money at par was refused in the defendant's butcher shop.[67] The "Knight of the Cleaver," ably defended by General James M. Varnum and Henry Marchant, maintained that a special court (not the superior court) should hear his case and that the penalty act was unconstitutional because of the no-jury provision. Consequently, Weeden asked the court to "take no Cogniscence of the Complaint" by Trevett.[68]

[66] *Ibid.*, September 28, 1786; Noah Mathewson to Noah Webster, September 28, 1786, in the Webster Papers, NYPL. Mathewson concluded that "A State Trade is now proposed & should it be adopted, would complete the mad system." No further mention of the Smithfield convention proposals exists.

[67] James M. Varnum, *The Case, Trevett against Weeden* (Providence, 1787), 1. See the report of this case in the *United States Chronicle*, October 5, 1786.

[68] Plea of John Weeden at the Suit of John Trevett . . . , in the Newport Historical Society [NHS]; *RSRI*, X, 219–220.

Four of the five justices of the court ruled that they had no juris-diction in the case. However, the court stated that the penalty act was, indeed, unconstitutional.[69]

It was in an atmosphere of discontent aroused by *Trevett v. Weeden* and the Smithfield convention that the special session of the state legislature met in early October, 1786. One of the first matters taken up was the case of the superior court. In Rhode Island the legislature was the highest judicial body.[70] Not only did the legislature appoint all judicial officers, but it also served as a court of appeals and possessed the sole power of pardon and impeachment. The Majority consequently thought it con-temptible of the underlings in the superior court to dare to rule unconstitutional an act of the supreme authority of the state. The legislature, therefore, summoned the justices and the clerk of the court "to assign the reasons and grounds of their judgment in adjudging an act of this assembly unconstitutional."[71]

The clerk and three of the five justices of the superior court appeared before the assembly and presented their side of the case. After hearing the justices, the assembly ruled that they had not given satisfactory reasons for their judgment, but that they would not be charged with any "criminality." Consequently they were discharged from attending the assembly. The next year, however, when the legislature appointed judicial officers, all four superior court justices who ruled in favor of Weeden were dismissed.[72]

On October 6, after reprimanding the superior court, the assembly selected a bipartisan committee to report measures that would support the credit of paper money and promote "union and harmony in the state." The committee's compromise plan, however, was rejected outright, and the Majority pressed pro-posals for strengthening the state's currency.[73] A bill was intro-duced to require every citizen and resident of the state to take an oath to support paper money. Any citizen who refused to sub-scribe to the oath would be disenfranchised; any lawyer who

[69] James Manning to Nicholas Brown, October 11, 1786, in the Brown Papers, JCBL; Wilkins Updike, *Memoirs of the Rhode Island Bar* (Boston, 1842), 199–200.

[70] Frank G. Bates, *Rhode Island and the Formation of the Union* (New York, 1888), 135–137.

[71] *RSRI*, X, 218; *United States Chronicle*, November 9, 1786.

[72] *RSRI*, X, 220.

[73] *Providence Gazette*, October 7, 14, 1786; *United States Chronicle*, October 12, 1786.

refused would be disbarred; any merchant who refused could not send or receive vessels; and any government official who refused would be turned out of office.[74] This "test act" was so controversial that the Majority decided to submit it to the towns for consideration.

Meetings were held in all thirty towns to discuss the proposed test act. "A Freeman" asked if anyone could honestly take the oath when the paper currency had already depreciated to "4 to 5 for 1." It appeared to him that the bill was "a State trick" to disenfranchise all honest men and thereby leave the government in the hands of the present rulers.[75] The Providence town meeting also denounced the proposed test act as a violation of the social compact. Enactment of the bill, it suggested, would signal the loss of both liberty and property.[76] Newport's town meeting agreed that the test act would herald a period of "Arbitrary Aristocracy" in Rhode Island.[77]

When the legislature reconvened on October 30, it found that only three towns had favored the bill.[78] All the other towns had voted, some unanimously, to reject it.[79] Consequently, when the vote was taken, only six deputies favored it. The Minority attempted to follow up its success by repealing the legal tender provisions, but the Majority managed to postpone consideration to the next session.

After the defeat of the test act, the Majority believed that the success of its program depended upon the further restriction of its opponents. A far-reaching, anti-Minority program was therefore enacted. First, an act was passed that made lodgments easier.[80] Next, a severe limitation was placed on mercantile credit instruments and promissory notes.[81] This was followed by the submis-

[74] *United States Chronicle*, October 12, 1786. It seems probable that the test act was merely a scare tactic aimed at getting the Minority to moderate its opposition to the paper money.

[75] *Providence Gazette*, October 14, 1786.

[76] William R. Staples, *Annals of the Town of Providence* (Providence, 1843), 306–308.

[77] October 24, 1786, Newport Town Records, in the NHS; *Newport Mercury*, October 30, 1786.

[78] Foster, North Kingstown, and Scituate voted in favor of the test act; *United States Chronicle*, November 2, 1786; *Newport Mercury*, November 13, 1786.

[79] Papers Relating to the Adoption of the Constitution, RISA.

[80] Money could be tendered to any justice in the state rather than only with a justice from one's own county. *RSRI*, X, 226, 230–231. This was enacted because some local judges refused to accept lodgments.

[81] *Acts and Resolves*, December, 1786, pp. 22–23.

sion of a petition for the repeal of Newport's city charter and an excise tax which fell heavily on the larger towns.[82] Finally, a motion was passed for paying one-quarter part of the state securities. This was the initial step in redeeming the entire state debt.[83]

Despite the harshness of these measures, some Rhode Islanders believed that these were but the first steps to be taken. To some freemen the only solution to the state's economic woes was an equal distribution of all property; and according to the *Providence Gazette*, such a bill was introduced in the legislature. The bill provided that:

> Whereas the God of nature made all men equal; from whence it is evident, that the different conditions among mankind have originated from ambition, avarice, and the lust of domination. And whereas, the great objects of the late war were the rights of equality, then violated by the rapacities of British power; notwithstanding which, many citizens among ourselves have acquired immense fortunes out of the earnings of others; and many also have claims and demands of a public and private nature, which they are as able to relinquish as the others to discharge. And Whereas it is essential to the ideas of sovereignty, that all nations should be equal; whereas France, Spain and Holland, make demands for money lent, which they stand in no need of, and which we are unable to pay.

> Wherefore, Be it Enacted by the General Assembly, and by the Authority thereof, That all debts, dues and demands, of whatever nature or kind, be forever abolished, extinguished and discharged.

> And be it further Enacted, That an equal distribution of all property, both real and personal, within this State, be made by the first day of May next, making as many allotments as there are heads of families; and that _____ be a Committee for that purpose.

> And whereas, the continuation of a republican government depends upon supporting the principles of equality: Be it therefore further Enacted, That forever hereafter, at the end of thirteen years respectively, there be a general abolition of debts, and an equal distribution of property.

> And whereas there may be some so bold and daring as to attempt the payment of debts, notwithstanding the good intentions of this General Assembly: Be it therefore Enacted, That every person offending herein, shall for every offence receive thirty-nine

---

[82] *United States Chronicle*, January 18, 1787. Newport's city charter was repealed in March, 1787.
[83] *RSRI*, X, 218, 230.

lashes, and be closely confined in gaol for the space of six months upon conviction before a Justice of Peace, or Warden; and shall moreover forfeit his proportion of property to be distributed as aforesaid.[84]

No evidence, other than this newspaper report, has been found substantiating the introduction of this bill; therefore, it is possible that it was a Minority plant. It is likely, however, that such a bill or proposals of a similar nature were presented in an effort to intimidate the Minority to soften its opposition to the paper money. Whatever the motivation for the newspaper report, there is little doubt that it contributed to the mounting fear of leveller tendencies in Rhode Island.[85] Consequently, a bill was proposed which, in essence, guaranteed the right of private property.[86] This bill was sent to the towns for the consideration of the freemen, but Minority fears persisted. An all-out effort, therefore, was made to unseat paper money men in the April, 1787, elections.

Shortly before the state elections, both parties declared their platforms. The Minority again appealed for compromise, vowing to back paper money if it was declared legal tender at a rate of four to one.[87] The Country Party rejected the compromise and passed an act appropriating money for the redemption of one-quarter part of all state securities.[88] Both parties' positions were clearly and emphatically stated; it was now the choice of the freemen.

The Country Party "carried all before them" in the election, polling majorities of over two to one in most contests. A newspaper writer complained that "where there have been any alteration among rulers, those alterations have been for the worse. Our situation for this year will be but one remove from the state of the d[amne]d."[89] The leaders of the Majority, with this over-

---

[84] *Providence Gazette*, January 6, 1787. This account was reprinted in at least ten different newspapers from Vermont to Georgia.

[85] For other accounts of the demand for an equal distribution of property see Merrill Jensen, *The American Revolution Within America* (New York, 1974), 80–84.

[86] *Providence Gazette*, January 13, 1787.

[87] *United States Chronicle*, April 5, 1787; *Pennsylvania Mercury* (Philadelphia), April 6, 1787.

[88] *Acts and Resolves*, March, 1787, pp. 11–12.

[89] William Ellery to Benjamin Huntington, May 10, 1787, in the Huntington Autograph Collection, JL; *Providence Gazette*, April 21, 1787.

whelming mandate, appointed their followers to most of the state offices. William Ellery lamented that "they have not re-elected one man to office who could interfere with their measures. They have removed all the judges of the Superior Court except the Chief Justice [Paul Mumford], and have introduced a lot of penniless, illiterate, ignorant men."[90] With the takeover of the government virtually complete, the Majority readied itself for the final phase of its redemption of the state debt.

Late in October, 1786, the legislature had appointed a committee to determine the extent of the state debt and to propose ways and means of redeeming it.[91] In March, 1787, the committee reported that the state owed about £160,000 or nearly $545,000.[92] The debt was composed primarily of two types of securities— £106,976 in 6 percent notes and £46,071 in 4 percent notes—both of which had gravitated into the hands of a relatively few public creditors.[93] The committee stated that the 6 percent notes should be redeemed quarterly starting immediately, while the 4 percent notes needed further consideration.[94]

The legislature accordingly called for the redemption of all 6 percent notes in four equal installments beginning in March, 1787. Subsequent acts were passed in June, 1787, February, 1788, and May, 1788, for the redemption of the second, third, and fourth quarters of the 6 percent notes.[95] Any public creditor who failed to submit his certificates to the general treasurer within six weeks would forfeit future claims on that quarter part of the securities.[96] The legislature ingeniously financed this redemption plan by levying taxes payable in paper money immediately after each quarter of the debt was paid. Thus a ready supply of paper money was

[90] To Benjamin Huntington, May 10, 1787, in the Huntington Autograph Collection, JL.

[91] *RSRI*, X, 218.

[92] *Ibid.*, X, 236–237, 451–453; General Treasurer's Accounts, 1781–1792, in Alphabet Book, No. 7, p. 321, RISA.

[93] The remainder of the debt was made up of orders on the treasurer granted for individuals' services rendered during the war. R.I. Records, Accounts for the Loan of 1790, 1790–1835, 32 vols., in RG 53, Vol. 454, Summary, NA.

[94] This was the exact plan established by the acts of December, 1786, and March, 1787.

[95] *RSRI*, X, 251, 273, 280, 286, 290.

[96] Extensions were frequently granted. See the *Newport Herald*, November 22, 1787.

available for the next quarter's payment on the securities. The result was that the 6 percent notes, redeemed with paper money that had depreciated to about fifteen to one, were canceled with no excessive amount of taxation.

In October, 1788, the legislature moved that the first quarter of the 4 percent notes be paid in paper money at their real value.[97] The Minority immediately condemned the Majority for not redeeming all of the 4 percent notes at once. The "procrastinating . . . payment" was "striking proof that the discharge of it was not the principal object with the Majority. Like a tub to amuse the whale, some part of it will be politically retained to throw out at the next election to induce the people to re-appoint them to complete so glorious a work."[98] To discredit this attack, the Majority, in December, 1788, passed an act requiring all public creditors to bring in their 4 percent notes to be redeemed in full by March, 1789.[99] In March, 1789, the legislature, demonstrating its professed concern for fair play, passed an act allowing creditors, who had forfeited their 6 percent notes by not submitting them to the state treasurer, to redeem them once more.[100] Few creditors, however, took advantage of this offer.

By the end of 1789 the state debt had been either redeemed or forfeited, while state expenses had been reduced to less than £10,000 annually, 40 percent of which was raised from the interest on paper money loans. Consequently, the assembly in September, 1789, temporarily repealed the tender provision until the next session a month later.[101] In October a bill was enacted making real estate and certain personal property, at an appraised value, payable for debts. The act also admitted officially that paper money had depreciated and set a fixed scale of depreciation at fifteen to one, paper to specie.[102]

[97] RSRI, X, 305–306; Newport Herald, November 6, 1787; Providence Gazette, November 8, 1787.

[98] Newport Herald, November 6, 1787; New York Daily Advertiser, December 15, 1787.

[99] RSRI, X, 312–313; Providence Gazette, January 10, 1789. The assistants wanted to make 4 percent notes collectible until May, 1789. This would have made the matter a more important political issue since the election took place in April. See the Newport Herald, January 8, 1789.

[100] RSRI, X, 317; Providence Gazette, March 21, 1789.

[101] Providence Gazette, September 26, 1789; United States Chronicle, September 24, 1789; Newport Herald, October 22, 1789.

[102] Providence Gazette, January 16, 1790; RSRI, X, 366.

The period of active political partisanship over paper money in Rhode Island had finally ended. Despite an act passed in September, 1790, allowing paper money loans to be repaid earlier than originally specified, much of the currency continued to circulate because of the need for a circulating medium of exchange.[103] The end of the paper money era, however, was heralded by a legislative resolution in 1792 that provided that all 1786 currency brought into the treasury be burned. Within two years, over half of the £100,000 was destroyed. The remaining currency trickled in until, in 1803, less than £5,000 remained unaccounted for.[104]

Despite the accusations of the Minority, creditors, both public and private, suffered relatively little from the state's paper money. The loan office, although it was a debtor-farmer institution, did not unduly benefit the country towns at the expense of the seaport towns. About 15 percent of the money loaned was issued in Newport and Providence. Of this sum, about 70 percent was loaned to merchants, many of whom had opposed the issuance of paper money. On a statewide basis, 60 percent of all money loaned went to merchants or wealthy landowners. Significantly, 554 men who borrowed the minimum amount of currency offered in their towns, took out a total of slightly over £10,000; the fifty largest borrowers received about £30,000 of the £96,000 issued. The state's ten largest borrowers together received a total of over £8,900, a sum more than £1,650 greater than that loaned in the six towns of Middletown, Jamestown, North Providence, Warren, Barrington, and New Shoreham. Thus both proponents and opponents of paper money, the rich as well as the debtors, took advantage of the loan offices.[105]

One of the major arguments against Rhode Island paper money was that it allowed debtors to tender depreciated currency to their creditors. Even if the creditors refused to accept the paper, the debt was considered paid. No doubt instances of fraud occurred, but most lodgments took place in the early months of paper currency at which time the money had depreciated little. In the last

---

[103] *RSRI*, X, 389.

[104] Henry Phillips, Jr., *Historical Sketches of the Paper Currency of the American Colonies, Prior to the Adoption of the Federal Constitution* (2 vols., Roxbury, 1865), I, 116. The outstanding currency was probably lost, destroyed, or saved as collectors' items.

[105] Grand Committee Office, Account Books, A and B, 1786–1803, RISA.

two years of the tender, moreover, relatively few debtors tendered
paper to their creditors.[106] A total of about £17,000 was lodged in
payment for private debts by about 200 men. Of this sum, £13,514
was forfeited to the state. The state, however, upon the requests
of debtors throughout this time period, allowed over £7,000 of this
forfeited money to be returned to the debtors, who then were still
obliged to their creditors. Consequently, a total of about £6,000
of private debt was annihilated—a relatively small sum when considered against the whole amount of paper money issued and the
amount of state debt redeemed with the currency.[107] The tender
law, therefore, in private transactions acted primarily as a stay law
which forced creditors to postpone foreclosure proceedings rather
than risk payment in paper.[108] Other creditors, who accepted
paper currency when tendered, lost money. Generally speaking,
however, these creditors used the paper currency they received to
pay their creditors, thus losing very little in the process. In essence,
then, the paper currency also served as a sort of indirect tax
on creditors.

Much more significant than the payment of private debts was
the redemption of the entire state debt. Rhode Island, saddled
with a state debt of about £153,000, paid an annual interest of
approximately £10,500 to its creditors. This sum was equivalent
to the total amount of regular annual governmental expenses. To
support such an onerous debt, the state was forced to raise taxes.
The Country Party believed that the only practical fiscal policy,
without overburdening the people, was to issue paper money,
allow it to depreciate, and then redeem the debt with it. This
policy, although it was bound to injure a few, was justified
because most of the state debt had been incurred at depreciated
levels anyway.[109] Many of the larger security holders, hoping for

[106] *United States Chronicle*, August 2, 1787; "Extract of a letter from South-Kings-
town, July 4, 1787," in the *Providence Gazette*, July 14, 1787. Debtors who lodged
money were sometimes socially ostracized or excommunicated from churches and fra-
ternal societies. See the *Providence Gazette*, July 4, 1789; *United States Chronicle*,
July 23, 1789; *Newport Herald*, November 22, 1787, February 26, 1789. Other debtors
felt obligated to justify their lodgments. See the *Providence Gazette*, December 27,
1788, May 2, 1789; *Newport Mercury*, July 30, October 8, 1787; *United States Chronicle*, September 13, 1787, April 30, 1789.

[107] Polishook, *R.I. and the Union*, 157.

[108] George Benson to Nicholas Brown, June 22, 1786, in the Brown Papers, JCBL.

[109] "A Friend to this State," Address to the Citizens of the State of Rhode Island, in
the *American Museum* (Philadelphia), IV (1790), 320–321.

better treatment from the national government, refused to present their certificates for redemption. Almost half of the state debt, therefore, was declared forfeited while the other half was redeemed in paper money.[110] The state debt was liquidated, but in the process, the Country Party alienated an influential segment of the population and aroused the suspicion and hostility of the other states.

Because Rhode Island's economic experience during the Confederation was unusually radical, it served as a symbol of the danger threatened by popularly controlled state legislatures. Every state in the union, to some degree, experienced a popular demand for government relief, and a majority of the legislatures succumbed to the most feared evil of all—paper money. The danger from violent factions, such as Shays's rebels in Massachusetts and the Exeter rioters in New Hampshire, was readily apparent, but it was believed that state and local governmental forces could suppress these illegal protesters. Nothing, however, could restrain the programs of radicals when they constitutionally captured the institutions of government at the polls. Therefore economic conservatives, after losing control of their state legislatures and failing to strengthen Congress through amendments, turned their efforts to a dramatic alteration in the country's central government. As Benjamin Rush stated in February, 1788, if the new Constitution

> held forth no other advantages [than] that [of] a future exemption from paper money & tender laws, it would be eno' to recommend it to honest men. To look up to a government that encourages virtue, establishes justice, insures order, secures property, and protects from every species of violence, affords pleasure that can only be exceeded by looking up in all circumstances to a GENERAL PROVIDENCE.[111]

[110] Phillips, *Sketches of Paper Currency*, I, 166–167. After Rhode Island ratified the Constitution, the state was given $420,000 by Congress under the provisions of the federal assumption program. The legislature then provided that those who still held state certificates (which had been declared forfeited) could bring their certificates to the general treasurer and receive payment from the assumption funds. In order not to discriminate against the state creditors who had received depreciated paper money for their certificates, the legislature provided that all certificates received by the treasurer be returned to the creditors with the amount of paper money received (and its corresponding specie value) endorsed on the back. These state creditors, then, could also take advantage of the assumption funds and apply for the balance of specie due them.

[111] Rush to Jeremy Belknap, February 28, 1788, in the Belknap Papers, MHS. Also see the *Pennsylvania Gazette*, August 29, 1787.

Most Rhode Islanders, however, had a different attitude toward the Constitution. Majority leaders had refused to appoint delegates to the federal convention supposedly because of a "love of true constitutional liberty." The Articles of Confederation set forth the mode of making alterations in the country's government. Any other method of altering the constitution was said to be dangerous to the liberties of the people.[112] In reality, the Majority feared a strengthened central government which might interfere in state matters, especially in fiscal matters. Since the proposed Constitution banned emissions of legal tender state paper money, there was some doubt about the effect ratification would have on the money in circulation. Would all money have to be recalled immediately? Could the state debt still be paid in depreciated currency? What measures could the assembly enact to support the currency? All these were critical questions that no one could answer with complete assurance.[113]

The Constitution also fared badly in Rhode Island for several other reasons, foremost among which was the state rights philosophy of the inhabitants. Because of their religious and economic unorthodoxy, Rhode Islanders for years had been maligned. Occasionally proposals were made to obliterate the state as a political entity. Similar suggestions increased because of the state's opposition to the new Constitution.[114] Such proposals merely strengthened the resolve of the Majority to maintain its opposition to the Constitution and to support the paper money.

By the beginning of 1788 the struggle over the new Constitution had reached major proportions. No longer able to avoid the issue, Majority leaders blocked ratification by submitting the Constitution to the freemen in town meetings where, on March 24, 1788,

---

[112] Governor John Collins to the President of Congress [Arthur St. Clair], September 15, 1787, in Letters Sent by the Governor, Vol. 4, No. 74, RISA. The only other mode that the Country Party accepted in altering the government was a constitutional convention elected directly by the people.

[113] William Ellery to Benjamin Huntington, September 30, 1788, in the Huntington Autograph Collection, JL.

[114] Francis Dana to Elbridge Gerry, September 2, 1787, in the L. W. Smith Collection, MNHP; *United States Chronicle*, November 1, 1787; *Providence Gazette*, February 7, 1788; "Extract of a Letter from a very distinguished Member of Congress to a Gentleman in this State, dated, New York, September 15, 1789," in the *United States Chronicle*, September 24, 1789.

it was defeated by a vote of 2,711 to 243.[115] In a letter to the president of Congress, the assembly justified the referendum as being based "upon pure Republican Principles" derived "from the Body of the People at large."[116] Although the Constitution was overwhelmingly defeated, the assembly stated that the new plan of government contained some necessary provisions that could be adapted to the Confederation government, but as for the Constitution as a whole, it was a dead issue.

With the ratification of the Constitution, economic and political sovereignty shifted from the states to the central government where fiscal conservatives hoped to thwart the efforts of the unorthodox. Not until May 29, 1790, however, after the state debt was completely canceled, did Rhode Island finally adopt the new Constitution. This obstructionist action antagonized the entire country, yet a majority of Rhode Islanders still endorsed the policies of the Country Party. Despite their tarnished image, Rhode Island paper money advocates were able to prevent the adoption of the new Constitution long enough to complete one of the most successful programs of debtor relief and public finance undertaken by any of the American states during the Revolution.

---

[115] Rhode Island was the only state that refused to call a convention to consider the Constitution. Supporters of the Constitution condemned the referendum because, in their estimation, pure democracy was impractical. For the names of men who voted in the referendum, see Papers Relating to the Adoption of the Constitution, RISA. The vote totals given here vary from most secondary sources because mistakes in addition by town clerks and assembly clerks have been corrected.

[116] Governor John Collins to the President of Congress [Cyrus Griffin], April 5, 1788, in Letters from the Governor, Vol. 4, No. 76, RISA.

The Impact of the Constitution on State Politics: New York as a Test Case

Steven R. Boyd

FEW EVENTS in American history have attracted as much attention as the adoption of the United States Constitution. Historians have examined the debate over the Constitution on the national, state, and local levels. They also have analyzed the economic interests, social characteristics, and political aspirations of the men who framed and adopted as well as those who opposed ratification of the Constitution.[1] The impact of the Constitution on the states themselves and on politics outside the state conventions, however, scarcely has been considered.[2] Yet the issue of the Constitution intruded upon and significantly altered state politics in the fall of 1787. It provoked widespread intra- and interstate political activ-

---

[1] Jack P. Greene provides a convenient survey of the historiography in his introduction to *The Reinterpretation of the American Revolution, 1763–1789* (New York, 1968). Alfred Young, *The Democratic-Republicans of New York: The Origins, 1763–1797* (Chapel Hill, 1967), discusses the literature as it relates to New York.

[2] This applies to both national and state studies. Thus Clarence E. Miner, *The Ratification of the Federal Constitution by the State of New York* (New York, 1921), and Robert A. Rutland, *The Ordeal of the Constitution: The Antifederalists and the Ratification Struggle of 1787–1788* (Norman, 1966), both concentrate on the conventions. Similarly E. Wilder Spaulding, *New York in the Critical Period* (New York, 1932), and Jackson Turner Main, *The Antifederalists: Critics of the Constitution* (Chapel Hill, 1961), while they discuss the political antecedents of the ratification controversy, focus on the state conventions in 1787 and 1788. Linda G. DePauw, *The Eleventh Pillar: New York State and the Federal Constitution* (Ithaca, 1966), also limits her study to the immediate issue of the Constitution and its ratification.

270

ity by Federalists and Antifederalists, and it led to the nationalization of the spring, 1788 and 1789, state elections.

This impact of the Constitution is best exemplified in New York. There incumbent Governor George Clinton and his supporters used their offices and influence to try to prevent unconditional ratification of the proposed Constitution by their state and the nation. Clinton brought considerable weight to this effort. He was a central figure in New York politics throughout the Confederation. First elected governor in 1777, he was re-elected several times, in part on the basis of his popularity as a war hero. He also developed a loyal following among local county officials by the use of his position as the head of the state council of appointment. In addition, Clinton had a core of loyal supporters among state legislators. Although the figure varied with each session, roughly one-third of the members of the legislature were "Clintonians," i.e., supporters of Clinton's programs and policies. Another third, "Anti-Clintonians," consistently opposed Clinton and his programs. A third group, usually smaller than either the Clintonians or Anti-Clintonians, consisted of political neutrals who shifted their support between the two major blocs on each vote or issue.[3]

Of the wide range of issues that divided the legislature during the Confederation, some are most indicative of Clinton and the Clintonians' views and aspirations. Clinton favored the confiscation of Tory estates and the rapid distribution of those estates and New York's unsettled western lands. The Clintonians advocated issuing paper money and endorsed other modest forms of debtor-relief legislation, but Clinton personally led the state's military action against Shaysites crossing into New York from Massachusetts in 1787. A nationalist during the war, Clinton came to see the states as the mainstay of the Confederation after war's end. Thus, in 1784 he favored passage of a state impost and three years later a measure providing for state assumption of the national debt. Committed to state solutions of the problems facing the Confederation, the Clintonians opposed various attempts to strengthen the Articles of Confederation: among them the trade regulation

<hr />

[3] E. Wilder Spaulding, *His Excellency George Clinton: Critic of the Constitution* (New York, 1938), *passim*; Young, *Democratic-Republicans*, chap. 2; and Jackson Turner Main, *Political Parties Before the Constitution* (Chapel Hill, 1973), chap. 5.

amendment, the impost of 1781, and the impost of 1783.[4] In January, 1787, the legislature appointed delegates to the Philadelphia Convention. But three weeks before the convention in Philadelphia adjourned, a newspaper writer, using the pseudonym "Rough Carver," warned that there were men in New York City "assiduously striving to form a party against Federal attachments," that is against the reforms proposed by the federal convention.[5] The city's newspapers soon reflected the efforts of these men. In July, 1787, Alexander Hamilton attacked New York's Governor George Clinton for criticizing the work of the federal convention.[6] On September 6 the *New York Journal* published a piece signed "A Republican" in which the author declared that it was the responsibility of every officer in government "freely and unreservedly to express his sentiments on public measures." A week later "Rusticus" openly attacked the "aristocratic junto" in New York, which presumably included both Hamilton and the author of the "Rough Carver" essay, for seeking to silence all "who do not subscribe to their political creed." Like "A Republican," "Rusticus" insisted it was the responsibility of every citizen to express his "approbation or disapprobation of public measures . . . ," including the convention.[7] As "Anti-Defamationist" expressed it, "If . . . our worthy Governor or any other man conceives that by attempting a cure . . ." the convention has instead increased the malady, "it becomes his duty, as far as in him lies, to stem the tide of congressional, legislatorial, or popular prejudice" in its favor.[8]

In the following weeks Clinton, Abraham Yates, Jr., and the remainder of the New York congressional delegation sought to do just that. On the floor of the Confederation Congress Melancton Smith, Yates, and John Haring supported Richard Henry Lee's attempt to submit the proposed Constitution to the states accompanied by a resolution pointing out that the convention had exceeded the authority of Congress by proposing an entirely new form of government. Defeated in that and a second effort to submit amendments to the Constitution for the consideration of the states,

[4] Spaulding, *New York in the Critical Period, passim.*
[5] *New York Daily Advertiser*, September 5, 1787.
[6] *Ibid.*, July 21, 1787.
[7] *New York Journal*, September 13, 1787.
[8] *Ibid.*, September 20, 1787.

Lee, Smith, Yates, and Haring, along with Arthur Lee, a member of the board of treasury, and Massachusetts convention delegate Elbridge Gerry—all then in New York—apparently met to plot strategy and to co-ordinate their efforts, which were to extend to every state in the union.[9]

Several key decisions were made by these men in early October and communicated by Richard Henry Lee to Antifederalists from Massachusetts to South Carolina. They first agreed that the state legislatures should delay action on the report of the federal convention until their spring sessions and that when they adopted resolves calling for conventions they schedule those conventions to meet simultaneously. Second, the Antifederalists decided to embark on an extensive, co-ordinated propaganda campaign designed to convince the public of the need for amendments and a second constitutional convention. Finally, they agreed that once the conventions did meet, Antifederalist delegates should communicate with one another, agree upon a specific list of amendments, and unite in the demand for a second constitutional convention.[10]

With their legislature not scheduled to meet until January, 1788, New York Antifederalists were able to concentrate their initial efforts during the fall months on the second phase of the Antifederalist attack. In newspaper essays, broadsides, and pamphlets they outlined their objections to the proposed Constitution, warned of the dangers inherent in adopting it in its current form, and proposed alternatives to unconditional ratification.

[9] There is no direct record of a meeting of Richard Henry Lee, Arthur Lee, and the New Yorkers—Clinton, Yates, Smith, and Haring. For indirect evidence that they did meet see "New England," in the *Connecticut Courant* (Hartford), December 24, 1787, and March 30, 1788. Gerry alluded to a meeting with Lee in his letter to James Warren, October 18, 1787, in the Sang Autograph Collection, Southern Illinois University. In addition, Lee knew all of these men personally, and it seems implausible at a minimum that they did not meet to plan strategy, given their common opposition to unconditional ratification.

[10] During October Lee outlined such a plan of action in letters to Samuel Adams in Massachusetts, William Shippen in Pennsylvania, and Edmund Randolph and George Mason in Virginia, in James C. Ballagh, ed., *The Letters of Richard Henry Lee* (2 vols., New York, 1911–1914), II, 430–447, 450–458. In each case Lee stressed the need for the recipients of his letters to convey his objections and solicit the support of former allies of Lee's in the Confederation Congress: Dr. Samuel Holten and James Lovell in Massachusetts; Dr. James Hutchinson in Pennsylvania; Thomas Stone in Maryland; Chancellor Edmund Pendleton in Virginia; and Henry Pendleton in South Carolina.

In essence Clinton and other New York Antifederalists objected that the proposed Constitution removed sovereignty from the states and vested it in one national government. That meant that powers previously exercised by the state governments henceforth would be wielded by the central government. The most significant of these was the virtually unlimited power to tax. The new government's mandate to legislate for the general welfare and to adopt whatever measures were necessary and proper to achieve that end were also alarming. With such legislation defined as the supreme law of the land and enforceable in national courts, the total destruction of the state governments would follow.

Antifederalists also charged that the new government would not be responsive to the majority of the people. The Senate was an aristocratic body, the President an elective King. Not even the House of Representatives, the one democratic element in the new government, would adequately represent the interests of small farmers, mechanics, and artisans spread across the land. The government would not only operate independent of, or even in opposition to, the wishes of the majority of the people, but the Antifederalists contended that it would silence all its critics. Finally, and in the popular mind most importantly, there was no bill or declaration of rights detailing the rights and the liberties of the people.[11]

Despite these objections and dire prognostications, Clinton and most New York Antifederalists did not call for rejection of the Constitution. Instead, they suggested that citizens should demand amendments and a second constitutional convention. A second convention could remedy the structural errors in the Constitution, restrict the powers of the new government, and secure the funda-

[11] Antifederalists' objections to the Constitution are summarized in Main, *Antifederalists*, chaps. 6 and 7. The specific objections are taken from one or more of the following: "Cato" [George Clinton], I–VII, September 27, 1787–January 3, 1788; "Brutus" [Robert Yates], I–XVI, October 18–April 10; "A Countryman" [DeWitt Clinton], I–IV, December 6 to January 10; "Cincinnatus" [Arthur Lee], I–VI, November 1 to December 6; and "Republican," October 25, all in the *New York Journal;* Robert Yates and John Lansing, Jr., to George Clinton, [December 21], in the *New York Daily Advertiser,* January 14, 1788; and a broadside signed by Jeremiah Van Rensselaer, chairman of the Albany Antifederal Committee, April 10, 1788.

[12] "Cato," I [George Clinton], in the *New York Journal,* September 27, 1787. Few New York Antifederalists explicitly recommended a second convention during the fall. The proposal was most frequently made by Pennsylvania Antifederalists whose essays were reprinted in the *New York Journal* and whose broadsides were distributed

mental rights of the people. It could also "give you another [Constitution] if it is required."[12]

The Antifederalist alternatives to ratification—amendments and a second constitutional convention—were implicit in most of the essays written by New York Antifederalists or published in the city's Antifederalist *New York Journal.* Clinton and his followers did not totally rely, however, on the normal circulation of the city's newspapers to carry their views to the people. They took special care, for instance, to see that certain pieces were printed in the Thursday issue of the *Journal* because of its more extensive country circulation.[13] They also organized themselves as a "Society of Gentlemen in New York" whose major purpose was to make Antifederalist objections to the Constitution widely known. In order to do this the society subsidized the printing of at least one edition of Richard Henry Lee's *Letters from the Federal Farmer,*

---

by New York Antifederalists. See, for example, "Centinel" I and II [Samuel Bryan], in the *New York Journal,* November 1, 1787; "An Officer of the Late Continental Army" [William Findley], *ibid.,* November 19, 1787; and "Old Whig" IV and V [James Hutchinson and others], *ibid.,* December 8, 10, 1787. All five of these essays were published as broadsides and were among the pieces distributed by John Lamb and other New York Antifederalists during the fall. In the spring New York Antifederalists also came out in favor of a second convention as an alternative to unconditional ratification. See, for example, the broadside signed by Jeremiah Van Rensselaer, chairman of the Albany Antifederal Committee, April 10, 1788; and "Plebian" [Melancton Smith], *Address to the People of the State of New York,* in Paul L. Ford, ed., *Pamphlets on the Constitution of the United States* (Brooklyn, 1888), 89–116. Paul Ford first attributed the "Cato" letters to Clinton in his *Essays on the Constitution* (Brooklyn, 1892). In *The Eleventh Pillar,* Linda G. DePauw challenges this attribution, suggesting instead that Abraham Yates, Jr., was the author.

I think the burden of evidence sustains Ford's identification. It certainly renders suspect DePauw's suggestion that Abraham Yates, Jr., was "Cato." In the first place Clinton's name was linked to the "Cato" essays in the contemporary press, a point denied by DePauw. In "Cato's Soliloquy," published in the *New York Daily Advertiser,* October 23, "Cato's" name is mentioned twice. In "Cato's Soliloquy Parodied," a satirical piece which appeared in the *Northern Centinel* (Lansingburgh) on December 25, 1787, each reference to "Cato" is replaced with "C*****n." Similar evidence casts doubt upon Dr. DePauw's "guess" that Yates was Clinton. An extract of a letter from a gentleman at Poughkeepsie, when the legislature assembled in January, 1788, and printed in the *Northern Centinel,* January 15, declares that "Cato and the Rough Hewer are both here." Since Yates was known to be the "Rough Hewer," it seems clear that he was not "Cato." Contemporaries believed Clinton to be "Cato." That belief, and Ford's attribution, eventually may be proven incorrect. But until evidence to the contrary becomes available, I think we should continue to attribtue the "Cato" essays to Governor George Clinton.

[13] Charles Tillinghast to Colonel Hugh Hughes, January 27–28, 1788, in the Hugh Hughes Papers, Library of Congress [LC].

which, with a broadside compilation of "Centinel" I and II and an essay signed "Timoleon," they distributed throughout New York and New England.[14]

The details of the society's distribution campaign cannot be determined with precision. In broad outline, though, John Lamb, an ally of Governor Clinton and collector of the impost for the state of New York, sent packets of pamphlets, newspapers, and broadsides to political leaders across the country during November–December, 1787. Lamb did so anonymously, using only an unsigned covering letter asking that the recipient (whom Lamb believed to be an Antifederalist) circulate the materials among the populace.[15] Federalists nevertheless quickly identified Lamb and the "Antifederal junto" in New York as the source of these packets.

The Federalist response to these shipments, both public and private, provides some measure of the breadth and persistence of

---

[14] In "The Authorship of the Federal Farmer Letters," in the *William and Mary Quarterly* [*WMQ*], 3rd Ser., 31 (1974), 299–308, Gordon S. Wood questions another of Paul L. Ford's attributions, that of *The Letters from the Federal Farmer* to Richard Henry Lee. The evidence which supports Ford's attribution is, I believe, twofold. First, the *Letters* were written and published during October, 1787, while Lee was in New York. Indeed, Lee's departure from New York coincided with their public release. Lee also had an opportunity to write and arrange for the publication of the second series of *Letters*. The *Additional Letters* are dated December 25 to January 25. Lee could have written them while at his plantation, Chantilly. An "Advertisement," which served as an introduction to the second volume, is dated January 30. That was the day Arthur Lee arrived in Virginia, on leave from the board of treasury which met in New York. Arthur Lee could have carried the manuscript north with him when he returned to New York. Delayed by bad weather he did not reach New York until March 11. But the *Additional Letters* were not published until May, 1788, allowing ample time for Lee to deliver the manuscript to Antifederalist printer Greenleaf before the publication date.

If Lee had the opportunity to write and arrange for the publication of both volumes of the *Letters*, some contemporaries also believed he was the author. A Federalist essayist, "New England," attacked Lee as the author in the December 24 *Connecticut Courant*. In January, 1788, the editor of the *Massachusetts Centinel* (Boston) criticized the *Letters* "said to be written by Richard Henry Lee," while a correspondent in the Antifederalist *American Herald* (Boston) defended Lee, whom he also believed to be the author (January 7, 1788). A year later the *Massachusetts Centinel*, reporting Lee's election to the United States Senate from Virginia, described Lee as a "celebrated writer" (January 4, 1789).

Certainly newspaper writers and their readers could have been mistaken in their identification of Lee as the author of the *Letters*. Still, given the widespread belief that Lee was the author, and in the absence of evidence to the contrary, I think we should attribute *The Letters from the Federal Farmer* to Richard Henry Lee.

[15] *New York Daily Advertiser*, December 4, 1787.

the Antifederalist onslaught. On November 22, for instance, the *New Haven Gazette* revealed that a "piece called 'Centinel' is circulating with great industry in this state [Connecticut]," having been sent there by John Lamb. An article which reported the arrival of packets of "Centinel" essays on November 12 appeared simultaneously in Hartford and Middletown.[16] In December this influx was followed, according to reports in the Hartford *American Mercury*, by several shipments of Richard Henry Lee's *Letters from the Federal Farmer*.[17] Federalist Jeremiah Wadsworth confirmed this when he complained to Henry Knox that Connecticut Antifederalists "daily receive pamphlets and newspapers from Antifederalists in New York and Pennsylvania."[18] Wadsworth told Rufus King that the pamphlets were sent to his cousin, Comptroller General James Wadsworth, congressional delegate Stephen Mix Mitchell, "and all others supposed to be against the Constitution."[19]

Although Federalist complaints originated in Connecticut, Lamb did not limit his efforts to that state. The *New Haven Gazette's* report on "Centinel" essays circulating in Connecticut was reprinted in New York, Albany, Northampton, Boston, and Portsmouth. A New York *Daily Advertiser* criticism of that city's Antifederalists for circulating handbills in Connecticut was reprinted in Lansingburgh, Boston, Portsmouth, and Exeter. Another *New Haven Gazette* attack on "Centinel" was reprinted in Middletown, Newport, New York, Poughkeepsie, and Boston.[20]

The printing of such complaints about Lamb, the "Centinel," and Richard Henry Lee implies that these Antifederalist pieces were circulating in the towns and counties which were served by

[16] *American Mercury* (Hartford) and *Middlesex Gazette* (Middletown), both November 26, 1787.

[17] December 17, 1787.

[18] December 12, 1787, in the Knox Papers, Massachusetts Historical Society [MHS].

[19] December 16, 1787, in the King Papers, New-York Historical Society [NYHS].

[20] *New Haven Gazette*, November 22, 1787; *New York Morning Post*, December 1, 1787; *Albany Gazette*, December 6, 1787; *Hampshire Gazette* (Northampton), December 6, 1787; *Massachusetts Centinel*, December 1, 1787; *New Hampshire Gazette*, (Portsmouth), December 5. 1787; *Daily Advertiser*, December 4, 1788; *Northern Centinel*, December 18, 1788; *Massachusetts Gazette* (Boston), January 4, 1788; *New Hampshire Gazette*, January 9, 1788; *Freeman's Oracle* (Exeter), January 18, 1788; *New Haven Gazette*, December 13, 1787; *Daily Advertiser*, December 19, 1787; Poughkeepsie *Country Journal*, December 26, 1787; *Massachusetts Centinel*, December 27, 1787.

the newspapers that reprinted the attacks. "A Customer" asked the printer of the Poughkeepsie *Country Journal* to reprint an article critical of Lamb and "Centinel" because the essay "has been circulated in this state no less than in Connecticut."[21] Correspondents in the Lansingburgh *Northern Centinel* and *Albany Gazette* also grumbled that "certain great characters in this state . . . have troubled this part of the country with false alarms (viz. George [*sic*] Bryan's 'Centinels') in great abundance."[22]

Lamb also saw to it that an ample supply of Lee's *Letters* were available to Massachusetts convention delegates. He did so through Edward Powars, editor of the *American Herald*, who advertised Lee's *Letters*, specifically the printing prepared for the "Society of Gentlemen in New York," for sale on December 31, 1787. This provoked a local controversy in Boston. A correspondent in the *Massachusetts Gazette* assured his readers that the pamphlet (which he admitted he had not read) contained "all the falsehoods, absurdities and improbabilities with which the scribbling sons of anarchism and Antifederalism abound."[23] Powars could only reply that he presumed "a free and impartial discussion of this important subject cannot be disagreeable to the HONEST part of the community," and that he hoped the pamphlets would be "generally purchased."[24]

The New York Antifederalists did not rely, however, solely on the merits of Lee's written arguments. They wrote to allies in Boston and sent "emissaries" to both the Massachusetts and New Hampshire conventions.[25] There they attended the debates of the conventions, and, according to reports in the *Massachusetts Gazette*, were "introduced into those nocturnal scenes of conspiracy carried on by the star chamber associates. . . ."[26] The leader of those associates was James Warren, who was urging Massachusetts convention delegates to adjourn until June. Such an adjournment was consistent with the initial Antifederalist goal of

---

[21] December 13, 26, 1787.

[22] *Northern Centinel*, December 25; *Albany Gazette*, December 20, 1787.

[23] December 28, 1787.

[24] *American Herald*, January 7, 1788.

[25] Archibald Maclaine to James Iredell, March 4, 1788, in Griffith J. McRee, *Life and Correspondence of James Iredell* (2 vols., New York, 1857–1858), II, 219–220; Peter Curtenius to George Clinton, March 2, 1788, in the George Clinton Papers, George Bancroft Transcripts, New York Public Library [NYPL].

[26] *Massachusetts Gazette*, February 8, 1788.

simultaneous conventions and perhaps reflected the efforts of Lamb's emissaries there.

TABLE I

STATE	LEGISLATURE CALLED CONVENTION	DATE OF CONVENTION	DATE OF RATIFICATION
Delaware	November 9–10, 1787	December 3–7, 1787	December 7, 1787
Pennsylvania	September 28–29, 1787	November 20–December 15, 1787	December 12, 1787
New Jersey	October 26–November 1, 1787	December 11–20, 1787	December 18, 1787
Georgia	October 26, 1787	December 25, 1787–January 5, 1788	January 2, 1788
Connecticut	October 16–17, 1787	January 3–9, 1788	January 9, 1788
Massachusetts	October 25, 1787	January 9–February 7, 1788	February 6, 1788
New Hampshire (first session)	December 11–14, 1787	February 13–22, 1788	
Rhode Island (referendum)	March 1, 1788	March 24, 1788	
Maryland	November 27, 1787	April 21–28, 1788	April 28, 1788
South Carolina	January 19, 1788	May 12–24, 1788	May 23, 1788
New Hampshire		June 18–21, 1788	June 21, 1788
Virginia	October 25–31, 1787	June 2–27, 1788	June 26, 1788
New York	January 31–February 1, 1788	June 17–July 26, 1788	July 26, 1788
North Carolina (first convention)	November 20, 1787	July 21–August 4, 1788	
North Carolina	November 30, 1788	November 16–23, 1789	November 21, 1789
Rhode Island (first session of convention)	January 17, 1790	March 1–6, 1790	
Rhode Island (second session of convention)		May 24–29, 1790	May 29, 1790

During the winter and fall months then, Lamb and members of the New York society mounted an extensive, co-ordinated, pub-

lic attack on the Constitution. They also co-operated with Massachusetts and New Hampshire Antifederalist convention delegates
in an attempt to adjourn those states' conventions. There were
deficiencies in their efforts, in Connecticut where packets of Antifederalist literature were distributed to Federalists; in Massachusetts where the legislature approved a January convention before
Antifederalist leaders in the state house and senate learned of the
plan for simultaneous conventions later in the year; and in New
Hampshire where the Federalist-dominated legislature approved
a February convention. Most of these shortcomings, however, were
beyond the control of New York Antifederalists, while others,
notably in New Hampshire, were at least temporarily overcome
with that state convention's adjournment. Furthermore, within
New York the initial "popular prejudice" in favor of the Constitution dissipated, though the Antifederalists were organizationally
prepared to conduct statewide campaigns for political office to
insure that New York would not unconditionally ratify the
proposed Constitution.

This effort did not take on real direction until February, 1788.
The state legislature, which was to call the convention, set the
date for the elections of delegates, and establish requirements for
voters, did not assemble in Poughkeepsie until January 11. Three
weeks later both houses approved a convention resolve which
made all white males over the age of twenty-one eligible to vote
for convention delegates on April 29. The convention was to
assemble in Poughkeepsie on June 17.[27]

One provision of this resolution, in particular, had a significant
effect on the shape of the ensuing Antifederalist campaign. The
elections for convention delegates coincided with those for state
legislators. In the following months this resulted in a blending of
the Antifederalists' campaigns for convention delegates and state
legislative seats into one united effort.

Once the legislature took action approving the convention
resolves, Federalist Egbert Benson expected "great politics to
cease."[28] Although the legislative session continued for another
month, Benson was essentially correct because following the pas-

[27] Broadside resolve, in the McKesson Papers, NYHS.
[28] To James Madison, February 1, 1788, in the Fogg Autograph Collection, Maine
Historical Society.

sage of the convention resolve members of the legislature concentrated their attention elsewhere. In Poughkeepsie they met to discuss strategy, and then many members of the house and senate left to establish county committees, nominate candidates, and begin the campaign for their election.[29]

Before the end of April Antifederalists created committees designed to "manage the elections for convention" delegates in twelve of the state's thirteen counties.[30] One of the first to organize was Albany County. There Antifederalists met on February 12 and appointed a committee to co-ordinate their efforts in the convention election. Two weeks later the same committee called for a meeting of "two or three gentlemen from the different districts in the county" to meet in mid-March and nominate candidates for the convention. At that meeting Antifederalists agreed upon a slate of candidates for the convention, assembly, and senate.[31]

Even before the nominations there was extensive campaigning in the county. Federalist Leonard Gansevoort remarked that the "opposers of the New Constitution here [Albany] are indefatigable in endeavouring to excite the people against it. . . ."[32] They also, as William North bitterly complained, scattered "the 'Centinel,' *The Farmers Letters* and every other publication against the Constitution . . . all over the county, while *The Federalist* remains at New York. . . ."[33] Following the nomination of candidates, a broadside composed of Antifederalists' objections to the Constitution and the Antifederalist nominees for the convention, assembly, and senate was also circulated throughout the county. As Jeremiah Van Rensselaer, chairman of the Albany Antifederalist committee, reported to John Lamb, "we are in close action from morning to night."[34] Lamb was equally active. During March, 1788, he sent John Lansing, Jr., a candidate for both the convention and assembly, 300 copies of Mercy Warren's *Observa-*

[29] Melancton Smith to [?], April 6, 1788, in the Lamb Papers, NYHS; Cornelius Schoonmaker to Peter Van Gaasbeek, April 4, 1788, in the Van Gaasbeek Papers, Roosevelt Library [RL], Hyde Park.

[30] The phrase was used by Federalist William North to describe the Albany County committee. To Henry Knox, February 13, 1788, in the Knox Papers, MHS.

[31] John Lansing, Jr., et al., to anon., handwritten broadside, in the Emmet Collection, NYHS; *Albany Journal*, March 15, 1788.

[32] To Peter Gansevoort, February 13, in the Gansevoort-Lansing Papers, NYPL.

[33] To Henry Knox, February 13, in the Knox Papers, MHS.

[34] *Daily Advertiser*, April 10, 1788.

tions . . . by a Columbian Patriot and 60 copies of the Antifederalist compilation, *Observations on the Proposed Constitution*,
with a request that they "be distributed amongst the inhabitants
of your county."[35]

Lamb, as a part of a distribution effort which ultimately
reached Antifederalists in twelve of the state's thirteen counties,
also sent Lansing an additional two hundred copies of the Warren
pamphlet with instructions to send them to men in Washington
and Montgomery counties who would disseminate them "with the
most expedition."[36] Even before these pamphlets arrived, "Antifederal business" had been carried on in Washington County with
great spirit. State Senator John Williams was a member of the
county Antifederalist committee and a candidate for the convention. Two other members of the Washington committee, David
Hopkins and Albert Baker, were also candidates for the convention, while a third, Alexander Webster, was renominated for a
seat in the assembly.[37]

In Montgomery County a meeting of the "four lower districts
of the county" nominated all four members of the Antifederal
committee—Christopher P. Yates, Volkert Veeder, John Frey, and
William Harper—and John Winn and Henry Staring for the convention. That meeting also named the same six candidates for the
assembly. Antifederalists circulated copies of the nominations and
their publications throughout the county.[38]

Columbia County Antifederalists met at Claverack on March 18
and nominated Peter Van Ness, Mathew Adgate, and John Bay as
candidates for the convention. All three men were members of the
county's Antifederalist committee, while the latter two and John
Korts were the Antifederalist candidates for the assembly. Van
Ness was a candidate for the senate.[39] Electioneering in Columbia County was widespread. Van Ness received 150 copies of

[35] Notation on an undated distribution list, in the Lamb Papers, NYHS. This list
includes the names of the members of each Antifederal county committee in the state.
[36] *Idem.*
[37] Abraham Yates to Abraham G. Lansing, February 28, 1788, in the Yates Papers,
NYPL.
[38] Christopher Yates to George Herkimer, April 9, 1788, in the Herkimer Papers,
Oneida Historical Society.
[39] *Hudson Weekly Gazette*, March 20, 1788. Van Ness's candidacy was mentioned
in Henry Oothoudt and Jeremiah Van Rensselaer to Jellis Fonda, April 5, 1788, in
the New York State Library.

Observations . . . by a Columbian Patriot and 35 copies of an Antifederalist compilation, *Observations on the Proposed Constitution* from the New York City committee. The latter included "The Reasons of Dissent of the Minority of Pennsylvania," a piece a correspondent in the *Hudson Weekly Gazette* complained was "circulating with amazing assiduity" in the interior parts of the county.[40]

Antifederalist business was also carried on "with spirit" in Orange, Ulster, and Dutchess counties. One sign of that "spirit" appeared in early February, 1788, when a group of Orange and Ulster county Antifederalists met at Montgomery and, "having . . . discovered a unanimous disapprobation of the system," committed the Constitution to the flames.[41] A week later a meeting of inhabitants of Kingston, Ulster County, also "unanimously disapproved" the Constitution. Members of that meeting proposed that Addison, Johannes Snyder, and Dirck Wynkoop attend a county-wide meeting at New Paltz in late February. Leaders there also recommended that Addison and Wynkoop be nominated candidates for the convention.[42]

Despite this display of unanimity, Antifederalists within Ulster were divided. Addison and Snyder secured their own nomination at the New Paltz meeting on February 28, but Peter Van Gaasbeek, a Kingston resident and "one of the major powers in Ulster County" politics, opposed their candidacies.[43] He maintained that Addison was not popular within his own precinct, Kingston, and that Snyder was in reality a Federalist. Van Gaasbeek, however, had another reason for opposing their nominations. He had met with county and state leaders and had drawn up a different slate of candidates which included Governor Clinton.[44] Resolution of differences did not come easily. Not until April 21, after consultation with Antifederalists in all the county's precincts and party leaders in New York, was Assemblyman Cornelius Schoonmaker able to propose a suitable ticket including Governor Clinton,

[40] April 10, 1788.
[41] *New York Journal*, February 23, 1788.
[42] "A Subscriber," *ibid.*, February 29, 1788.
[43] Michael D'Innocenzo and John Turner, "The Peter Van Gaasbeek Papers: A Resource for New York History, 1771–1797," in *New York History*, 47 (1966), 153–159.
[44] Cornelius Schoonmaker to Peter Van Gaasbeek, April 4, 1788, in the Van Gaasbeek Papers, RL.

James Clinton, Ebenezer Clark, John Cantine, Dirck Wynkoop, Ezra Thompson, and himself.[45]

The dispute over the choice of convention candidates also disrupted the early selection of nominees for the assembly and agreement upon a man for the senate. In early April Schoonmaker proposed a list to Peter Van Gaasbeek, but as late as the seventeenth no list had been agreed upon. Only on April 21 were the candidates selected, and copies of the nominations for assembly, senate, and convention distributed throughout the county.[46]

In Dutchess County citizens from the ten precincts met at Oswego in late February and named seven candidates for the state convention. A month later the Constitutional Society of Dutchess County gathered in Amenia and nominated the same slate—Judge Zephaniah Platt, Ezra Thompson, Gilbert Livingston, John DeWitt, Jonathan Akins, and Melancton Smith. However, the Oswego meeting had not nominated candidates for the assembly. The constitutional society did. The seven assembly candidates included two convention nominees, John DeWitt and Jonathan Akins, and two members of the county Antifederalist committee, Lewis Dubois and Matthew Patterson.[47]

Melancton Smith's nomination to the convention provoked some local criticism. A correspondent, adopting the pseudonym "Many Antifederalists," attacked the nomination because Smith was no longer a resident of Dutchess County. Playing upon local pride, "Many Antifederalists" urged local voters to reject those men from outside the county thrust upon them by a small number of local politicians and offered an alternative list of men from the seven "most considerable precincts" in the county. In response to this charge "Cassius" declared that Smith was a property holder in Dutchess as well as a patriot, republican and worthy citizen," i.e., an Antifederalist. "Cassius" further asserted that "Many Antifederalists" was in reality a Federalist attempting to split the Antifederalist vote in the county.[48] Smith was, of course, as "Many Antifederalists" charged, a merchant residing in New York. But the convention resolves did not include a county residency

---

[45] A copy of the list is in Joseph Gasherie to the Citizens of Kingston, April 21, 1788, in the Van Gaasbeek Papers, Senate-House Museum [S-HM], Kingston.

[46] *Idem.*

[47] Poughkeepsie *Country Journal,* March 4, April 15, 1788.

[48] *Ibid.,* March 4, 18, 1788.

requirement. Thus party leaders like Governor Clinton and congressional delegate Smith, although residents of New York City where the Constitution was overwhelmingly popular, could be nominated in upstate counties and be relatively sure of a seat in the convention.

This is not to conclude that Antifederalists conceded the elections in the southern counties. On the contrary, Westchester, Kings, Queens, Suffolk, and New York County Antifederalists established county committees, distributed literature, nominated convention, assembly, and senate candidates, and worked for their elections.

In Westchester the current assembly delegation and the Antifederalist county committee were the same, except that Philip Pell replaced Ebenezer Lockwood on the latter. Committee members received copies of *Observations . . . by a Columbian Patriot* and the compilation *Observations on the Proposed Constitution* from the New York City committee. By late February Abraham Yates thought the prospects for the county were favorable.[49]

In Kings and Queens counties the outlook was less promising. An anonymous newspaper correspondent attacked Doughty and Wyckoff, the county's assemblymen, for voting against the resolution calling for a state convention, and for being under the "absolute sway" of Queens County Assemblyman Samuel Jones.[50] Jones was a member of the city committee, leaving Stephen Carmen as the sole Queens County committeeman. Carmen, Jones, John Schenck, and Nathaniel Lawrence stood for election to the convention, while Whitehead Cornwell ran with Carmen, Schenck, and Jones for re-election to the assembly.

By comparison, the Suffolk County committee was larger. It included Antifederalist publicist Thomas Treadwell and three of the county's assemblymen. Yet by early April no list of candidates for the convention had been agreed upon. David Gelston, the Antifederalist nominee for the senate from the southern district, carried 200 copies of the *Observations . . . by a Columbian Patriot* to the county and exhorted committeeman John Smith to "stir yourself—meet your friends somewhere—agree upon a good

---

[49] Abraham Yates to Abraham G. Lansing, February 28, 1788, in the Yates Papers, NYPL.

[50] *New York Daily Advertiser*, February 20, 1788.

list—hold them up—persevere!"[51] Eventually Antifederalists drew up a good list—one that included Treadwell, Jonathan N. Havens, John Smith, David Hedges, and Henry Scudder. All the candidates were members of the county committee, and, with the exception of Treadwell, were candidates for re-election to the assembly.

In contrast to the counties where Antifederalists nominated a single slate of candidates and actively worked for their election, New York City Antifederalists proposed several lists, some of which included the names of Federalists. If, through such confusing nomination tactics, the Antifederalists could attract enough votes to deprive even one Federalist of a seat in the convention, it would be a gain for the Antifederalists.[52]

The Antifederalists' electioneering paid handsome dividends everywhere in the state except New York City and its immediate vicinity. The final vote count showed an overwhelming Antifederalist victory as their candidates were elected in Washington, Montgomery, Albany, Ulster, Columbia, Dutchess, Orange, Queens, and Suffolk counties. Only New York, Westchester, and Kings elected Federalists. Forty-six of the sixty-five convention delegates were Antifederalists; seventeen were Federalists. The sentiments of the two delegates from Richmond were "unknown."[53]

In addition to securing a major victory in the convention elections, Antifederalists won a majority of the assembly contests. Indeed, the results in the assembly elections paralleled those for the convention. The same nine counties that elected Antifederalist convention delegates chose Antifederal assemblymen. The three counties that chose Federalist convention delegates elected Federalist assemblymen. Furthermore, the counties which individually elected Antifederalists to the convention, collectively chose Antifederalist senators. Those that elected Federalist convention delegates chose Federalist senators.[54]

One reason the returns paralleled one another so closely was that the three elections involved the same men. Antifederalists nominated sixty-three candidates for the convention. Of those

---

[51] April 9, 1788, in the John Smith of Mastic Papers, NYHS.

[52] Nominations were printed in the *Daily Advertiser*, April 26; and the *New York Journal*, February 19, March 13, April 4, 5, 19, 22, May 1, 1788. Melancton Smith insisted that Clinton be nominated in Ulster County, arguing that it was better that he "be chosen in two places than not at all." To [?], April 6, 1788, in the Lamb Papers, NYHS.

[53] *New York Journal*, June 5, 14, 1788.

[54] *Idem.*

sixty-three, thirty-five were also candidates for the assembly. Seven Antifederalist convention candidates were members of the state senate, two of whom were seeking re-election in the spring. Thirty Antifederalist county committeemen were candidates for a seat in the legislature. In addition, the same issues dominated the convention and legislative elections. Antifederalists appealed to the voters to elect men to the assembly because they were "men who have uniformly manifested their attachment to the liberties of America," "so that the suffrages of the county may be more united," and because their legislative candidates were "against adopting the new Constitution without previous amendments."[55]

The Constitution apparently was the decisive issue in the legislative elections. All of the state's counties elected men of the same party to the convention and legislature. They did so in four counties at the expense of incumbents of the opposite party. Thus voters in Columbia and Albany counties chose Antifederalist convention delegates and legislators over Federalist incumbents. In Westchester and Kings counties incumbent Antifederal assemblymen were defeated as Federalist challengers swept both the legislative and convention elections.

The Constitution had a direct bearing on the outcome of the legislative elections because Antifederalists chose to make it an issue. They campaigned for seats in the legislature because they saw the state legislature as a second line of defense in the drive for revision of the proposed Constitution. As Mercy Warren explained in her *Observations . . . by a Columbian Patriot*, if the Constitution were ratified and the new government set into operation, the state legislatures would remain a source of power from which legally to sustain the drive for a second constitutional convention.[56]

In the weeks following the elections, however, New York Anti-

---

[55] *New York Journal*, April 1; Joseph Gasherie to the Citizens of Kingston, April 21, in the Van Gaasbeek Papers, S-HM; and a broadside signed by Jeremiah Van Rensselaer, chairman, Albany Antifederal Committee, April 10, 1788.

[56] Mercy Warren, *Observations on the New Constitution . . . by a Columbian Patriot*, in Ford, ed., *Pamphlets*, 1–24. Ford identifies Elbridge Gerry as the author. For a correction of that attribution see Charles Warren, "Elbridge Gerry, James Warren, Mercy Warren and the Ratification of the Federal Constitution in Massachusetts," in the Massachusetts Historical Society *Proceedings*, 64 (1932), 143–164.

Federalists also nominated candidates for state legislative seats and campaigned for their election in part on the basis of their support for the Constitution. Antifederalists, however, because of their own political philosophy, placed particular emphasis on the state legislatures, while Federalists generally deprecated them.

TABLE II*

County	County Committee	Convention Candidates	Assembly Candidates
Washington	David Hopkins Ebenezer Russell John Williams Alexander Webster Albert Baker Peter B. Freicel	DAVID HOPKINS ICHABOD PARKER JOHN WILLIAMS ALBERT BAKER	JOSEPH M'CRACKEN PETER B. TEARSE EDWARD SAVAGE ALEXANDER WEBSTER
Montgomery	Christopher P. Yates Volkert Veeder John Frey William Harper	CHRISTOPHER P. YATES VOLKERT VEEDER JOHN FREY WILLIAM HARPER JOHN WINN HENRY STARING	CHRISTOPHER P. YATES VOLKERT VEEDER JOHN FREY WILLIAM HARPER JOHN WINN HENRY STARING
Albany	John Lansing Jr. Henry Oothoudt Jeremiah Van Rensselaer Abraham G. Lansing Peter W. Yates	JOHN LANSING JR. HENRY OOTHOUDT ROBERT YATES PETER VROOMAN DIRCK SWART ANTHONY TEN EYCK ISRAEL THOMPSON	JOHN LANSING JR. JOHN YOUNGLOVE JEREMIAH VAN RENSSELAER CORNELIUS VAN DYCK JOHN THOMPSON JOHN DUNCAN H. K. VAN RENSSELAER
Columbia	Peter Van Ness John Bay Mathew Adgate William B. Whiting	PETER VAN NESS JOHN BAY MATHEW ADGATE	JOHN KORTS JOHN BAY MATHEW ADGATE

* Those men whose names are in capitals were elected.

County	County Committee	Convention Candidates	Assembly Candidates
Ulster	Nathan Smith Patrick Bailey Cornelius C. Schoonmaker Dirck Wynkoop Johannes Snyder	GOVERNOR GEORGE CLINTON JOHN CANTINE CORNELIUS C. SCHOONMAKER DIRCK WYNKOOP EBENEZER CLARK JAMES CLINTON	NATHAN SMITH JOHN CANTINE CORNELIUS C. SCHOONMAKER DIRCK WYNKOOP EBENEZER CLARK CHRISTOPHER TAPPEN
Dutchess	Peter Tappen Lewis Dubois Theodorus Bailey Matthew Patterson	ZEPHANIAH PLATT MELANCTON SMITH JACOBUS SWARTOUT JOHN DE WITT GILBERT LIVINGSTON EZRA THOMPSON JONATHAN AKINS	ISAAC BLOOM JACOB GRIFFEN MATTHEW PATTERSON JOHN DE WITT GILBERT LIVINGSTON SAMUEL A. BARKER JONATHAN AKINS
Orange	John Hathorn Coe Gale Reubin Hopkins Thomas Moffatt Peter Taulman John [——]	JESSE WOODHALL HENRY WISNER JOHN HARING JOHN WOOD	JEREMIAH CLARK HENRY WISNER JOHN CARPENTER PETER TAULMAN
Westchester	Philip Pell Jr. Jonathan G. Tompkins Abijah Gilbert Thomas Thomas Joseph Strong Samuel Drake	Ebenezer Lockwood Jonathan G. Tompkins Abijah Gilbert Thomas Thomas Joseph Strong	Ebenezer Lockwood Jonathan G. Tompkins Abijah Gilbert Thomas Thomas Joseph Strong

(Continued on next page)

County	County Committee	Convention Candidates	Assembly Candidates
New York	Melancton Smith John Lamb Marinus Willett Samuel Jones James M. Hughes	Melancton Smith John Lamb Marinus Willett Samuel Jones John Lawrence Isaac Stoutenburgh Governor George Clinton William Malcolm William Denning	Melancton Smith Nicholas Bayard Marinus Willett Aaron Burr Henry Rutgers Isaac Stoutenburgh Gabriel Ludlow Thomas Stoughton William Denning
Kings	Charles Doughty Hendrick Wyckoff	Charles Doughty Cornelius Wyckoff	Charles Doughty Cornelius Wycoff
Queens	Stephen Carmen	STEPHEN CARMEN SAMUEL JONES JOHN SCHENCK NATHANIEL LAWRENCE	STEPHEN CARMEN SAMUEL JONES JOHN SCHENCK WHITEHEAD CORNWELL
Suffolk	Thomas Treadwell David Hedges John Smith Jonathan Havens Henry Scudder Thomas Wickes Caleb Cooper Epenetus Smith	THOMAS TREADWELL DAVID HEDGES JOHN SMITH JONATHAN HAVENS HENRY SCUDDER	NATHANIEL GARDNER DAVID HEDGES JOHN SMITH JONATHAN HAVENS HENRY SCUDDER
Richmond			

federalists set out to insure that they would not be forced to rely on the state legislatures to achieve the political goals they desired. In early May Governor Clinton responded to Virginia Governor Edmund Randolph's letter of late December, 1787. In that letter Randolph had enclosed the Virginia resolution of mid-December with its provisions for co-operation and communication among the conventions. In his reply Clinton wrote of the appropriateness of communications between the two states relative to the Constitution. The initiative, Clinton presumed, would come from Virginia "as the session of your convention will take place before that of this state."[57]

However, ten days later John Lamb launched a broader initiative. Writing on behalf of the New York Federal Republican Committee, he supplemented Clinton's letter to Randolph with a circular letter to Antifederalists in New Hampshire, Rhode Island, Pennsylvania, Maryland, Virginia, and the Carolinas.[58] His object was the amendment of the Constitution "previous to its adoption." The means of "accomplish[ing] this desirable end" was twofold. First, Lamb suggested that Antifederalists in New

[57] Randolph's letter and Clinton's reply are in Moncure D. Conway, *Omitted Chapters in the Life and Papers of Edmund Randolph* (New York, 1889), 110–111.

[58] Lamb wrote to New Hampshire Antifederalists Joshua Atherton and Nathaniel Peabody. The letter to Peabody, May 18, is in Personal Miscellany, LC. Atherton's replies, June 11, 14, are in Isaac Q. Leake, *Memoir of the Life and Times of General John Lamb* (Albany, 1857), 312–313. On May 29 the *Newport Herald* identified Lamb as the source of anonymous letters and Antifederalist pamphlets sent from New York to Rhode Island Antifederalists. Lamb sent his letter to Pennsylvania Antifederalist George Bryan under cover of Philadelphia broker Edward Pole. Pole's reply, June 20, is in the Lamb Papers, NYHS. In his reply Samuel Chase of Maryland mentioned letters from Lamb to Chase and Maryland Governor William Smallwood. Chase to Lamb, June 13, Leake, *Lamb*, 310–311. Lamb wrote to Virginia Antifederalists Patrick Henry, George Mason, William Grayson, and Richard Henry Lee. The letter to Lee is in the Lee Family Papers, University of Virginia. Mason's reply of June 9 is in Robert A. Rutland, ed., *The Papers of George Mason* (3 vols., Chapel Hill, 1970), III, 1057–1058; that of Lee, June 27, is in Ballagh, ed., *Letters of Richard Henry Lee*, II, 474–475; and those of Henry and Grayson, both June 9, in Leake, *Lamb*, 307–308, 311–312. Willie Jones, Thomas Person, and Timothy Bloodworth, all of North Carolina, also received copies of the Circular Letter from Lamb. The one to Jones is in North Carolina Manuscripts, Duke University. Bloodworth's reply, July 1, and Person's, August 6, are in William K. Boyd, comp., "News, Letters, and Documents Concerning North Carolina and the Federal Constitution," in Trinity College Historical Society *Historical Papers*, 14 (1922), 77–81. The only other known recipients of the letters were South Carolinians Rawlins Lowndes, Aedanus Burke, and Thomas Sumter. Lowndes reply, June 21, is in Leake, *Lamb*, 308; Burke's, June 28, 1788, is in the Lamb Papers, NYHS.

Hampshire, New York, Virginia, and the Carolina conventions "open a correspondence and maintain a communication that they should understand one another on the subject and unite in the amendments they propose" to be adopted prior to ratification.[59] Once they agreed upon a specific set of amendments, Lamb wanted them to "act in concert" with some "rational plan" that would insure their adoption.[60] Although Lamb did not spell out the details of the plan for unified action, presumably the list of amendments would have been submitted to the Confederation Congress, supported by Antifederal majorities in the New Hampshire, New York, Virginia, and the Carolina conventions, the Rhode Island legislature, and by Antifederalist minorities in Massachusetts, Pennsylvania, and Maryland. Unified action would have demonstrated widespread support for amendments prior to ratification and provided proof of agreement among Antifederalists on specific amendments.

Although Lamb's attempt to link Antifederalists across the nation in the demand for previous amendments failed, it was not because of a late start by the Federal Republican Committee or delays in the delivery of the mails.[61] Lamb's letters were a logical outgrowth of the original proposal for interconvention co-operation made in October, 1787. They were intended to resurrect at least part of that plan by stimulating interconvention communication and co-operation between the New York, New Hampshire, and Virginia conventions which were to meet simultaneously in June, 1788. Furthermore, Lamb's letters reached their intended recipients in New Hampshire and Virginia, and their responses arrived in New York before any of the three conventions reached a final decision.

[59] See letters to Peabody and Jones, *ibid*. Nowhere did Lamb stipulate the previous amendments he and the members of the "Republican Committee" desired. However, judging from Melancton Smith's *Address to the People of the State of New York . . . By a Plebian*, which Lamb forwarded with the mid-May letters, it seems clear that the New Yorkers wanted at least a stipulation that all powers not expressly granted to the central government were reserved to the states; an increase in the number of representatives in the House; some limitations on the central government's power to tax; a restriction on the jurisdiction of the federal courts; and guarantees regarding the right to, time, and place of national elections. See Ford, ed., *Pamphlets*, 102–104.

[60] See the draft of Lamb's letter to members of the Virginia and New Hampshire conventions, June 6, 1788, in the Lamb Papers, NYHS.

[61] See Main, *Antifederalists*, 236; Rutland, *Ordeal of the Constitution*, 210; Young, *Democratic-Republicans*, 111; DePauw, *Eleventh Pillar*, 211.

New Hampshire Antifederalists Nathaniel Peabody and Joshua Atherton received Lamb's letter with the enclosed Antifederalist pamphlets before the opening of the second session of the New Hampshire convention. In response Atherton informed Lamb that the majority of New Hampshire delegates were still in favor of amendments prior to ratification. He warned, however, that "no amendments" had been agreed to or even attempted by the convention delegates. If New York were to resolve "not to adopt without the necessary amendments," and forwarded that news to Exeter, then the New Hampshire convention would almost certainly "close with your wishes and views." If New York failed to take such a positive step, then rejection by New Hampshire was in doubt.[62]

Lamb's letters to Virginia's Antifederalist convention delegates George Mason, Patrick Henry, and William Grayson reached Richmond on June 7, in ample time for interconvention correspondence on the subject of amendments.[63] In fact, a "committee of opposition" discussed amendments before Eleazer Oswald, the Antifederalist printer who served as a messenger for the New York and Virginia Antifederalists, reached Richmond. There he "closeted" himself with Mason, Grayson, Henry, and other members of the Antifederalist opposition, presumably to discuss strategy, specific amendments, and Lamb's proposal for interconvention co-operation.[64] The Virginians endorsed the latter proposal and forwarded a tentative list of amendments to New York through Oswald when he departed on June 11.

Even as these initial negotiations were being carried on, Lamb, encouraged by the outcome of the New York convention elections,

---

[62] June 11, 14, Leake, *Lamb*, 312-313.

[63] William Grayson to John Lamb, June 9, *ibid.*, 311-312. The same day James Madison informed Alexander Hamilton that Oswald arrived on Saturday, which was June 7, 1788; Harold C. Syrett et al., eds., *The Papers of Alexander Hamilton [PAH]* (New York, 1961 to date), V, 4.

[64] Madison to Hamilton, June 9, *ibid.* For additional comments on Oswald's role see Madison to Washington, June 13, in the Washington Papers, LC; Henry Lee to Hamilton, n.d., in *PAH*, V, 10, and Washington to Henry Knox, June 17, in John C. Fitzpatrick, ed., *The Writings of George Washington* (39 vols., Washington, 1931–1944), XXIV, 518.

Oswald irked Federalists because of his efforts. Henry Chapman, a New York merchant, complained to a friend in Philadelphia: "That restless firebrand the printer in your city is running about as if driven by the devil, seemingly determined to do all the mischief he can. Indeed in my opinion he is an actual incendiary and ought to be the object of legal restraint." To Stephen Collins, June 20, 1788, in the Papers of Stephen Collins, LC.

wrote again to New Hampshire and Virginia Antifederalists, reiterating the importance of co-operation among the three conventions on specific amendments prior to ratification. Joshua Atherton received Lamb's letter at Exeter on June 21.[65] However, it did not contain what Atherton had previously stipulated as necessary for an Antifederalist victory: news of New York's refusal to ratify the Constitution in its present form and a list of specific amendments. Subsequently, and despite Atherton's best efforts, New Hampshire ratified by a 57 to 47 margin.

It is not clear if a similar letter was sent to Virginia. A draft exists in the Lamb papers, but there is no mention of it in any of Mason's ensuing correspondence with the New York committee. A second letter was less necessary in this instance because the Virginians were in direct contact with their New York counterparts, and because the news of the New York Antifederalist election victory reached Richmond independently of the Lamb committee letter as early as June 18.[66]

There was no breakdown in interstate communication among the Antifederalists in the three state conventions which were to meet in June and whose co-operation was to form the framework for the entire drive for previous amendments. Neither was there a disruption in the delivery of Lamb's letters to North Carolina and Rhode Island Antifederalists. In mid-May Lamb wrote to Willie Jones, Timothy Bloodworth, and Thomas Person, Antifederalist members of the North Carolina convention. Those letters apparently reached Wilmington, North Carolina, by June 11. On that date the *Wilmington Centinel* advertised for sale a number of Antifederalist pamphlets "just arrived from New York." Among them were Mercy Warren's *Observations . . . by a Columbian Patriot*, Melancton Smith's *Address to the People of New York . . . by a Plebeian*, and Luther Martin's *Genuine Information*. Lamb enclosed these and other pamphlets in each of his letters. The notice of their availability in Wilmington serves to date the arrival of the Lamb letters in North Carolina a full six weeks before the opening of their convention.

This provided ample time for the North Carolinians to reply

[65] A draft of letters to members of the New Hampshire and Virginia conventions, June 6, 1788, is in the Lamb Papers, NYHS.
[66] *Virginia Independent Chronicle* (Richmond).

to Lamb. Thus on July 1 Timothy Bloodworth, an Antifederalist from Wilmington and chairman of the North Carolina Antifederalist committee of correspondence, endorsed Lamb's proposal for previous amendments. Because the sentiments of North Carolina's convention delegates could not be collected prior to the opening of the convention, Bloodworth urged Lamb to forward the "proposed amendments" agreed upon by the three June conventions so that the North Carolina convention could act consistently with them.[67]

Willie Jones did not reply personally to Lamb's letter, presumably because he was a member of the committee of correspondence on whose behalf Bloodworth wrote. The third recipient of the letter, Thomas Person, did not receive his letter until "the 23rd of July, and then open." At that late date there was little Person could do. Bloodworth had already written on behalf of the Antifederalist committee. Thus Person waited another two weeks and then informed Lamb of North Carolina's refusal to ratify the Constitution by a vote of 184–83.[68]

According to reports in the *Newport Herald,* letters from Lamb, "accompanied by a fresh packet of pamphlets against the proposed Constitution," were delivered to Rhode Island's Governor John Collins and several other prominent Antifederalists during May.[69] Although not extant, the anonymous letters to which the *Herald* alluded almost certainly outlined the national plan for previous amendments proposed by Lamb. The pamphlets probably included copies of Lee's *Letters from the Federal Farmer* since they stated well the New Yorker's objections to the Constitution and indirectly outlined the kind of amendments envisioned by the Federal Republican Committee.[70]

There were some delays in the delivery of Lamb's letters. Those to George Bryan in Philadelphia, Samuel Chase in Baltimore, Richard Henry Lee at Chantilly, Virginia, and Aedanus Burke, Rawlins Lowndes, and General Thomas Sumter in Charleston, were all in transit approximately a month. In none of these cases, however, did the protracted delivery significantly affect Lamb's plans. The South Carolina convention was overwhelmingly Feder-

---

67 To John Lamb, July 1, 1788, in Boyd, ed., "News, Letters and Documents," 77–79.
68 To John Lamb, August 6, 1788, *ibid.*
69 May 29; "A Rhode Islander," June 12, 1788.
70 See Lamb's letters of May 18, cited in footnote 58.

alist and it is doubtful that the decision of the convention would have been different had Lamb's letters been presented to it. Pennsylvania ratified the Constitution in December. George Bryan and Dr. James Hutchinson, Antifederalist leaders in Philadelphia, learned of the negotiations between New York and Virginia from Eleazer Oswald, who stopped over in the city on his way north.[71] Lee, on the other hand, was not a member of the Virginia convention, although communication between the Virginia and New York conventions continued unabated.

During May and June, then, New York Antifederalists initiated a nationwide correspondence on the amendment subject. The responses to their initiative were positive and included pledges of support from Antifederalists in both ratifying and nonratifying states. New York Antifederalists in the convention did not, however, immediately act upon these responses and implement the next step in their drive for previous amendments. They did not because of the discouraging news from Virginia, a state they viewed as an essential ally if the drive for previous amendments was to succeed.

Eleazer Oswald returned to New York on the evening of June 16 with letters from Mason, Grayson, and Henry to the Federal Republican Committee. Captain Tillinghast immediately carried the letters to Governor Clinton in Poughkeepsie.[72] The news in those letters was less than promising. All three Virginians believed the balance between the two parties in the convention was extremely close, although Grayson gave the Federalists a three-vote plurality, with "seven or eight dubious characters . . . on whose decision the fate of this important decision will ultimately depend."[73]

In Poughkeepsie Governor Clinton turned the letters over to Robert Yates, chairman of an Antifederalist committee of correspondence. On June 21 Yates, in a private letter to Mason, explained that while New York Antifederalists were "willing to open a correspondence with your convention" in an official capacity, "the doubtful chance of your obtaining a majority—and the

---

[71] Thomas Willing to William Bingham, June 29, in the Gratz Collection, Pennsylvania Historical Society.

[72] John Lamb to George Clinton, June 17, in the Lamb Papers, NYHS; George Clinton to John Lamb, June 21, 1788, in Leake, *Lamb*, 315–316.

[73] To John Lamb, June 9, 1788, *ibid.*, 311.

possibility that we will complete our determination before we could avail ourselves of your advice are the reasons we pursue the present mode of [unofficial] correspondence." Despite the resigned tone, Yates stressed the "fixed determination" of the New York Antifederalists not to adopt "without previous amendments"; he kept alive a hope for an unexpected Antifederalist victory in Virginia.[74] Arrival of the news of Virginia's unconditional ratification ten days later shattered these hopes.

Virginia's ratification significantly altered the political situation in Poughkeepsie. There was no longer any real doubt that the new government would be put into operation, although the Confederation Congress did delay for over two months setting up the machinery for elections of a President, Vice President, and members of Congress. With the certainty that the new government would become operational, with or without New York, the possibility of previous amendments on the terms initially proposed by the Federal Republican Committee and sought by the Antifederalists in convention was gone.

Apparently at this point, overwhelmed by events outside their own state, the Antifederalist majority in the New York convention "determined they could not reject" the Constitution. Instead, the question became "which was the mode most eligible to insure a convention of the states to reconsider it, to have the essential amendments engrafted to it."[75] There were several possibilities, and the delegates debated all of them in the ensuing weeks. On July 10, following presentation of the Antifederalist amendments, John Lansing introduced a motion providing for ratification with recommeded, conditional, and explanatory amendments. Federalists countered with a motion for unconditional ratification with recommended amendments. After three days of debate Melancton Smith introduced another alternative: ratification upon condition only that the proposed amendments be submitted to a constitutional convention and that congressional powers over the state militia, elections, and taxation be suspended until a final determination was made by the convention. Federalists, in order to forestall adoption of Smith's proposal, proposed an adjournment

---

[74] See his covering letter to Lamb, June 21, 1788, *ibid.*, 315–316.
[75] See the report of the debates in the *Country Journal* (Poughkeepsie), July 29, 1788.

of the convention to allow the delegates to consult their constituents. Instead, the convention simply recessed for the evening.[76]

The next day, July 17, Federalists proposed ratification "in full confidence" that the New York amendments would be considered by Congress. Smith, realizing that Congress could not, consistent with the provisions of Article V, call a convention on its own initiative, proposed that the convention ratify the Constitution with the condition that the state retain the right to secede if two-thirds of the states did not petition Congress to call a convention within a specified number of years. A circular letter was to be sent to the states encouraging them to do the same.[77]

Smith's motion seemingly exhausted the various alternatives. It also introduced a crucial feature in terms of Smith's own decision to acquiesce in unconditional ratification: a circular letter to the states calling upon them to petition Congress to convene a second convention. When he introduced it, however, the majority of Antifederalists opposed the idea. Hence on July 19 John Lansing reintroduced Smith's earlier motion, which was debated for three days.[78] Finally, on July 23 the conditional clause of the motion was amended to "in full confidence" that the proposed amendments would be submitted to a general convention.[79] On July 24 Lansing made a last effort, offering his earlier motion with its reservation of the right to secede if a convention was not convened. That part of the motion was defeated, but the delegates did appoint a committee to draft a letter to the states. Written that evening, the New York Circular Letter, with its request that the states petition Congress to call a second convention, was approved by the delegates the next day.[80]

---

[76] Portions of the debates are printed in Jonathan Elliot, ed., *The Debates in the Several State Conventions on the Adoption of the Federal Constitution* (5 vols., Philadelphia, 1886), II, 205–414. More complete are Gilbert Livingston's "Notes on Debates in the New York Convention, 1788," in the Yates Papers, NYPL. For an analysis of the notes taken by Livingston, Francis Childs, John McKesson, and Melancton Smith, see the editorial note in *PAH*, V, 11–13. There is no one complete secondary account of the proceedings of the convention. For a summary see Young, *Democratic-Republicans*, 110. Robin Brooks, "Alexander Hamilton, Melancton Smith, and the Ratification of the Constitution in New York," in *WMQ*, 3rd Ser., 24 (1967), 339–358, concentrates on the latter days of the convention. A sketch emphasizing the debates on the judicial clause may be found in Julius Goebel, Jr., *History of the Supreme Court* (New York, 1971), I, 396–412.

[77] Livingston Notes, in the Yates Papers, NYPL.

[78] Elliot, ed., *Debates*, II, 411–412.

[79] *Ibid.*, 412.

[80] New York *Independent Journal, Supplement Extraordinary*, July 28, 1788.

Historians have noted a number of factors which collectively induced twelve Antifederalists to vote with nineteen Federalists in favor of unconditional ratification. The threat of secession by the southern counties, the potential loss of the national capital, and the *de jure* ratification by ten states all took their toll.[81] All of these notwithstanding, New York Antifederalists could have refused to ratify the Constitution, just as their North Carolina counterparts did two weeks later. They chose, however, to ratify and to work for reform of the system from within. They did so, in large part because of the responses to Lamb's letters of mid-May. Article V of the proposed Constitution required Congress to convene a constitutional convention if petitioned to do so by two-thirds of the ratifying states. Letters received in Poughkeepsie during June and July from Antifederalists in other states seemed to indicate that the likelihood of Congress calling a second constitutional convention would be greater if New York ratified the Constitution. Thus Joshua Atherton, even as he encouraged the New York Antifederalists not to yield, declared that "there is a great majority in our House of Representatives unfavorable to the Constitution."[82] Certainly they could be counted on to petition Congress for a convention.

Massachusetts had been the first state to ratify in full confidence of amendments, and as in New Hampshire, its lower house, or so Antifederalists believed, favored amendments. Furthermore, Antifederalist leaders in Massachusetts were encouraging New York to ratify.[83] If New York became the third state that could be relied upon to petition Congress, then Pennsylvania would be the fourth. Although the state had ratified unconditionally, and without recommended amendments, there was a sizable and vociferous group in the state which endorsed the idea of a second convention. In addition, like Massachusetts Antifederalists, state leaders in Pennsylvania encouraged New York to ratify.[84]

Farther south the prospects of the state legislatures continuing to press for a second convention seemed equally strong. In April

[81] The best account is in Young, *Democratic-Republicans*, 110–114, who expands Main, *Antifederalists*, 238–239. On Smith's role see Brooks, "Alexander Hamilton," *passim.*

[82] To John Lamb, June 23, 1788, in the Lamb Papers, NYHS.

[83] DeWitt Clinton Notes, July 16–19, 1788, in the DeWitt Clinton Papers, Columbia University. Clinton does not identify either the Massachusetts or Pennsylvania Antifederalists by name.

[84] *Idem.*

Maryland ratified by an overwhelming margin. Still, during June Antifederalists informed the Federal Republicans in New York that the citizens of the state supported amendments 4 to 1, and that the question of amendments was a major issue in the forth-coming state elections.[85] The logical conclusion to be drawn from that report was that the state legislature, after the October elec-tions, would also be in favor of amendments, and receptive to a request from the state of New York that Maryland petition Congress to convene a second convention.

Virginia was an Antifederalist stronghold. The state legislature elected in April was even more Antifederalist than the convention which had just ratified the Constitution with recommended amendments.[86] Virginians were the first to propose a circular letter to the states encouraging them to petition Congress to convene another convention, although as part of a conditional ratification. Certainly they would be responsive to a similar suggestion from New York. Timothy Bloodworth was uncertain what course North Carolina would follow if Virginia ratified the Constitution, but he pledged to support amendments emanating from New York. So did Aedanus Burke from South Carolina.[87] Burke main-tained that despite South Carolina's ratification, the majority of the state's white population opposed unconditional ratification. And he pledged that any communication from Lamb or the Federal Republican Committee would "be duly attended to."

The exact date these replies to Lamb's letters of May and June reached New York, and then Poughkeepsie, are not all known. Those of the Virginians reached Poughkeepsie prior to June 21. In the case of those from New Hampshire, Maryland, and the Carolinas, it can only be noted that there was ample time for the letters of Atherton (June 23), Chase (June 13), Bloodworth (July 1), and Burke (June 19) to reach the Antifederalists at Poughkeepsie while the convention was in session. There they pro-vided testimony of the likelihood of a favorable response to an appeal by New York that the state legislatures petition Congress on the subject of a second convention.

The New York Circular Letter was instrumental in persuad-ing Antifederalists to acquiesce in unconditional ratification.

[85] Samuel Chase to John Lamb, June 13, 1788, in Leake, *Lamb*, 310.

[86] James Madison to Alexander Hamilton, June 22, 1788, in *PAH*, V, 61–62.

[87] Bloodworth to John Lamb, July 1, in Boyd, ed., "News, Letters, and Documents," 77–79; Burke to John Lamb, June 23, 1788, in the Lamb Papers, NYHS.

Approval of the circular letter as the "condition" of ratification, in turn, was a direct result, not of the failure of the Federal Republican Committee's efforts, but their success. The responses to the Lamb letters of May and June indicated a willingness on the part of Antifederalists throughout the union to follow the lead of New York in the quest for substantive reform of the Constitution. The rational plan for securing amendments, mentioned but never detailed by Lamb in the letters of May and June, became the New York Circular Letter of July 26, 1788.

Between October, 1787, and July, 1788, then, the question of ratification "nationalized" electoral politics in New York. It also prompted substantial, organized, statewide Antifederalist activity which culminated in the adoption of the New York Circular Letter as a quid pro quo for ratification by the New York convention. Following ratification, national issues continued to shape electoral politics and to stimulate organized Antifederalist activity in New York. Amendments and the demand for a second constitutional convention remained issues in the spring, 1789, gubernatorial, state legislative, and first federal elections because Antifederalists still believed they could achieve substantive reform of the Constitution, either by the state legislatures petitioning Congress to call a second convention or by electing Antifederalists to both houses of the federal legislature.

The first option, that of the state legislatures petitioning Congress, was the mode favored by Antifederalists in July when they obtained unanimous approval of the circular letter as a condition of ratification by New York. In August Governor Clinton sent the circular letter to the chief executives of every state; over forty newspapers in twelve states reprinted it.[88] To the chagrin of Antifederalists throughout the union, Federalists publicly condemned the letter while privately impugning the integrity of New York Federalists for agreeing to it.[89]

---

[88] The Letter was first printed in the *Country Journal*, August 5. It was reprinted as far north as Portland, Maine, on August 21, and as far south as Savannah, Georgia, the same day. No printing has been located in any Delaware newspaper.

[89] See, for example, the *Pennsylvania Gazette* (Philadelphia), August 6, 13; "X to the Governors of the States," in the *Connecticut Gazette* (New London), August 16; "Republican," in the *Virginia Independent Chronicle*, August 27; and "Solon" [William Heath], in the *Independent Chronicle* (Boston), August 28. For criticism of Federalist acquiescence to the Circular Letter see James Madison to George Washington, August 11, in the Washington Papers, LC, and Washington to Madison, August 17, in the Madison Papers, LC.

Even more damaging to Antifederalist hopes were the responses of the state legislatures—responses which proved the optimism of July to be delusory. During the fall Federalist majorities in New Jersey, Connecticut, and Pennsylvania blocked positive action by those state legislatures on the circular letter.[90] Even in states where they were a majority in only one house, Federalists dominated. Thus during November the Massachusetts and New Hampshire legislatures also failed to act.[91] Equally frustrating to New York Antifederalists, the Antifederalist-dominated Rhode Island legislature insisted on submitting the circular letter to the freemen in the towns for their consideration instead of petitioning Congress.[92] Only the Virginia legislature complied with the recommendation of the New York convention. On November 20, 1788, they approved a petition asking Congress to call a convention of "deputies from the several states, with full power to take into consideration the defects of the Constitution. . . ."[93]

Rebuffed by the other state legislatures, New York Antifederalists turned to the forthcoming state and federal elections in the pursuit of their elusive goal. Governor Clinton, himself a candidate for re-election, Melancton Smith, Abraham Yates, Jr., and a majority of the party's leaders agreed that New York Antifederalists must unite in a concerted effort to elect Antifederalist officeholders on the state and federal level. State legislators could then choose Antifederalist United States Senators and instruct the state's congressional delegation to "exert all their influence and

[90] October 30, 1788, *Votes and Proceedings of the Thirteenth General Assembly . . . New Jersey* (Trenton, 1788), 7–9. Jonathan Trumbull described Connecticut's action: "The Circular Letter for the Convention of the State of New York being among the letters which the Governor laid before the assembly, [it] had of course a reading. . . . This was all that passed respecting it for although we had in our assembly the champion of the Antis [James Wadsworth], with some of his principal aides, yet no one had hardiness enough to call up the consideration of that letter. . . ." To George Washington, October 20, 1788, in the Washington Papers, LC. The Pennsylvania Assembly acted on September 8 and October 4; *Minutes of the Twelfth General Assembly . . . Pennsylvania* (Philadelphia, 1788), 219–221, 276.

[91] In Massachusetts the letter was referred to committee, but no report was made during the session. House Journals, October 31, 1788, in the Massachusetts Archives. New Hampshire Antifederalist Joshua Atherton complained that all opposition had ceased in that state, the language of former opponents being that "it is adopted, let us try it." To John Lamb, February 23, 1789, in the Lamb Papers, NYHS.

[92] November 1, 1788. Rhode Island Acts and Resolves, in the Rhode Island State Archives.

[93] November 20, *Journal of the House of Delegates* (Richmond, 1828), 66.

use all reasonable means" to obtain ratification of the amendments proposed by the New York convention or to secure the calling of a second constitutional convention.[94] Antifederalist campaigning in the spring, 1789, elections paralleled that of 1788. This time, however, the Federalists won a majority in the assembly and maintained control of the senate. That meant both of New York's Senators turned out to be Federalists. Only Governor Clinton, a minority in the lower house, and three Antifederalist candidates for the United States House of Representatives stood victorious against the Federalist tide.[95]

Antifederalists gained invaluable experience on the state and interstate levels during the campaigns of 1788 and 1789. That experience proved important because Article I, Section II, of the Constitution (the direct election of U.S. Representatives) created a mechanism by which national questions could be debated on the local level. National issues would continue to shape the focus and conduct of New York politics in the years to come.

[94] The quotation is from Abraham Yates, Jr., to the Members of the New York Legislature, December 8, in the Yates Papers, NYPL. Clinton's views are expressed in his message to the legislature, December 11; *Daily Advertiser*, December 15. A "Federal Republican," whom Alfred Young identifies as Melancton Smith, urged the voters of the state to choose men "to represent them as will firmly pursue the plan recommended by the convention of this state," i.e., men who would support the call for a second constitutional convention. See the *New York Journal*, December 11, 1788.

[95] Young, *Democratic-Republicans*, chap. 6.

The Murder of the Militia System in the
Aftermath of the American Revolution

Richard H. Kohn

MORE than a quarter century after the Constitution was adopted, Gouverneur Morris, who, as chairman of the committee of style, authored much of the Constitution's final language, explained that in shaping the militia provision, the framers "meant chiefly to provide against . . . the hazarding of the national safety by a reliance on that expensive and inefficient force. An overweening vanity leads the fond many, each man against the conviction of his own heart, to believe or affect to believe, that militia can beat veteran troops in the open field and even play of battle. This idle notion, fed by vaunting demagogues, alarmed us for our country," Morris remembered. "To rely on undisciplined, ill-officered men, though each were individually as brave as Caesar, . . . is to act in defiance of reason and experience." "Those, who, during the Revolutionary storm, had confidential acquaintance with the conduct of affairs, knew that to rely on milita was to lean on a broken reed."[1]

In spite of their own doubts, the framers of the Constitution understood the tremendous popular affection for the militia, how greatly Americans looked to militia for the nation's protection,

AUTHOR'S NOTE: An earlier version of this paper was presented at the Sixth Military History Symposium, U.S. Air Force Academy, October 11, 1974.

[1] Gouverneur Morris to Moss Kent, January 12, 1815, in Max Farrand, ed., *The Records of the Federal Convention of 1787* (rev. ed., New Haven, 1937), III, 420–421.

how deeply ingrained was the concept and tradition of the citizen-soldier in American defense. Some of the most politically conscious of the nation's military leaders after the Revolution, although not themselves champions of militia, felt compelled to acknowledge its primacy: "The first principle of the Security of the United States," conceded Henry Knox; "the only palladium of a free people," intoned Timothy Pickering; "this Great Bulwark of our Liberties and independence," echoed George Washington.[2] In numerous debates after the war, in the Congress and outside, the militia was defended and glorified in the same terms.[3] When Alexander Hamilton publicly denigrated "small fugitive bodies of volunteer militia" as the "mimicry of soldiership" in a July 4, 1789, New York City speech attended by some of the nation's top leadership, it was interpreted as a general attack on the militia.[4] Nearly a year later, in the House of Representatives,

[2] Henry Knox to George Washington, April 17, 1783, in the George Washington Papers, Library of Congress [LC]; Timothy Pickering to George Washington, April 22, 1783, in Octavius Pickering and Charles Upham, *The Life of Timothy Pickering* (4 vols., Boston, 1863–1867), IV, 432; George Washington, "Sentiments on a Peace Establishment," enclosed in George Washington to Alexander Hamilton, May 2, 1783, in John C. Fitzpatrick, ed., *The Writings of George Washington* [*WGW*] (39 vols., Washington, 1931–1944), XXVI, 387. Washington revealed just how opposed to the militia he really was when he complimented Steuben on the latter's plan to abolish the state militias as they were then constituted. See George Washington to Baron von Steuben, March 15, 1784, in *WGW*, XXVII, 360.

[3] See, for example, the Massachusetts delegates to the Massachusetts Assembly, June 4, 1784, in Edmund C. Burnett, ed., *Letters of Members of the Continental Congress* (8 vols., Washington, 1921–1936), VII, 543; committee report, Massachusetts Assembly, July 9, 1784, in the Samuel Adams Papers, New York Public Library [NYPL]; "Democratic Federalist," in the *Pennsylvania Packet* (Philadelphia), October 3, 1787; "Cincinnatus," in the *New York Journal*, November 22, 1787; *William Thompson in Debates and Proceedings in the Convention of . . . Massachusetts . . . which finally ratified the Constitution* (Boston, 1856), 180; Patrick Henry, George Mason, and Alexander Grayson in Jonathan Elliot, ed., *The Debates in the Several State Conventions on the Adoption of the Constitution* (5 vols., Washington, 1854), III, 314, 378–381, 385, 388, 412, 415–420, 422–424; Petition of the Franklin County Freemen, in the *Independent Gazetteer* (Philadelphia), February 19, 1788, reprinted in John Bach McMaster and Frederick D. Stone, eds., *Pennsylvania and the Federal Constitution, 1787–1788* (Lancaster, 1888), 502. For statements in Congress during the 1790's, see the debates in Joseph Gales and W. W. Seaton, comps., *Debates and Proceedings in the Congress of the United States* [*Annals of Congress*] (Washington, 1834–1856), 2 Cong., 1 sess. (1791–1792), 337–348, 2 Cong., 2 sess. (1792–1793), 762–768, 779–802, 5 Cong., 2 sess. (1797–1798), 1525–1545, 1631–1707, 1725–1772, 6 Cong., 1 sess. (1799–1800), 247–369.

[4] Eulogy on the late Major General Greene, July 4, 1789, in Harold C. Syrett et al., eds., *The Papers of Alexander Hamilton* [*PAH*] (New York, 1961 to date), V, 350.

South Carolina's Aedanus Burke rose to the defense: "I now declare, that the assertion was false," Burke declared heatedly, and then, turning to the crowded gallery where he thought Hamilton sat, "I throw the lie in Colonel Hamilton's face."[5] Burke later apologized, but not before he extracted from Hamilton an explicit denial of any intention to slur the militia's effectiveness.[6] Endorsement of the militia's importance went beyond public displays for popular consumption. As John Adams traveled through Europe in the 1780's, he repeatedly cited the militia, along with the "Towns, . . . Schools and Churches as the four Causes of the Growth and Defence of N[ew] England" and the source of "the Virtues and talents of the People"—"Temperance, Patience, Fortitude, Prudence, . . . Justice, . . . Sagacity, Knowledge, Judgment, Taste, Skill, Ingenuity, Dexterity, and Industry."[7]

American trust in their local forces reflected over a century's political and military development. From the first years of settlement colonists had relied on the citizenry in local units for defense against Indians; the militia responded in nearly every major conflict involving European foes up until the Revolution. By the middle of the eighteenth century, however, colonists were relying more heavily on British forces for protection, while serving as volunteers in specially organized expeditions or in crown units. But provincial regulars were a rarity except for patrols or garrisons on the frontier or in seacoast forts, and the men were usually drafted or volunteered out of local militia organizations. Even while the system was deteriorating markedly during the generation before the Revolution and falling into disuse in older settled areas, American faith in it remained unshaken. On the surface, the system seemed to work and to be flexible, to allow different colonies to adapt their forces to special local conditions or, if performance dropped, to modify fines, training, organization, or the conditions of service.[8]

---

[5] Aedanus Burke speech, March 31, 1790, in the *New York Journal*, April 15, 1790, and Otho H. Williams to Philp Thomas, April 8, 1790, both in *PAH*, V, 334n, 335n. See also William L. Smith to Edward Rutledge, April 2, 1790, in George C. Rogers, ed., "The Letters of William Loughton Smith," in the *South Carolina Historical Magazine*, 69 (1968), 112.

[6] Aedanus Burke to Alexander Hamilton, April 7, 1790, in *PAH*, V, 358.

[7] John Adams diary, July 21, 1786, in L. H. Butterfield, ed., *Diary and Autobiography of John Adams* (4 vols., Cambridge, 1961), III, 195.

[8] An excellent discussion of the militia system is Douglas Edward Leach, *Arms for Empire: A Military History of the British Colonies in North America, 1607–1763 (The*

More important still, Americans depended on the militia for political reasons, because they feared and distrusted standing armies, and because they knew of no other institutional alternatives. Through most of the colonial era, their experience with the British military establishment was one of friction and antagonism, of arrogant, snobbish, or dictatorial officers and officials, of harsh and brutal discipline in the army, of shady enlistment practices— all of which was fortified and given spectacular notice by radical Whig literature which became so influential before the Revolution. In all of their writings, radical Whig opponents of standing armies presented the militia as the safe, proper force for a peaceful people who valued liberty. As John Trenchard put it as early as the 1690's, "there can be no danger where the Nobility and chief Gentry . . . are the Commanders, and the Body [is] made up of the Freeholders, . . . unless we can conceive that the Nobility and Gentry will join in an unnatural Design to make void their own Titles to their Estates and Liberties: and if they could entertain so ridiculous a Proposition, they would never be obeyed by the Souldiers."[9]

The Revolution, as historians have always known, strengthened the militia tradition immeasurably. The emplacement of a substantial British force in the colonies, its gradual transfer to urban

---

Macmillan Wars of the United States, New York, 1973), chap. 1. Standard published works are Louis Morton, "The Origins of American Military Policy," in *Military Affairs* [*MA*], 21 (1958), 75–82; Jack S. Radabaugh, "The Militia of Colonial Massachusetts," in *MA*, 18 (1954), 1–18; E. Milton Wheeler, "Development and Organization of the North Carolina Militia," in the *North Carolina Historical Review* [*NCHR*], 61 (1964), 307–323; Philip Alexander Bruce, *Institutional History of Virginia in the Seventeenth Century* (New York, 1910), II, 3–70; and especially John W. Shy, "A New Look at Colonial Militia," in the *William and Mary Quarterly* [*WMQ*], 3rd Ser., 20 (1963), 175–185. The most complete analyses of the system are in unpublished dissertations, the best of which are David Richard Millar, "The Militia, the Army and Independency in Colonial Massachusetts" (doctoral dissertation, Cornell University, 1967); Richard Henry Marcus, "The Militia of Colonial Connecticut, 1639–1775: An Institutional Study" (doctoral dissertation, University of Colorado, 1965); Archibald Hanna, Jr., "New England Military Institutions, 1693–1750" (doctoral dissertation, Yale University, 1950); and Frederick Stokes Aldridge, "Organization and Administration of the Militia System of Colonial Virginia" (doctoral dissertation, American University, 1954).

[9] John Trenchard, *An Argument Shewing, that a Standing Army is Inconsistent with a Free Government* (London, 1697), 22. I have covered the origin of the prejudice against standing armies in chapter 1 of *Eagle and Sword: The Federalists and the Creation of the Military Establishment in America, 1783–1802* (New York, 1975). For an excellent discussion of the subject see Don Higginbotham, *The War of America Independence: Military Attitudes, Policies, and Practice, 1763–1789* (*The Macmillan Wars of the United States*, New York, 1971), 7–53.

areas, the resulting conflict, and finally the explosion of the Boston Massacre in 1770 emblazoned the hatred of standing armies into the Revolutionary experience. As the British army and standing armies generally became fixed as the symbols of monarchy, of European corruption, of tyranny, and of the ministry's conspiracy against liberty, so too did the militia become identified with America, with freedom, with republicanism, and with colonial virtue. In the outpouring of self-congratulations after the war, battles like Bunker Hill enshrined the militia in popular mythology. And the central element in the militia tradition, the concept of the citizen-soldier, became basic to the language and history of independence and nationhood. As recently as 1940, the chairman of the Senate Military Affairs Committee publicly proclaimed that the American "people . . . are different from the peoples of virtually every other country . . . from the standpoint of natural, inherited national defense." The Senator announced, "I am not . . . 'afear'd' of Hitler coming over here because if he does, he will get the worst licking he ever had in his life, because our boys have been trained to shoot."[10] Yet in spite of the Senator's extravagance, one of the little remembered results of the Revolution was that it set in motion forces that ultimately destroyed the militia as the primary institution for the defense of the United States.

*   *   *   *

One of the oldest controversies in the history of warfare and already, by 1776, the subject of a century's debate in England and America was the effectiveness of regulars versus militia in battle. The Revolution, though it reinforced the political popularity of militia, provided no definitive military answers. The war was too complex, the fighting too varied; a comparative assessment was impossible because the struggle was for national independence and all too often made a mockery of orthodox strategy and tactics. For one group, however, the lessons were anything but ambiguous. To Washington and most of the leaders of the Continental

---

[10] Senator Robert R. Reynolds (N. C.), quoted in Louis Smith, *American Democracy and Military Power: A Study of Civil Control of the Military Power in the United States* (Chicago, 1951), 252.

army, who were working desperately to maintain in the field a stable force capable of defeating the British in open, eighteenth-century battle, the militia appeared undisciplined, ill-organized, and unreliable. They concluded early in the war that militia were inferior, and they never changed their minds. Militia "come in you cannot tell how, go, you cannot tell when; and act, you cannot tell where," Washington wrote in dismay. They "consume your Provisions, exhaust your Stores, and leave you at last in a critical moment."[11]

Recent scholarship, of course, indicates that the militia were central to the winning of independence: screening the Continental army; preventing the British from maneuvering, foraging, raiding, or pursuing an "oil-slick" strategy without mounting major expeditions; and helping to pen up British forces in urban areas until by the end they depended on overseas transport for nearly all their supplies (an unbearable financial, administrative, and logistical burden for the government in London).[12] The militia also operated as a political force, intimidating individuals into declaring their allegiance, enforcing loyalty, retaliating against Tories, and, when the British invaded an area, drawing the indifferent and the lukewarm into the maelstrom of revolution.[13] Many British officers learned a grudging respect for American troops no matter what their origin. As Lord Cornwallis

[11] George Washington to the President of Congress, December 20, 1776, in *WGW*, VI, 403. This is the standard quotation of Washington's opinion on militia. See, for example, John C. Miller, *Triumph of Freedom, 1775–1783* (Boston, 1948), 237; John K. Mahon, *The American Militia: Decade of Decision, 1789–1800* (*University of Florida Monographs Social Sciences No. 6*, Gainesville, 1960), 5.

[12] See Piers Mackesy, *The War for America, 1775–1783* (Cambridge, 1965), 36, 141, 143, 252, 256, 343–344, 404–407; David Syrett, *Shipping and the American War, 1775–1783* (London, 1970), 125–129, 248; and the complaints by British officers and officials: Charles Stuart to Lord Bute, July 10, 1777, in E. Stuart Wortley, ed., *A Prime Minister and His Son* (London, 1925), 112–113; Sir William Howe to Lord George Germain, January 5, 1777, and January 19, 1778, Lord George Germain to Sir Henry Clinton, June 4, 1781, Alexander Leslie to Sir Henry Clinton, December 4, 1781, all in Colonial Office [CO] 5, 94/31–32, 95/86–87, 102/1, 104/162, Public Record Office.

[13] Higginbotham, *War of American Independence*, 273–275; John Shy, "The American Revolution: The Military Conflict Considered as a Revolutionary War," in Stephen G. Kurtz and James H. Hutson, eds., *Essays on the American Revolution* (Chapel Hill, 1973), 121–156.

[14] Earl of Cornwallis to Sir Henry Clinton, June 30, 1781, CO 5, 102/506.

lamented in mid-1781, "I will not say much in praise of the Militia of the Southern Colonies, but the list of British Officers & Soldiers killed & wounded by them since last June, proves but too fatally that they are not wholly contemptible."[14]

What counted most after the war, when Washington questioned his staff and the department heads of the Continental army in response to a congressional request for ideas on a permanent system of national defense, was the perception of what had occurred and what was needed for the future. From their perspective, Washington and his advisers saw militia as difficult and unpredictable in nearly every military situation. All believed the United States had to have a national army to guard the country's natural invasion routes and to possess the West, where state jurisdiction did not extend. A peacetime force was needed to keep alive military knowledge, to prepare, and to act as the nucleus for wartime. To Washington's officers warfare demanded practice and expertise; officers had to be professional, and, if possible, trained at military academies. Last of all, Washington and the officers of the Continental army, who had fought for *all* the states and who by the end of the war supported efforts to strengthen the central government, recognized in the support of militia very disturbing political implications. Should the new nation decide to rely solely on local institutions for defense, the states and not the Confederation would possess the power of the sword, an essential power of government, one that along with the power of the purse defined ultimate sovereignty in the body politic.

In 1783 the nationalists faced a difficult dilemma: how to defend a republic which rejected standing armies when they themselves rejected militia for political and military reasons. The solution appeared to be reform and nationalization of state forces. Washington and others in the army believed three essential changes necessary, none wholly susceptible to action by the states individually. First, all the militias must become uniform in equipment, organization, and doctrine so that they could fight together effectively in the field. Second, training must increase dramatically, with annual bivouacs and stiffer fines regularly enforced for absence from muster or failure to possess the stipulated arms or accoutrements. Some of Washington's advisers wanted federal inspectors appointed to harden training and monitor the reforms. Third, because adequate training and preparation of the entire male population seemed impractical and wasteful, Washington and the officers advocated classing: singling out the young men (in Washington's words the "Van and flower . . . ever ready for Action and zealous to be employed") for special units, extra training, greater readiness, and additional obligations in military emergencies.[15] All of these reforms, endorsed by Washington and adopted eventually by the nationalists and later the Federalists, required central co-ordination and management—in short, the assumption of some degree of national control over what had always been purely state institutions.[16]

For the next ten years the question of a national military establishment and reform of the militia were inextricably linked together and pushed by nationalists and their Federalist successors in the belief that the United States must maintain some system in peacetime for frontier protection, for internal security, for possible war, and because defense was the responsibility of the central government. Because of the popular prejudice against standing armies, because of disagreements over the relative merits of regulars and citizen-soldiers, and most importantly because of the delicate issue of state or national supremacy, both met stiff opposition. Many Americans, unable to distinguish between a national military establishment and the classic standing army of European history, undoubtedly opposed a regular army. But few could dis-

[15] George Washington, "Sentiments on a Peace Establishment," enclosed in Washington to Alexander Hamilton, May 2, 1783, in *WGW*, XXVI, 390.

[16] For the various plans advanced in 1783 see the documents cited in footnote 2, above, and John Paterson to George Washington, April 16, 1783, and Frederick Stueben, plan for a peace establishment, enclosed in Frederick Steuben to George Washington, April 21, 1783, both in the Washington Papers, LC; Jedidiah Huntington to George Washington, April 16, 1783, in Jared Sparks, ed., *Correspondence of the American Revolution . . . Letters to George Washington* (4 vols., Boston, 1853), IV, 278; William Heath to George Washington, April 17, 1783, *The Heath Papers*, Massachusetts Historical Society *Collections*, 7th Ser., 65 (1905), 386–388; Rufus Putnam to George Washington, 1783, in Rowena Buell, ed., *The Memoirs of Rufus Putnam* (Boston, 1903), 198–215; George Clinton to George Washington, April, 1783, in the *Public Papers of George Clinton* (10 vols., New York, 1899–1914), VII, 144–147; Edward Hand, "On a Peace Establishment," 1783, in the Edward Hand Papers, Peter Force Transcripts, LC. See also Benjamin Lincoln's report to Congress, March 3, 1783, and his letter to Alexander Hamilton et al., May, 1783, both in the Papers of the Continental Congress, item 38, Record Group 360, National Archives; the two plans dated 1783, in the F. W. A. Steuben Papers, New-York Historical Society [NYHS]; Steuben's *A Letter on the Subject of an Established Militia, and Military Establishments* (New York, 1784); and Alexander Hamilton, "Report on a Military Peace Establishment," May–June, 1783, in *PAH*, III, 378–379.

approve of reforming the militia. After the war, several states moved to revise statutes and improve their forces.[17] Logic dictated that any future war would require integrated plans and leadership from the central government. Not even opponents of nationalizing the militia disputed the advantages of increased training, standardization of organization and equipment (although a few Congressmen later raised questions), or providing realistic enforcement procedures. Granted the plans advanced in public in the 1780's by Steuben and Knox were extreme—Steuben advocated abolition of all state authority and reduction of the forces to 25,000 enlisted volunteers and Knox called for classing, with enough training to make the total annual expense unbearably large. But for the future the nation needed armies capable of fighting outside state boundaries, of garrisoning the frontiers, and of defeating either the Indians or European adversaries. Clearly the old colonial militias—a patchwork of indifferently prepared and haphazardly armed units—were unsuitable legally and militarily. On their reform rested their future in the defense system of the United States.

*   *   *   *

The first obstacles to reform the nationalists faced in the 1780's were the ambiguity in the Articles of Confederation about Congress's ability to raise peacetime armies and the unmistakable absence of any congressional authority over the militias. In the Constitutional Convention, nationalists moved resolutely to overcome these barriers. On the army power, opposition was negligible except for Elbridge Gerry, who almost singlehandedly had blocked the creation of a national establishment in 1784. But the proposal for control of the militias sparked a fierce exchange. When Virginian George Mason moved to allow Congress "to regulate the militia," a power included in several plans of union before the convention, several delegates pointed out that the states

---

[17] See the laws in Lt. Col. Arthur Vollmer, comp., *Military Obligation: The American Tradition. A Compilation of the Enactments of Compulsion From the Earliest Settlements . . . Through the Articles of Confederation 1789 (Backgrounds of Selective Service. Special Monograph No. 1, Volume II*, Washington, 1947), Part 2 (Conn.), 250–263, part 3 (Del.), 26–35, part 4 (Ga.), 141–152, part 6 (Mass.), 261–267, part 11 (Pa.), 116–123, part 13 (S.C.), 102–104, part 14 (Va.), 422–440.

would never assent to their own disarmament.[18] "They would pine away to nothing after such a sacrifice of power," objected Oliver Ellsworth.[19] Gerry was adamant. "[T]his [was] the last point remaining to be surrendered"; if adopted, "the plan will have as black a mark as was set on Cain."[20]

As so often happened in the convention, a compromise quickly emerged to allow state and national governments to share authority over the militia, just as they were to exercise the taxing power jointly. The Committee of Eleven offered a clause permitting Congress "[t]o make laws for organizing, arming, and disciplining the militia, and for governing such part of them as may be employed in the service of the United States, reserving to the States . . . the appointing of the Officers, and . . . training . . . according to the discipline prescribed" by the central government.[21] Again a bitter fight erupted over the extent of national control. According to Rufus King of the committee, "organizing" meant specifying the size and composition of units; "arming" meant stipulating the weapons; and "disciplining" meant "prescribing the manual, exercise, evolutions, etc."[22] Gerry saw through that interpretation immediately: "a system of Despotism," he charged, "making the States drill-sergeants."[23] Yet neither Gerry nor other dissenters could block the nationalists who demanded uniformity and reform, or southerners who wished the militia strengthened for internal purposes or for their open frontiers. James Madison at one point suggested limiting the states to the appointment of officers below the rank of general, but that went too far even for many nationalists.[24] In the end the convention adopted the committee's recommendation, and, along with provisions for federalizing militia under the President as commander-in-chief, gave the new government substantial new military power.

What looked on the surface to be a nationalist victory—and was

[18] James Madison's notes, August 18, 1787, in Farrand, ed., *Records of the Federal Convention*, II, 326. Earlier suggestions in the convention for putting the militia under national direction are in *ibid.*, I, 293, II, 136.

[19] Madison's notes, August 18, 1787, *ibid.*, II, 331.

[20] Madison's notes, August 18, 1787, *ibid.*, 332.

[21] Journal of the convention, August 21, 1787, *ibid.*, 352.

[22] Madison's notes, August 23, 1787, *ibid.*, 385.

[23] Madison's notes, August 23, 1787, *ibid.*, 385.

[24] Madison's notes, August 23, 1787, *ibid.*, 388.

in terms of military sections generally—was in reality the first step in the eventual demise of the movement to reform the militia. As bitter fights in Congress during the next decade testified, the convention never adequately defined the powers of the states and Congress. New Hampshire's John Langdon had warned his fellow delegates about "the confusion of the different authorities on this subject," but most in the convention, wanting to nationalize the militia but apprehensive about the reaction in the coming fight over ratification, evidently preferred to leave the government's powers open to interpretation.[25] For the next ten years at least a conflicting welter of local interests, personal views, and partisan disagreement, all played out against a background of strife over national and state jurisdiction, was destined to stymie legislation which could strengthen the militia system. The Constitution was merely the first step, as Gouverneur Morris knew when he pressed Washington to accept the Presidency. "No Constitution is the same on Paper and in Life."[26]

* * * *

President Washington first began pressing Congress to reorganize the militia a few months after taking office, but other business prevented a congressional committee from drafting any legislation. Before the next session started, the President studied various European and American systems and forwarded his ideas to Secretary of War Knox, who then submitted a revised version of his 1786 plan to Congress. The Knox plan of 1790 was the culmination of nationalist thinking about ways to transform state forces into "powerful" and "energetic" armies. The central ideas were classing and nationalization. An "advanced corps" of eighteen- to twenty-year-olds would attend thirty-day "camps of discipline" (the twenty-year-olds would attend ten days only), where, "remote from . . . the vices of populous places," they would learn the trade of war. Afterwards they would pass into a "main corps" (twenty-one- to forty-five-year-olds), the reserve pool from which armies would be drawn for war and which, while mustered only four times yearly, would maintain its efficiency by the "con-

---

[25] Madison's notes, August 18, 1787, *ibid.*, 331.

[26] Gouverneur Morris to George Washington, October 30, 1787, in the Washington Papers, LC.

stant accession" of well-trained youth. (The oldest group would muster twice yearly and act as a home guard against invasion.) Furthermore, Knox proposed division of all companies into twelve-man sections so that federal authorities could draft individuals up to three years if enough volunteers did not come forward in an emergency. Naturally the federal government specified a single, uniform organization and oversaw all training. And in a major reversal designed to insure military readiness, all arms, equipment, and clothing would come from federal supplies—even pay for the men on bivouac. To deal with the problems of enforcement and exemptions, Knox proposed that instead of fines, graduation from the advanced corps would be a prerequisite to "exercising any of the rights of a free citizen." While he accepted exemptions in principle, "measures of national importance never should be frustrated for accommodation of Individuals."[27]

Congress and the public greeted the administration's plan with shock and disbelief—"so palpably absurd and impolitic," reacted DeWitt Clinton, "that I take it for granted it will meet with no success."[28] Obviously Knox wanted the militias nationalized completely; the states would be left merely to appoint officers and arrange exemptions. Even state inspectors, quartermasters, and adjutant generals would be required to report to federal officials. And the administration probably phrased its recommendations purposely in extreme terms in hopes that after debate and compromise Congress would still accept major changes in the system. But nearly every aspect of Knox's plan brought heavy criticism: the expense, estimated at $400,000 yearly; classing, which would take apprentices and young laborers away from employment for a month annually; the bivouacs, which some felt would militarize the nation and corrupt the youth; and the stingy exemption policy, so anti-Quaker that one Congressman refused to send the plan to the printer lest Quakers desert the Federalist party. "There are a number of opinions," Knox learned from a Massachusetts friend, "all tend[ing] to damn it."[29]

[27] For Knox's plan, see the *Annals of Congress*, 1 Cong., 2 sess. (1789–1790), 2088–2107.

[28] DeWitt Clinton to Charles Clinton, February 8, 1790, in the Miscellaneous Collection, NYHS.

[29] Henry Jackson to Henry Knox, February 21, 1790, in the Henry Knox Papers, Massachusetts Historical Society [MHS]. For other reactions, see Benjamin Goodhue

For the next two years Congress struggled to produce a national law and in the process stripped away virtually every meaningful proposal for reform. In the wake of the hostile reaction to Knox's plan, a congressional committee weakened classing, reinstituted the old fine system, and changed the arming provision back so that individual militiamen supplied their own equipment. The only tough sections remaining in the draft legislation were administrative: the addition of state adjutants, commissaries of military stores, and presidentially appointed inspectors to attend regimental musters and direct training. In July, 1790, the House cautiously ordered the bill printed in order to test public reaction. Like nearly all the proposals for change, it pleased few, including some of its authors. "I do not look upon it [as] a very perfect system," admitted George Thacher, a member of the committee. "[E]very time I run it over, I think I can point out imperfections."[30]

In truth, the idea of a national system made most Congressmen very uncomfortable. Any law, no matter what the benefit to the country as a whole, might tread heavily on local interests and very

---

to Stephen Phillips, January 25, 1790, in the Phillips Family Collection, MHS; Henry Wynkoop to Reading Beattie, January 21, 1790, in Joseph M. Beatty, Jr., ed., "The Letters of Judge Henry Wynkoop," *Pennsylvania Magazine of History and Biography*, 38 (1914), 187; James Madison to Thomas Jefferson, January 24, 1790, in Julian P. Boyd, ed., *The Papers of Thomas Jefferson* (Princeton, 1950 to date), XVI, 125; James Madison to _____, February 2, 1790, in the Roberts Autograph Collection, Haverford College Library; William Ellery to Benjamin Huntington, February 2, March 8, 1790, in the Benjamin Huntington Papers, Rhode Island State Archives [RISA]; J[oseph?] B. V[arnum?] to [George Thacher?], February 7, 1790, in the George Thacher Papers, Boston Public Library; William Irvine to John Nicholson, February 21, 1790, in the Simon Gratz Collection, Historical Society of Pennsylvania; Edward Carrington to James Madison, March 2, 1790, in the James Madison Papers, NYPL; Paine Wingate to Timothy Pickering, March 7, 1790, in Charles E. L. Wingate, *Life and Letters of Paine Wingate* (2 vols., Medford, 1930), II, 353; Henry Van Schaack to Theodore Sedgwick, March 10, 1790, in the Theodore Sedgwick Papers, MHS; "A Mechanic," in the *Freeman's Journal* (Philadelphia), March 17, 1790; John Quincy Adams to John Adams, April 5, 1790, in Worthington C. Ford, ed., *Writings of John Quincy Adams* (7 vols., New York, 1913–1917), I, 54; William Maclay journal, April 16, 1790, in Charles A. Beard, ed., *The Journal of William Maclay* (New York, 1917), 235.

[30] George Thacher to General Goodwin, July 8, 1790, in the Thacher Papers, MHS. The bill was printed in the *Gazette of the United States* (Philadelpha), July 14, 1790, July 17, 1790, July 21, 1790.

likely preclude needed local variations in organization or equipment. In towns classing would hurt tradesmen who employed
apprentices. In the South a uniform tactical structure might
threaten the employment of extra cavalry units for slave patrol.
The expense of a national system, especially the cost of arming
and training by the federal government, seemed huge. Quakers,
who mounted a potent lobby against a strong system, feared that
any law out of Philadelphia might prevent exemptions for reason
of conscience. Every voter, as Rhode Island's Senators openly
admitted, would feel the effect of more training or stiffer fines, or
view the schedule of exemptions with jealousy.[31] Many Senators
and Representatives, themselves veterans or active in the militia,
had pet theories as to the changes needed or desired. And lurking
in the background was the explosive question of just how far
federal authority over the state forces actually extended.

The first extensive debate in December, 1790, in part the
product of General Josiah Harmar's defeat at the hands of the
Indians in Ohio and the President's continual prodding, reflected
the jumble of interests and opinions. Every provision in the bill
was dissected and disputed—"too much into the minutiae of the
business," complained one Congressman; "puerile," snapped Jonathan Trumbull of Connecticut.[32] Gradually, inexorably, every
strong provision was stripped away to satisfy the chorus of conflicting views. Classing was erased, opposed by several Federalists as
discriminatory against tradesmen and by others because young
men might live so scattered as to make their mustering impossible.
Federal inspectors were transferred to state control in order to
avoid expense and because the Constitution seemed to mandate
all militia appointments by the states exclusively. After ten days
the bill was, in Trumbull's words, "so mutilated, maimed, & mur-
dered" that the House appointed a committee to prepare another
draft, but the new version solved little. Quakers in Philadelphia
and Rhode Island intensified their opposition to any specification

[31] Joseph Stanton and Theodore Foster to the Governor of Rhode Island, February
17, 1790, in the Governor's Correspondence, RISA.
[32] Timothy Bloodworth, in the *Annals of Congress*, 1 Cong., 3 sess. (1790–1791),
1817; Jonathan Trumbull to William Williams, December 25, 1790, in the Autograph
Collection, Harvard University Library.

of exemptions, and dissent from other quarters diminished not the slightest.[33] Knowledgeable observers predicted that Congress would not produce any legislation in the foreseeable future.[34]

Then in December, 1791, news of General Arthur St. Clair's defeat in Ohio rocked the capital. The regular army was annihilated, and the President's authority to mobilize the militia or reimburse militiamen called out by state officials had lapsed. The frontiers were all but naked.[35] To meet the threat, the administration proposed a 5,000 man army, the third request for more regulars in three years.[36] Never was the need for either reform of the militia or a national military establishment clearer to the nation's leaders, or the need for a militia law more desperate. As the President wrote bitterly in response to a letter from Federalist Senator Benjamin Hawkins which opposed the administration's western military program, "No man wishes less than the P_____to see a stand[in]g army established; but if Congress will not Exact a *proper* Militia law (Not such a milk and water thing as I expect to see if I ever see any) Defence and the Garrisons will always require some Troops."[37] Republican James Monroe agreed, "Anything is preferable to nothing as it takes away one of the argu-

[33] See Benjamin Bourn to Moses Brown, December 25, 1790, January 12, 1791, both in the Moses Brown Papers, Rhode Island Historical Society [RIHS]; James Pemberton to Moses Brown and Thomas Arnold, January 19, 1791, in the Almy-Brown Papers, RIHS; various constituents to Theodore Foster, January, 1791, in the Theodore Foster Papers, RIHS.

[34] William Smith to Otho H. Williams, December, 1790, in the Otho H. Williams Papers, Maryland Historical Society; Edward Carrington to James Madison, February 2, 1791, in the James Madison Papers, LC; George Thacher to William Wedgeny, November 11, 1791, in the Thacher Papers, MHS. For the debate see *Annals of Congress*, 1 Cong., 3 sess. (1790–1791), 1804–1828, 1837, 1840.

[35] Under the act of March 3, 1791 (*Annals of Congress*, 1 Cong., 3 sess. [1790–1791], 2351), the President could "engage a body to serve as cavalry" and, if a new regiment could not be recruited "in time to prosecute such military operations as exigencies" required, he could substitute an equal number of militia. The authorization was obviously meant to be temporary and, except for cavalry, limited to less than a thousand militia. Knox pointed out the lack of proper mobilization procedures when preparing temporary defense measures, telling the President that the only alternative was to request the governors of exposed states to call out the militia themselves. See Henry Knox to George Washington, January 1, 1792, in the Washington Papers, LC.

[36] For the administration's military program see Walter Lowrie and Matthew Clarke, eds., *American State Papers . . . , Indian Affairs* (Washington, 1832), I, 197–202.

[37] George Washington, "Errors of Government Towards the Indians," February, 1792, in *WGW*, XXXI, 494. The letter from Benjamin Hawkins to George Washington, February 10, 1792, is in Elizabeth G. McPherson, ed., "Unpublished Letters from North Carolinians to Washington," in *NCHR*, 12 (1935), 162–165.

ments for a standing army."[38] In February, 1792, discussion began anew on the weakened congressional bill; this time debate hinged on the extent of national control, the most divisive issue and one increasingly central to the emerging party struggle. Opponents attempted to block every assertion of national authority, at one point even moving to abandon the requirement for uniform caliber muskets. Finally, in order to achieve any agreement at all, Congress struck out every controversial provision, heeding the reasoning of Elias Boudinot (who pleaded at the outset that "a plan of conciliation alone would ever procure . . . a militia bill") to make "the law . . . very simple in its construction, and refer to as few objects as possible."[39]

In the end, the Uniform Militia Act passed in 1792 (and signed by the President at the last possible moment so as, undoubtedly, to register his disgust) was so weak that many Federalists could not bear to support it. Gone was every vestige of the reforms nationalists and Federalists had advocated for a decade: classing, increased training, and guarantees of uniformity. The law contained no provisions for fines, or officials specially charged with upgrading standards or reporting to the federal government, and no procedures for insuring a national system. Militiamen (all eighteen- to forty-five-year-olds) were to arm and equip themselves; states were to adopt the tactical organization prescribed if "convenient"; and training was to conform to Steuben's wartime manual unless "unavoidable circumstances" dictated otherwise. If the states or individuals ignored the law, the government was powerless to intercede.[40]

---

[38] James Monroe to Archibald Stuart, March 14, 1792, in the James Monroe Papers, Virginia Historical Society.

[39] Elias Boudinot, *Annals of Congress*, 2 Cong., 1 sess. (1791–1792), 419.

[40] The law is in *ibid.*, 2 Cong., 1 sess. (1791–1792), 1392–1395. Debate in the House, Senate action, and the voting can be followed *ibid.*, 2 Cong., 1 sess. (1791–1792), 103, 104, 111, 112, 113, 114, 115, 122–123, 128, 418–424, 432, 433, 435, 436, 552–553, 577, 578–579. The House vote was 31 to 27 and did not follow any sectional or party patterns. Staunch Federalists like Fisher Ames, Theodore Sedgwick, and Elias Boudinot voted for it, as did nearly all the antiadministration Virginians like Madison and Abraham Venable. Opponents included important Federalists like Jeremiah Wadsworth and George Thacher, as well as administration enemies William Findley, Nathaniel Macon, and Thomas Sumter. A more complete account of the drafting of the law is Richard H. Frazer, "The Foundations of American Military Policy, 1783–1800" (doctoral dissertation, University of Oklahoma, 1959), 259–284. See also Howard White, *Executive Influence in Determining Military Policy in the United States (University of Illinois Studies in Social Sciences*, XII, Urbana, 1924), 92–93; Mahon, *American Militia*, 17–18.

Almost universally, contemporaries viewed the act as unsound and inadequate. State laws passed to implement it contained tremendous variations, from unit structure to fines to number of musters.[41] After his legislature wrestled with the statute, Federalist Senator Charles Carroll of Carrollton concluded that "never . . . did a body of wise men pass so mischievous an act."[42] Every Congress for the next thirty years attempted to strengthen it, but even in the aftermath of the Whiskey Rebellion, when Secretary Knox reported that the War Department had been forced to furnish two-thirds of the men mobilized with arms, and Congressman Samuel Smith, who had commanded the Maryland contingent in the march to Pittsburgh, berated his colleagues with tales of the militia's dismal performance (in response to one order to load, fifty men had "put down the ball before the charge of powder"), Congress could not agree on another law.[43] Because of the pressure of Harmar's and St. Clair's defeats, Congress had been forced to fulfill its duty to implement the militia provision of the Constitution.[44] True reform could have cost tens of thousands of dollars annually, forced changes the states did not want, worked hardships on special groups, and certainly increased the burden on individual voters. No one could agree on fines, exemptions, whether training camps would school youth to defend the country or debauch their morals, or indeed whether nationalization would

---

[41] Fraser, "American Military Policy," 229–330, 451–452.

[42] Charles Carroll of Carrollton to John Henry, December 3, 23, 1792, both in Kate Mason Rowland, *The Life of Charles Carroll* (2 vols., New York, 1898), II, 190, 193–194. For other expressions see the debates in the *Annals of Congress*, 2 Cong., 2 sess. (1792–1793), 701–702, 708–711, 3 Cong., 2 sess. (1794–1795), 1067–1071, 1214–1220, 1233–1237, 4 Cong., 2 sess. (1796–1797), 1675–1691, 2223–2224, 5 Cong., 1 sess. (1797) 340–341, 642, 5 Cong. 2 sess. (1797–1798), 1384–1386, 1524, 1525, 1559–1560, 1772–1773, 6 Cong., 1 sess. (1799–1800), 201, 523.

[43] Knox also estimated that three-quarters of the nation's militiamen lacked arms. Henry Knox to the House, with enclosure, December 10, 1794, in the *Annals of Congress*, 3 Cong., 2 sess. (1794–1795), 1396–1399; Samuel Smith, *ibid.*, 3 Cong., 2 sess. (1794–1795), 1069. John A. Logan, *The Volunteer Soldier of America* (Chicago, 1887), 164–165, states that "almost every session" from 1794 to 1819 considered revising the 1792 act.

[44] A good example of the way this pressure worked was North Carolinian William Barry Grove's comment that the law "is not altogether what I could wish, but the necessity in my opinion of having some general principles for the States to act on induced me to give it my assent. I am persuaded if We had had a Militia Law in existence so many Regular Troops would not have been needed to defend the frontier from a Set of Naked *Indians*." Grove to Governor Alexander Martin, March 17, 1792, in the Governors' Papers, North Carolina Division of Archives and History, Raleigh.

revitalize the system or destroy it. And as the party struggle hardened, the disagreement over the extent of congressional authority grew more heated and partisan. Federalist military theoreticians might want classing, but party stalwarts from seaboard constituencies saw difficulties for their towns, and some in the party undoubtedly realized that a weak militia enhanced the need for a strong military establishment. (Republican Senator William Maclay accused Knox of proposing a purposely extreme plan in 1790, knowing that it could never pass, and that Congress would be forced to accept a standing army.[45]) Republicans might wish to improve the militia to avert a military establishment, but too many in the party wanted to keep federal budgets small and federal authority over the states at a minimum. As Dwight Foster explained in 1795, after a long and fruitless debate over revising the law, "this is a subject which affects the various Interests of Individuals in every part of the United States and consequently many great and various are the Sentiments and opinions which are formed by different persons on Questions of this Nature."[46]

*　*　*　*

With the passage of the 1792 act and the failure of the reform movement, the colonial militia system ⸱continued to decline as a viable military force until it finally passed into oblivion, in ridicule and disorganization, before the Civil War.[47] Ironically, those

---

[45] William Maclay journal, April 16, 1790, in Beard, ed., *Journal of Maclay* 235.

[46] Dwight Foster journal, February 17, 1795, in the Dwight Foster Papers, American Antiquarian Society.

[47] With the exception of Jim Dan Hill, *The Minute Man in Peace and War: A History of the National Guard* (Harrisburg, 1964), 9–10, military analysts and historians have emphasized the weakness of the 1792 act. See Brevet Major General Emory Upton, *The Military Policy of the United States* (62 Cong., 2 sess., Senate Document No. 4941, Washington, 1912), 85; John McAuley Palmer, *America in Arms: The Experience of the United States with Military Organization* (New Haven, 1941), 50–53; Walter Millis, *Arms and Men: A Study in American Military History* (New York, 1956), 50–52; Arthur A. Ekirch, Jr., *The Civilian and the Military* (New York, 1956), 33–35; Frazer, "American Military Policy," 449–462; T. Harry Williams, *Americans at War: The Development of the American Military System* (Baton Rouge, 1960), 18–19; C. Joseph Barnardo and Eugene H. Bacon, *American Military Policy: Its Development Since 1775* (2nd ed., Harrisburg, 1961), 77–82; Mahon, *American Militia*, 18–21; Russell F. Weigley, *Towards an American Army: Military Thought from Washington to Marshall* (New York and London, 1962), 20–21; Russell F. Weigley, *History of the United States Army* (New York, 1967), 93–94. The best description of the militia's decline in the early nineteenth century is Marcus Cunliffe, *Soldiers & Civilians: The Martial Spirit in America, 1775–1865* (Boston, 1968), chaps. 6 and 7, See

who had opposed increasing federal military powers were in part responsible for the ultimate triumph of the national government in military affairs. But it was also true that once the mantle of the British army had been removed, the old militia system of universal service and state control could not alone provide for America's military security. The new nation needed co-ordinated, trained armies commanded by skilled officers and equipped with standard arms and equipment, forces that would respond to the will of a central government, fight outside a particular state or overseas, and stay abreast of changes in warfare and technology. The leaders of the Continental army and many nationalists recognized the problem as early as 1783, and, as would happen often after American wars, military programs were proposed that proved unacceptable for essentially political reasons.

And yet by 1800, after a decade of Indian conflict, rebellions in Massachusetts and Pennsylvania, a war scare with Britain and a quasi war with France, after the smashing triumph of France's new legions across Europe, some of the militia's fervent champions began to realize that even citizen-soldiers must be well-trained and the defense of the republic managed with efficiency by a single authority. "We are all Republicans, we are all Federalists," declared Thomas Jefferson in his inaugural address. Nowhere did Jefferson prove the point more clearly than in a statement which, because it revealed a consensus on the role of militia, marked the true epitaph for those institutions in the American defense system: "a well-disciplined militia," proclaimed the new President, "our best reliance in peace and for the first moments of war, *till regulars may relieve them.*"[48]

---

also William H. Riker, *Soldiers of the States: The Role of the National Guard in American Democracy* (Washington, 1957), chap. 3; Paul Tincher Smith, "Militia of the United States from 1846 to 1860," in the *Indiana Magazine of History*, 15 (1919), 20–47; and a typical local study, Anthony Marro, "Vermont's Local Militia Units, 1815–1860," in *Vermont History*, 40 (1972), 28–42.

[48] Emphasis added. Thomas Jefferson, First Inaugural Address, March 4, 1801, in James D. Richardson, ed., *A Compilation of the Messages and Papers of the Presidents, 1789–1897* (8 vols., Washington, 1896–1899), I, 323.

A Fond Farewell to Henry Adams:
Ideas on Relating Political History to
Social Change During the Early National Period

Van Beck Hall

THE POLITICAL HISTORY of the early national period presents a great challenge and opportunity to historians interested in relating political decision making to stability and change in the economic and social-cultural structure of the society. Change certainly occurred. The American people reproduced rapidly and moved westward. Capitalists and states built new transportation systems. Religious denominations experienced a second Great Awakening. Postal riders circulated throughout the nation and carried an increasing number of newspapers and magazines to more subscribers. Americans formed and joined voluntary political, social, and cultural organizations in ever-increasing numbers. American merchants took advantage of European wars to change the routes of their trade. Farmers grew and supplied ever greater quantities of cotton for the developing English mills. By 1830 the United States had arrived at the threshold of the Industrial Revolution. Yet these changes, though significant, were neither as rapid nor as all encompassing as those occasioned by the rapid industrialization that took place after 1830. This period gives us the opportunity to analyze the connections between social change and political decision making before the upheaval of industrialization.

To generate insights into the relationship between politics and stability and change within the society, historians must use a variety of historical methods. Henry Adams, in his magisterial *History*

323

of the United States, gives us an exciting narrative description of the administrations of Jefferson and Madison.[1] Hundreds of historians since Adams have developed his narrative, written biographies, described politics and politicians, and analyzed ideologies; while others have borrowed ideas from the social scientists and have used techniques devised by statisticians and political scientists to examine the types of changes taking place between 1790 and 1830. Unfortunately, at times, historians seem more interested in attacking other approaches than in developing their own ideas about the period. In fact, all approaches are useful. Intuition and statistical rigor and flowing narrative and social-scientific analysis are all important tools and approaches for any historian attempting to deal with the complex problems of politics and change.

The thesis of this essay is that it is possible to integrate these disparate but mutually supportive methods in exploring the relationships between politics and social-economic change. In order to accomplish this we will have to adopt appropriate definitions and analytical procedures for each side of the relationship. A first task is the expansion of the definition of politics and the scope of political history. To define politics as the use of governmental power to make and enforce decisions expands the scope of political history and produces a better understanding of the relationship of politics to other social and economic changes. Under such a definition political historians would no longer be primarily interested in the intricate development and machinations of parties and party systems but could expand their analysis to cover "nonpartisan" political decisions and a wide range of nonlegislative institutions ranging from Supreme Courts to local overseers of the poor. A second task is to describe and analyze social-economic change in terms appropriate to linkages with political decision making. For this purpose we will have to uncover sources and develop methods which permit the measurement, not only of over-all rates of change, but also of differences in these rates among regions, states, and localities and of associated changes in classes, groups, and organizations. This will permit us to compare and contrast the characteristics of individuals, of social groups, and of localities, both with regard to differences among them at any particular time and as they are affected by changes over time.

[1] *History of the United States* (9 vols., New York, 1889–1891).

Finally, the redefinition of politics and the appropriate measurement of social-economic change should make it possible to discover those specific linkages between the two that can vastly expand our understanding of the political process.

*   *   *   *

A narrow definition of politics and political history as partisan differences or the history of political parties makes it difficult for us to relate political decisions to many of the changes taking place within a society. Historians have too often considered political history as party history and have used the party as the starting point of the research. Historians of the early national period have focused on the two parties, Federalist and Democratic-Republican, that formed the first American party system. They have described, in detail, the strength, organization, ideology, and composition of these parties for the nation and the states.[2] They have produced studies based on roll call analysis of the Congress and state legislatures, on voting patterns of towns and other constituencies, and on the collective biographies of the competitors.[3] Others have examined the 1820's and have described the formation of the second party system from the groups and factions that survived the collapse of the first system or that organized themselves during that decade.[4] All of this is important, but the narrow emphasis on parties ignores many other important political developments dur-

---

[2] A few of the recent studies include: Paul Goodman, "The First American Party System," in William Nesbit Chambers and Walter Dean Burnham, eds., *The American Party Systems: Stages of Political Development* (New York, 1967), 56–89; David Hackett Fischer, *The Revolution of American Conservatism* (New York, 1965); Norman K. Risjord, *The Old Republicans: Southern Conservatism in the Age of Jefferson* (New York, 1965); and Shaw Livermore, *The Twilight of Federalism* (Princeton, 1962).

[3] Jackson Turner Main, *Political Parties Before the Constitution* (Chapel Hill, 1973), 18–43, provides an excellent discussion of methodology. Rudolph M. Bell, *Party and Faction in American Politics: The House of Representatives, 1789–1801* (Westport, 1973), gives anaylsis of national politics. Manning J. Dauer, *The Adams Federalists* (Baltimore, 1953), uses an older but still effective method.

[4] The best starting point for this is Richard P. McCormick, *The Second American Party System: Party Formation in the Jackson Era* (Chapel Hill, 1966), and his essay, "Political Development and the Second Party System," in Chambers and Burnham, eds., *American Party Systems*, 90–116. See also Lee Benson, *The Concept of Jacksonian Democracy: New York as a Test Case* (Princeton, 1961), for method. For one state with direct links from the first to second party system see John A. Munroe, *Federalist Delaware, 1775–1815* (New Brunswick, 1954).

ing the period. It fails to describe what happened politically when well-organized parties disappear, as they did in many states between 1801 and 1826 and in the nation between 1816 and 1824.[5] It fails to explain the importance of so-called nonpartisan issues that came before Congress and the state legislatures. It fails to analyze political decision making, except in terms of parties and personalities.[6] It fails to explain decisions made by judicial and administrative institutions. Finally, it fails to examine the links among local, state, and national politics, except through parties.[7] In order to begin to cover these other areas we must expand the scope of political history to include much more than the partisan differences within a "party system."

The broader definition of politics, which I suggest, would be based upon all of the uses of governmental power to achieve a wide range of goals. It would enable us to broaden the scope of political history to examine nonpartisan divisions in legislative bodies, to analyze and describe the procedures within legislatures and other political institutions, to search for executive influence and explain the decisions made by executive agencies, to examine the courts and judicial decisions, to describe decisions made by public or semipublic bodies, ranging from boards of works to boards of state banks, and to examine the operations of local governmental institutions such as county courts, selectmen, and overseers of the poor.

Thus there are at least six ways we can broaden the scope of political history. We can analyze issues that cut across or ignore party lines; we can describe the operations of legislatures; we can analyze the political role of the courts; we can discuss the politics of state agencies; we can examine the importance of local politics; and we can investigate the links that connected local, state, and national politics.

The first is, of course, to begin to analyze issues that seemed to have little relevance to the divisions of partisan politics. Scholars who have analyzed party voting in Congress or in state legislatures

[5] One effort to do this for the national level is James Sterling Young, *The Washington Community, 1800–1828* (New York, 1966).

[6] One study that attempts to explain the politics of judicial reform in the context of partisan politics is Richard E. Ellis, *The Jeffersonian Crisis: Courts and Politics in the Young Republic* (New York, 1971).

[7] One of the best examples of a study that develops these linkages through an analysis of party is Carl E. Prince, *New Jersey's Jeffersonian Republicans: The Genesis of an Early Party Machine* (Chapel Hill, 1967).

have discovered that many important issues simply do not fit into a partisan mold.[8] Legislators and Congressmen lined up in their partisan ranks in electing speakers, in replying to executive messages, or in responding to foreign policy and a wide range of other issues. But these neat divisions became blurred or obliterated when bank charters, internal improvements, changes in social-welfare systems, and many other important questions came on the floor. Historians have also discovered that for long periods between 1789 and 1827 it is difficult if not impossible to uncover lasting party divisions in either Congress or in many of the state legislatures.[9] This failure to find partisan behavior and the difficulties of even describing, let alone analyzing, nonpartisan divisions leads to totally impressionistic and narrative statements and analysis about the relationship of politics to ideology, personalities, and issues.

Jackson Turner Main has used one technique that can begin to bring some order to this nonpartisan chaos. Main, studying the 1780's when legislators simply did not fit into neatly divided parties, used computer analysis of all the roll call votes to uncover voting blocs of legislators who, over time, tended to vote together on a wide range of issues.[10] Several students have applied his technique to later periods and have begun to uncover similar blocs in various states and in different time periods.[11] These blocs should not be confused with highly organized parties. Additional analysis often shows some important differences, depending upon issues, among legislators who stand within the same bloc. This means that in addition to analyzing the total voting pattern their patterns of voting on clusters of related issues must also be analyzed.[12] By doing this the researcher can determine which members of a

---

[8] This is especially true in many of the narrative works on state politics where issues are discussed but little effort is made to analyze them if they fail to correspond to party or "factional" divisions. Two interesting exceptions are Charles H. Ambler, *Sectionalism in Virginia, 1776–1861* (Chicago, 1910), and Dixon Ryan Fox, *Decline of Aristocracy in the Politics of New York* (New York, 1918).

[9] Young, *Washington Community*. Also notice studies on politically oriented topics, such as David J. Rothman, *The Discovery of the Asylum: Social Order and Disorder in the New Republic* (Boston, 1971), that pay little attention to political divisions.

[10] Main, *Political Parties*, 18–43.

[11] An example is Leonard J. Sneddon, "State Politics in the 1790's" (doctoral dissertation, State University of New York at Stony Brook, 1972).

[12] In other words an analysis of divisions based on all the roll-call votes for a particular session permits the researcher to classify the legislators into two or more groups or "blocs," but an analysis of specific issues may indicate different patterns.

legislature voted together while at the same time he can also discover which legislators and constituencies supported or opposed bank charters, internal improvements, judicial and constitutional reforms, and a wide range of other proposed legislation.[13] The scholar can then show continuity or change over time that may be totally unrelated to the blocs that an individual legislator votes with. These methods, when used in conjunction with an analysis of partisan divisions, will for the first time give us an awareness of the complexities of politics during periods when parties were developing, disintegrating, or nonexisting.

Legislators did not confine their political operations to roll calls. We need to know a great deal more about the actual operations of legislative politics during this period. Jack Greene and Robert Zemsky have demonstrated the importance of small groups of legislators who controlled the important committees that drafted most of the important legislation.[14] It is obvious that the same thing occurred during the early national period. All legislators were not equal; some had prestige and important assignments while others attended, voted, and returned home. Legislatures passed or defeated important measures without taking roll call votes; this forces us to examine the composition of the committees that reported bills and recommended action for clues about the goals of specific groups and regions. Legislation passing through one house often died in the other; bills would be amended beyond recognition; houses would refuse to compromise on their position; important legislation died in conference committees. When one considers the large number of legislative and parliamentary traps waiting for bills, it is sometimes amazing that any important legislation could be pushed through.[15] These legislatures also found themselves overwhelmed with petitions and bills that today would be submitted to the courts. In Virginia relatively well-organized

[13] Thus the researcher can determine the major "blocs" and at the same time can analyze the differences among legislators on specific groups of issues.

[14] Jack P. Greene, The Quest for Power: The Lower Houses of Assembly in the Southern Royal Colonies, 1689–1776 (Chapel Hill, 1963), and Robert Zemsky, Merchants, Farmers, and River Gods: An Essay on Eighteenth Century American Politics (Boston, 1971).

[15] The photoduplication revolution has made it much easier for the historian to return to the original legislative records. The best guide is William Sumner Jenkins and Lillian A. Hamrick, eds., A Guide to the Microfilm Collection of Early State Records (Washington, 1950), for the legislative journals. The general lack of archival committee materials means that historians must comb through these journals to discover committee assignments, reports, etc.

legislatures spent weeks going over time consuming minor matters like the remission of individual militia fines, the unpaid accounts of sheriffs, and divorces.[16]

Professional politicians have always been acutely aware of these subtleties of the legislative process which escape notice in most histories. They know the importance of nonpartisan issues and the methods by which bills can be guided through the legislative maze. Careful analysis of the membership on important committees and detailed studies of the legislative process will give us additional insights about the political process within legislative bodies.

Politics was not confined to legislatures. The state and national governments created agencies that made important political decisions. There have been relatively few studies of the politics within these bodies. The judiciary, both national and state, made an enormous number of decisions that had a political impact on an incredible number of issues ranging from the punishment of criminals to the legal role of corporations. The courts untangled conflicting land claims, defined the rights and privileges of citizens, interpreted the laws passed by the legislatures, and in some states continued to operate under the principles and procedures of the common law with relatively little legislative interference.[17] These judicial decisions had an enormous impact on political change. Certain decisions expunged or changed legislative action; others swept away restrictions on social and economic change. Historians have written a great deal about the national Supreme Court but very few analytical studies have been written about the lower federal or state courts that might place them in a political context of making decisions with enormous potential for stability

---

[16] Session laws that were printed at the time appear in Charles Evans, ed., *American Bibliography* (13 vols., Worcester, 1903–1955), and the continuations after 1800 in Ralph R. Shaw and Richard H. Shoemaker, eds., *American Bibliography* (New York, 1958–1967), through 1819; Richard H. Shoemaker, ed., *A Checklist of American Imprints* (Metuchen, 1967–1971), through 1829, and Gayle Cooper, ed., *A Checklist of American Imprints* (Metuchen, 1972) for 1830. Roger P. Bristol, ed., *Supplement to Charles Evans American Bibliography* (Charlottesville, 1970) fills in through 1800. These are keyed to the microcard collection of Clifford K. Shipton, *Early American Imprints* (Worcester, 1956 to date), which now runs through 1812. There is also a project under way to reproduce the session laws of all the states through 1899.

[17] There are some general surveys of American law for the period, but anyone wanting detailed information about court procedures, etc., in the various states enters into a veritable wilderness. L. Kinvin Wroth and Hiller B. Zobel, eds., *Legal Papers of John Adams* (3 vols., Cambridge, 1965), I, xxi-xciv, suggest what can be done in this area.

or change. The study of the personal characteristics of the judges and the importance of their decisions on political, social, and economic development has just begun.[18] Indeed, we may find that many of the most important changes came about between 1790 and 1830, not through the elective or legislative process but through the vast number of decisions of state and lower federal courts.

In addition to the courts all of the states and many smaller political divisions established or possessed special boards and commissions that exercised broad power. These administrative bodies attempted to settle land disputes; cared for the mentally ill; administered the penitentiaries; planned, built, and supervised internal improvements; expended public funds for education; and performed countless other services for states and local communities. Every one of these agencies made political decisions. Sometimes co-operating with, but at other times ignoring, the legislative and executive authorities, they made decisions concerning the types of improvements to be made, the way that the poor, prisoners, and students would be supported, and many other decisions that influenced the development of states and communities.[19]

These governments also created primitive bureaucracies. Historians have produced some good institutional studies of the national bureaucracy and have begun to describe the characteristics of important national officeholders during the period.[20] But little has been done to even describe the powers and functions of

[18] The history of American law for this period seems to seep down from the top. Julius Goebel, Jr., *Antecedents and Beginnings to 1801* (Vol. I, Oliver Wendell Holmes Devise History of the Supreme Court of the United States, New York, 1971), covers more ground than usual. Dwight F. Henderson, *Courts for a New Nation* (Washington, 1971), has material on lower federal courts; findings by Douglas W. Catton, "A Study of the State and Federal High Courts in the Law and Politics of Pennsylvania" (doctoral dissertation, University of Illinois-Champaign-Urbana, 1973), and Mark K. Bousteel Tachau, "The Federal Courts in Kentucky, 1789–1816" (doctoral dissertation, University of Kentucky, 1972), break some new ground.

[19] Virginia, for example, established several of these bodies. See *The Revised Code of the Laws of Virginia* (2 vols., Richmond, 1819), I, 412–418, for the mental hospital; I, 82–90, for the Literary Fund; II, 121, for examiners of pilots; 201–205, for the fund for internal improvements (or the board of public works); and II, 264–269, for the county overseers of the poor.

[20] The two books by Leonard D. White, *The Federalists: A Study in Administrative History, 1789–1801* (New York, 1948), and *The Jeffersonians: A Study in Administrative History, 1801–1829* (New York, 1951), offer a concise overview. Sidney H. Aronson, *Status and Kinship in the Higher Civil Service: Standards of Selection in the Administrations of John Adams, Thomas Jefferson, and Andrew Jackson* (Cambridge, 1964), represents a ground breaking study.

the state and local bureaucracies.[21] In Virginia, for example, the executive council made many important decisions when the legislature was not in session. The state auditor controlled the methods of collecting and auditing taxes, and the treasurer voted the states' shareholdings in banking corporations.[22] We need many more institutional histories of these early bureaucracies.

The national and state governments established large numbers of mixed private and public boards to control banks and colleges and to oversee many major transportation improvements. All of these mixed bodies had considerable decision making powers. The state-appointed directors of a bank could determine to grant or withhold loans to certain groups or individuals, and this decision could have important consequences for the economic development of a state or town. The focuses of political history must be expanded beyond the horizon of legislative roll calls and popular voting. We must begin to develop some processes which describe and analyze the decisions made in these important judicial and administrative bodies.

A massive amount of work, furthermore, needs to be done on the nature of local politics. Every town, township, or county had numerous officers who controlled the expenditures for social welfare, education, road construction and maintenance, led the militia, and monitored taverns. In some states voters or taxpayers elected these officials; in others, the county courts or some other body appointed them; regardless of the method of selection they had considerable local power and their decisions could be related to all sorts of economic and social-cultural change.[23] Besides analyzing the decisions of these officers the historian can also ascertain the characteristics of individuals who held these offices and whether these characteristics changed over time. Indeed, in counties and towns where they were elected by the voters changes in the characteristics of these officers could be related to changes within the entire community.[24]

21 A recent exception is Robert M. Ireland, *The County Courts in Antebellum Kentucky* (Lexington, 1972).

22 *Revised Code (1819)*, II, 1–6, for the Auditor; and II, 85–86, for the directors of the Farmer's Bank of Virginia.

23 Bray Hammond, *Banks and Politics in America: From the Revolution to the Civil War* (Princeton, 1957), esp. 144–196, gives some information about state banks.

24 Most local studies have used local returns and politics to explain the development of parties. Some of these are John W. Brant, "Analysis of Anti-Masonic and Whig Voting in Somerset County, Pennsylvania, 1828–1840" (seminar paper filed

The complex linkages among state, national, and local politics must also be examined in greater detail. Some scholars have already presented excellent studies in describing how party organization linked these political levels.[25] This work, however, tends to ignore the issues and decisions that lay outside the area of partisan politics. We need some studies of the types of influence and pressure that a community or constituency could bring to bear on its legislator or Congressman. In many instances the legislator himself had a direct stake in legislation favoring a particular community. He could, for example, be involved in the chartering of a local bank or corporation. The community might bring pressure to bear through petitions and memorials or by writing letters to their legislator. The legislative journals and manuscript collections of Congressmen and legislators give us an indication of these pressures.[26]

The passage of a bank charter can illustrate the importance of the broader definition of politics and the use of the six methods to broaden the scope of political history. In most cases bank charters were nonpartisan, "private" questions that seldom required a roll call vote. Yet the success or failure of efforts to charter a bank could have an enormous influence on the future development of a community or of certain groups and individuals within a town.[27] The extended definition includes this sort of political activity. The analysis of local politics gives us an indication of where the supporters of the bank charter fit into the social, economic, and political structure of their community. The supporters then either influence or put pressure on their legislator, and this

---

in History Department Library, University of Pittsburgh, 1969); Whitman H. Ridgway, "A Social Analysis of Maryland Community Elite, 1827–1836; A Study of the Distribution of Power in Baltimore City, Frederick County, and Talbot County" (doctoral dissertation, University of Pennsylvania, 1973); and Kathleen Smith Kotolowski, "The Social Composition of Political Leadership: Genesee County, New York, 1821–1860" (doctoral dissertation, University of Rochester, 1973).

[25] Prince, *New Jersey*, is an excellent example.

[26] Petitions are especially useful for these purposes. They can be located and traced through the legislative journals, and most states have retained them in their archives. In Virginia they are filed by county, and in Massachusetts they are filed with the appropriate legislation. Many of them also have lists of names appended so that a researcher can trace these individuals back into the local county or community.

[27] One of the basic reasons for the rapid expansion of banking facilities was the rivalry among communities and among groups of businessmen and capitalists in the same community.

illustrates the links between local and state politics. The petition or memorial arrives in the legislature. We can now follow it through the intricate process of committees, reports, readings, amendment, and passage in both houses. We can analyze the structure and procedures of the legislature and perhaps determine why this particular charter passed while others failed. In some cases a roll call vote might be taken, and this gives us an opportunity to analyze support and resistance to the charter in terms of the characteristics of the legislators and their constituencies. Even after the governor approves the bill, the process has not been completed. In many cases the state may appoint some of the directors, and we have to analyze the impact of the decisions of these directors on the operations of the bank. The very existence of the new institution may depend upon the decisions of the courts regarding its charter, its issuance of paper money, and its operations. Finally, the supporters, after their success, must be on guard against efforts to modify their charter or restrictive general banking laws.[28] This merely illustrates how all the factors involved in such an operation can only be described by expanding our definition of politics and the scope of political history, and by developing some new approaches to nonpartisan political decision making.

* * * *

The second task is to describe stability and change within the society and to develop methods that will enable us to relate this mass of information to the processes of political change. Our description of stability and change depends upon the availability of research materials and on the particular unit that we intend to analyze. A close analysis enables us to differentiate among individuals and various political units in terms of their economic and social-cultural characteristics and of the varied rates of change that take place in these characteristics over time.

The description of the economy involves the development of materials and ideas dealing with demography, commerce, internal transportation, agriculture, manufacturing, and finance. Impor-

[28] All of these steps can be traced through available records. The legislative journals give information about the appearance and commitment of petitions; many of the petitions are available, and the journals enable us to follow the action through one or both houses. The session laws give the final outcome. In many states the chartered banks had to report to the legislature or the executive.

tant changes occurred in all these categories between 1790 and 1830. Population grew rapidly and moved westward. The patterns of international and domestic trade changed. States and individuals built turnpikes and constructed vast canal systems. Agricultural methods and crop systems changed. Banks, which were rare in 1790, became commonplace by 1830. All of these economic changes influenced the political behavior of states, towns, and communities, and many resulted from political decisions championed by certain individuals and communities.

People were the basis of politics. Their increase or loss, migration, age structure, residence in urban and rural regions, and racial and ethnic composition all had a political impact. Rapid population growth and the westward movement of migrants did not affect all states, regions, or communities in the same way. Certain states and regions and counties within states, including eastern ones, grew very rapidly; others remained stationary or lost population. The timing of growth also varied throughout the forty-year period. Immigration flowed from and to different regions depending upon the decade; an area that grew rapidly between 1790 and 1810 might be almost stagnant by 1830.[29] These differences in population growth, emigration, and immigration must have had a tremendous physical, psychological, and political impact upon populations. Those who remained in stagnating towns and communities would develop a totally different perspective about the world and its future from those who lived in booming and growing regions. Age structures and sex ratios also varied as working age males tended to migrate into the cities or toward the West.[30] This rapid movement of population worried many who

---

[29] There is a large amount of demographic material available for this period. The population schedules were published for each of the first four census years. Existing manuscript returns have been printed for 1790, and the available manuscript returns for 1800, 1810, 1820, and 1830 are available on microfilm. There is some manufacturing and agricultural material mixed in with some of the 1810 and 1820 population returns for certain counties in Virginia. The best single printed source for county data for the entire period is United States Bureau of the Census, *Statistics of Population: Ninth Census of the United States* (Washington, 1872), 68–72, which gives Virginia and West Virginia. The Historical Archive, Inter-University Consortium for Political Research at Ann Arbor, Michigan, has a data file containing census data by county and/or state from 1790 through 1970.

[30] Some recent studies on the demography of this period include J. Potter, "Growth of Population in America, 1700–1860," in D. V. Glass and D. E. C. Eversley, eds., *Population in History: Essays in Historical Demography* (Chicago, 1965), 631–688, and Colin Foster and G. S. L. Tucker, *Economic Opportunity and White American Fertility Ratios, 1800–1860* (New Haven, 1972).

believed that older ideas of community were being shattered by rapid movement and feared that various types of religious, social, and political controls might be required to bring order to the boom and chaos of the West and the cities. Rapidly growing units with a psychology of growth and development demanded banks, internal improvements, settlement of land disputes, and many other changes from their state and national governments in which older, stagnant, or better serviced communities had less interest. The basic data are available to provide detailed studies of population growth and stagnation among small subdivisions. The decennial, published census provides a wealth of information about population growth and gives increasing detail about sex and age composition. Additional material is also available in the remaining manuscript census returns for the period.[31]

Urbanization and the proportion of inhabitants in rural and urban areas is more difficult to handle. The large towns and cities did not grow too much more rapidly than the population as a whole and the proportions of Americans living in urban areas, as defined by the census, declined between 1810 and 1820. Yet in many states and regions within states urban population did grow more rapidly than the population of the particular state or region and the census definition fails to indicate the importance of small towns and hamlets of from 250 to 2,500 population. Many of these were, in reality, small urban areas that had totally different occupational structures and population patterns from the surrounding countryside.[32] These hamlets served as the headquarters of local professionals, merchants, and speculators who possessed connections with similar individuals in larger cities who often spearheaded political efforts to charter banks and supported the news-

---

[31] One of the basic problems, due to the rapid formation of counties and other minor civil divisions throughout the period, is to analyze units that cover the same area over time. Many of the states have published handbooks that give the formation of these units. Boundaries can be determined from maps and from the acts creating new units in the session laws of the various states.

[32] One of the best recent studies on early urbanization is Allan R. Pred, *Urban Growth and the Circulation of Information* (Cambridge, 1973). His *Spatial Dynamics of United States Urban-Industrial Growth* (Cambridge, 1966) also is very suggestive. See also the collection of essays in David T. Gilchrist, ed., *The Growth of the Seaport Cities, 1790–1825* (Charlottesville, 1967). The printed census material lists only the larger towns. In many cases small towns and hamlets can be discovered through the use of the manuscript census returns. The 1820 census gives a crude occupational breakdown; in Virginia there were significant differences between the occupational structures of even the smallest towns and the surrounding rural countryside.

papers and voluntary societies that became increasingly important during the early national period. In short they differed from the surrounding rural areas, and the existence of several of these centers could make a county, region, or state support different types of political demands than those backed by totally rural areas. A close study of this process of urbanization and partial urbanization would uncover some very important differences among units and regions within the same state. Unlike the basic study of population growth and composition, the analysis of this sort of urbanization will often depend upon a very careful analysis of manuscript census materials. In Virginia, for example, only a handful of towns have separate listings in the published returns, but many others are listed in the manuscript volumes.[33]

These early census materials give us a great deal of information about race and almost none about ethnicity. We can use the printed returns to determine the proportion and relative growth of the slave, the free black, and the white population for particular units over time.[34] The manuscript returns and tax returns enable us to reconstruct the slaveholding patterns for counties, families, and sections. Such information again allows us to underline some significant differences among political units in terms of their ratio of slave to free population and the relative importance of slaveowners. In many southern and border states a wide range of political issues became involved with slavery, and these population characteristics thus had a direct connection with political decisions.[35] Some researches have attempted to overcome the lack of ethnic census data by using surnames to determine the ethnic characteristics of the population, and this at least reveals some hints about the location of certain groups.[36] The location of

[33] Gazetteers are also useful for determining the location and population of towns not listed in the published census. These can be discovered by examining the Evans *Bibliography* and its various continuations.

[34] Since the manuscript census returns are by households, slaves sometimes are included in the listings for overseers, tenants, and others who did not actually own slaves.

[35] Tax returns are important in this context, since they give the ownership and not the physical location of slaves. In Virginia the state archives at Richmond has an almost complete set of personal property tax books for every county from the 1780's through the 1850's. This enables us to compare slave ownership with the listings in the manuscript census.

[36] See the American Council of Learned Societies, "Report of Committee on Linguistic and National Stocks in the Population of the United States" (based on studies

churches of ethnic denominations, the existence of ethnic newspapers, and gazetteers and travel accounts also provide some impressionistic information about the ethnic characteristics of counties and regions. Although historians can assess the presence or absence of particular ethnic groups, it is very difficult to determine the proportion of various groups within a particular unit, especially when a given town or county contained several groups.[37]

Economic development and change are also difficult to approach. The research problem is rooted in the paucity, special characteristics, and noncompatibility of early economic records. The statesmen of the early national period had not mastered the intricate methods of computing national product, personal income, and all the other data available to modern economic historians. There was no agricultural census until 1839; the early, 1810 and 1820, manufacturing censuses are spotty; each state operated a different tax system and levied taxes on different types of property assessed at different values. These are only some of the better-known problems. Yet despite the difficulties, we can use the available sources and make some generalizations about commerce, transportation facilities, manufacturing, finance, and agriculture.

The *American State Papers,* congressional documents, newspapers, and some manuscript customs house records contain a massive amount of information about international and coastal commerce. The published materials were broken down by states and customs districts but generally included only the total tonnage held in the district or the total imports and exports by state or district. In order to determine the export of particular commodities or the actual trading patterns of the merchants for individual ports and districts, we must turn to the newspapers and manuscript evidence. The papers often included lists of ships clearing in and out. These assist the historian in analyzing the trading patterns of a particular port. At the very least he can locate the ports, decide their relative importance, and form some idea of their flow of commerce.[38]

---

by Howard F. Barker and Marcus L. Hansen), in American Historical Association *Annual Report,* 1931 (1932), Vol. I, which explains the surname analysis.

[37] Lists of churches, by denomination, especially those of specific immigrant groups, i.e., German Lutheran or Reformed, are especially helpful.

[38] *The American State Papers: Documents Legislative and Executive of the Congress of the United States, 1789–1833* (38 vols., Washington, 1832–1861), contain a

Data on internal commerce are even more diffuse. Manuscripts, newspapers, and state legislative records give information about the quantities of certain types of produce that paid tolls on turnpikes and canals; that were inspected by state or local authorities; and that give some indication of the credit and trading patterns between inland and coastal merchants.[39] Some idea about interior commerce and merchandising can also be garnered from tax lists, directories, and other sources. Many states levied taxes on inventories and others required merchants, druggists, or peddlers to purchase wholesale or retail licenses. This enables the historian to locate merchants and mercantile communities within specific communities and to distinguish among these communities in terms of their varying levels of commercial-mercantile activity.[40] All of this can, at least, give us an impressionistic picture of inland commerce.

Better information exists with which to plot the outlines of the developing transportation system. Reports to legislatures and to commissions by engineers and committees give an amazing amount of detail about navigable rivers, improvements to the navigation of rivers, and the construction of canal systems.[41] It

---

massive amount of commercial data. The best guide for similar material after 1817 is *Checklist of United States Public Documents, 1789–1909* (3rd ed., Washington, 1911), of which Vol. I gives a listing of congressional and departmental publications. These documents have been photoreproduced and are available as *Senate* and *House Documents* for the early period.

[39] Newspapers, especially those with a commercial leadership, contain reports of local produce inspected, the amounts of produce shipped over nearby canals, and statistics about prices. The best guides to available newspapers are Clarence S. Brigham, ed., *History and Bibliography of American Newspapers, 1690–1820* (2 vols., Worcester, 1947), and United States, Library of Congress, *Newspapers on Microfilm: United States, 1948–1972* (Washington, 1973), which, despite its title, gives the newspapers available on microfilm for this period. There are also large quantities of published and unpublished state materials. In Virginia, for example, the legislative journals after 1817 contain lengthy supplements with reports of various executive agencies and legislative committees and the Auditor's Papers in the State Archives in Richmond contain reports of shipments from tobacco warehouses. Other states have additional data, and many of the published reports can be found through using Evans, *American Bibliography* and its continuations.

[40] Virginia, for example, required merchants to procure licenses every year and returns were made annually from each county. In Massachusetts taxes were levied on stock in trade, or inventory. My *Politics Without Parties: Massachusetts, 1780–1791* (Pittsburgh, 1972), 1–22, gives some account of this material.

[41] In Virginia, beginning in 1817–1818, lengthy reports by the board of public works are appended to the legislative journals. Similar bodies and reports existed in many other states. They offer an excellent idea of the state of inland water transportation at any given time.

thus becomes possible to plot and gauge the development of internal navigation. Roads are more difficult to locate. Contemporary maps help; the charters and reports of turnpike companies reveal the location of improved roads; and the postal records, especially those concerning mail contracts, give a concise description of at least a part of the road network at any given time.[42] Despite the problems, a historian can gain a fairly good hold on the presence or lack of certain types of transportation facilities for any particular unit at any given time.

Agricultural change and development and the description of the agriculture of specific units is also a difficult chore. Much of the information for this depends on tax lists, travel accounts, records of transportation companies, inspection data, and a wide range of incompatible data. Yet enough material has survived to enable the researcher to reach some conclusions about the agricultural basis of many towns and counties. In New England and some other states the tax records offer an extraordinary amount of information about the use of land, livestock holdings, the ownership of orchards, and the production of certain types of crops.[43] Materials for other states are unfortunately more limited. Some taxed only slaves or specific types of livestock; others levied a flat rate on the value of land without differentiating it as to tillage, pasturage, or waste.[44] In these states where tax records are limited, other evidence can help us to locate the production of certain types of crops and livestock. Reports generated by inspection systems for flour and tobacco are available in newspapers or in state archives. In Virginia, for example, one can trace the southern and western shift of tobacco production by noting the location and the volume of business of the tobacco warehouses during this period.[45] Gazetteers, reports of agricultural societies, travel accounts, and local newspapers help to fill the gaps with their descriptions of farms, cat-

---

[42] Most states, sometime during this period, produced official maps. The session laws of the various states give the charters of the turnpike corporations, and these generally contain the location of the road, its capitalization, specifications for construction, etc. Postal records may be found in the *American State Papers, Class X, Miscellaneous*, and in *House* and *Senate Documents* for the period after 1817.

[43] See *Politics Without Parties*, 1–22, for a discussion of these New England materials.

[44] Virginia generally levied taxes on certain categories of slaves, horses, and lots, but did not differentiate various classes of land. In 1814 and 1815 the state expanded taxation to include mills, coal pits, cattle, furniture, and many other items.

[45] The tobacco warehouse shipments are available in the Auditor's Papers at the Virginia State Archives in Richmond.

tle drives, and local market conditions.[46] Crops are easier to locate than livestock production. This is unfortunate since even during this early period a high proportion of farm income came from livestock instead of from crops.[47] Although much must remain impressionistic, the researcher can at least make some statements about the agricultural economy of specific regions and counties and how this changed or remained stable through time.

The size of farms and the types of labor used can also be determined for this period. Census and tax information gives the owners and numbers of slaves for the southern and border states.[48] Tax lists for the entire nation give the size and ownership of farms. The use of hired labor on larger, commercial northern farms is more difficult to discover, but close studies of particular towns and counties will yield some indication about the use of labor and the scale of operations.[49] Thus we can begin to differentiate agricultural regions by product, by size of operation, and by the type of labor used, and we can also determine if these changed or remained constant over time.

Manufacturing is easier to trace than agriculture. The 1810 and 1820 census materials, though spotty, at least present one with a starting point. The 1820 census of population contains some information about households involved in manufacturing. A careful use of city directories, local gazetteers, travel accounts, and other sources gives the researcher some sense of the presence or absence of certain types of manufacturing activity. A careful scrutiny of newspapers uncovers advertisements for mills, iron works, indi-

---

[46] The best way to locate gazetteers, books, almanacs, etc. dealing with agriculture is to comb through the Evans *American Bibliography* and its continuations. Magazines on microfilm can be located through the indexes to the *American Periodical Series, 1741–1799*, and the same, 1800–1850. Small, inland newspapers, even with broken runs, often reveal information about local conditions.

[47] Robert E. Gallman, "Commodity Output, 1839–1899," and Marvis M. Towne and Wayne D. Rasmussen, "Farm Gross Product and Gross Investment in the Nineteenth Century," both in National Bureau of Economic Research, *Trends in the American Economy in the Nineteenth Century* (Studies in Income and Wealth, Princeton, 1960), 13–71, 255–315.

[48] By combining the manuscript census with the real and personal property tax books one can determine, at least for Virginia, how many households owned land and slaves and the size of slaveholdings. We can also discover changes in patterns of ownership through time.

[49] Some of the techniques used by James T. Lemon, *The Best Poor Man's Country: A Geographical Study of Early Southeastern Pennsylvania* (Baltimore, 1972), would be useful, especially when combined with census materials.

vidual artisans, and a wide range of minor manufacturing. Several studies have been written about specific types of manufacturing in specific states or regions, and these frequently contain a massive amount of information about the location of these activities.[50] Ship registrations give the name of the town in which the vessel was built. Many states levied taxes on certain manufacturing activities, and these can be found in the tax lists.[51] The federal direct taxes levied during the War of 1812 also aid us in locating a range of manufacturing activities.[52] Generally, it is easiest to locate the larger units. The iron works, arsenals, textile mills, shipyards, and rope walks can be found more easily than the activities of individual artisans. But at least the researcher who finds and uses this material can plot the location and development of larger scale industrial units.

The location and relative importance of banks and other financial institutions can also be plotted. The session laws of the various states give the names, locations, and usually the capitalization of all the chartered banks. In addition many states required that banks submit annual reports which included information about capitalization, deposits, and note issue.[53] The location of incorporated insurance companies can also be determined from the session laws. It is more difficult to fix the location of private, unchartered banks and insurance companies, but local newspapers often contain information about these activities.[54] At

---

[50] Both of these are terribly incomplete. The 1810 census is printed in [Tench Coxe, ed.], *A Statement of the Arts and Manufacturers of the United States of America . . . for the Year 1810* (Philadelphia, 1814). The 1820 census is in *Digest of Account of Manufacturing Establishments in the United States* (Washington, 1823). The 1820 manuscript returns have been microfilmed. Advertisements in the newspapers are excellent for locating mills, early factories, and other activities.

[51] For examples from Massachusetts see *Politics Without Parties*, 1–22. Virginia in 1814 and 1815 taxed coal pits, tan yards, printers, mills, and ice houses.

[52] These lists are now available for some of the states.

[53] Fortunately most states had not passed general incorporation laws by this period. This means that corporate charters can be located in the session laws, and these often give details about location, capitalization, and frequently offer the names of the original directors. Legislative documents, especially the petitions, give additional information.

[54] Incorporated insurance companies can be located through the session laws. Private banks and insurance companies can sometimes be located through advertisements in local newspapers. In Virginia the passage of legislation to prevent the existence of unchartered banks ignited a debate that produced a great deal of information about the location and operations of these private, unchartered banks.

the very least one can ascertain which towns and counties had banks, get some idea about the size and relative importance of their operations, and find regions that lacked chartered banks or other financial facilities.

The description of social-cultural characteristics of individuals or of communities and counties requires the generation of data dealing with social-economic class, professions, and occupations, the relationships among upper-class groups and individuals, the growth of voluntary organizations, the development of postal and other communications facilities, the spread of newspapers and magazines, religion, and intellectual and ideological change. All of these changed considerably between 1790 and 1830. Families and individuals rose or fell from one social-economic group to another; the social-economic characteristics of counties and communities changed over time; more individuals went into professions whose power and influence increased through time, and towns and communities attracted a greater or lesser share of these professionals; members of the upper class from different communities began to intermarry and develop other social links; voluntary organizations sprang up to achieve political, social, religious, and cultural goals; postal service spread throughout the nation; editors printed newspapers and magazines and strengthened older institutions; and even the style of literature changed. Thus the nation and its states altered their social-cultural characteristics, and these changes varied in impact and intensity from community to community and from individual to individual.

Historians have masses of data to determine social-economic class. State, local, and national tax lists provide data about land holding patterns, ownership of slaves, and personal property, and scattered information about holdings of inventory and other forms of liquid wealth.[55] Fortunately, this information is listed by the name of specific individuals so that from these lists we can determine the distribution of several types of property. Unlike other extant material about this period such information permits one 1) to show the distribution of total wealth and of holdings in certain types of property, such as slaves, livestock, land, or liquid

---

[55] Unfortunately these lists vary considerably from state to state. The location of these lists and books is also a serious problem. In Massachusetts they may be found in the various towns. In Virginia there are copies for every county and every year which are available in the state archives at Richmond.

wealth, among deciles of the population; 2) to begin to identify the various social-economic classes; and 3) to relate officeholders and politicians to their social-economic positions and to the types of property they held.[56] In addition to dealing with individuals the historian can show how property distribution and class structure changed within a particular community over time or compare among groups of communities for one time or over time.[57]

These differences among communities and individuals could be related to the political process in at least two ways. Units with different types of wealth or with varied patterns of distribution of wealth would support different policies on many issues. At the same time individual legislators, local officers, executives, and judges could be analyzed to find where they fit in the social-economic structure of their communities and in their states or the nation. Groups of such individuals, sharing certain social-economic characteristics, might operate together or apart depending on the issues involved.

The period also witnessed the rapid growth of professions. Law and lawyers became increasingly important as the society and economy became more complex and as corporate bodies played a more significant role. The lawyers and the legal profession, Janus-faced, looked backward to tradition and the common law at the same time that many lawyers developed new procedures to promote corporate development, economic growth, and social change.[58] Lawyers played a leading part in most legislative bodies where their expertise gave them a tremendous advantage in drafting new legislation. Lawyers tended to locate in developing communities where they serviced the merchants, wealthy farmers and planters, and rising manufacturers who needed their services to handle their growing legal problems. Many of the lawyers played important roles in business, finance, and politics, and became

[56] Some examples of the use of these lists are in Sam B. Warner, *The Private City: Philadelphia in Three Periods of its Growth* (Philadelphia, 1968), 1–45, and James A. Henretta, "Economic Development and Social Structure in Colonial Boston," *William and Mary Quarterly*, 3rd Ser., 22 (1965), 75–92.

[57] One of the best examples is James T. Lemon and Gary B. Nash, "The Distribution of Wealth in Eighteenth Century America: A Century of Change in Chester County, 1693–1802," in the *Journal of Social History*, 2 (1968), 1–24.

[58] An excellent description of this process that analyzes the connections of lawyers with rising corporations is Edwin M. Dodd, *American Business Corporations Until 1860: With Special Reference to Massachusetts* (Cambridge, 1954).

wealthy and joined the upper classes.[59] Their meteoric rise suggests that entrance to the bar was one of the smoothest paths to fame and fortune.

Lawyers, like businessmen or farmers, did not always think alike; they certainly did not form a monolithic group on most issues, but their common approach to legal problems resulting from their legal training certainly influenced the tone of politics and the nature of development in many states and units throughout the nation. The location and importance of this group can be charted in two ways. Lists of lawyers are readily available, and their position in the social-economic structure and their service in legislatures, administrative boards, and executive bodies can easily be traced. At the same time we can compare counties and communities in terms of the relative presence or absence of attorneys.[60]

Other professions did not offer the same opportunities for advancement, but most developed a growing consciousness which was reflected in a broader concern over professional standards. States and medical associations became interested in the training and licensing of doctors. Medical schools developed to train physicians and doctors published their research and ideas. A few doctors even became important political or economic figures. They did not have the connections of lawyers, but their location tells us something about the needs and advantages of the communities in which they practiced.[61] During this period states and corporations began to look for trained civil engineers; bankers and financiers desired trained clerks and bookkeepers; and manufacturers searched for trained managers and skilled artisans. In Virginia Thomas Jefferson and his associates even engaged in a little raiding to assemble a faculty for their new university.[62] All of this reflected the growing demand for professionals, and we can discover the location of these individuals and the growth of the schools and institutions that produced them.

---

[59] Location of lawyers can be determined from lists in almanacs and other sources. For large cities local directories are very useful. See Dorothea N. Spear, *Bibliography of American Directories Through 1860* (Worcester, 1961), which lists all directories available in microform.

[60] See *Politics Without Parties*, 20–21, 45–46, for some examples.

[61] The same sources used for lawyers often give information about doctors, but they tend to be more scattered and difficult to find.

[62] There are constant references in the supplements to the Virginia legislative journals to the need for trained engineers. Jefferson's activities are in Paul L. Ford, ed., *The Writings of Thomas Jefferson* (10 vols., New York, 1892–1899), esp. vol. X.

Based on our examination of the social-economic structure and our analysis of the professions, we can begin to analyze the inter-connections among the professional, economic, and political elites within particular communities or in the states and the nation. We can, for example, examine the marriage and educational patterns of upper-class individuals and groups in various communities and states and determine how and when certain groups became inter-related. We can also examine the vacation patterns of individuals and groups as they fled the coastal cities for inland springs or cooler climates.[63] Even in an era before Blue Books and Social Registers, we can at least begin to describe the upper classes in various settings and the connections or lack of connections among them. In addition to the connections among the upper classes we can use manuscript correspondence to uncover the links among lawyers, merchants, storekeepers, intellectuals, ministers, and many other social and professional groups.[64] All of this can give us some insights about the flow of information and the methods through which various individuals and groups mobilized to achieve political aims.

Americans became more organized during this forty-year period. In 1790 relatively few nongovernmental organizations existed. There were religious denominations, a handful of banks and other economic corporations, a few colleges and academies, and some miscellaneous organizations interested in everything from history and science to dancing. During the next forty years such organizations multiplied at a rate far in excess of the increase in population. In the economic sphere capitalists chartered banks, turnpikes, internal improvement companies, and even a hand-ful of manufacturing corporations. This flurry of organization resulted in bringing banking and finance almost totally under cor-porate control. Internal improvements became either a state or corporate responsibility, and corporations had some control over insurance. Commerce, agriculture, and manufacturing, however, tended to remain in private hands.[65] In the religious sector organi-

[63] Almost all newspapers yield brief notices of marriages that give the names and residence of the parties involved. The Virginia papers print large numbers of adver-tisements about springs. These often suggest accommodations and prices.

[64] Although most manuscript material, especially of less important families, has not survived, the existing collections can be analyzed to illustrate the correspondence patterns of various occupations and classes.

[65] One of the best methods is to go through the session laws for several states, year

zations sprang up to create Sunday schools, to distribute Bibles, to regulate morals, and to finance missionaries.[66] In politics persons formed not only parties but local lodges with social as well as political functions. Ethnic groups, artisans, merchants, and others organized chambers of commerce, relief organizations, social groups, and early trade unions or masters' associations.[67] States chartered more and more colleges and academies, historical societies, and other organizations.[68] Americans quickly took to organization. Every important political issue spawned mass meetings of interested persons who always elected officers and appointed committees to draft resolutions and plans for action.

Newspapers, directories, and many other sources give the location and officers of many of these voluntary organizations. Institutions chartered by the states can be located through the session laws or in reports to the legislature. Newspapers also reveal enormous amounts of information about mass meetings, and their advertisements contain valuable clues about the existence of many other types of organizational activity. This information enables the researcher to relate towns and communities to each other in terms of the total amount of such activities or by the presence or absence of particular types of activities.[69] We can also, in many instances, locate the officers of these organizations and, through tax lists and other information, relate them to the social-economic structure of their communities. Thus all sorts of voluntary activities can be related to particular communities or to individuals within those towns.

The revolutionary expansion of postal facilities between 1789

---

by year, beginning in 1790, noting the number of charters granted by the legislature. The old classic, J. S. Davis, *Essays in the Earlier History of American Corporations* (2 vols., Cambridge, 1917), offers a running start through 1800.

[66] Charles I. Foster, *An Errand of Mercy: The Evangelical United Front, 1790–1837* (Chapel Hill, 1960), is an excellent overview. The newspapers are filled, especially after the War of 1812, with reports of local Bible societies and Sunday school unions.

[67] The ones chartered through the legislature can be found in the session laws. Others can be uncovered through notices in local newspapers.

[68] The session laws contain details about the organization, location, and governance of these institutions.

[69] Massive amounts of newspapers are now available in microform. The best guide is *Newspapers on Microform*. One of the major problems is that good runs of many important papers have not survived. In Virginia there are only scattered copies of the *Richmond Compiler*, which seems to have printed large quantities of economic and commercial information.

and 1830 changed the communications pattern of America. In the 1790's only the larger coastal and a handful of inland towns held post offices. By the mid-1820's even the most obscure rural county had a post office and a postmaster. The development and use of these postal facilities, in themselves, serve as an index of certain types of development. Examination of the printed and manuscript postal records would give the researcher an idea of how towns, counties, and other units utilized their postal facilities over time. The increase in the use of these facilities did not remain constant over time or among communities and sections. A comparative study of these records might uncover a great deal about the local or cosmopolitan characteristics of many communities for which we have little population or economic information.[70] These facilities carried an enormous increase in letters, documents, newspapers, and magazines. Anyone searching through a newspaper for this period finds good evidence for the close relationship between the rules and regulations of the post office and the circulation of newspapers.

The rapid development of newspapers and other publications depended upon and insisted on this postal revolution. Relatively rare outside the major towns in 1790, newspapers became widespread by the mid-1820's. Any town with pretentions had its own newspaper and bank by 1830. Although circulations remained small, the increasing number of papers, together with their local control, had a considerable impact on the reading and intellectual habits of the population. Even papers in isolated areas carried market reports from the larger commercial centers, news of world, national, and state events, and masses of national and state documents. The advertisements, even in these small towns, showed the growing complexities of society as ads appeared for theaters and manufacturers. The editors printed essays by local citizens or lifted from other newspapers that dealt with economic development, religion, politics, and many other important topics.[71] The historian can locate these papers, can compare the towns and com-

---

[70] Pred uses this information extensively in his *Urban Growth*. The basic sources are the *American State Papers—Class* X, and the *House* and *Senate Documents* for the period after 1817. The best institutional study remains Wesley E. Rich, *The History of the United States Post Office to the Year 1829* (Cambridge, 1924).

[71] Papers can be located through Brigham, ed., *History and Newspapers in Microform*.

munities with and without newspapers, can analyze the growth of newspapers in certain areas, regions, and units; all of this when combined with the postal records gives us a fascinating picture of the development or lack of development of particular communities.

America experienced a religious revolution between 1790 and 1830. Denominations, spearheaded by the evangelical churches and sects, worked to turn a secular society back into a religious one. They developed and adapted new methods and activities ranging from camp meetings to Sunday schools to attract Americans to particular denominations or to a more vague Protestant evangelical Christianity. Bible societies poured out their testaments; Sunday schools taught reading, writing, and evangelical morality; camp meetings reached the rural unchurched; revivals flourished in Kentucky and at Yale; various "front" organizations preached morality and temperance, and by the 1820's the evangelicals moved into politics to support "reforms" that would make America "once more" a religious nation. In short a muscular evangelical Protestant Christianity arose that used a wide range of new techniques and increased the intensity of religious feeling. Too many historians have examined this so-called second Great Awakening as a sort of western, frontier, camp meeting phenomenon that appealed to emotionally starved farmers without realizing that this was merely one section of the "Christian Front" offensive that was sweeping the entire world and inspiring the fervent dream that not only America but the entire world could be brought to the feet of the Christian Redeemer.[72]

A careful analysis of the impact of this movement on different individuals and communities is difficult, but three approaches might warrant investigation. The first, and easiest, would be to analyze the positions and strengths of individual denominations over time and within specific sections or communities. Denominations varied in their theological beliefs, their organization, and their involvement in "front" activities. Most of the denominations, at some time, kept or printed reports of their conferences, synods, and other administrative bodies which locate congregations and ministers and often give data about the membership and financial support of particular local congregations. Although

[72] Basic patterns are discussed in Foster, *Errand of Mercy*. Clifton E. Olmstead, *History of Religion in the United States* (New York, 1962), presents materials on denominations. John B. Bole, *The Great Revival, 1787–1805: The Origin of the Southern Evangelical Mind* (Lexington, 1972), is a good account of revivalism in the South.

difficult to analyze and not compatible across denominational lines, the use of this material gives the researcher at least an impressionistic notion about the strength and weakness of particular denominations in specific regions or units and the changes in strength within or among these units over time. Local church records can be related to tax lists and other data to present the reader with an idea of the religious choices and preferences of individuals or groups within a particular community.[73] These would give us a feel for the relative strength of denominations and of the groups and classes that they appealed to.

But any discussion of the religious impact of the second awakening must do more than merely plot the strengths and locations of the various denominations. The popular front spawned large numbers of new organizations, and these must also be analyzed. The earliest and largest, the American Bible Society, established local auxiliaries throughout the country which distributed thousands of Bibles and testaments. The Sunday school unions and societies also played an important role. Many of the religious reformers saw the Sunday school as a handmaiden of the Bible society. To read the Bible one had to be literate, and the Sunday schools, by creating literacy through the use of religious tracts and Bible stories, must have had a tremendous impact on the world view of young Americans who would not have darkened the door of a church thirty years earlier. In addition to organizations that included several denominations, individual denominations established their own societies, especially those interested in home and foreign mission efforts. The popular front also founded a wide range of other organizations that lacked direct affiliation with denominations but which were headed or staffed by churchmen and used churches for their facilities and meeting places. Temperance societies, moral organizations, and even the well-known American Colonization Society could be included in this category.[74] All of these organizations have left published or manu-

[73] The general histories offer little assistance in pinning down denominations in particular counties and communities. Many denominations published their conference and organizational records. These can be uncovered in the Evans *Bibliography* and its continuations. Newspapers often carried reports of local conferences as well as notices of camp meetings, church dedications, and services.

[74] Denominational histories usually give a great deal of material about the relations of the particular church with other denominations and with the various "front" activities. Local church records are available but are often hard to uncover and use. The newspapers often carry the annual reports of local auxiliaries of the American

script evidence about their membership, activities, and finances. Plotting the location and activities of these societies gives the historian an idea of the extent of the Christian Front. In particular communities the individuals involved in these societies can be related to their denominational membership and to their position in the community.[75] This analysis would enable us not only to compare communities in terms of their involvement in these activities but would also shed light on the bitter schism that occurred in many denominations over involvement with extra-denominational organizations.[76]

In addition to this type of analysis a third approach is required in order to come to grips with the increased religiosity in American life. We can analyze the growth, spread, and relative power of the denominations and societies, but we need another method to measure the way in which religion began to permeate American society by 1830. The content analysis of newspapers and manuscripts might give us some clues. Anyone reading large numbers of files of American newspapers for the entire period between 1790 and 1830 is struck by the appearance of essays dealing with religious topics and the increasing use of Biblical and religious images in essays dealing with political and nonreligious topics. Usage seems to vary from region to region, even within the same state, and although some of this development may depend upon the religious idiosyncrasies of the editors, the impressionistic evidence indicates that, regardless of editors or location, this sort of imagery increased through time.[77] Besides the images in secular publications, religious denominations issued their own newspapers and magazines, and religious pamphlets flooded the nation. Content analysis and the use of this publication data could give us some interesting hypotheses about the relative importance of these developments within particular units and sections.

Bible Society, the Sunday School Union, the American Colonization Society, and many other organizations.

[75] Newspapers frequently contained lists of officers and managers of these organizations; religious newspapers and magazines are also helpful, and these can be located through *Newspapers in Microform* and the *American Periodical Series*.

[76] An excellent example of this type of research is Robert Doherty, *The Hicksite Separation: A Sociological Analysis of Religious Schism in Early Nineteenth Century America* (New Brunswick, 1967).

[77] An example of this type of analysis is Richard L. Merritt, *Symbols of American Community, 1735–1775* (New Haven, 1966).

Intellectual and ideological change is especially difficult to grasp. Many historians have produced excellent studies dealing with the structure and changes in intellectual patterns during the period, and some have attempted to relate these changes to other economic, social, or political developments. Hopefully, we can build on these studies and find some methods through which they can be analyzed and related to political decision making. We could, for example, analyze the entire intellectual community, discover where the authors and intellectuals lived, what types of connections they had with upper-class or other groups, their involvement in religious and other types of activities, and how their ideas changed or remained constant with time. We might also be able to analyze the distribution of their ideas through their books and the newspapers. All of this would take a great deal of careful research, but fortunately some of the work has already been accomplished.[78]

*   *   *   *

All of these detailed descriptions can be used to compare individuals and communities at one particular time or to compare the amounts of change through time. In both cases we can use an almost infinite assortment of differences that would depend upon the goals of the historian and the availability of sources. In Virginia in 1810, for example, we can differentiate the rapidly growing from the stagnating counties, those with larger proportions of slaves from those with a lower proportion; counties with different transportation systems; those with or without newspapers, voluntary organizations, lawyers, doctors, or intellectuals; those that contained or lacked cities and hamlets; and those with particular religious or ethnic characteristics. We can also place individuals, such as legislators, administrators, or judges in terms of these differences and within the context of their counties and communities. Then we can relate the differences that seem appropriate for our purposes to the decisions made through the political system.

Instead of looking at one particular year we can compare units and individuals as they changed over time. We can, for example, in Virginia between 1810 and 1830 differentiate rapidly growing

---

[78] An example is George H. Daniels, *American Science in the Age of Jackson* (New York, 1968), esp. 6–33.

from stagnating counties; counties in which the proportion of slaves rose or fell; counties that remained more rural from those containing rapidly growing towns and hamlets; counties that remained isolated compared to those through which roads were built; counties that attracted or failed to attract newspapers and voluntary organizations; and counties that changed their ethnic, religious, or economic characteristics from those that retained their older patterns. Families and individuals can also be analyzed to determine if their residence, social-economic status, or occupations changed through time.

It is obvious that the large number and complexities of these descriptions compel us to develop new methods to deal with them. Consequently, many historians have developed "scales" with which differences and changes can be related to one another or to political behavior. Our first inventions may be simple, and perhaps even simple-minded, but, at least, the use of these scales will begin to give us a working description that can be related to our extended definition of politics.

Historians have used two basic types of economic continuums or scales. One that is especially revealing because it analyzes individuals is that of ranking individuals on the basis of wealth on an upper-to-lower-class continuum. The historian can then find where particular legislators, administrators, and judges fit and can ascertain if politicians occupying similar positions on the continuum voted or acted together. The researcher can relate this scale to religious, occupational, ethnic, or other data. He can find where members of a particular religious denomination, profession, or even social club fit and can make some statements about the social-economic characteristics of these groups.[79] The basic weakness of this scale is the impossibility of applying it to counties, communities, or voting units. Voting data for the early national period generally exist only for entire townships or counties. Although some distinctions by social-economic class can be made about these units, it remains impossible to range a large number of these units along a class-based continuum. Some states, which practiced open voting, have retained poll lists giving the names and choices of individual voters. This data could be related

[79] Most political historians do this in an impressionistic way. See Henretta, "Economic Development and Social Structure," and Warner, *Private City*, for some methods.

to such a social-economic scale.[80] It seems that the chief usefulness of this scale will be to analyze individual politicians or members of specific organizations.

The other economic continuum attempts to take units such as towns and counties and arrange them in terms of their economic development or activity. The researcher places at one extreme the large, diversified metropolitan towns or counties and at the other the subsistence areas. Then he attempts, on the basis of available data, to rank the towns and units inbetween the two extremes. He can then use the continuum to explain or describe the voting of representatives of particular types of constituencies or the types of political pressures that come from particular towns and counties.[81] This method offers a good way to relate discrete units to politics, a good description of the economic structure at a particular time, and can serve as the basis for showing how an economy changed over time.

Social and cultural features can also be placed on some kind of continuum. A local-to-cosmopolitan scale can be worked out for both individuals and counties and towns. The researcher may argue that certain occupations, classes, religious denominations, or types of military service are more or less "cosmopolitan" or "local." He can then rank a large number of individuals on his scale and relate this to their political activities. The historian can also use information about the location of courts, newspapers, churches, amount of postal receipts, and many other items to arrange a number of towns or counties along a similar continuum. At one extreme he can place the larger and more complex communities, while the other end would contain the relatively more isolated towns and counties.[82] This type of scale could be integrated with the continuum of economic diversity or development, but such a merger would have to be done with considerable care.[83] These cosmopolitan-local scales for both individuals and communities can, of course, also be related to changes among the units or to specific political issues or changes.

---

[80] A recent example of the use of poll books is John M. Rozett, "The Social Bases of Party Conflict in the Age of Jackson: Individual Voting Behavior in Greene County, Illinois, 1838–1848" (doctoral dissertation, University of Michigan, 1974).

[81] See *Politics Without Parties*, 1–22.

[82] *Idem.*, and Main, *Political Parties*.

[83] See *Politics Without Parties*, 1–22, for a crude way to attempt this.

*   *   *   *

This leads us to our third major task, the development of ideas and techniques that will enable us to define and locate political change and to relate it to the patterns of stability and change within the society. This complex task must be broken down into at least four parts: the development of a working definition of political change; the description of the process of political change relating these processes to our broader definition of politics; relating these political changes to our descriptions of society; and then discovering the sections of the society responsible for change, in general, or for specific changes.

The working definition of political change will depend upon the goals of each individual historian. The researcher may be interested only in certain types of decisions. He may deal with specific topics such as internal improvements, banking, education, or penal reform. In this case he will confine his attention to the political decisions made in his area of interest by a single state or the national government. He can expand his study to compare, among several states, the decisions made for specific topics. For example he can compare the politics of banking or penal reform in Virginia, New York, and South Carolina. He can also expand his topic to include political decisions made on a broader range of issues for a particular state or region. He can limit the study to the analysis of decisions for a particular level of government, for example the county, or he may concentrate on a particular town or county. One can also study the decisions of specific institutions, ranging from legislatures through county courts. Since every piece of legislation, court decision, and administrative rule becomes by definition a "change," the historian, in addition to limiting his topic, must also use his intuitive knowledge of the society and the political process in an effort to differentiate important from less important changes. If this is done openly, other scholars who disagree with his analysis or selection may still be able to use his work as a foundation for more sophisticated studies.

The basis for a working definition will depend upon a systematic analysis of the narrative records left by governments. Session laws, now available for most of the states, provide the most convenient starting point. A careful study of legislation, over time, gives us a considerable amount of information about all sorts of political change.[84] The researcher can organize this material by topics and make a detailed study of the changes taking place through time. He can, for example, select bank charters and examine decisions about policies concerning the location of banks, the amount of capitalization, the presence or absence of state control, the legal restrictions on banks, and many other topics. Or he might take statutes dealing with the penal system and note changes concerning corporal punishment and imprisonment, solitary confinement, and the use of the penitentiary as a profit making factory. This careful use of session laws also permits the historian to compare the activities of different states or of state and national governments. Based on this research, the historian can begin to make some decisions about the relative importance of the political changes taking place through legislation. In addition to the session laws we must also analyze judicial decisions. In the various states superior and inferior courts ruled on a wide range of issues.[85] Some of these cases involved the interpretation of statutes, while others shaped custom and common law to fit new situations. Many historians have analyzed the national Supreme Court, but few have researched the decisions of the circuit and district courts. The decisions of the higher courts have generally been published, but the papers of the lower courts are harder to obtain. Historians must begin to locate and analyze this material, which gives an additional dimension to political change. For example, the courts made most of the basic decisions concerning the powers, privileges, and responsibilities of corporations. Historians working on many topics will have to subject these judicial decisions to the same scrutiny as they give the session laws. Administrative records and the proceedings of local governments may also be important to many historians. The rulings made by administrators or commissions that controlled penal institutions, the construction of internal improvements, inspection of various commodities, and many other agencies are often available, either in manuscript, or through reports to state legislatures and to Con-

---

[84] Thanks to the recent microform project, the session laws of all the states are now available to most good academic libraries. The ones printed during the period can be located through the Evans *Bibliography* and its continuations.

[85] Any good law library should have the decisions of most of the state higher courts. Those printed during the early nineteenth century can be located in the Evans *Bibliography* and its continuations.

gress.[86] In many cases these men made their decisions by selecting from a series of alternatives that had been permitted in the basic legislation. In some cases the administrators made rules and regulations that seemed to stretch if not openly violate the meaning of the laws under which they acted. Records of local governments and their agencies open up a final area for research. Many of these have been destroyed or poorly preserved, but the records of county courts, selectmen, overseers of the poor, school commissioners, surveyors, and many other agencies give us some idea about the implementation of laws and regulations at the local level.[87]

Narrative historians have worked with this material for centuries. They have used session laws and Supreme Court Reports to chart political history but have neglected the records of the lower courts, administrative bodies, and local governments. Historians can borrow their techniques and many of their results and then analyze this mass of records in a more systematic fashion to discover what, in their opinion, is important political change.

Constructing a working definition of political change forces us to consider the components of political change and how each of these components can be integrated with our broader definition of politics. One could describe this process in terms of innovation, dissemination, and response. Although most political historians have tended to analyze changes through looking at the responses of legislators, social classes, and regions that opposed or supported certain policies, our broader definition may enable us to build some bridges to intellectual historians interested in the development and dissemination of ideas and to social and cultural historians who have described methods of disseminating ideas. An idea for a political change could involve anything from a vague desire for some general social or economic change to specific details about a bank charter, a canal, or a new penal system. Upon investigation we may find that certain sorts of ideas for change come from certain regions or groups and that during specific time periods ideas for certain types of changes will seldom develop. This would indicate that in any society, at any given time, people's ideas

[86] Administrative records can sometimes be obtained from supplements to the *Legislative Journals*. Others were published by the states and can be located through the Evans *Bibliography* and its continuations. Many exist only in manuscript and must be used in the various state archives.

[87] These records are unfortunately difficult to locate and hard to use. They are usually available only in courthouses and city halls.

will fall within some flexible framework of thought. Thus, during the early national period practically no American thinkers would be expected to develop ideas of change that would lead to a military coup, the establishment of monarchical rule, or the implementation of Marxist ideology. Too frequently we forget that the intellectual choices open in a particular society at a particular time may be as limited as the economic or social options.[88] The historian can seek out these ideas from letters, newspapers, pamphlets, books, and many sources, and in a systematic way build up a notion of the range of ideas being developed within a particular state.

The use of these sources leads us into the second phase, that of describing the dissemination of ideas for change. These can be traced in many ways. In addition to looking at newspapers, essays, books, and pamphlets we can investigate the proceedings and presentments of grand juries, the petitions that constituencies sent to their legislators, the resolutions of mass meetings, the correspondence to legislators, and many other sources. This evidence can give us some indication of the range and spread of certain ideas of change, which regions, individuals, and groups supported these ideas, and the variety of pressures that they put on specific political institutions. Agitation for the construction of a canal illustrates this. The original idea had been implemented for centuries in Asia and Europe but at some specific time an individual in a particular town or county had to develop an idea proposing the construction of a specific canal. His idea was disseminated, and other individuals and groups began to favor or oppose the project. Communities petitioned their legislature, mass meetings passed resolutions, and in this case the pressure was applied directly to the state legislature to grant a charter. In other instances different forms of pressure could be placed on the judiciary, administrative agencies, or local governments to implement other types of change.

While the idea was being disseminated, a response began to build. In some instances a vast majority believed the idea to be totally unacceptable and, like St. George Tucker's suggestion for ending slavery in Virginia, it simply disappeared.[89] Or the idea for

[88] Two good examples of an intellectual study of a particular state are Richard Beale Davis, *Intellectual Life in Jefferson's Virginia, 1790–1830* (Chapel Hill, 1964), and Richard D. Birdsal, *Berkshire County, A Cultural History* (New Haven, 1959).

[89] St. George Tucker, *A Dissertation on Slavery With a Proposal for the Gradual Abolition of It in the State of Virginia* (Philadelphia, 1796).

change might be totally accepted and a charter for a new turnpike company meet no local, state, or national opposition. In many instances the dissemination of an idea for change also brought resistance. The group pushing for a new bank might run into opposition from other groups that wanted their particular bank or from groups that opposed all banking corporations. In these cases lines form, and the issue may be fought over for years. The pattern of response in the legislature or through popular voting is relatively easy to follow. Even without roll call votes a close examination of the legislative journals tells us a great deal about conflicting pressures that can be analyzed through committee membership and reports, amendments, and differences between two houses in a bicameral legislature. Response in judicial, administrative, and local governmental units becomes more difficult to analyze. More studies on the role of the courts and judges as decision makers, the types of personnel who staffed these courts, and the various ways through which attorneys developed and presented ideas to these judges would give us some real insights into this area. At least we can begin to examine systematically the patterns of ideas and the responses of a wide range of political institutions to these ideas of change.

Next we must relate our descriptions of society to this process of political change. The historian can apply his scales describing the social-cultural and economic structure of the state to the process of political change. He can find where the individuals who develop new ideas for change come from. They may be lawyers or Presbyterians or upper-class merchants or middle-class artisans, and they may live in rapidly developing commercial towns or stagnating subsistence farming counties. He can trace the dissemination of ideas. He can show that petitions came from counties that lay along navigable rivers, from towns that had overseas trade, or from regions that had few newspapers. If the proposal for change went into the legislature, he can analyze the composition of the committees that reported or killed the proposal. These committeemen belonged to certain churches, lived in particular towns, and practiced specific occupations. If fortunate, he may find one or a series of roll call votes. In some instances he may find roll call votes on similar proposals that emerged session after session. In these cases one can analyze both the legislators and their constituencies in terms of all the characteristics that had been described.[90] Even if the changes were implemented through courts, administrative agencies, or local governments, we can still analyze the composition of the bodies that made decisions. In the courts we can analyze the background of the judges and lawyers. These men could have resided in rapidly growing commercial towns and had a very different outlook from men living in stagnating counties. Appeals to a higher court may have resulted in different decisions because the judges had different characteristics or different intellectual training. We can use similar analysis about the administrative agencies. Local government can also be analyzed in terms of the types of persons who made decisions. We can also analyze decisions made by these bodies in terms of the interests and characteristics of their communities. In the 1820's, for example, many states gave local bodies a considerable amount of power over education.[91] In some communities local officials pressed for schools, while in others they did very little. Decisions of all sorts, even by local units, can be related to where they fit on scales that measure a wide range of variables. Thus the juxtaposition of the description and scales with the process of political change enables us to pin down the location and characteristics of individuals and communities that fought for, opposed, or remained apathetic to a wide range of political changes.

After integrating the political process with our description we can begin make some conclusions about pressure for and resistance to change and begin to discuss some of the old radical versus conservative, democratic versus nondemocratic, and region versus region arguments that have been advanced to explain the politics of the early national period. We can do this in as broad or narrow a manner as we desire. One historian, for example, may be interested in the pressures for change in banking. He can locate the types of communities and individuals who pushed for charters and the individuals and groups that opposed them. He can determine if opposition resulted because of groups which opposed all banking corporations or because of groups which generally favored

[90] Efforts to "scale" over several sessions are *Politics Without Parties*, and Main, *Political Parties*.

[91] *Virginia Code (1819)*, I, 87–89, for school commissioners, and I, 90–93, for the University of Virginia.

banks but opposed the competition of a particular bank. He can continue his study over time and illustrate the connections, over time, between a changing social-cultural, economic structure of a state and the changing or consistent position of individuals and communities within that state. He can also analyze the court decisions concerning banking and the regulations issued by state owned or influenced banks to determine if important changes developed outside of the legislative arena. He can analyze the backgrounds of these individuals and relate them to the groups favoring or opposing bank charters. He might find, for example, that the groups favoring banking had much more, or much less, power in the courts than in the legislature. He could then complete a similar study for other states, and this would enable him to place the politics of banking in a comparative context that would enable him to claim that certain groups and communities, regardless of state lines, tended to support or oppose banks.

Instead of taking one issue, a historian could analyze a wider range of topics. He could examine banking, internal improvements, constitutional reform, and educational reform for a single state. He could determine if pressures for change, in this wide array of issues, came from similar areas. He might find that commercial towns supported all these reforms, or he might find that poor, subsistence counties supported constitutional reform while opposing educational changes and internal improvements. But we would have, at least, a concise description of the communities and individuals favoring or opposing wide ranges of change, and we could begin to make some comments about the relationship among social-cultural, economic, and political change for a nation that was advancing into the industrial revolution.

This analysis, when integrated with narrative and partisan political history, will add immeasurably to our knowledge of the period. Instead of taking the party as the crucial point of departure, we would be examining change. We might find that counties and individuals supporting a particular party tended to favor or oppose certain types of change, and this would increase our insights into the characteristics of the first and second party systems. In addition it will enable us, for the first time, to come to grips with those political issues that cut across party lines or the important divisive issues that erupted during periods when organized parties simply did not exist. It will also enable us to begin to make some good, analytical statements about the interrelationships of politics and change. Political historians by broadening the scope of political history can begin to come to grips with all of those issues and changes that affected a much larger group in the population than the handful of white, adult, and, in many instances, taxpaying males who voted at elections.

I am not presumptuous enough to argue that these ideas and suggestions are the best or only solutions for arriving at an understanding of the period, but I hope that they will lead other political historians to do some hard thinking and to join in a debate about the methods we can use to come to grips with the problem of relating politics to social change. It will take more than using computers or organizing our evidence to apply modern social scientific theories that, in any case, may not fit an earlier age. Henry Adams and many others, fortunately, long ago laid down a framework for the history of this period. We must always be grateful for their skill, their scholarship, and their insights, but we must use different materials and respond to different questions. We pay these giants a far greater compliment by standing on their shoulders to look farther and wider than we do by hiding behind their backs—which is what a continued reliance on the narrative method amounts to.

A Listing of Merrill Jensen's Publications

Books

The Articles of Confederation: An Interpretation of the Social-Constitutional History of the American Revolution, 1774–1781. Madison, 1940. [Paperback edition, 1959; Seventh printing, 1970.]

The New Nation: A History of the United States During the Confederation, 1781–1789. New York, 1950. [Paperback edition, 1965.]

Editor, *Regionalism in America.* Madison, 1951. [Paperback edition, 1965.]

Editor, *English Historical Documents, Volume IX: American Colonial Documents to 1776.* London and New York, 1955.

The Making of the American Constitution. New York, 1964.

Editor, *Tracts of the American Revolution, 1763–1776.* New York, 1967.

The Founding of a Nation: A History of the American Revolution, 1763–1776. New York, 1968.

The American Revolution Within America. New York, 1974.

Articles

"The Cession of the Old Northwest." *Mississippi Valley Historical Review,* 23 (June, 1936), 27–48.

"The Articles of Confederation: A Re-Interpretation." *Pacific Historical Review,* 6 (June, 1937), 120–142.

"The Creation of the National Domain, 1781–1784." *Mississippi Valley Historical Review*, 26 (December, 1939), 323–342.

"The American Revolution in American History." *Proceedings of the Middle States Association of History and Social Science Teachers*, 39 (1941–1942), 12–18.

"The Idea of a National Government During the American Revolution." *Political Science Quarterly*, 58 (September, 1943), 356–379.

"Preface to the Second Printing." *The Articles of Confederation* (August, 1947), vii–xiv.

"European Colonial Experience, A Plea for Comparative Studies." *Studi in Honore Di Gino Luzzato*. 4 vols. Milan, Italy, 1950, IV, 75–90. (With Robert L. Reynolds.)

"The American Union: Its Interpretation and Its Historical Origins." Inaugural Lecture as Harmsworth Professor, University of Oxford, 1950. 23 pp.

"Democracy and the American Revolution." *Huntington Library Quarterly*, 20 (August, 1957), 321–341.

"Preface to the Third Printing." *The Articles of Confederation* (January, 1959), xv–xxiii.

"Introduction." Randolph G. Adams, *Political Ideas of the American Revolution*. Reprint, 1959, 5–31.

"The Origins of the Democratic Tradition in America." *American Studies in India*. New Delhi, India, 1965, 109–134.

"The Origins of American Federalism." Doshisha University, *American Studies Quarterly*, 3 (Kyoto, Japan, 1966), 17–56. (In Japanese.)

"Historians and the Nature of the American Revolution." Ray Billington, ed., *The Reinterpretation of Early American History*. Huntington Library, 1966, 101–126.

"The Colonial Phase." C. Vann Woodward, ed., *The Comparative Approach to American History*. New York, 1968, 18–33.

"The Popular Leaders of the American Revolution." Union College, 1968. 16 pp.

"The American Revolution and American Agriculture." *Agricultural History*, 43 (January, 1969), 107–124.

"The American People and the American Revolution." *Journal of American History*, 57 (June, 1970), 5–35. (Presidential address to the Organization of American Historians, April 16, 1970.)

"Introduction." Joseph Galloway, *Historical and Political Reflections on the Rise and Progress of the American Rebellion.* [London, 1780]. New York, 1973. 24 pp.

"The Articles of Confederation." *Fundamental Testaments of the American Revolution.* Library of Congress, Washington, 1973, 49–81.

Work in Progress

Editor, *The Documentary History of the First Federal Elections, 1788–1790.* 3 vols. projected. Madison, 1975_____.

Editor, *The Documentary History of the Ratification of the Constitution.* 14 vols. projected. Madison, 1975_____.

Ph.D. Students Under Merrill Jensen's Direction at the University of Wisconsin

Jackson Turner Main, "The Anti-Federalist Party, 1781–1788" (1949).

E. James Ferguson, "Revenue Power and the Movement for National Government, 1780–1790" (1951).

Whitney K. Bates, "The Assumption of State Debts, 1783–1793" (1952).

Frank W. Crow, "The Age of Promise: Societies for Social and Economic Improvement in the United States, 1783–1815" (1952).

Siegfried B. Rolland, "Cadwallader Colden: Colonial Political and Imperial Statesman, 1718–1760" (1952).

Kenneth Coleman, "The American Revolution in Georgia, 1763–1789" (1953).

Arthur L. Jensen, "The Maritime Commerce of Colonial Philadelphia" (1954).

Carl W. Ubbelohde, Jr., "The Vice-Admiralty Courts of British North America, 1763–1776" (1954).

Robert P. Thomson, "The Merchant in Virginia, 1770–1775" (1955).

Phyllis R. Abbott, "The Development and Operation of an American Land System to 1800" (1959).

Roger J. Champagne, "The Sons of Liberty and the Aristocracy in New York Politics, 1765–1790" (1960).

Terrance L. Mahan, S.J., "Virginia Reaction to British Policy, 1763–1776" (1960).

Thomas R. Meehan, "The Pennsylvania Supreme Court in the Law and Politics of the Commonwealth, 1776–1790" (1960).

Leslie J. Thomas, "Partisan Politics in Massachusetts During Governor Bernard's Administration, 1760–1770" (1960).

William D. Barber, "The West in National Politics, 1784–1804" (1961).

Joseph Albert Ernst, "Currency in the Era of the American Revolution: A History of Colonial Paper Money Practices and British Monetary Policies, 1764–1781" (1962).

Neil R. Stout, "The Royal Navy in American Waters, 1760–1775" (1962).

Van Beck Hall, "The Commonwealth in the New Nation: Massachusetts, 1780–1790" (1964).

Gaspare J. Saladino, "The Economic Revolution in Late Eighteenth-Century Connecticut" (1964).

Jerome J. Nadelhaft, "The Revolutionary Era in South Carolina, 1775–1788" (1965).

Stephen Saunders Webb, "Officers and Governors: The Role of the British Army in Imperial Politics and the Administration of the American Colonies, 1689–1722" (1965).

Jonathan G. Rossie, "The Politics of Command: The Continental Congress and Its Generals" (1966).

Kenneth R. Bowling, "Politics in the First Congress, 1789–1791" (1968).

Richard H. Kohn, "The Federalists and the Army: Politics and the Birth of the Military Establishment, 1783–1795" (1968).

Russell S. Nelson, Jr., "Backcountry Pennsylvania (1709 to 1774): The Ideals of William Penn in Practice" (1968).

Stephen E. Patterson, "A History of Political Parties in Revolutionary Massachusetts, 1770–1780" (1968).

John N. Shaeffer, "Constitutional Change in the Unicameral States, 1776–1793" (1968).

John F. Walzer, "Transportation in the Philadelphia Trading Area, 1740–1775" (1968).

George W. Geib, "A History of Philadelphia, 1776–1789" (1969).

Ronald Hoffman, "Economics, Politics and the Revolution in Maryland" (1969).

James Kirby Martin, "Political Elites and the Outbreak of the American Revolution: A Quantitative Profile in Continuity, Turnover, and Change, 1774–1777" (1969).

Edward F. Robinson, "Continental Treasury Administration, 1775–1781: A Study in the Financial History of the American Revolution" (1969).

Neil T. Storch, "Congressional Politics and Diplomacy, 1775–1783" (1969).

George M. Curtis III, "The Virginia Courts During the Revolution" (1970).

Peter R. Barry, "The New Hampshire Merchant Interest, 1609–1725" (1971).

Robert A. Becker, "The Politics of Taxation in America, 1763–1783" (1971).

Walter S. Dunn, Jr., "Western Commerce, 1760–1774" (1971).

LeGrand L. Baker, "The Board of Treasury, 1784–1789: Responsibility Without Power" (1972).

Gordon DenBoer, "The House of Delegates and the Evolution of Political Parties in Virginia, 1782–1792" (1972).

Joseph L. Davis, "Sections, Factions, and Political Centralism in Confederation America, 1774–1787" (1972).

John P. Kaminski, "Paper Politics: The Northern State Loan-Offices During the Confederation, 1783–1790" (1972).

David E. Maas, "The Return of the Massachusetts Loyalists" (1972).

Steven R. Boyd, "The Constitution in State Politics: From the Calling of the Constitutional Convention to the Calling of the First Federal Elections" (1974).

Marc M. Egnal, "The Pennsylvania Economy, 1748–1762: An Analysis of Short-Run Fluctuations in the Context of Long-Run Changes in the Atlantic Trading Community" (1974).

Ph.D. Candidates:

Douglas Clanin	William O'Brien
Glenn Jacobsen	Joel Shufro
Rupert C. Loucks	John Suter

Notes on the Contributors

STEVEN R. BOYD, a faculty member at the University of Texas, San Antonio, is completing a study of the impact of the Constitution of 1787 on the states during the process of its writing and ratification. He also is finishing an essay on the objections of nationalists to the Constitution.

KENNETH COLEMAN has published extensively on colonial and revolutionary Georgia, including his well-known book *The American Revolution in Georgia* (1958). A member of the history department at the University of Georgia, he has undertaken editorial responsibilities for further volumes in *The Colonial Records of Georgia* series, and he is completing a general investigation of Georgia in the colonial period.

GEORGE M. CURTIS III is research associate, *Papers of John Marshall*, the College of William and Mary, Williamsburg, Virginia. His research interests include Virginia's provincial legal history, and he is working on a study of Virginia courts on the eve of the American Revolution. A recent article on the Goodrich family and Virginia's revolution appeared in the *Virginia Magazine of History and Biography*.

JOSEPH L. DAVIS has recently completed a book-length manuscript on the impact of sectional attitudes on politics during the Confederation years. He was a recipient of a post-doctoral research grant from the National Endowment for the Humanities in support of that investigation.

E. JAMES FERGUSON, a faculty member at Queens College of the City University of New York, has written *The Power of the Purse: A History of American Public Finance, 1776–1790* (1961), and *The American Revolution: A General History, 1763–1790* (1974), among many other publications. He has served as visiting editor of publications for the Institute of Early American History and Culture, and he is currently editor-in-chief of the *Papers of Robert Morris* project.

VAN BECK HALL is the author of *Politics Without Parties: Massachusetts, 1780–1791* (1972). A member of the history department at the University of Pittsburgh, his research interests include Virginia and the early national republic, 1790–1830.

JOHN P. KAMINSKI, associate editor of the *Documentary History of the Ratification of the Constitution* project, University of Wisconsin, Madison, recently had an article published in the *Georgia Historical Quarterly* on the adoption of the Constitution of 1787 in that state. He also is working on a number of essays and a book-length manuscript covering aspects of the ratification struggle, including the public debate and attempts to stifle that debate through intimidation, violence, and suppression of the mails; and on an article for *Rhode Island History*.

RICHARD H. KOHN, the author of *Eagle and Sword: The Federalists and the Creation of the Military Establishment in America, 1783–1802* (1975), is a member of the department of history, Rutgers University, New Brunswick, New Jersey. Recent articles have appeared in the *William and Mary Quarterly* and the *Journal of American History*, among other scholarly journals.

JACKSON TURNER MAIN, a faculty member as well as the director of the Institute for Colonial and Intercultural Studies at the State University of New York at Stony Brook, has published numerous scholarly books and articles. His two most recent volumes include *The Sovereign States, 1775–1783* (1973), and *Political Parties Before the Constitution* (1973).

JAMES KIRBY MARTIN, a member of the Rutgers University faculty, New Brunswick, New Jersey, has published *Men in Rebellion:*

Higher Governmental Leaders and the Coming of the American Revolution (1973), and *Interpreting Colonial America: Selected Readings* (1973). He also is serving on the editorial advisory board of the *Papers of William Livingston* project.

STEPHEN E. PATTERSON, the author of *Political Parties in Revolutionary Massachusetts* (1973), is a member of the faculty at the University of New Brunswick, Frederickton, N.B., Canada. His current research projects include an investigation of the origins of American conservatism as well as a documentary collection on the role of common people in the American Revolution.

JONATHAN G. ROSSIE, a member of the faculty at St. Lawrence University in Canton, New York, is the author of *The Politics of Command in the American Revolution* (1975). He also has served as a visiting faculty member at the University of Wisconsin, Madison.

STEPHEN SAUNDERS WEBB is a member of the department of history at Syracuse University. He has held fellowships with the Institute of Early American History and Culture and the Charles Warren Center for Studies in American History. Recent essays on British imperial and American colonial relations have appeared in *Perspectives in American History* and the *William and Mary Quarterly*.